MEXICO
in the 1940s

MEXICO
in the 1940s

Modernity, Politics, and Corruption

STEPHEN R. NIBLO

SR BOOKS

A SCHOLARLY RESOURCES INC. IMPRINT

Wilmington, Delaware

Scholarly Resources Inc.
104 Greenhill Avenue
Wilmington, DE 19805-1897
www.scholarly.com

Library of Congress Cataloging-in-Publication Data

Niblo, Stephen R., 1941–
  Mexico in the 1940s : modernity, politics, and corruption / Stephen R. Niblo.
      p.   cm. — (Latin American silhouettes : studies in history and culture)
  Includes bibliographical references and index.
  ISBN 0–8420–2794–7 (cloth : alk. paper)
  1. Mexico—Politics and government—1910–1946.
2. Mexico—Politics and government—1946–1970. 3. Political corruption—Mexico—History—20th century. 4. Mass media—Political aspects—Mexico. I. Title. II. Series: Latin American silhouettes.
F1234.N495   1999
972.08'2–dc21   99-28870
                                                                          CIP

*F
1234
. N 495
1999
June 200
A BM 5842*

♾ The paper used in this publication meets the minimum requirements of the American National Standard for permanence of paper for printed library materials, Z39.48, 1984.

To my son Christopher

Contents

Acknowledgments, **ix**

Abbreviations and Acronyms, **xi**

Introduction, **xvii**

Chapter 1   Mosaic of an Era, **1**

Chapter 2   Avila Camacho's Moderation, **75**

Chapter 3   The 1946 Selection, **149**

Chapter 4   Alemán's Counterrevolution, **183**

Chapter 5   The Politics of Corruption, **253**

Chapter 6   The Battle for the Mexican Media, **311**

Conclusion, **361**

Bibliography, **369**

Index, **387**

Acknowledgments

I am especially grateful to William Beezley and Judy Ewell for their editorial comments and encouragement throughout this project. Richard Hopper, Carolyn Travers, and the anonymous reviewers at Scholarly Resources also provided the kind of support that is vital to researchers.

Many friends and colleagues helped me in various ways: Barry Carr, Luis Javier Garrido, Benjamin Keen, Alan Knight, David La France, Moises González Navarro, Kenneth Polk, Enríque Semo, and Paul Vanderwood. A special thanks goes to John Mraz for help in locating the photographs. These generous people should rest assured that I acknowledge that the shortcomings of this book are entirely my own.

Without exception, the archivists at the Archivo General de la Nación, the National Archives of the United States, the Roosevelt Library, and the Truman Library, as well as the librarians at Borchardt Library and the staff and my colleagues in the Department of History of La Trobe University were extremely helpful. Without the university's overseas study program it would not have been possible for me to work from such a distance. The endless support of my wife Diane and our families has made this project a joy.

Abbreviations and Acronyms

A.C. & Co.	Anderson, Clayton and Company
AFL-CIO	American Federation of Labor-Congress of Industrial Organizations
AMC	Asociación Mexicana de Caminos (Mexican Association of Roads)
AN	Acción Nacional (National Action Party)
AOCM	Alianza de Obreros y Campesinos de México (Alliance of Workers and Peasants of Mexico)
AP	Associated Press
ARMCO	American Rolling Mills Company
ASARCO	American Smelting and Refining Company
ASU	Acción Socialista Unificada (Unified Socialist Action Party)
BANAMEX	Banco Nacional de México (National Bank of Mexico)
BBC	British Broadcasting Corporation
BEW	Board of Economic Welfare
CCC	Confederación de Cámaras de Comercio (Confederation of Chambers of Commerce)
CCI	Confederación de Cámaras Industriales (Confederation of Industrial Chambers)
CCRM	Cámaras de Comercio de la República Mexicana (Chambers of Commerce of the Mexican Republic)
CEIMSA	Compañía de Exportaciones e Importaciones Mexicana S.A. (Mexican Export and Import Corporation)
CEMOS	Centro de Estudios del Movimiento Obrero y Socialista (Center for Studies of the Labor Movement and Socialism)
CFB	Combined Foods Board

CFE	Comisión Federal de Electricidad (Federal Electricity Commission)
CFR	Council on Foreign Relations
CGOCM	Confederación General de Obreros y Campesinos de México (General Mexican Confederation of Workers and Peasants)
CGT	Confederación General de Trabajadores (General Confederation of Workers)
CIA	Central Intelligence Agency
CIO	Congress of Industrial Organizations
CITSA	Compañía de Inversiones y Transportes S.A. (Investment and Transport Company)
CNC	Confederación Nacional de Campesinos (National Confederation of Peasants)
CNIT	Cámara Nacional de Industrias de Transformación (National Chamber of Industries of Transformation)
CNT	Confederación Nacional de Trabajadores (National Confederation of Workers)
COCM	Confederación de Obreros y Campesinos de México (Mexican Confederation of Workers and Peasants)
CONCAMIN	Confederación de Cámaras Industriales (Confederation of Chambers of Manufacturing)
CONCANACO	Confederación Nacional de Cámaras de Comercio (National Confederation of Chambers of Commerce)
COOC	Coalición de Organizaciones Obreras y Campesinas (Coalition of Worker and Peasant Organizations)
COPARMEX	Confederación Patronal de la República Mexicana (Employers Confederation of the Mexican Republic)
CPN	Confederación Proletaria Nacional (National Proletariat Confederation)
CROM	Confederación Regional Obrera Mexicana (Regional Confederation of Mexican Workers)
CTAL	Confederación de Trabajadores de América Latina (Latin American Confederation of Workers)

CTM	Confederación de Trabajadores Mexicanos (Mexican Confederation of Workers)
CUT	Confederación Unica de Trabajadores (The Only Confederation of Workers)
DDF	Departamento del Districto Federal (Department of the Federal District)
D.F.	Districto Federal (Mexico City)
EXIMBANK	Export-Import Bank
FBI	Federal Bureau of Investigation
FNTIE	Federación Nacional de Trabajadores de la Industria Eléctrica (National Federation of Workers in the Electrical Industry)
FPPM	Federación de Partidos del Pueblo Mexicano (Federation of Political Parties of the Mexican People)
FROC	Frente Regional de Obreros y Campesinos del Estado de Puebla (Regional Front of Workers and Peasants of the State of Puebla)
FSTSE	Federación de Sindicatos de Trabajadores al Servicio del Estado (Federation of Unions of Workers at the Service of the State)
FUPDM	Frente Unico Pro Derechos de la Mujer (The Only Front Supporting the Rights of Women)
IBRD	International Bank for Reconstruction and Development (World Bank)
IEM	Industrias Electrónicas Mexicanas (Mexican Electronics Industries)
IMF	International Monetary Fund
INS	Immigration and Naturalization Service
ITII	Instituto Technológico de Investigaciones Industriales (Technological Institute of Industrial Research)
ITT	International Telephone and Telegraph Company
MEXLIGHT	Mexican Light and Power Company
MEXTELCO	Mexican Telephone Company
MIT	Massachusetts Institute of Technology
MPPDA	Motion Picture Producers and Distributors of America
NAFISA	Nacional Financiera S.A. (National Finance Bank)

NAM	National Association of Manufacturers
NBER	National Bureau of Economic Research
N.D. & R.	Nacional Distribuidora y Reguladora S.A. (National Distributor and Regulator)
NPA	National Planning Association
NRA	National Recovery Administration
OIAA	Office of Inter-American Affairs
OPA	Office of Price Administration
OSS	Office of Strategic Services
PAN	Partido de Acción Nacional (National Party of Action)
PAW	Petroleum Administration for the War
PCM	Partido Comunista Mexicano
PEMEX	Petróleos Mexicanos (Mexican Petroleum Company)
PIPSA	Productores e Importadores de Papel S.A. (Producers and Importers of Paper)
PNLM	Partido Nacional Liberal Mexicano
PNR	Partido Nacional Revolucionario
PRI	Partido Revolucionario Institucional (Institutional Revolutionary Party)
PRM	Partido Revolucionario Mexicano (Revolutionary Mexican Party)
RFC	Reconstruction Finance Corporation
SITMMSRM	Sindicato Industrial de Trabajadores Mineros, Metalúrgicos y Similares de la República Mexicana (Industrial Union of Mining, Metallurgical and Similar Workers of the Mexican Republic)
SITTFDS	Sindicato Industrial de Trabajadores Textiles de Fibras Duras y Similares (Industrial Union of Textile Workers of Hard Fibers and Similar Occupations)
SME	Sindicato Mexicano de Electristas (Mexican Electricians Union)
SNTE	Sindicato Nacional de Trabajadores de la Educación (National Union of Education Workers)
SOFINA	Belgian holding company that owned MEXLIGHT
SRE	Secretaría de Relaciones Exteriores (Foreign Relations Secretariat)

STERM	Sindicato de Trabajadores Electricos de la República Mexicana (Union of Electrical Workers of the Mexican Republic)
STFRM	Sindicato de Trabajadores Ferrocarrileros de la República Mexicana (Union of Railroad Workers of the Republic of Mexico)
STIC	Sindicato de Trabajadores de la Industria Cinematográfica (Union of Workers in the Film Industry)
STPC	Sindicato de Trabajadores de la Producción Cinematográfica (Union of Workers in Film Production)
STPRM	Sindicato de Trabajadores Petroleros de la República Mexicana (Union of Petroleum Workers of the Mexican Republic)
UGOCM	Unión General de Obreros y Campesinos de México (General Union of Workers and Peasants of Mexico)
UNAM	Universidad Nacional Autónoma de México (National Autonomous University of Mexico)
UNS	Unión Nacional Sinarquista (National Union of the Enemies of Anarchy)
UPI	United Press International
USDA	United States Department of Agriculture
USIS	United States Information Service
USSR	Union of Soviet Socialist Republics
WFTU	World Federation of Trade Unions
WPB	War Production Board

Introduction

The history of Mexico seems to have ended in 1940, at least in the work of many practicing historians. Examples of analytical history that combine solid research with a sense of historical perspective are rare for the final three-fifths of the twentieth century. For some, an aversion to developments after 1940 and sympathy for earlier versions of the Mexican Revolution may contribute to this barren historical landscape. Historians have been quick to cede the post-1940 terrain to economists, students of politics, and sociologists. Yet to understand Mexico today it is essential to examine the way the country's recent past evolved.

There have been some important overviews, in the tradition of textbooks for teaching,[1] and social scientists have offered many valuable contemporary analyses.[2] Some excellent studies of specialized topics, especially in the areas of labor, education, and land reform, are beginning to emerge.[3] Regional studies have boomed in Mexico since Luis González's *Pueblo en vilo*, and a few of these have touched the recent past.[4] Fortunately, there are some excellent young scholars who have produced outstanding studies, including Seth Fein, Anne Rubenstein, and Friedrich Schuller.[5] Many authors react quickly to the extraordinarily stunning events of recent decades.

Yet overall historical studies of the political and economic life of the nation are extremely rare. This is peculiar since the central government is strong, to the point of being a system of presidential autocracy, and the stunning shifts in the country's model of development have had profound impact on people's lives. Moreover, a high level of nationalism has accompanied the state-building project that has dominated a great deal of public life in this century. Historians of Mexico have been extremely reluctant to undertake projects of contemporary history. Even venerable academic journals treat 1940 as an absolute divide, beyond which they do not tread.[6] As of 1996, neither the *Hispanic American Historical Review* nor *Historia Mexicana* had published an article dealing with post-1940 Mexico in the past decade—perhaps ever. Since 1985 the *Journal of Latin*

American History had only two original articles based on solid historical research,[7] plus another seven articles written by social scientists on specialized topics.[8] The interdisciplinary nature of *Mexican Studies/Estudios Mexicanos* makes comparisons difficult; this journal is only beginning to publish examples of contemporary history, and most recent material has been produced by social scientists who rarely consult the historical record.

Historians' reluctance to examine the recent public record denies the country an adequate sense of perspective. Because recent decades have been so tumultuous, lack of understanding of the recent past also makes it difficult to formulate policies to deal with even the most severe contemporary problems. The absence of a body of historical analysis also handicaps scholars working in the social sciences, in social and regional history, and on cultural topics. As Alan Knight recently noted when trying to extend his analysis beyond the 1930s, "I omit reference to the 1940s since we have few studies of popular protest in that decade."[9] One might add that popular protest is not the only topic on which there is a paucity of research.

Perhaps the contrived, even choreographed nature of official political discourse has made it difficult to deal with Mexico's recent political history. There is nothing inherently wrong with focusing on the six-year terms of office of the nation's presidents; however, when that emphasis is joined with excessive reliance on the problematics and evidence provided by the leaders of the day, the result can be stultifying. Just as diplomatic history can become more interesting if one escapes the diplomats' agenda, political history soars as new perspectives emerge. Yet recently a new aversion to politics, which has flowed from a wave of nihilism posturing under the guise of postmodern discourse, may have made the study of politics and economics less fashionable. As a result of internal professional crises, the end of the Cold War, and the collapse of the ˙Left, historians have avoided postrevolutionary Mexico. Consequently, with some honorable exceptions, the historiographical landscape for the final three-fifths of the twentieth century looks bleak indeed.

When there have been efforts to press on with contemporary history, some historians have been limited by their acceptance of a far too narrow definition of politics.[10] A fundamental difference between a political historian and a political commentator is the willingness of the former to go beyond the political agenda set by the politicians and journalists of the day and ask new questions, consult alternative sources, and suggest new perspectives. In Mexico, political history has too frequently been determined by the political agenda of the ruling party and the logic of the presidential term of office, the *sexenio*. Perhaps the country's extreme version of presidential centralism accounts for this. Nevertheless, it is striking that so few serious attempts have been made to use the rich public record for the period to write the country's recent history.[11]

One pioneering attempt was made to write the contemporary political history of Mexico in the series Historia de la Revolución Mexicana, by researchers at the Colegio de México. This project was initatiated after President Luis Echeverría awarded Daniel Cosío Villegas the Premio Nacional de Letras in 1971 upon Cosío Villegas's completion of his ten-volume *Historia moderna de México*. Echeverría had met several times in private with don Daniel as part of the president's "democratic opening," and this was the high point in their relationship. According to the historian's biographer, Enrique Krauze, Echeverría offered both to fund the new project and to help researchers gain access to official records.[12]

Teams of historians and graduate students from the Colegio de México were quickly organized to study each presidential term of office. It was an important, if an uneven, effort given the archival window of opportunity that Echeverría promised to open. As these teams rushed into action, they relied heavily upon newspapers, not as a source to explain political factions and networks of influence, but as factual accounts of political events. Although researchers made some use of the rich collections of primary documents in the National Archives of the United States, they generally ignored the Archivo General de la Nación in Mexico City.

At the best moments of the series, its twenty-three volumes provide real insights, as in the work of Lorenzo Meyer, Rafael Segovia, and Luis González. At the worst moments, the teams went to the Hemeroteca Nacional, the national newspaper library, and their seminars merely link newspaper summaries into narratives as the core of these volumes. As a result, the logic of presidential centralism and the contemporary political agendas continued to dominate some historical analyses.[13] It was disappointing when this effort produced the kind of history that reads like a summary of press clippings, especially for the period after 1940. The point is not to fault this pioneering effort, however, because even the weakest volumes filled in a great deal on what had been virtually empty historical canvases. What remains disappointing is that this series has not stimulated subsequent efforts to build upon these early initiatives.

Historical narratives that stay slavishly within the parameters provided by governments offer a too narrow view of politics and discourage the integration of political and economic factors with other approaches. Innovative units of analysis are required to provide vital new perspectives, especially in a world that has lost fundamental organizational principles with the decline of the Left and the end of the Cold War. A broader definition of politics must include—but also must go beyond—the accomplishments, perspectives, myths, and illusions that prevailed among the narrow circle of decision makers and commentators of the day. Analyses of the way alternative political agendas developed, flourished, and withered can expand the meaning of politics in one direction. A perceptive individual's political perspective and even forlorn efforts to affect change can also lead beyond a narrow reiteration of official positions and open a dialogue with other social and cultural forces in society. Studies of the links between national agendas, local histories, and daily life cry out for historical treatment.

There are obvious problems in penetrating the secrets of the narrow circle of power brokers in what is, after all, one of the world's most closed political systems. These difficulties have led to a tradition in which oral interviews are used to try to capture fading memories. The Instituto Mora has produced many commendable results; however, too many of those interviews are closed to researchers, and only infrequent attempts are made to preserve interviews in any area other than social history. There is real potential if candid oral evidence—some quite erroneously call it oral history—can supplement the surviving written record. Yet there are also pitfalls in this approach. Apart from the well-known problems of confabulation and fading memory, there is the danger that some of these efforts can become highly dependent upon personal relationships between the researcher and the powerful figures being interviewed. There can be an unwillingness to challenge the perspective of powerful individuals or even to ask unfriendly questions that might indirectly challenge the subject's version of events. In the worst of cases, these interviews can border on hagiography.[14] In other instances, institutional relationships have led to extreme examples of self-censorship. Whereas it was probably impossible at their meeting in 1970 in Austin for a distinguished group of historians of contemporary Mexico to ask Miguel Alemán about allegations of corruption, it was, nevertheless, a terrible waste of an opportunity not to deal with specific aspects of his administration.[15]

When these problems are added to the reluctance of public figures in Mexico to talk or write candidly about their experiences, the danger is that the recent history of Mexico may be lost definitively.[16] There is, therefore, no alternative to using the rich archival sources in the national archives of Mexico and the United States, which historians have tapped only lightly to this point. Perhaps then the benefits of historical perspective can begin to emerge, to reshape and enrich our understanding. With a solid base of political and economic analyses, innovative approaches focusing upon regional, social, and gender topics can contribute additional insights. To skip the politics and economics, however, would be to leave the skeleton out of the body. Some parts might still be around, but they would scarcely hang together.

This study, therefore, is fundamentally concerned with political and economic issues at the national level. Perhaps this is unavoidable, given the conjuncture of the autocratic system of presidential centralism in Mexico and the unusually broad coalition of forces in support of the Allied cause during World War II. Analyses of the relationship between local and national politics— be it in either a reform movement or the initiatives of a regional cacique—have been producing some of the most interesting work on Mexican politics in recent years.[17] But the 1940s may be quite different. There certainly were regional protests, as events demonstrated in Monterrey and in León at the end of the Avila Camacho administration, and workers clearly felt tremendous pressure from the crisis of *carestía*, as attested to by the large number of wildcat strikes. Still, whenever a movement started to develop, it was isolated and contained; even the Left joined the government and the United States in opposing anything that might threaten the Grand Alliance. Moreover, after the war, the great project of industrialization held the broad antipopular coalition together for some time. Never was this more obvious than in the case of Lombardo Toledano's apologetic for the antilabor onslaught of the Alemán years or in the case of the political isolation of the Hunger Caravan in 1947.

This analysis of the interaction of political and economic forces defines politics as a twofold struggle: first, as a struggle to attain and use state power, and second, as a concomitant contest over the way to look at public issues—the battle for hearts and minds. From a chronological point of view, this study examines Mexican politics in the wake of Cárdenas, that is, in the decade of the 1940s, although the analysis of Alemanismo continues into the early years of the presidency of Adolfo Ruíz Cortines.

In an attempt to set the scene by giving an impression of what life was like in the 1940s, Chapter 1 focuses on the concept "the past is a foreign country," which already applies to that period so great have been recent changes in Mexico.[18] The chapter's technique might be likened to that of an impressionistic painting in which a series of small pieces are juxtaposed to create an overall image. Of course, no such effort can ever completely capture the richness and complexity of the life of an era. Moreover, references to local and regional developments are uneven, in part reflecting the unevenness of the literature. The discussion is also inevitably slanted toward the regions of Mexico with which I am most familiar. "Mosaic of an Era" evokes the spirit of an age and gives glimpses of some of the different realities that existed then.

Chapters 2, 3, and 4 are political histories of the presidencies of the 1940s, offering an interpretation of political events that are on the verge of being lost. As an illustration of this point, it is revealing to ask how many students of Mexican politics can remember the specific context in which the governing party changed its name from the Partido Revoluciónario Mexicano (PRM) to the Partido Revoluciónario Institucional (PRI). My hope is that these efforts may stimulate others to undertake a systematic look at the recent past based upon different units of analysis. It is fascinating to have lived through a period and then to see the historical studies that emerge. Although I did not first visit Mexico until the late 1950s, my years in that country were close enough to events of the 1940s to at least tap the memories of many who had lived through that period.

Some may find Chapter 5 to be controversial. There are so many ways to look at corruption that it presents a challenging topic of analysis for the historian. Not only is the public record of corruption in this period rich and abundant, but corruption was so dominant at the time that it shaped many aspects of life and even molded the country's model of development. Thus, corruption cannot be viewed as a minor aberration: It provides another fundamental explanation for many acute problems of poverty and underdevelopment that still exist and that are again increasing in the 1990s. Even the most seemingly reasonable, balanced, dispassionate, and detached historical narrative cannot be objective if it ignores the massive record of corruption in the 1940s. More important, until there is a clear understanding of how these astonishing abuses of public trust occurred, there is little chance of averting the forward retention of these practices.

To return to the idea of politics as a battle over the way we look at public issues, Chapter 6 examines how in the 1940s new channels of communication and influence were allocated. National politics became intimately linked to the power of the media as domestic entrepreneurs played an intricate game, using the new technologies that came from the advanced industrial countries while opposing powerful European and U.S. interests. Although this story is fascinating in its own right, it also looks toward the present in that many of those individuals who gained control of the media of communication, or who later inherited that control, still play an important role in setting the public agenda of today.

Finally, the reader should be aware that *Mexico in the 1940s: Modernity, Politics, and Corruption* is intended to complement my earlier study of the relations between Mexico and the United States in the same period.[19] That volume examined the international relationship between the two countries at the level of diplomatic, military, economic, and business relations. This volume, by contrast, is fundamentally an analysis of the domestic history of Mexico after the presidency of Cárdenas.

Notes

1. Among the better overviews are Judith Alder Hellman, *Mexico in Crisis*; Héctor Aguilar Camín and Lorenzo Meyer, *In the Shadow of the Mexican Revolution*; and Colin MacLachlan and William Beezley, *El Gran Pueblo*. James Cockcroft's, *Mexico: Class Formation, Capital Accumulation, and the State*, devotes one-half of his book to the post-1940 period.

2. Luis Javier Garrido's *El partido de la revolución institucionalizada* deals only with the early 1940s in the last chapter. See also Frans J. Schryer, *Ethnicity and Class Conflict in Rural Mexico*; Soledad Loaeza, *Clases media y política*; Douglas C. Bennett and Kenneth Sharpe, *Transnational Corporations vs. the State*; Dale Story, *Industry, the State, and Public Policy*; and Roderic Ai Camp, *Polling for Democracy*. Alfonso Taracena has produced one of the most concrete studies of the period; unfortunately, it was written before the major archives of the period were opened. See Alfonso Taracena, *La vida en México bajo Avila Camacho*.

3. Commendable monographs included Barry Carr, *Marxism and Communism in Twentieth-Century Mexico*; Rafael Loyola Díaz, *El ocaso del radicalismo revolucionario*; Joe Foweraker, *Popular Mobilization in Mexico*; Aurora Loyo Brambila, *El movimiento magisterial de 1958*; David E. Lorey, *The University System and Economic Development in Mexico*; Susan R. Walsh

Sanderson, *Land Reform in Mexico, 1910–1980;* and Mary Kay Vaughan, *Cultural Politics in Revolution.*

4. Jeffrey Brannon and Eric N. Blankoff, *Agrarian Reform and Public Enterprise in Mexico;* Gilbert M. Joseph, *Rediscovering the Past of Mexico's Periphery;* Thomas Benjamin, *Rich Land, Poor People.*

5. Seth Fein, "Hollywood and United States-Mexican Relations in the Golden Age of Cinema"; Anne Rubenstein, "Mexico 'sin vicios': Conservatives, Comic Books, Censorship, and the Mexican State, 1934–1976"; Friedrich E. Schuller, "Cardenismo Revisited: The International Dimensions of the Post-Reform Cárdenas Era, 1937–1940."

6. A few recent examples of this tendency are John Tutino, *From Insurrection to Revolution in Mexico;* Marta Elena Negrete, *Relaciones entre la Iglesia y el Estado en México;* Stephen H. Haber, *Industry and Underdevelopment;* Francie R. Chassen de López, *Lombardo Toledano y el movimiento obrero mexicano;* Anna Macías, *Against All Odds;* Shirlene Soto, *Emergence of the Modern Mexican Woman;* Alexander M. Saragoza, *The Monterrey Elite and the Mexican State;* Jaime E. Rodríguez O., ed., *The Revolutionary Process in Mexico;* and Mark Reisler, *By the Sweat of Their Brow.*

7. Barry Carr, "Mexican Communism, 1968–1981: Eurocommunism in the Americas?" 271–319; Frans J. Schryer, "Peasants and the Law: A History of Land Tenure and Conflict in the Huasteca," 238–311.

8. Marilyn Gates, "Codifying Marginality: The Evolution of Mexican Agrarian Policy and Its Impact on the Peasantry," 277–311; Kevin J. Middlebrook, "The Sounds of Silence: Organised Labour's Response to Economic Crisis in Mexico," 195–220; Leigh Binford, "Peasants and Petty Capitalists in Southern Oaxaca Sugar Cane Production, 1930–1980," 33–55; Miguel Angel Centeno and Sylvia Maxfield, "The Marriage of Finance and Order in Mexican Political Elite," 57–85; Jeffrey W. Rubin, "COCEI in Juchitán: Grassroots Radicalism and Regional History," 109–36; Yemile Mizrahi, "Rebels without a Cause? The Politics of Entrepreneurs in Chihuahua," 137–58; Carlos Elizondo, "In Search of Revenue: Tax Reform in Mexico under the Administrations of Echeverría and Salinas," 159–90; David E. Davis, "Failed Democratic Reform in Contemporary Mexico: From Social Movements to the State and Back Again," 375–408.

9. Alan Knight, "*Cardenismo:* Juggernaut or Jalopy?"

10. Sadly, the most recent study of the Alemán years falls into this category. See Tzvi Medin, *El sexeño alemanista.*

11. An important exception is Rogelio Heránandez Rodríguez, *La formación del politico mexicano.*

12. Enrique Krauze, *Daniel Cosío Villegas,* 255–57.

13. Luis Medina, *Historia de la revolución mexicana, periodo 1940–1952;* Luis Medina and Blanca Torres, *Historia de la revolución mexicana, periodo 1940–1952.*

14. See James W. Wilkie and Edna Monzón de Wilkie, *México visto en el siglo XX.* The unwillingness to discuss seriously allegations of corruption with Ramón Beteta provides a case in point.

15. The painfully obsequious questions put to Miguel Alemán at the University of Texas in Austin in 1970 offers a further example. From the perspective of this researcher, not a single question on a specific historical issue relating to his term of office was directed to the former president, although it was abundantly clear that several distinguished historians—most notably Daniel Cosío Villegas and Friedrich Katz—engaged him in

tense and subtle political debate. Perhaps considerations of international academic diplomacy took precedence over research. See Miguel Alemán Valdes, *Miguel Alemán contesta* (Austin: Institute of Latin American Studies, University of Texas, 1975).

16. Among the memoirs that fail to discuss concretely the internal political life of the governing party are Eduardo Villaseñor, *Memorias-testimonio,* and Francisco Javier Gaxiola, *Memorias.* The memoir that comes closest to discussing political issues with candor is Luis Alamillo Flores, *Memorias: Luchas ignorados al lado de los grandes jefes de la revolución mexicana.* It is less helpful for the post-Cárdenas period. Recently, David Barkin has conducted extensive interviews with Salvador Lemus Fernandez who was a close associate of Cárdenas in Michoacán. The level of candor in this interview promises to open new dimensions in memoir literature in Mexico.

17. Paul Friedrich, *The Princes of Naranja;* Jeffrey W. Rubin, "Decentering the Regime: Culture and Regional Politics in Mexico" (unpublished manuscript), and idem, "COCEI in Juchitán: Grassroots Radicalism and Regional History," *Journal of Latin American Studies* 26 (1994): 109–36; Wil Pansters, *Politics and Power in Puebla;* Alicia Hernández Chavez, *La mecánica Cardenista;* Enríque Márquez, "Political Anachronisms: The Navista Movement and Political Processes in San Luis Potosí."

18. David Lowenthal, *The Past Is a Foreign Country* (New York: Cambridge University Press, 1985).

19. Stephen R. Niblo, *War, Diplomacy, and Development.*

1
Mosaic of an Era

Mexico in 1940 was profoundly different from Mexico today. For a start, there was only one Mexican for every five who live there now. The 1940 census estimated that the population was just under 20 million, up from 13.6 million at the beginning of the century when all of Latin America had only 60 million people. Even by the end of the decade, there were only 25.7 million Mexicans. At the time, no one was so extreme as to suggest that more people would live in Mexico City by the year 2000 than would live in the entire country in 1950.[1] Or to put it another way, the population that had doubled between the first census in 1895 and 1950 virtually doubled again by 1970.[2]

Today's skyrocketing rate of population growth hides the fact that Mexico was then sparsely populated. Including the urban population, there were fewer than ten people per square kilometer throughout the land, including the 1.75 million who lived in Mexico City, where the population had grown to 3.05 million by the 1950 census. That meant that for the rural majority there was a considerable degree of isolation. Although some rural Mexicans traveled to the cities to find work—and a few occasionally ventured as far as the United States—the village remained the center of the world. It was divided into small barrios, usually along dirt tracks. *Campesinos* went out from clusters of simple adobe dwellings to work the fields. Although the Mexican Revolution had increased the sense of national identity, for most people in the countryside there were only the neighboring pueblos, and the complexity of interpersonal relationships over the generations made each region into a universe of its own. In many villages the rule of law was still remote and local tyranny prevailed.

Official census data claimed that 64.9 percent of the population lived in rural areas in 1940, a figure that declined to 57.2 per-

cent by 1950. However, there is a fundamental statistical flaw behind these figures. Statisticians seriously overstated the case for
urbanization by defining any town over fifteen thousand as urban,
thus alleging an inflated 5.7 percent rate of increase for urbanization in the 1940s.[3] In Mexico, high urban density amazes outsiders
in that far more people live in towns than seems possible. This statistical methodology defines small towns as urban, even where the
culture is still overwhelmingly rural. If cultural criteria were to be
used to set the divide between rural and urban, rather than an arbitrary round population number, it would be necessary to increase
significantly the rural estimates.

   Mexico was not just a land of peasants. The ascendancy of the
central government was assured after the state-building project of
Cardenismo had more than reversed the erosion of central authority during the revolution.[4] Numerous caudillos were crushed by
the central government in the 1930s, including Saturnino Cedillo
in San Luis Potosí, Tomás Garrido in Tabasco, Adalberto Tejeda in
Veracruz, and Fidencio Osornio in Querétaro.[5] In addition, the federal government was in the process of taking on a wide range of
tasks, from health and education to the great project of industrialization. Federal expenditures reflected these new functions, growing from 631.5 million pesos in 1942 to 3.46 billion pesos in 1950.
Using James Wilkie's schema of budgetary analysis, there was a
shift in government expenditure toward economic projects over the
decade from 37.6 percent under Cárdenas, to 39.2 percent under
Avila Camacho and 51.9 percent under Alemán—away from social
expenditures: 18.3 to 16.5 to 13.3 percent, respectively.[6] The census
divided Mexicans' working lives into the following categories:

Activities	1940	1950
Total population	19,653,552*	25,791,017*
Agriculture	3,826,871	4,823,901
Mining	106,706	97,143
Industry	836,143	1,222,020
Transportation and communications	149,470	210,592
Commerce and finance	518,295	684,092
Services	257,921	600,559
Government	191,588	278,820
Others [n.b.]	163,658	354,966
Women at home	6,303,028	7,003,735
Children under 12	6,981,763	6,981,763
Economically active population	6,054,652	8,272,093

*Error in the data figure reflects the quality of statistical estimates in the 1940s.

Several observations are in order. All statistics from the period must be taken lightly. Dr. Josué Sáenz, director of credit in the Ministry of Finance, met with U.S. embassy officials on this point in July 1948. His estimate was that agricultural statistics were "200 percent on the low side." They systematically ignored peasant production, whereas industry statistics—which were based on voluntary monthly questionnaires sent to factories—were "75–100 percent on the low side." Even mining statistics, which should have been easy to measure, were fudged since reporting was for tax purposes, as was also the case for exports. Sáenz thought that even these problems paled next to the series on wages and employment, which he referred to as "the biggest gap in Mexican official statistics."[7] Census data for 1940 was especially unreliable due to the unrest surrounding the elections; one random review of a *delegación* (ward) in the D.F. found a 60,000 person error. Thus all data must be used as a general indication, at best, to be complemented or overruled by other information. Those who accept census data and national income accounting figures as the sole and absolute epistemological basis of their understanding are being naive.

Although the rural population was still growing rapidly, the modern vision of an industrial future seemed assured. Industry, commerce and finance, services, transportation and communication, and government were more than keeping up with the population growth. The fall in employment in mining could be explained with reference to the peculiarities of demand associated with World War II. The terrible reality of industry's not generating enough new jobs to stay abreast with, much less gain on, population growth was still in the future. Given the country's traditional poverty, it was quite possible to focus on the new jobs created in the 1940s rather than on the allegation that only 32 percent of the labor force were, in one economic diplomat's revealing phrase, "gainfully employed."[8]

Boy selling candies, Mexico City. *Courtesy Hermanos Mayo, Archivo General de la Nación, Mexico City*

A new business elite had emerged. It combined powerful politicians with the most important figures in the private sector in ways
that were not obvious. It represented the new vision of industrial
modernity, linking national and international capital, that had captured the imagination of the era. Even the census data reflected the
dominant values by grossly underestimating the importance of the
peasant and artisan economies, since those activities seemed part
of a fading past. In addition, concrete mechanisms quickly guaranteed that these new values distributed income away from peasants
and workers and toward those groups at the top of society during
the period. Although she did not project her work back to 1940,
Ifigenia M. de Navarrete's classic study of income distribution demonstrated that in 1950 whereas the bottom 20 percent of society received only 6.1 percent of the national income and 50 percent of
society shared only 19 percent, the top 10 percent enjoyed 49 percent of the national income, and this inequality grew in subsequent
decades.[9]

Although public investment in agriculture grew in the 1940s,
the number of ejiditarios who benefited from the land reform fell
from 54,678 in 1940 to a low of 9,092 in 1948, although official figures claimed a recovery to 24,391 by 1950. The bottom 70 percent
of the population had a smaller share of the nation's agricultural
land in 1950 than a decade earlier, and the landowners in the
top decile increased their share of the cultivated land from 47.76 to
51.42 percent.[10]

Real wages continued to fall even after the wartime emergency
measures lapsed. The "official" public index of average real wages
for workers in Mexico City, in which 1939 = 100, continued to fall
to 88.8 by the end of the decade, or to 82.1 in 1947 if one uses the
secret index of real wages prepared by the Ministry of Labor for
Miguel Alemán.[11] Statistical experts generally understood that by
limiting this index of real wages to paid workers in the capital, in
industries where federal industrial awards were implemented, these
figures significantly understated the decline in real wages suffered
by the population as a whole.[12] More recently, Jeffrey Bortz has re-
worked the figures for industrial workers in Mexico City. His index, in which 1938 = 100, shows deterioration in real wages to a
low of 46.4 in 1947, with only marginal recovery after that. Not
until 1971 did the purchasing power of industrial wages regain the
1938 level.[13]

In the countryside, wages varied significantly from area to area.
One study of rural wages for 1949 showed a high of 10 pesos per

day along the U.S. border to a low of between 2 to 3 pesos in the central plateau with an average of 5 to 6 pesos along either coast.[14] In remote villages in the south, cash virtually disappeared from many labor relationships. By using the force of law to prevent the prices of basic staples from rising, even in the face of shortages, the entire Mexican industrialization push of the 1940s was based upon a major transfer of resources from the rural population to the investors, private and public. At times blatant political intervention was used. In Yucatán, on the last day of 1942, Governor Canto Echevarría convinced the state legislature to pass a law—unanimously—reducing the weekly wage to between 2 and 3 pesos, instead of the 8 pesos then considered basic. In the face of on-going announcements of new lands being turned over to ejidos, one peasant observed, "Now that they have said the land is ours, we are dying of hunger."[15] The legislature had the capacity to reduce wages because the law not only required the production of henequen, which was a near exigency of nature, but also forced all finance and sales through a state monopoly.

In pueblos such as San José de Gracia, Michoacán, as Luis González explained in his splendid study, the desire for autonomy was paramount. *Campesinos* understood that land meant life. On a single hectare of arable land, 15 kilos of corn seed yielded 700 kilos of corn at harvest, and 10 kilos of beans produced 200, enough to sustain a family of six for the year. While waiting for their petitions for land to be granted, ejiditarios worked as farmhands or day laborers, or they tried to find something rustic to sell, perhaps firewood or herbs, if they could find an unclaimed source of supply.[16] Even in 1944 a day's labor earned only 1.5 pesos.[17] As one *campesino* who left for the city put it, "Without land, do you think that a day's labor will allow me to feed my kids?"[18]

Another kind of description of rural Mexico came from an anthropologist working at the time. In 1947, Oscar Lewis went to the village of Tepoztlán in the state of Morelos, which had been the site of an early village study by Robert Redfield in the 1920s. Lewis selected Tepoztlán not only to deepen Redfield's understanding but also to see what changes had occurred in the past twenty years:

> Upon my arrival in the village it seemed to be in many aspects as Redfield had described it. Its physical appearance had changed but little. Once off the highway which runs to the plaza, there were the same unpaved streets and adobe houses, the barrio chapels, the people carrying water to their homes from the nearest fountains, the men wearing their ancient white *calzones* and

huaraches, the barefoot women with braids and long skirts. But the signs of change could also be seen. There were the new asphalt road, the busses, the tourist cars, the Coca-Cola and aspirin signs, the Sinarquist placards on a roadside wall, the queue of women and children waiting to have their corn ground at the mills, the new stores and poolrooms in the plaza, and a few women with high bobbed hair and high-heeled shoes. Moreover, school enrollment had increased from the "few score" of Redfield's time, to over six hundred, and the village had obtained ejidos under the national ejido program.[19]

These people owned few possessions, traveled infrequently, and were almost always destitute. Many spoke bitterly to Lewis about how little the arrival of the tourists had helped them: "We have a new road and many tourists but our children are still dying."[20]

Maid washing dishes. *Courtesy Hermanos Mayo, Archivo General de la Nación, Mexico City*

Power was usually exercised over the rural poor by a local landowner called a caudillo, a local political boss or cacique, or a *jefe político*, who may have still exercised the arbitrary power to discipline and punish on the basis of a fairly raw application of force. An extreme example of a local machine was in Puebla where Maximino Avila Camacho, doubtlessly aided by his brother's position as minister of war, was strong enough by 1939 to force all members of the state legislature to sign a *pacto de honor* swearing fidelity to him and their willingness to sacrifice themselves for Maximino's "cause."[21]

And when caudillos were in collision, local violence could create the worst of times. There were laws, of course, and the revolution had promised major changes; however, the right to legal redress against an abuse of power by a powerful local boss was still negligible. For most rural people, daily life was more similar to that in earlier centuries than in the world we know today, although things were changing rapidly in the towns and cities. It was more prudent to overlook and try to deflect the unjust use of force than to confront authority.

Maximino Avila Camacho in the bullring in Puebla. *Courtesy Hermanos Mayo,
Archivo General de la Nación, Mexico City*

Local tyranny was not the only problem. To a considerable degree, peasants viewed the outside world with deep suspicion. For it was from beyond the village that the worst depredations came: marauding armies and tax collectors to take any surplus the peasants produced, and in the second half of the nineteenth century, smart lawyers to help the hacendados take traditional village lands. The revolution had restored some village lands, but to many, daily life seemed only slightly changed. In remote areas, strong mechanisms of self-defense had developed over the centuries. In 1951, Dr. Gonzalo Aguirre Beltrán encountered extreme resistance from the Chamula Indians in the small villages around San Cristóbal, Chiapas, as the Instituto Nacional Indigenista tried to bring the first medical clinic to the region. "The implementation of this was extremely difficult, since the Chamulas have always resisted the incursion of outsiders in their territory."[22]

Yet the revolution had also injected the countryside with major new variables—education and land reform. The old order of the *gente de orden*, in which land could only be purchased or inherited, had been changed by the Mexican Revolution. Villagers who formed an ejido could apply for grants of land, and if luck or political connections were favorable it might be forthcoming. A highly complex rural scene emerged. Although the old landowning elite was bitterly opposed to the ejido movement, through the government, as represented by local PRM officials, the *comisariado ejidal*, and the CNC, peasants might succeed in attaining a grant of land.

At the point of land reform, rural divisions deepened between the winners and the losers. The *agraristas* who gained land owed a lot to the political machine. However, other rural people, especially the *acasillados* who did not get land, or perhaps even lost their place on a confiscated estate, could easily be manipulated by the old owners. Alternatively, private landowners found fiscal and financial arrangements that helped them push the recipients of

ejidal land aside, even in the Cardenista heartland.[23] Lourdes
Arizpe, in her study of migration to Mexico City, noted that "once
the land was divided, violence did not disappear; it was channelled
into a struggle for control of the ejido, which was the real factor
underlying the apparent ethnic conflict [between Indians and mes-
tizos]."[24] And any local leader who used a position of power to take
land as his own property, or was especially arrogant or authoritarian, could easily spawn a heated opposition.[25]

In Naranja, Michoacán, generations of conflict pitted two families of would-be caudillos, the Casos and the Ocampos, against each
other on the basis of their ethnic differentiation and religious attitudes—always against the background of local violence (fifteen
possibly political murders during the decade), agrarian politics, and
claims on ejido lands. Levels of state and national politicians then
lined up with local factions. As Paul Friedrich put it, "Repeatedly
one notes in Michoacán politics that majority support and convincing principles are never enough: the winning factions are those with
the organization, the strongest fighters, ideological fervor, and the
support of Cárdenas and his network."[26] The dominance of the cacique, "Scarface" Caso, was unbroken throughout the 1940s—although there were numerous challenges to his rule.[27]

In Puebla as well, machine politics took precedence over ideology, although the battle centered upon the relationship between
the state government and labor as well as rural power structures.
As Wil Pansters explained: "The Puebla countryside was characterized by multifarious conflicts among peasants, *caciques*, ejido
leaders and large landowners . . . [where] the new governor immediately launched a military campaign against these groups. . . . Many
caciques understood that serving as intermediaries within the new
State and party structures would enable them to maintain local
control. Those who were unwilling to adjust to [Maximino] Avila
Camacho's supremacy suffered repression." Thus, despite considerable personal bitterness, Cárdenas sided with the reactionary
Maximino Avila Camacho (see Chapters 2 and 5) against the CTM-
affiliated Frente Regional de Obreros y Campesinos of Puebla
(FROC) in the complex struggles between 1937 and 1939.[28] Frequently abrasive changes came to a traditional rural world as local
power structures adjusted to central influences—and sometimes
the other way around. However, the changes of the 1940s were not
all political.

Light was different in the 1940s. The world was not yet electri-
fied. When day gave way to night it became dark in a way that we

can no longer know. In the cities there were only a few street lights; street lighting was being extended quite unevenly around the country in three stages: from lamp oil, to natural gas, to electricity. The best illumination was dim by today's standards; there would be dark areas on busy streets even after electric street lights had been installed on each corner. As one left the central areas of a large city, the artificial light quickly dissipated. In small towns and in the countryside, the dark of night enveloped everything. Sources of light were few: open fires, oil lamps, and candles. (A Coleman lamp was a rare luxury in the 1940s.) People lived closer to the cycles of nature. There was a great difference between nights with a full moon and nights with no moon, and each day everyone knew what stage the moon would be in. The sky was ablaze with the light of stars on a moonless, clear night in a way that many urban dwellers today have never seen. (The electric lights of even the smallest town on the horizon reduce the view of the night sky significantly.) People tended to go to bed earlier, and they rose with the light of day. With the first hint of the pre-dawn, the work of the world began again.

There was tremendous enthusiasm for the arrival of electricity. In the United States, the folksinger Woody Guthrie wrote songs about the Grand Coulee Dam's "turning the night into day," and, a bit north of the post-1835 Mexican border, a young congressman, Lyndon B. Johnson, built a political constituency that lasted a lifetime by bringing electricity to the hill country of Texas. The level of enthusiasm was no less in Mexico. One person from the coast of Veracruz recalled as a tremendous advantage of electricity that it dramatically reduced the number of fires since it was so easy to lose control of an open flame. Electricity extended the day and made work easier, although home appliances and electronics would take another decade to make an impact. The 1940s was a decade in which many great hydroelectric projects were built. As electric lines took vastly increased flows of power to cities and factories, people learned that by throwing two wires over the new lines they could, very carefully, organize their own small project of electrification. Mexican Light and Power Company (MEXLIGHT) bitterly complained to the government about the piracy of electricity and used it as justification for increases in the tariffs.

Petroleum also played a role in bringing light to the country. From its inception in 1938, Petróleos Mexicanos (PEMEX), recognized that it had to price kerosene well below the cost of production as a way of turning people away from the use of firewood in their braziers for heat and light. (In 1941 the poor were ordered to get rid of their wood-burning braziers within a year and replace them with oil stoves.) This was the only conservation measure that was significant in the 1940s, and the importance of this measure was universally accepted although the depletion of the forests continued.

Still, the nation was energy poor. Without reservoirs, most of the rivers were fairly useless for power generation; coal reserves were meager, and the great reserves of natural gas were totally unknown. In the far north of the country the distance required to bring petroleum products to the cities, and especially to the factories of Monterrey and Guadalajara, added considerably to the cost of production, as local chambers of commerce complained. During the war, Mexican officials begged for an allocation of natural gas from Texas for the northern factories—a request that was repeatedly denied in the name of wartime production priorities.[29] Therefore, when a hot fire was required in workshops, foundries, or factories, the country was still dependent on a rural industry that converted wood into charcoal or coke.[30] For decades, the first automobiles shared the growing network of roads with burros laden with enormous burlap bags of charcoal. Visiting social scientists watched donkeys and trucks contest the new highways and devised theories of a dual economy.

Just as the night was darker, the world was also smaller for most people. The railroads had opened up Mexico to an unprecedented degree by the end of the nineteenth century; however, for most people, a journey by rail was still exceptional and, by today's standards, very long. Only slowly did trucks displace porters and mule trains to carry the nation's freight. In 1940, there were only 93,623 cars (of which 77,812 were used privately) and 41,932 trucks in the entire country. In the main, people walked, traveled in carriages, rode horses, or led burros—which were then very common. (They became rare in later decades, a sacrifice to the urban pet food industry.) For the country's *campesinos*, it was still a world in which one normally traveled not far beyond the distance one could walk or ride. And in such small worlds, a local landmark, a distinctive geographic feature, even a rock or a tree might be so important it could be given a proper name.

Roads were few and in poor condition. However, the sense of liberation and control that driving down a road offered made endless converts to motoring. Some people still remember the extraordinary pleasure of traversing the grand boulevards that the French had built in the capital, admiring the elegant buildings with the snowcapped volcanoes in the distance.[31] Before congestion and pollution triumphed, it was truly one of the world's great cities. Although only a few sealed ribbons connected the major cities of the central highlands, road construction was high on the national agenda. The first federal highways were built in the 1930s connecting México-Laredo, México-Veracruz, México-Guadalajara, and Puebla-Oaxaca. The extremely mountainous nature of much of the country meant that unpaved roads could easily turn into dusty trails in the dry season. And when the rains came, from June to October, mud was sovereign.

The federal highway network covered only 9,929 kilometers at the beginning of the decade, a figure that increased to 21,422 kilometers by 1950. After building the highways connecting Oaxaca-Tuxtla Gutiérrez, México-Ciudad Juárez, and Guaymas-Hermosillo-Nogales, a new stage was reached in 1947 when the Caminos Vecinales was instituted to provide smaller feeder roads.[32] Mexico's 1941 agreement with the United States to purchase $10 million of road bonds, as a way of absorbing wartime surpluses without interrupting production for the war effort, provided an important stimulus to road building.[33] As soon as roads were completed, the telegraph arrived and bus service followed. Luis González recorded that in 1943 the Flecha Roja bus service first came to San José de Gracia as the México-Manzanillo route became passable, although work was suspended for a while after the end of the war. Still, a partially completed road meant a mere twelve-hour journey to Mexico City, or three hours to Guadalajara, and within a year, cinema and radio came to town.[34] For the villagers, the world was becoming larger.

Petroleum consumption nearly quadrupled over the decade as people quickly made use of the new highways. Another benefit of wartime cooperation was the acceptance by U.S. diplomats of the great Pan-American Highway project. Although a great deal of sentimental nonsense was uttered about linking the hemisphere from pole to pole, or about its effect on tourism, U.S. diplomats clearly understood that this project was essentially a way to increase exports. By contrast, the railroads suffered considerable deterioration over the decade because of extremely heavy usage during the war. On the eve of the Korean War in 1950, it was estimated that the railroad network would be of minimal value if another war were to again require Mexico's resources. In 1950 there were 105,162 trucks and 17,872 busses in the country. But trucks lasted an average of only six years, so rough were the roads.[35] Tramways made it easy to get around in most major cities, and the occasional line even extended out into the countryside, as from Puebla to Cholula.

One U.S. embassy official took the adventurous course of driving from Texas to Mexico City to take up his posting immediately after the war.[36] Traveling south from Texas, the roads were passable on the northern deserts. Leaving Saltillo, however, he recorded that the roads petered out, and the motorists had to dead reckon over the mountains, judging which route would get them back to the completed section of the highway closest to San Luis Potosí as they climbed to the central plateau. The photographic record of the period of wartime cooperation richly illustrates the extreme difficulties of road travel in the 1940s.[37] As an alternative, aviation grew rapidly as a half-million flights carried 5.5 million passengers during the decade.[38]

Yet for the vast majority, work on the land was still the basis of the social order. According to the 1940 rural census, some 193,000 owners held 290,000 rural properties larger than five hectares, covering 29,600,000 hectares. It also reported that there were 929,000 units smaller than five hectares, of which 497,000 were less than one hectare—true *minifundias*. The country's 14,681 ejidos had grown, at least in government reports, to rival private landholding by encompassing 28,900,000 hectares by 1940.

Campesinos

Rural life was based on the agricultural cycle. For the men, there was the endless labor on the land. Life came with the rains to the *milpas* (cornfields) in central and southern Mexico. Before the rains arrived the land had to be cultivated, fertilized, and planted. So fundamental was this cycle to peasant society that at one point during the Caste War of Yucatán, a century earlier, as the Indians in rebellion were on the verge of casting their masters out of the peninsula, they broke off the battle—on the very brink of victory— to return to the planting.[39] Food for the next year took precedence over victory, for there was no one else to plant the corn. The agricultural calendar was absolute.

As the rains arrived, the weeding and tending of the crops took on a new dimension. Modern plows were beginning to come into the fields; however, in many areas, traditional plows pulled by oxen were still common. (Tractors, first imported in large numbers for the war effort, represented a different universe.) The machete, the first item of hardware to come to the *campo*, made it easier to weed, but it also made the weeds come back stronger. Stones and raw-hide were still the tools the rural worker used for digging, smoothing, and moving the earth.[40] Fields were not fenced off, and humans or animals could easily threaten the crop. Vigilance might ward off an animal and protect the precious corn, but it was of little use against the marauding bands that history too readily called armies. If a crop was lost the peasant had no insurance or alternative cash crop to fall back upon—only famine. An innovation that went astray was life-threatening, and that lesson, driven home over the centuries, made peasants extremely wary of new methods of production.

After the harvest there was some time to rest as the dry season set in. After all, the *zacate* was as well stored where it stood in the fields as it was in a shed until it could be used for fodder and fires. Even the odd corn rain mattered very little before the signs in the late spring sky alerted peasants to the need to finish their preparation of the land, as the endless cycle came around again. Animal fertilizer and seeds had to be added to the prepared land in the hope that the timing was right to catch the first rains in May or June. More than a hundred varieties of corn had evolved over the millennia as each strain of seed settled into its most suitable ecological niche.

The peasants' homes were simple and their possessions were few. Typically, house walls were made of adobe and roofs were terra-cotta tiles. The floors were hard-packed dirt; there was neither running water nor toilets. The walls were covered with whitewash that came from ground limestone, or *cal*. In the highlands, where fuel was scarce, few houses had chimneys for the cooking fire, since charcoal does not smoke. Open cooking fires had been outside. (In the hot country, where fuel was abundant, smoke helped keep insects at bay.) If adobe and roof tiles were beyond the family's means, the roofs would be made of thatch and the walls would be a mixture of mud, sticks, and corn stalks, or *zacate*. Furnishings were sparse; personal possessions were stored in clay pots. Whereas traditionally people had slept without bedding on straw mats, called *petates*, with *sarapes* and *rebozos* offering their only protection from the night air, prosperous individuals were acquiring beds in the 1940s.[41] At the other extreme, Lourdes Arizpe records that for occasional fieldhands in the 1940s, there was frequently only a ditch in which to sleep.[42] There was, however, another formidable sign of change. Cement production tripled over the decade to 1,387,000 metric tons, and this implied that a change in the landscape was on the horizon; cement cubes would soon replace traditional adobe and terra-cotta dwellings, and the atrium, or *patio*, style of architecture would fade.

For women, work revolved around the home and the preparation of the corn. Before the electricity-powered grinding mill that captured Oscar Lewis's attention came to the village, the daily grinding of corn into powder was done on the ancient grinding stone. A bit of limestone and some water were added to make the *masa*, or dough, which was then cooked on a flat surface to make tortillas. And they had to be fresh—so the water was hauled, the fire was tended, and the meals prepared. Laundry could be done with an amazingly small amount of water, and the simple trick of splashing an extra bit of water on the clothing as it dried made bleach redundant. (This was the key to the amazingly clean and white clothing that peasants wore in the fields and about which travelers marveled.) A woman wore the traditional *rebozo* while she worked, enabling her to carry an infant while keeping her hands free.

Women washing clothes. *Courtesy Hermanos Mayo, Archivo General de la Nación, Mexico City*

The sexual revolution had not yet come to the *campo*, and notions of romantic love of the sort now proffered in *telenovelas* (soap operas) were virtually unknown. Knowledge about sexuality was minimal, misinformation was common, and existing attitudes favored sexual restraint—although such restraint was not necessarily based upon a sense of guilt. Although he was talking about the towns, Carlos Monsiváis explained the use of the *sábana santa*, "corte en el medio para evitar el conocimiento de desnudez de la esposa."[43] The chaperon or *dueña* system was reserved for the more affluent youths in the towns, just as the brothel and *casa chica* were for prosperous men and poor women. In the countryside, neither dating nor kissing were practiced, although courtship was beginning to replace arranged marriages. Women commonly described pregnancy as "being ill with child" and frequently viewed men's attentions as an abuse. Lewis reported that adolescent girls believed sexual intercourse was painful and thought sexual organs to be ugly.[44] Nevertheless, the children somehow arrived. Each child minded the younger, collected firewood, and watched over the animals. The family was usually said to be patriarchal and hierarchical, although, upon close observation, some women were found to exercise extremely important roles in the markets and village economy.

Market day was vital. In small villages, it came once a week, although it became more frequent as the size of a town grew. In the towns and cities in the 1940s, a frequent municipal project was to clear an area and build a permanent market that would operate regularly. Sanitation improved, since at the end of each day the cement stalls could be hosed down. In addition to providing items that could not be produced at home, the market was the focus of social life. Not only food but also cheap clothing, simple hardware, tools, and folk medicines were available. People would travel a long way to attend, and the night before the market, there was good cheer before people fell asleep around the market. In the *campo*, there could be no running to the shops to buy something if one forgot it on market day. Indeed, the villages and many small towns had neither restaurants nor shops.

It was a world without clocks, calendars, cinema, television, newspapers, books, electricity, or appliances; even the transistor radio was still more than a decade away. (For many rural Mexicans, the first films they saw were wartime propaganda efforts screened around the country by U.S. embassy propaganda officers, using portable generators and projectors, to build support for the war effort.) Pleasures were immediate. In the evening, conversation recalled the events of the day in great detail, and the oral tradition made storytelling an art form. A guitar or an accordion might provide music, and pulque was the reward for the light work of tending the maguey cactus; however, beer and tequila—distilled in a factory from the agave cactus—were pushing that cottage industry aside with astonishing speed.

Pain was common since a simple cut could become infected and fester, or a toothache could generate agony. The local *curandera*, or healer, tapped ancient knowledge of natural cures, and some local remedies actually worked. However, the lack of clean water and sewage systems constantly generated disease. In the 1930s health workers were proud of the government's effort to bring potable water to rural areas; yet by their count they extended clean water to only 263 villages in the entire country. In 1943 a major step was taken with the founding of the Secretaría de Salubridad y Asistencia. A national network of hospitals was started, and a program of inoculation against infectious diseases was also begun. Although headway was being made in health care, many peasants still had only the solace they found in the Church's assurance that for the dutiful the next world would be better.

Above all, there were few choices—one did what one was born to do. As had been true from the most ancient times, life was sustained by four staples: corn for tortillas, beans, chiles, and zucchini. Clothing was still spun in remote villages; however, cheap manufactured textiles were available in the markets, and dress instantly revealed the division between the traditional sector and the modern. In 1943 the price of a kilo of *masa* was 0.09 peso or, 115 pesos per ton, and *manteca*, the lard that was used in the preparation of beans and for cooking, was inflated to a scandalous 2.50 pesos per kilo (a day's wage for a rural laborer in the central highlands or a week's wage in Yucatán). It provided a successful diet if all of the components were present. In the absence of even one of these items, however, malnutrition quickly occurred.

Festivals and Celebrations

The agricultural calendar was intimately linked to the cycle of religious celebrations. Over the years, ceremonies and festivals were superimposed one over the other, and the village calendar revolved around them. The anti-clerical prohibition of religious processions in the 1917 constitution was a forlorn gesture in many rural areas. In Michoacán the Church served as a rallying point for local culture against the incursions of centralism, from the *reforma* to the *cristiada*, and into the Cárdenas era, much to the consternation of the central authorities.[45] Even the design of Tarascan houses and churches announced immediately that different cultural forces were at work, some of which were very old. Yet that state also produced Lázaro Cárdenas.

Local culture was a complex amalgamation of influences, accumulated layer by layer over the centuries. Just as the "Flowery Wars" parades at Easter may have evoked some remote and distorted memory of things Aztec, they also allowed the prosperous to show off their coaches and horses. In Papantla, Veracruz, the "flying Indians" amazed visitors from around the world with their ability to combine dance with aerial acrobatics. Those dances were clearly pre-Columbian in origin. By contrast, in Tonantzintla the passion plays and street theater at Easter used the forms and masks that the early friars had brought to Mexico to instruct the Indians in the rudiments of Christian theology and iconography. The Moors, cast as eternal villains from the Spanish reconquest, paraded each year in their gruesome masks, although popular understanding of the rituals had evolved beyond recognition. In neighboring Cholula the colonial influence was closer to the surface. As the rains approached, a special statue was taken from the church, Nuestra Señora de los Remedios, on top of the great Pyramid of Quetzalcoatl, down to one of the hundreds of churches in the town. The accompanying celebrations and processions were important in their own right, but this was also the signal to plant the corn.

So deeply were the agricultural cycles integrated with the religious calendar that they seemed equally a part of nature to many villagers. It was this link, rather than mere religious superstition, as the liberals of the *reforma* and many revolutionaries believed, that forged the fundamental bond between the villagers and the Church. The *tequilíliztle,* or communal work for the Church or municipality, was still common, and villagers also had perpetual obligations associated with celebrations and festivals. (Pop economists, ignoring the rights of landowners, interest rates, and mandated prices for corn, complained that this village cargo system was what had decapitalized the *campo.*) Yet for the Church authorities "their" traditions frequently became unrecognizable as ancient popular traditions mixed with and at times contaminated "proper" theology from Rome.

In Cuetzalan, in the Sierra de Puebla, the festival named in honor of San Fernando de Asís lasted three or four days in October, always including a weekend. The tradition of the cargo cult allocated the organization of the festival to the *mayordomo* of the saint being honored. Substantial costs fell on him, including a great feast of *mole poblano* for the entire town, but there was great prestige as well. Dances, religious processions, and festivals mixed with strong drink just as pre-Columbian and Christian religious elements intermingled. Different groups performed the dances/ceremonies of *Voladores, Quetzales, Negritos* (from Cuba), *Santiagos, Españoles y Moros,* and *malinches.* Fireworks and candle processions, costumes and masks, the magnificent headpieces of the Quetzales—all made the world magic for a few days. Some anthropologists think that the very measurements, the speed and rate of descent of the *hombres pajaros* who fly out from a forty-meter post, reflected the Aztec measurement of time.[46] Such festivals marked the passing of the seasons and were a break from rural labor.

Peasant unwillingness to embrace "progressive" urban-generated reform movements, from the *reforma* to the *cristiada,* infuriated political leaders. A striking example of the cultural chasm that could exist between the country and the city was the response of the workers of the Red Brigades to the entrance of Emiliano Zapata's army—their allies—upon the conquest of Mexico City in 1915. The workers were incredulous. How could Zapata's triumphant forces carry banners of the Virgin of Guadalupe as they marched into the capital that they had conquered? To the urban workers, this banner was a symbol of Spanish, and later of upper-class, domination. For the rural majority, traditional religious celebrations were still an essential part of village life.

There was also a counterforce. In some rural areas, most notably but not only in Tabasco, anticlericalism developed deep roots, and people in this tradition remembered odious religious sanctions: the enforcement of religious vows, forced tithes, Church taxes, and the Church's monopoly over the civil register—issues that we tend to forget about today.[47] Even in less radical areas, a new set of secular celebrations was challenging the old religious monopoly over festivals. The burning of the Judas at the end of Lent had not really been a religious festival, although it was linked to the Church's calendar. In Mexico City, the social inversion associated with the Judas burnings remained popular in Tepito, Colonia del Valle, and La Merced through the 1940s.[48] Increasingly, celebrations of national independence on September 16 were becoming far more common, and the *bodas de oro* became secular village celebrations. Even simple pleasures like playing cards and billiards created alternative social clusters in the smallest village.[49]

For rural Mexicans, work followed the cycle of the agricultural calendar, and the issue was what claim on production the workers would have. Payday was a foreign concept in the *campo.* For the owners of land, the crops were sold at harvest time, yet even they usually depended on the local *agiotista*, or moneylender, who charged extraordinarily high rates of interest (around 40 percent) from planting to harvest. In 1947 the government was unable to sell its development bonds at 6 percent. Prime bank rates were around 12 to 18 percent, but the Banco de Pequeño Comercio charged 5 percent per day.[50] For the rest of the rural population, the use of a plot of land for subsistence farming was the best alternative, far better than the occasional work that provided the most precarious living in the country. The various mechanisms that extracted surplus from rural Mexico were so effective that at the end of each year's labor, there was little new accumulation for those who actually produced the crops.

The cash economy was quite limited, although there were some rural industries that brought currency to the villages. Market gardening was a possibility if one were close to a town, mine, the railroad, or some other enterprise. Sadly, the techniques of grafting had been largely lost after independence, and orchards had deteriorated in many places. Almost anyone could make adobe, although kiln-fired bricks were still rare. Adobe blocks and the ubiquitous terra-cotta roofing tiles were rural industries that required only access to the right clays, manure, water, and firewood. Outcroppings of limestone provided the whitewash for the traditional rural building before paint became generally available. And Mexican stonemasons were among the best in the world when a major project was undertaken.

Most important was the horse and livestock industry. The breeding of animals for burden and transport was a traditional staple of the village economy. Fine animals from rural Mexico were desired by even the highest and most powerful. At the other end of the livestock scale, pigs were kept by poor families as a form of family savings. Before they were able to work in the fields, children little older than toddlers were assigned an animal to watch over all day. It was a grave responsibility. In central and southern Mexico raising livestock was a cottage industry; however, the great pastoral estates still dominated in the north where sparse rains and the proximity of U.S. markets combined to ensure that herding would be on a large and more commercial scale.

There was also a robust tradition of folk medicine in which herbs and charms were used for medicinal and superstitious purposes. In a society where medical relief was in its infancy and what existed was poorly distributed, the need for relief from pain was great.

People lived with some degree of pain for most of their lives, and the medicinal and psychological impact of the folk cures and artifacts kept the women who specialized in the sale of these items busy in the markets. Belief structures were tightly integrated with these practices, and it was common to see people cover their mouths with a handkerchief as temperatures changed—to avoid illness. In remote regions these practices continue today and give us a glimpse of the pre-modern medical past.[51] Today there are still sections in markets where traditional remedies are sold, and the great pharmacological companies have studied many of the properties of folk medicines in recent decades. Although traditional remedies still played a major role in people's lives, when quinine, penicillin, and sulfa drugs became available in the 1940s, modernity took a great step forward.

For the vast majority of rural people, the family and village economies dominated their working lives. Their rewards were rarely in cash, unless they made something they could sell beyond the village. For many individuals the village economy was still fairly self-sufficient—although not in the sense of the importance of its production for the national economy—and villagers resisted reformers and land-grabbers alike in trying to keep their lands and run their own affairs. The effort expended in the village economy was necessary so that the individual could enjoy sustenance from the family's labor. One worked to eat; it was not the same as what urban people thought of as having a job.

Paid Work

The Mexican census of 1940 characterized only 32 percent of the labor force, or 5.8 million Mexicans, as economically active. Yet two out of three adults of working age did not just sit around; they produced items of subsistence in the peasant or artisan economy. Of those who produced for the marketplace directly or had paying jobs, 5.4 million were men. The 4.2 million men and 9.5 million women listed as "inactive" were found largely in the villages.[52] By 1950 the census reported that apart from the 8.8 million children under twelve, 7.6 million women and 900,000 men were still economically inactive. To the purveyors of modernity, the village economy counted very little, and this was as much a matter of culture as of economics.

What these categories missed was the movement from country to town and at times the other way around. Families would fre-

Women sweeping up rice after wedding in order to feed themselves, Mexico City. *Courtesy Hermanos Mayo, Archivo General de la Nación, Mexico City*

quently split their chances by covering both worlds. If a paid job was forthcoming, it opened the way for the family to participate in the cash economy; however, people were not yet entirely dependent on the cash economy, and wages could be supplemented by petty commodity production on a small parcel of land. There was also the common practice of pursuing multiple tasks rather than the single job by which urban folk increasingly define themselves.

Artisans

The other vast network to which decision makers were indifferent as they committed the country to the industrial push of the 1940s was the artisan economy. Small workshops, frequently linked to the home, occupied a central place in the period. It is difficult to get a sense of the size of this sector of society, for artisans, independent producers, and small merchants tended to merge in different reports. Nevertheless, there is a suggestion that the 1940s were part of an early stage of petty commodity production that was on the increase, before the final ascendancy of the factory system. José Calixto Rangel Contla recalculated census data and concluded that independent producers increased from 44.8 percent to 52.8 percent of the labor force between 1940 and 1950.[53]

It is rare to get a detailed glimpse of this world, as one does in 1943 when a U.S. association of women's clubs organized a tour of a glass-making factory in Mexico City. When the group found abuse and endemic disease among the barefoot children working in the factory, they were so shocked that they challenged their embassy officials, under the United States' New Deal labor legislation, to block exports of its fine glassware to expensive department stores including Marshall Field's in Chicago and Lord and Taylor's in New York City. Their effort convinced diplomats of the truthfulness of their allegations, but got them nowhere.[54]

Although census data purported to capture artisan activity, it was difficult to estimate, and artisans were relegated to the category of "others." Their statistical irrelevance clashed quite starkly with their importance in society. Extremely small-scale production was precarious and frequently highly exploitative of the workers. This was production on a financial shoestring in an environment that was, at least for artisans, highly competitive. Banks were reluctant to loan to this sector, and government programs ignored them. When artisans tried to band together in cooperatives in order to pool capital and benefit from economies of scale, private enterprise and the government worked against them. Even people on the left applied Marx's theory of surplus value or notions of the "aristocracy of labor" to their operations. In short, artisans were without political cover.[55]

The problem was that as the more efficient factories inevitably took their toll on these workshops, it had a terrible effect on employment, since this had been a labor-intensive sector. The rise of the factories, based upon the logic of capital and cost-per-unit production, was inevitable, and increasing unemployment—even in periods of rapid growth—was the price of this efficiency. To take the example of the soap industry, there were some two hundred ninety factories and workshops producing soap in Mexico in 1949, when all but a handful were forced out of business.[56] As the war started, there were new military demands for the glycerin the industry produced; however, other forces doomed the soap makers. Wartime propaganda teams using trucks carrying portable generators, sound systems, and projectors brought film footage to remote villages. These propaganda films came bundled with soap advertisements that were so effective that after the propaganda teams worked an area, Colgate Palmolive's sales went up and the domestic soap producers faced declining sales.[57]

Certain sectors such as glass making, *artesanías*, or wood or leather craft work established a real presence as tourists and exporters discovered unbelievable bargains. Mexican craftspeople brought great style and beauty to many of their products. Even folk arts found a market niche. Travelers were amazed to find Tarascan potters "so devout they will only ply their hereditary trade on the feast days of St. Ursula and St. Martín."[58] However, most artisans had an up-hill battle against the relentless efficiency of the factory. As foreign machines designed in an environment of high labor costs came to Mexico, they made industrial jobs even fewer. But the full impact of this phenomenon was still decades away. In the 1940s the triumph of the factory over the artisan was definitely considered progress.

In regional centers such as Guadalajara, which serviced large agricultural districts and had a few specialized industries—tanning, tequila, beer, soft drinks, animal feeds, and shoes—the problems of urbanization were less severe as their suburbs rather than slums grew.[59] The high concentration of workshops and small industries was provided with considerable stimulus by production for the war effort, and those individuals who benefited spurred a building boom. Whereas from 1900 to 1943, eighteen new zones for residential housing were approved, from 1944 to 1949 alone, another thirty-two residential zones were started.[60] Then in 1945 the governor, General Marcelino García Barragán, founded an industrial zone along the railroad line to Nogales.

There were also new sectors of the economy that prospered in the decade. The harvest of fish quadrupled, from 6.3 million kilos in 1941 to 25.4 million in 1950. Mining, which had boomed during the war years, stabilized after 1947. An aggregate index in which 1929 = 100 showed that the norm for the decade was around 75–77, with the boom year of 1942–43 jumping to 87. Manufacturing figures showed a rapid acceleration of production as an overall index of industrial production (by amount produced, in which 1929 = 100), reaching 119.6 in 1940 and growing to 192 in 1950.

Industrial Workers

Workers who found jobs in the new industries faced a different world. The tyranny of time and the discipline of the factory forced them into a harsh world. The "dark Satanic mills" of the early industrial revolution were inhospitable places, where health and safety were routinely ignored. Balanced against their good wages, workers in PEMEX's petroleum refineries found their health at risk; even their right to free medicine was eliminated under President Alemán. In the nationalized factories, striking against the government was a great deal more difficult than taking on an unpopular foreign employer.

Mexico was both old and new in the 1940s. It was the location of the oldest permanent human settlements in the Americas. Cholula, with its grand pyramid that was rebuilt seven times before the Spaniards even dreamed of its gold, claims the longest continuous human settlement in the Western Hemisphere. The cities of Mexico were established long before the industrial revolution

changed the world beyond recognition. When the railroads came
to Mexico they did not change the pattern of human settlement as
they had in the United States as people pushed beyond the Missis-
sippi River. The railroads virtually bypassed major provincial cities such as Guanajuato or Querétaro since the core of these cities
had been finished centuries before. Yet, from the perspective of the
second industrial revolution and the expansion of the modern corporation, Mexico had only been slightly touched during the
porfiriato. Although during the revolution, as Alan Knight has demonstrated, fury was not directed against large U.S. corporations,
the fighting inevitably reduced business activity, and the long battle
between the state and the petroleum companies scared off many
foreign businesses.[61] On the eve of World War II, Alan Bateman,
head of the Metals Reserve Corporation, the agency in charge of
providing minerals for the war effort, admitted that Mexico's natural resources were virtually uncharted.[62] To the world of international business, Mexico was virgin territory in the 1940s.

Production that Mattered

What did count in the international arena was the expansion of the
modern corporation into Latin America. As Mark Berger points out,
Adolf A. Berle, Jr., the long-time Latin America specialist in the
State Department, called this expansion "a general advance in civilization," a phrase that Yale's diplomatic historian Samuel F. Bemis
and businessmen of the day such as Lamar Flemming, the president of Anderson, Clayton and Company, found so exciting that
they used it repeatedly, although the term "Pan Americanism" eventually replaced it as less offensive.[63] In the context of the first half
of the decade, the phrase meant production for the war effort.
Mexico's production of nonferrous minerals and strategic agricultural products was of great importance to the war effort. After production for the war effort peaked there was a painful period of
adjustment, after which Berle's "advance" meant the expansion of
the international corporation into Latin America.

Foreign investment flooded Mexico, and a new arrangement
linked foreign investors with the local power structure. The promise was for a modern, prosperous future and that meant urbanization. There was no romanticization of rural life, and no rewards
were extended for ethnographic authenticity. The rural past was
viewed as uncivilized, and even dress standards instantly signaled
a world of difference between the *campesino*, in traditional, home-

spun white cotton garb; the ranchero, dressed in the style of the *charro*; and the urban professional, in a European-style dark suit. The urban was the progressive, and industrialization was the goal. To the poet José Emilio Pacheco, the ubiquitous visual image of Miguel Alemán personified the official dream of an industrial utopia:

> The smiling face of Misterpresident everywhere: immense draw-ings, idealized portraits, ubiquitous photographs, allegories of progress with Miguel Alemán as God the Father, laudatory char-acterizations, monuments. Public adulation, inescapable private misery. We wrote a thousand times in notebooks as our punish-ment: I must be obedient, I must be obedient, I must be obedient with my parents and with my teachers. They taught us patriotic history, the national language, geography of the Federal District: the rivers (there were rivers then) the mountains (you could still see the mountains).[64]

The other kind of production that mattered was that associ-ated with the dream of modernity. Although there had been tenta-tive projects of modernization as far back as the eighteenth century, industrialization became a passion in the 1940s. The attraction of an affluent urban lifestyle was indisputable:

> Without any doubt there was hope. Our textbooks affirmed it: seen on a map, Mexico has the shape of a cornucopia or a horn of plenty. By the unimaginable 1980—without specifying how we were going to achieve it—there would be a future of universal plenty and well-being. Clean cities, without injustice, without the poor, without violence, without congestion, without garbage. For every family there would be an ultra modern, aerodynamic house (favorite words of the epoch). No one would want. Machines would do the work. Resplendent streets with trees and fountains, crossed by vehicles without smoke or pollution, without colli-sions. Paradise on earth. Utopia at last conquered.[65]

Some products seemed to represent the cutting edge of this modernity. The automobile industry came to play a central role here. After the war, cars and trucks of the Ford Motor Company (Ford and Mercury), of General Motors (Cadillac, Buick, and Pontiac), of Chrysler (Dodge, Plymouth, and De Soto), as well as of Packard, Nash, Hudson, Studebaker, Mack, and International Harvester, were all sold in Mexico.[66] The ascendancy of the motor car was a matter of state policy, although there was a constant battle over the quota that each company could import. PEMEX kept the price of gasoline low, although businesses complained to the president in

1948 about the price of fuel, which was then 35 centavos, or 12 U.S. cents, per gallon.[67] Motor vehicle registration grew in the Federal District as neither congestion nor pollution was a problem.[68]

Vehicles	1949	1952	1953
Autos	52,835	93,576	96,931
Busses	4,221	6,282	7,174
Trucks	12,538	22,717	23,477
Motorcycles	2,538	3,501	3,823
Total	72,190*	126,076	131,405

*Error in the total data figure reflects the quality of statistical estimates in the 1940s.

Antonio Ruiz Galindo, an industrialist and a frequent economic minister, tried several times to build a national automobile. First, he assembled several D-M Nacional autos, surrounding them with considerable publicity, even displaying the cars in the window of the Distribuidora Mexicana building on Madero Avenue. Only the body was produced in his factories; the engine was a Ford V-8. Then he attempted to come to an agreement with Fiat and/or Opel to put domestic bodies on European chassis. However, none of his efforts was successful.[69]

When, after the war, the Mexican government commissioned the production of Carmen Toscano's film *Memorias de un Mexicano*, it clearly revealed the importance of this vision of industrial modernity. The film magnificently used contemporary footage of the great revolution to recount the winner's version of events, from Madero's triumphal entrance into Mexico City to Carranza's departure on the *tren dorado*. In the final sequences of the film, shot in the late 1940s, factory assembly lines in full production were clearly represented as the ultimate meaning of the epic struggle. Even as it was being made, the film was viewed as a national treasure.[70]

Support for modern industries was at the top of the public agenda. In analyzing the changes in the federal budget between 1947 and 1948, one U.S. economic diplomat stated, "The largest single increase, 'additional expenditures,' is believed by Mrs. [M. S.] Tomich, the fiscal expert in the embassy, to be largely subsidy payments or rebates on taxes paid by import and export groups and tax exempt new industries. As this item has never entered fully into the public accounting of the Nation, its inclusion [would be] good fiscal practice."[71]

Stimulating the modern lifestyle was a paramount goal of decision makers. To own a home in Mexico City was a golden dream. Some people made headway fulfilling this ideal, so much so that

by 1942 journalists writing for *Hoy* complained that the old neigh-
borhoods (*colonias* Roma, Anzures, Juárez, and so on) had been superseded by seventy-one new colonies too numerous for anyone to
know.[72] To fill these homes, the latest products were displayed at
the Palacio de Hierro and the Puerto de Liverpool, and there was
tremendous excitement when, later in the decade, Sears, Roebuck
opened a chain of quality department stores in Mexico. Within this
context the films of the era played a greater role than mere entertainment. By portraying a modern, consumer-oriented lifestyle of
opulence, they were also creating a demand for producers. And
the battle for control of the media of mass communications—examined in Chapter 6—represented domination of the future to the
industrial magnates who fought for the privilege.

For those who could afford to keep up with *la nueva honda*, a
modern lifestyle meant *hamburgesas* and *jotdogs* rather than tacos
and *refrescos en botella* rather than *tepache*; it meant that a *jaibol* of
whisky or a cognac was preferable to tequila, to say nothing of the
now contemptible pulque. If an item came from Sears, Roebuck or,
better still, from California—it was something to talk about at
Sanborne's. And the English classes at the USIS center on Calle
Hamburgo in the *zona rosa* were booming, much to the pride of the
U.S. ambassador. According to one industry estimate, 1,854 television sets had been sold by the end of 1950.[73]

Newspapers brought signs of change, sometimes in surprising
ways. The war between the Arab League and Israel had Mexican
children playing *árabes y judíos*, from which José Pacheco took the
title of his reminiscences. Although the readership of newspapers
was growing, by today's standards their circulation in the D.F, even
in 1954, was extremely limited.

Newspaper	Daily	Sunday
Excélsior	116,277	140,500
El Universal	110,038	139,585
Novedades	77,000 (est.)	n.a.

The circulation of weekly magazines was also very limited in a
country of twenty million people.[74]

Magazine	Circulation	Owner
Manaña	18,820	Daniel Morales
Hoy	17,433	Lebrija & Arrache
Todo	60,500	E. Salcedo Ledesma
Siempre	17,500	José Pages Llergo

Tiempo	16,698	M. Luis Guzmán
Revista de Revistas	28,294	Excélsior
Sucesos	64,174	Francisco Sayrols

Tourists and Braceros

One of the new luxuries of the period was the emergence of mass tourism for pleasure. A daily Pullman sleeper train made the trip from Saint Louis to Mexico City (in 48 hours), and similar fast trains came from El Paso (46 hours), Laredo (29 hours), and Nogales (65 hours). Although foreign travelers had been attracted by Mexico's charms for centuries, working tourists on holiday were beginning to come to Mexico in 1940 in large numbers. In that year 139,000 visited the country, a number that increased to 305,561 by 1949. And when tourists found their way to Antonio Ruiz Galindo's exquisite new hotel at Fortín de las Flores, Veracruz, where fresh gardenias floated on the swimming pool each morning, many thought they had found the Platonic ideal of tourism.

Mexico set up a surprisingly powerful Department of Tourism to help tourists find their way and also to protect them from official abuse; the police quickly learned that the *mordida*, or semiofficial bribe, was not to be applied to these new visitors. Prices were regulated to avoid gouging and from their prominent offices on Juárez Avenue officials attended to complaints. Uniformed and licensed bilingual guides complemented the new highways that welcomed visitors, and a new industry emerged to provide a wide range of associated services for tourists. And in some years, more Mexicans visited the United States than the other way around.

In 1940 *The South American Handbook* described Mexico City: "It is laid out prettily with trees and flowers, and has fine modern buildings." It covered only fifteen square miles, and there was extensive open land in the D.F. Chapultepec Park, with its thousands of *ahuehuete* trees, was among the most beautiful park in the world. The core of the city could still be traversed by walking, and the name of a street changed each block in some areas of the *zócalo* and city center, revealing the mental landscape of a smaller urban world. History was close by on a walk along Avenue Balderas around the old Ciudadela, the armory where shot and artillery marks could still be seen in the walls from the *decina tragica* during the revolution. And the great boulevards—especially the Paseo de La Reforma and the Avenues Juárez and Insurgentes—remained as lavish gifts from a failed conqueror.

The capital boasted nine hotels with rooms from 5 pesos, eleven hotels with rooms from 10 pesos, and the two top hotels—the Hotel Anzures and the Hotel Reforma—with rooms costing over 15 pesos. (A decade later, hotels in the city were too numerous to list.) An extra 1.5 pesos added board in the moderate hotels, or travelers could dine at one of sixteen American, German, Spanish, French, or Italian restaurants, of which Sanborne's and the Bellinghausen are still in business today; alarmingly, there was also a Restaurante Swastika. There were seven cabarets—Ciro's had not yet been built—and six cocktail bars. The foreign community lived well in the Swiss, British, American, German, Spanish, or Rotary clubs, or at the Chapultepec Heights Golf Club above the park, and tennis clubs were fashionable. On a weekend, an excursion to the British, German, or Spanish boating clubs at Lake Xochimilco was popular, or an ascent of the volcano Popocatepetl could be attempted from Amecameca. Alternatively, a weekend in the perpetual springtime of Cuernavaca could be reached in two hours by car or four hours by train.

Mixcoac with its large nursery gardens was still nine miles southwest of the city, and San Angel was at the heart of a fruit-growing district. Tacubaya, "seven miles south-west, is one of the most populous and fashionable suburbs, with large country houses." Even a pilgrimage to the shrine of the Virgin of Guadalupe at Tepeyac, with its twenty-seven-ton silver railing, took the faithful two and one-half miles beyond the edge of the capital city. And the truly adventurous traveler who went to Acapulco in 1940 found four tourist hotels—El Miradór, La Quebrada, Homos, and the Tropicál—in that town of six thousand, where the main industry was distilling the oil of limes.[75] Within a few years the presidents of the 1940s would transform the town definitively as they promoted it as a location for the international jet set. Ultimately, President Alemán used the pleasures of the resort to entertain the foreign corporate elite and to cement business deals.

Besides the old wealthy travelers and the "Hawaiian shirt" set, many of the tourists were a new breed, including, for the first time, large numbers of teachers and students coming for a holiday on which to learn as well as to enjoy. Some liked the country so much that they returned to it to study after the war. U.S. soldiers discovered that their GI Bill entitlements for education enabled them to live quite well and to study at the new Mexico City College, located at kilometer sixteen on the México-Toluca highway. Over the next three decades this bilingual institution attracted many

distinguished scholars: Mexicans who sought relief from the bureaucracy at UNAM, and foreign academics who treasured the opportunity to live, teach, and study for prolonged periods in
Mexico.[76]

Braceros were the reciprocal of tourists, at the poverty end of
the scale. The bracero program, which was revived to provide unskilled labor to replace soldiers, had been initiated on U.S. demand
in the early years of the war, so quickly had the war shifted conditions from depression levels of unemployment to labor shortages.[77]
Even though the program tapered off after the war, U.S. diplomats
wanted to retain the program for several years, and Mexican diplomats used the continuation of the bracero program as a bargaining chip.[78] Texas was officially prohibited from participating during
this period because racism against Mexicans was so extreme in the
state, although that restriction was easily circumvented in practice. Nevertheless, millions of peasants endured racism, back-
breaking labor, and appalling living conditions to earn dollars to
send home to help their families and, they hoped, purchase a small
plot of land.[79]

So it was a complex picture, one in which unskilled rural laborers and larger numbers of Mexican tourists entered the United

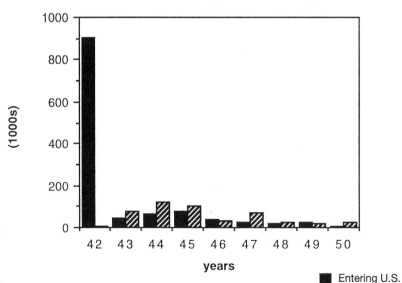

Braceros entering and leaving U.S.

States at the same time as foreign investors, tourists, researchers, teachers, and students discovered Mexico. Attempts to control the border were loose, and Mexico established, in effect, a second frontier at kilometer eighteen, where serious customs and immigration checks were made. In the actual border zones, only token attempts were made to enforce customs regulations; U.S. automobiles and products circulated freely. In that milieu, ideas and customs flowed both ways even as Mexico's decision makers looked north for the latest innovations, products, and styles.

Science

The 1940s saw important scientific innovations. U.S.-Mexican agricultural cooperation in the war effort had led the Rockefeller Foundation to become involved with agricultural research. Vice President Henry Wallace's role was critical. He introduced the foundation's president, Raymond B. Fosdick, to the country by providing agricultural experts, first to support war production and later to develop continuing research projects. This was the origin of the research into hybrid seeds by Norman Borlaugh that eventually led to the "green revolution." It gave an enormous boost to agribusiness, which treated agricultural production as any other business, to be augmented by research and governed by market considerations alone.[80] Thus as Cynthia Hewett de Alcántara demonstrated for newly irrigated land in Sonora, a new kind of scientific agriculture was generated on private lands that were owned by a politically connected elite and watered by the new irrigation projects built with public funds. "At every stage in the process of technification of big agriculture in Sonora, monumental government investments were forthcoming, justified always on the grounds that the nation must become self-sufficient in wheat and that Sonora was the future wheat producing emporium of Mexico."[81]

The immediate scientific challenge of the decade was to contain an outbreak of deadly *aftosa*, or hoof-and-mouth disease. It was necessary to kill tens of thousands of cattle for fear that the disease would wipe out the rest. The prevalence of polio also reminded everyone of how far science still had to go. Still, the wartime seizure of the chemical and pharmaceutical companies forced a new wave of innovations on these firms, and penicillin, sulfa drugs, and the first antibiotics made a tremendous impression.

In 1943 the Secretaría de Salubridad y Asistencia was established with a dual mission of establishing a national network of hospitals and combating infectious diseases by means of national sanitation and inoculation campaigns. In association with the new national law of the professions, medical doctors were required to spend a period of internship in the countryside, and the impact of this rule on rural health was great. To their credit, medical practitioners—unique among Mexican professionals—maintained a commitment to rural Mexico and to the Secretaría de Salubridad y Asistencia health system. There was also an effort to link their programs to the efforts of the Instituto National Indigenista after its creation in 1948. The health system claimed to have reduced the number of deaths due to gastroenteritis from 487 to 280 per 100,000 over the decade of the 1940s. In addition, Mexican doctors achieved international distinction in areas such as cardiology.[82]

The birth control revolution of the 1950s was made possible by the work of an isolated scientist named Russell Marker, who discovered, in the Mexican desert in 1940, a wild yam that yielded prodigious amounts of progesterone. According to David Halberstam, "By 1943 he [Marker] was able to walk into a small wholesale pharmaceutical company in Mexico City with two pickle jars filled with powder worth more than $150,000 [dollars] on the open market. Did the owners want some progesterone, he asked."[83] The company's eager acceptance of Marker's innovation eventually provided the central hormone for the team led by Goody Pincus that gave the world the birth control pill.

In 1945, Nelson Rockefeller's sacking by Truman, because the president considered him a potential Republican rival, convinced the young billionaire to set up his own company, the International Basic Economy Corporation (IBEC), to demonstrate to the Latin Americans—and to President Truman—how to develop Latin America. The IBEC provided venture capital, primarily in Brazil and Venezuela. However, it also funded some businesses in Mexico in addition to indirectly supporting the Rockefeller Foundation's hybrid corn project.[84]

There were many areas that were still in their professional infancy. For example, in the entire country in 1940 only six people—half of them women—registered under the professional act in the career of psychology, a figure that grew to over 42,000 in the next three decades.[85] Or, for a more immediate kind of pain, only 1,424 of the country's 6,000 practicing dentists held a recognized degree in 1947, according to the Unión Mexicana de Dentistas Libres.[86] Modernity was not just a theoretical construct. The negative side of science was thrust upon the world in August 1945 when the United States detonated the only two atomic bombs ever dropped in anger. In Mexico the initial relief over the end of the war quickly turned to horror as the extent of the destruction became clear. Angel Lázaro, writing in *El Nacional*, quickly set the dominant tone on August 8, by calling the dropping of the atomic bomb on Hiroshima a war crime and comparing it to the German death camps. After Nagasaki was also destroyed by an atomic bomb, these events were increasingly characterized as "acts of terror." There was, however, an alternative view expressed on August 11, when *El Universal* called the bomb, "The dove that flew over the Pacific."

Manuel Sandoval Vallarta led a "small but active scientific community" in calling upon the government to support science in the universities to help the country keep abreast of these events, as Regis Cabral has demonstrated. The government moved to protect its new strategic minerals—uranium, thorium, and actinium—which were found in the Placer de Guadalupe region in Chihuahua, Durango, and Guerrero. All of the great issues of responsibility and the implications for the great power rivalries were quickly explored as the atomic age caught up with Mexico.[87]

Still, the positive side of science and technology was paramount. The country was committed to a rapid push for industrialization, which meant that those who understood the secrets of a factory were welcome in Mexico. In *War, Diplomacy and Development*, I argued that underconsumption theory served as the vital link between Mexico's revolutionary past and its new development strategy, at least before the Alemán administration closed off that option. Whereas old ideas of the inherent racial inferiority of the Indian had provided a fundamental understanding of poverty, such views were now less acceptable. It is instructive to see how Dr. Manuel Gamio, director of the Instituto Indigenista Interamericano, tried to combine the rejection of racism with underconsumption theory. In a letter to President Alemán, he congratulated the president for placing such importance on the need to increase production, both industrial and agricultural.

Gamio distinguished between what he called "integral" consumers, who "do not make up even 25 percent," and the poor, or "partial consumers," in the country. The solution was to make them all consumers. This was pure underconsumption theory. In Gamio's view, the goal was to teach the vast majority to "live better" and to "increase and diversify their needs, satisfying them with goods and services they do not enjoy, thus overcoming the old customs that oppose every change." The usual homilies against vice and low national self-esteem were trotted out. However, his fundamental premise was that it was the backward outlook of the bottom 75 percent of society, not their lack of income, that kept them bogged down in tradition. Even for the founding director of the Instituto Indigenista Interamericano, it was safer to call for education rather than policies to change income distribution.[88]

By the end of the decade, the range of acceptable opinion no longer tolerated a general objection to the presence of foreign capital in the country: "the Cámara Nacional de Industrias de Transformación does not oppose in principle direct industrial investments by foreign capital." But they had concluded that foreign investment was frequently negative because it displaced domestic industry, aimed at foreign markets, and eliminated national employment opportunities. The hopelessness of their position, however, was revealed by their forlorn effort to quote the 51 percent law to the president in the hope that he would follow more nationalist economic policies.[89]

It is interesting to watch how Alemán's closest advisers shifted their arguments away from the underconsumptionist analysis. The grand prize for contradictory analysis went to Antonio Carrillo Flores, director of Nacional Financiera. In 1948, at the time of a devaluation, he wrote a long and compassionate letter to President Alemán. In the letter he commiserated with the president in his difficult decision, acknowledging how lonely it was at the top for the nation's leader. He then reiterated the underconsumption analysis, even praising a timber company in Durango that subsidized food for its workers. At the same time, however, he maintained that there was an undeniably urgent need for austerity and order. The public would not be able to avoid many new sacrifices. Life would become dearer and more difficult for the great mass of people. The least that could be demanded of the rest was austerity. The president had the right to ask it of those who would not suffer and might even benefit through their business dealings.[90]

Finally, Carrillo Flores suggested that workers ought to invest more in the country's productive activities, even as they were suffering from the crisis of *carestía*. Being a high official meant it was essential to modify one's belief structure as the president revealed the next policy. (As the CTM's Fidel Velázquez stated every six years, as the next official candidate, or *tapado*, was announced: "Mr. President, you read our minds.") To more fully understand this process, it is useful to look at the variety of cultural responses to the changing political agenda.

Cultural Affirmations, Cultural Denials

The scale of life in the 1940s was more personal, as people in any field tended to know each other, and on a daily basis one could pass the famous and the infamous on the streets. The raw material with which the country's cultural figures constructed their world views emerged in a fairly self-contained world. There was always deep interest in Europe, although in the early part of the century the slavish replication of the latest trends had had a detrimental impact on the country's intellectual life.[91] Unevenly, the Mexican Revolution had unleashed powerful creative currents. The love-hate relationship with the United States was always central; the rest of the world, even the other countries in Latin America, had surprisingly slight impact.

The cultural and intellectual life of the country was concentrated in Mexico City, although a degree of autonomous local culture developed in the larger provincial cities such as Guadalajara, Veracruz, and Monterrey. Yet it was an uphill battle against the arrogance of the *chilangos*. Centrifugal cultural forces, not to mention money, irresistibly attracted the best and the brightest to the capital. Only recently have Mexicans at the top of their fields begun to think that their futures might have to be outside of the hypertrophic city. Historically, European and Latin American traditions equated civilization essentially with urban life, to the considerable annoyance of the provinces. And the nation's leaders knew how to spread their message.

Indisputably, one of the great triumphs of the Mexican Revolution was its success in bringing some education to an amazingly broad section of society. From the 1920s, push after push extended the quality and quantity of education, as the official party was proud to boast. On the fiftieth anniversary of the outbreak of the Mexican Revolution, the Fondo de Cultura Económica—itself a Cardenista project to use the great skills of the Spanish refugees who sought refuge in Mexico after Francisco Franco's victory in the Spanish Civil War—commissioned the poet and diplomat Jaime Torres Bodet to organize a volume on *La cultura* in the semiofficial series *Mexico:*

50 años de revolución. Nearly 40 percent of the volume was dedicated to education in its various forms.[92] And the numbers were truly impressive.

In 1940 nearly four million children attended 18,469 primary schools with nearly 44,000 teachers; however, this still left 41 percent of the school-age children out of the system. Spending on education increased from 73.8 million pesos in 1940 to 312 million pesos a decade later, although as a percentage of the total federal budget this represented a decline of from 16 to 11 percent.[93] In spite of the growth of the schools, towns and villages invariably had a professional scribe to whom people unaccustomed to writing could turn if they needed a letter written or—increasingly—some kind of form filled out. The link between literacy and agrarian claims made this service of vital importance. If a person or family had extra money to spend, a visit to town in the 1940s might also include having a photograph taken by an itinerant photographer in the square or having a letter written to a relative working in Mexico City or as a bracero in the United States.

A range of free public education developed that went from *casas de cuna* and *guarderías infantiles* through six years for both primary and secondary school. Beyond that, university education began to expand. The National University (UNAM) had been autonomous since 1929, which had improved the quality of the institution considerably as academics replaced bureaucrats—for a while—in decision-making positions. UNAM's student population grew from 17,090 students in 1940 to 24,929 students a decade later, a figure that exploded after UNAM moved to its new *ciudad universitaria* in the south of the city in 1953.[94] State universities were established in Sonora, Nuevo León, Veracruz, Guanajuato, and Querétero during the decade.[95] Lombardo Toledano organized the Universidad Obrero de México to compete with the university system on the basis of state subsidies; it had an overtly Marxist curriculum. However, after opening with 715 students in 1936, enrollment fell to between 493 and 579 in the first half of the decade and after that the effort faded further.[96]

By contrast, a world-class postgraduate research institution grew out of the Casa de España en México, which had been founded in 1938 to attract intellectual refugees from Franco's Spain. Formalized in 1940 as El Colegio de México, it specialized in history and the social sciences and went from strength to strength; from 1941 it attracted funds and legitimization from overseas organizations such as Harvard University and the Rockefeller Foundation.

Under the intellectual leadership of Silvio Zavala, Daniel Cosío Villegas, José Gaos, and Alfonso Reyes, new generations of distinguished researchers were developed. The privately supported Instituto Tecnológico de Monterrey also achieved distinction in science and engineering.

The Fondo de Cultura Económica evolved into the most prestigious publishing house in Latin America in the 1940s. Although it had only ten employees in 1940, the Fondo grew rapidly as Eduardo Suárez (Hacienda), Aarón Sáenz (Seguros de México S.A., Asociación Hipotecaria Mexicana, Banco Internacional, and the Asociación Nacional de Productores de Azúcar), Antonio Carrillo Flores (Nacional Financiera), and Roberto López (Banco de Comercio Exterior) used their official positions to finance the publishing house lavishly. In 1950 it produced fifty-one new titles and sold more than three million volumes.[97]

Education was a cultural battleground over the years. Compulsory public education and free government textbooks afforded at least the illusion that it was possible to control the views of the next generation. On the surface, the battle was joined between supporters of the Cárdenas administration, who were inspired by what was called socialist education. They included the leadership of the teachers union, the Sindicato Nacional de Trabajadores de la Educación (SNTE), and many dedicated teachers. They faced great opposition from the governments of the 1940s, as we shall see in Chapters 2 and 3.

Beyond the Cardenista and Alemanista varieties of education, nationalism provided a deeper common denominator for the educational system. *"La moral de la revolución,"* as it was called, linked national pride in things *autenticamente mexicano* to the state and the government of the day. A heavy dose of patriotism was the obligatory core of the curriculum. The economically active state provided a new set of leaders and a more institutional focus intended to supersede older loyalties to Church, caudillo, cacique, or *patria chica.* Mass organizations and institutions of the state provided new patron-client relationships that were far more effective than the crude propaganda efforts in which the government occasionally indulged, as any listener to "La Hora Nacional" on Sunday at 10:00 P.M. on every radio station in the country quickly realized.[98]

Nevertheless, the accomplishments of the official culture were real. The percentage of the population that the census classified as illiterate dropped from 51.5 percent in 1940 to 35.2 percent a decade later, although that figure was based simply on asking people at census time if they could read. Yet mass education was not the only phenomenon that was constructing a new national outlook, and when government programs were supplemented creatively by less official efforts, the results could be impressive.

Art and Revolution

The Mexican muralist movement was undoubtedly one of the great artistic and cultural movements of the twentieth century. Not only were Diego Rivera, José Clemente Orozco, and David Alfaro Siqueiros among the greatest individual artists of this century, but they also shared a vision of the cultural emancipation of their nation, freed from the racism and oppression of the past. Who has not been moved by seeing poor Mexicans explaining to their children the history lessons explicit in Rivera's murals in the National Palace or by listening to the positive side of nationalism from the guides in the Museo Nacional de Historia in Chapultepec Park? This muralist school was one of the most successful attempts ever to wed politics and art. Although there were moments of excess— as with Rivera's representation of Cortés and the *conquistadores* or with his near worship of the state—a new vision of Mexican pride emerged as a corrective to Porfirian positivism.

The centrality of the muralists' representations of the Indian and the working poor gave their art its enduring power. The dignity of the Indian is clear in Diego Rivera's murals in the Secretariat of Public Education and in Orozco's paintings of the peasantry. In recent decades this tradition has continued to evolve in Francisco Zuñiga's drawings and sculptures of Indian women; in commercial terms, his work is now among the most highly valued of all living sculptors. Other fine artists continued elements of this tradition: Miguel Covarrubias, Frida Kahlo, Manuel Rodríguez Lozano, Xavier Guerrero, Fernando Leal, Pablo O'Higgins, Julio Castellanos, Celia Calderón, Ricardo Martínez, and many others.

The recovery of the daily life of the Aztecs as it is depicted in the bottom half of the peerless murals in the National Palace, in a technique highly dependent on the classical European heritage, also pioneered the union of ethnography and art. That tradition thrived in the paintings of the mural school as they juxtaposed the integrity of the Indian and *campesino* ever more vividly against what they viewed as the decadence of the bourgeoisie and the political class. Examples include José Clemente Orozco's *Law and Justice* and

Diego Rivera's *The Night of the Rich* in the Secretariat of Public Education.

The dignity of manual work, as represented in the murals in the New School, is combined with the march of technical progress to construct a vision of a new scientific and industrial future, as can be seen in Orozco's murals at Dartmouth College. There is a direct line of descent from Rivera's murals in the Secretariat of Public Education and the Palace of Fine Arts to Orozco's *Prometheus* at Pomona College and eventually to Siqueiros's work in the Poliforum. This vision of the future was firmly located in the ideals of the revolution. Never was this more powerfully expressed than in Rivera's mural in the Secretariat of Public Education, in which the revolutionary soldier is guarding, and perhaps listening to, the "Village Schoolteacher" as she instructs the children.

The Church took a battering from the muralists. The friars watched as the encomenderos branded the Indians after the conquest, and each generation of oppressors had their spiritual adviser at hand as depicted in the great historical murals. But in spite of the deep liberal and radical traditions of anticlericalism, the depiction of the Church was not entirely onesided. Diego Rivera depicted Bartolomé de las Casas and Toribio de Benavente Motolinía favorably in his murals, and José Clemente Orozco also delivered a complex view of religion in his painting *A Franciscan Bending over a Leper*. The symbol of the corrupted Church was present, as the serpent coiled around the cross made clear; however, also present was great tenderness, as the friar comforted the leper. Whether intentional or not, the painting anticipated the later regeneration of religious traditions that we now know as liberation theology.

Part of the strength of the muralist tradition flows from the technical brilliance with which Rivera solved problems of composition as his major murals took advantage of public walls, staircases, and other irregular and difficult spaces. His design and composition triumphs in the National Palace and the Talleres Gráficos de la Nación were astonishing. The uniqueness of these technical accomplishments alone places the Mexican muralist movement in a category by itself.

The muralists also provided a coherent and highly revisionist view of Mexican history, from the murals in the National Palace to *Sunday Dream in the Alameda Park* in the Hotel del Prado (1947–48). Rivera's depictions of Cortés and las Casas roughly paralleled scholarship done on the treatment of the Indians by Charles Gibson, Juan

Friede, and Benjamin Keen, and even the most staid researcher
working on the documents of the independence period would now
find it difficult to ignore Rivera's portrayal of Agustín de Iturbide.
Or again, John Womack's treatment of Emiliano Zapata is fundamentally consonant with Rivera's representation of that revolutionary in the Palacio de Cortés in Cuernavaca.

In other words, it is possible to read works representing the
highest standard of historical scholarship and still agree with the
essence of much of Rivera's reading of Mexican history, although
one will not find Inga Clendinnen's reconstruction of Aztec sacrifice or Laurens Perry's work on Benito Juárez anticipated there. It
is even rumored that there are those who find the muralist school's
treatment of the machine politicians of the PRM relevant to the standards of political behavior in the 1990s. Classic treatments of revolutionaries who have gone astray are Rivera's *General Porkbarrel
Dancing with Miss Mexico* in the Hotel Reforma, Rivera's murals in
the National Palace and in the agricultural college at Chapingo,
and Orozco's *Latin America* at Dartmouth College, as well as his
Allegory of Mexico (1940), *Justice* (1941), and, above all, *The "Leaders" and the Masses* at the University of Guadalajara.

Artistically, Rivera's work was so good that he could indulge
his volatile political passions without condemning his work to the
category of mere editorial art. Thus he could paint Marx, Lenin,
and Trotsky into the mural at Radio City Music Hall in Rockefeller
Center, at least until Nelson Rockefeller caught him at it, or even
write *"Dios no existe,"* as a response to Manuel Avila Camacho's
1940 statement *"Soy creyente,"* in the mural in the lobby of the Hotel del Prado without destroying his art.[99] However, he pushed the
limit in *The Nightmare of War and the Dream of Peace* at the time of
the Korean War.[100]

One of the most interesting art forms of the period evolved from
the remarkably original *calaveras,* or political engravings, of the
Porfirian artist José Guadalupe Posada. By the 1940s this tradition
was centered in the Taller Gráfica Popular, run by Leopoldo
Méndez. The workshop produced prints and engravings, illustra-
tions, and posters that were frequently linked to *corridos,* or bal-
lads. The best of these artists included Alberto Beltrán, Raúl
Anguiano, J. Chávez Morado, Pablo O'Higgins, and Castro Pacheco.
Among the *corridos* that caught the attention of U.S. diplomats were
the "Corrido de la persecución de Pancho Villa," which made fun
of U.S. intervention in Chihuahua in 1916; the "Corrido del 'Buen
Vecino,' " which an embassy official characterized as "a gross com-

ment on the late President Franklin D. Roosevelt and Mrs. Roosevelt"; "Cuatro corridos vaciladores de la intervención Americana"; and the "Corrido del eclipse del peso," which blamed the United States for the devaluation of 1948. U.S. diplomats hated the radical perspective of this tradition but so admired the skill of the artists that they commissioned the "Corrido de la fiebre aflosa" to publicize the work of the Aflosa Commission to rural Mexico.[101]

Anthropology and Archaeology

Anthropology and archaeology provided dynamic fields of cultural emancipation, which had not always been the case. Before the revolution, the nation's problems were frequently blamed on "the backward Indians." There was the—probably apocryphal—story that Porfirio Díaz used face powder to make himself look less "Indian." Whether this was true or not, racist assumptions about national characteristics had intermingled with the Porfirian theory of development that led the governments of the nineteenth century to take the villagers' land, the *terrenos baldíos*, in the name of liberal progress and to introduce immigration schemes to "improve" the race.[102]

The first generation of European and U.S. anthropologists frequently favored theories of race to explain their nations' wealth or theories about "the criminal type" to explain the dissidence of the poor.[103] In the worst instance, these theories led to a variety of selective breeding schemes for humans, known as the eugenics movement, and, in its most extreme form, to the anthropology of the Third Reich. Fortunately, the second generation of anthropologists and social analysts began the process of reversing these tendencies in Mexico.[104] The eruption of national pride unleashed by the revolution stimulated archaeologists to study and celebrate the accomplishments of the Indian past, and their discoveries were both exciting and politically potent. Bertram Wolfe recounted that on the weekends Diego Rivera would take a break from painting his murals and join friends on archaeological digs. Toward the end of his life Rivera even built himself a pyramid in the Pedregal that Wolfe described: "As one looks at it, one cannot say whether one is looking at a temple, a pyramid, a museum, an artist's studio or a tomb."[105]

Just as archaeology introduced the world to the greatness of the ancient Indian civilizations by developing such sites as Mitla, Monte Albán, and Teotihuacán, anthropology began to reverse the racism that had been directed against the living Indians. Indeed, Manuel Gamio, the first director of the Department of Anthropology, tried to link archaeological excavations with projects of development for Indians. The political impact of a demonstration of past Indian accomplishments was not lost on many, certainly not during the administration of Lázaro Cárdenas, and these concerns were quickly institutionalized. The Departamento de Asuntos Indígenas and the Instituto Nacional de Antropología e Historia were formed in time to host the conference that established the Instituto Indigenista Interamericano in 1940.

The 1940s saw the institutionalization of Mexican anthropology and archaeology even as positive models of nationalism emerged. Exciting discoveries at Tula in 1941 and Bonampak in 1946 further demonstrated that Mexico was one of the world's richest zones for archaeological excavations. This was one aspect of Cardenismo that was not reversed in the 1940s. It was, however, contained. As the great ethnographer Fernando Benítez lamented, it was necessary to maintain a strict divide between sympathy for dead Indians and support for the callous policies affecting their living heirs. A sure sign of the success of the anthropological movement was the famous "battle of the bones." On November 24, 1946, the alleged discovery of the bones of Cortés was announced only to be quickly countered by the unearthing of the bones of Cuauhtémoc. The dispute over the authenticity of both discoveries pitted the *indigenistas* against the *hispanistas* in a shadow battle paralleling the politics of *indigenismo*.[106]

Cinema

Film culture in Mexico in the 1940s offers a challenging topic for analysis. Cinema was becoming a mass passion, first in the cities and then in provincial towns. As the popularity of films soared, the increased size of each new theater amazed people. The opulent decorations in the theaters built during the period were remarkable, as the Teatro Alameda and the Teatro Reforma still testify. A few hours in these elaborate, ornate buildings made the imagination soar to complement the fantasies on the screen; outside, sidewalk vendors created the atmosphere of a carnival. The government heavily subsidized the cost of tickets, and a weekend visit to the cinema became a regular and affordable pleasure to a wide range of Mexicans. Moreover, it fit neatly into the tradition in which men spent Sundays with their families.

In part, the popularity of the cinema represented official policy. The state subsidized films from the 1930s as part of the Cardenista project. News trailers were organized by propaganda teams during the war years, and, thereafter, the government learned that propaganda shorts could serve a useful purpose with the theaters' large captive audiences. Visual reports on development projects were genuinely popular. Yet it was not all one way. Carlos Monsiváis points out that the cinema also allowed people to see themselves in a new public space. Empathy and fantasy merged in the imagination as people enjoyed the stunning new technology. Still, there were problems with the films.

In the early years Europe and the United States were obvious influences in the development of Mexican cinematography, and some early films were slavish in their emulation of foreign fashions. Mexico's love-hate relationship with the United States was clear from the beginning. Some U.S. films that seemed similar on the surface, especially melodramas and westerns, did not travel well because they reflected the anti-Mexican racism of the era. Racial epithets such as "greaser" and "wetback" were altogether too common in the United States. In an extreme example that nearly caused a diplomatic incident, Woodrow Wilson had to ask William Randolph Hearst to withdraw the film *Patria* because it was so inflammatory.[107] (Hearst's racist attitudes, however, did not stop him from acquiring vast amounts of land in Mexico.) Even well-meaning people in the United States were influenced by racist views. Children in liberal homes in the United States were frequently taught it was more polite to call their southern neighbors "Spanish-Americans" rather than "Mexicans." Years later Alejandro Galindo confronted this racism directly with his film *Espaldas mojadas* (1953). Although the film was criticized at the time for overstating the case—with high fences, watchtowers, and spotlights overlooking the Rio Grande—reality has subsequently caught up with Galindo's creative imagination.

Sergei Eisenstein was the first great foreign filmmaker to go to Mexico, where he made ¡*Que Viva México!* Surviving segments of his work still resonate in their own terms today. There was a world of difference, technically and in content, between Eisenstein's films and earlier Mexican melodramas such as *Santa* (1931), in which a young country girl is led astray by a soldier, disgraced, forced to work in a brothel and finally, suffering from cancer, dies conveniently at the most opportune moment—all within eighty minutes. Eisenstein's frustration with Hollywood made him open to an invitation from Diego Rivera to film in Mexico. He brought a new level of technical accomplishment and artistic vision to Mexico, although extreme difficulties never allowed him to finish the film. His film footage was blocked in California by Upton Sinclair and his wife, and eventually sold; upon Eisenstein's return to the USSR he fell under Stalin's disfavor.[108] Nevertheless, his record of actual life—not to mention his fascination with the bizarre—recorded a world of new images that eventually circulated in different versions of *¡Que Viva México!* [109]

Perhaps the most important film of the 1930s was *Vámanos con Pancho Villa* (1935), which Carl J. Mora described as "the last Mexican motion picture to deal honestly with the country's recent past."[110] To that point, it seemed as if the Mexican film industry might evolve into an art form that would upon occasion deal with Mexican realities. Such was not to be. Sadly, the Mexican cinema's relationship to history became, in Jorge Ayala Blanco's phrase, "*una historia mi(s)tificada.*"[111] One Mexican film that did deal honestly with a contemporary issue, however, was Roberto Gavaldón's *La barraca*; but it was safely located in Valencia, and its European ethnographic social context was so formal that the film had little appeal in Mexico. By the end of the 1930s, the triumphant regime of the melodrama endlessly exploited themes of sexual misery, *el jodidismo*, and the nobility of poverty.

The mythology of a golden rural past grew in the cinema, and no one better exemplified the divergence of myth and reality than Jorge Negrete, the singing cowboy. On one level Mexican cowboy films were overtly influenced by their U.S. equivalents. Tom Mix and Tito Guízar shared a striking physical resemblance, and cowboy films in both countries tapped many similar responses. There was the physical beauty of the mountains of Mexico and those of the American West. It was quite easy to slip back and forth between the two locations, and Durango eventually became the favorite state for U.S. filmmakers to use in countless westerns without their audiences being any the wiser.

Cowboy films in both countries tapped a simple good and evil dichotomy and evoked a romantic image of an earlier age. Not surprisingly, the ranchos of the far north tended to be the site of these films because the forced labor systems, against which the Mexican Revolution had at least in part rebelled, were too recent a memory. And nobody was going to romanticize the forced labor system of the Porfirian *enganche*. However, the astonishingly sentimental *comedia ranchera* became the staple of Mexican filmmaking. Tito

Guízar, a cowboy in the tradition of Tom Mix, Roy Rogers, and Gene Autry, made the genre permanent in *Allá en el Rancho Grande* (1936). There was, however, a vital difference between the cowboy and the *charro*. Whereas the cowboy in the West frequently clashed with the law, the railroads, or the large ranchers, "the charro or *ranchero* was generally trying not to initiate social change but rather to maintain the status quo. He came to represent the traditional and Catholic values in defiance of the leftist, modernizing tendencies emanating from the cities."[112] In his worst moments, the *charro* celebrated his ability to abuse those over whom he held power, a phenomenon well noted in recent times by women's movements.

Another difference between the two cowboy genres was that there was a social cap in Mexico above which the romantic cowboy rapidly lost his appeal. Urbanity and cowboys were mutually exclusive categories in Mexico, and westerns never evolved over the decades in Mexico to the degree that they did in the United States, where Indians were transformed from bloodthirsty savages into victims, if not spiritual or ecological heroes. There was a constancy in the Mexican western that made it, to a considerable extent, frozen in time and space. Just as *mariachi* music is always played in the key of A, the evolution of the Mexican western was cut short.

Jorge Negrete gained major stardom in *¡Ay, Jalisco no te rajes!* (1940), and he continued to make extraordinarily similar films for years.[113] He was born in Guanajuato, grew up in Mexico City, was fluent in English and German, and was educated in the Colegio Militar (Mexico's military academy). In the media, he evolved from a singer on XEW to a romantic film *charro* from Jalisco. He was soon followed by Pedro Infante, and their films evoked a safely romanticized version of the rural past for the millions who were moving to the cities. However, the closer the cinema was to the *zócalo*, the less frequently their films were projected.

In a different vein, there was a short tradition of *indigenista* films that offered a vision of the Indian as a pure, uncorrupted being. This genre was initiated by the innocent image of Emilio "El Indio" Fernández, who starred in *Janitzio* (1934). This powerful romanticizing of the Indians emphasized their innate nobility, not the politics of *indigenismo*. Fernández's magnificent photography represented the quality end of the spectrum. By 1943 his films *María Candelaria* and *Flor Silvestre*, which are frequently viewed as his best efforts, marked the high point of this tradition. What is notable about these films is that today they seem like an idealized and highly sanitized version of rural life. (Dolores del Río's dress and coiffures were always immaculate, even when she emerged from a hut made out of mud and *zacate*.) At the time these films were made, however, class sensibilities were so outraged by a favorable depiction of Indians that Emilio Azcárraga, soon to be Mexico's first media mogul, refused to show them in his Teatro Alameda.[114]

Perhaps the most astonishing aspect of the era is that none of the radical reforms of the Cardenista period found expression in Mexican filmmaking. Nothing of the nationalization of the railroads or petroleum, the experiment in workers' administration, the workers' militias, socialist education, or any of the other highlights of Cardenismo made its way into the cinema. Just the opposite! In 1939 the most successful film was Juan Bustillo Oro's nostalgic evocation of prerevolutionary Mexico, *En Tiempos de Don Porfirio*. Still the 1940s saw a steady growth in filmmaking in Mexico after a difficult period. By 1946 the industry was well enough established to found the Academia Mexicana de Ciencias y Artes Cinematográficas.

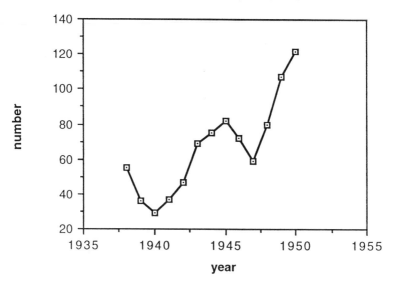

Films Produced in Mexico

More than just the quantity of films, the growth of the star system brought forth a new generation of actors who attracted large audiences to the cinema. A sign of the growing confidence of these

Mexican movie stars emerged in April 1944 when Jorge Negrete and Mario Moreno "Cantinflas" challenged the internal organization of the Sindicato de Trabajadores de la Industria Cinematográfica (STIC). Before that point, actors had been considered the same as any other employees and had been merged with the technicians and construction workers on the film sets in Section 2 of the STIC. A strike in April drove home the actors' claim to superior status, and the new movie stars were eventually allowed to form their own union, the Sindicato de Trabajadores de la Producción Cinematográfica (STPC). Typical of the era, the dispute between the unions was extremely bitter and came close to being violent. Accusations of corruption also highlighted the dispute. Mario Moreno's popularity, and his personal relationship with the president, carried the day as the new union openly defied Fidel Velázquez and the CTM. Eventually, the government embraced the stars and their new union. It was at this point that Moreno, Negrete, and María Félix appeared publicly on the balcony of the Palacio Nacional with President Avila Camacho and Miguel Alemán as the STPC offered the government a parade of thanksgiving for its support against the STIC.[115] The Mexican presidents of the 1940s were among the first heads of state to learn the public relations value of

Cantinflas marching with the leaders of the electricians' union. *Courtesy Hermanos Mayo, Archivo General de la Nación, Mexico City*

associating with movie stars. They also screened and monitored new movies regularly from the presidential residence Los Pinos.

It was ironic that the leader of the film workers' union, Mario Moreno "Cantinflas," served as the main link between political leaders of the 1940s and the film industry because it was through his acting that the common man first found expression in Mexican film culture. A remarkably talented stand-up, or *carpa*, comedian, Cantinflas had had as his first full-length hit *Ahí Está el Detalle* (1940). The film pitted the streetwise but innocent lad—the *pelado*—against the authorities. A master of evasion, the lad uses laughter, a remarkably circular kind of language, and other weapons of the weak to slip out of trouble. By the end of the film, even the judge has absorbed his street slang. In this film Cantinflas challenged the pomposity of social hierarchy rather than evoke the politics of the revolution.[116] His next film, *Ni Sangre ni Arena* (1941), was a parody of a popular U.S. bullfight film of the day, and as such was itself very popular. The authorities smarted from Cantinflas's ability to ridicule the police, as he did in *El gendarme desconocido* (1941), which was instantly appealing to anyone who knew about the abuse of police authority; however, this film too was a cultural dig, not a call to an alternative political or social vision.

Cantinflas "bullfighting," Mexico City. *Courtesy Hermanos Mayo, Archivo General de la Nación, Mexico City*

Cantinflas was so good that by the end of the decade he had sparked an imitator. Germán Valdez, known as "Tin Tan," emerged in his shadow in *Hay Muertos que No Hacen Ruido* (1946), *Calabacitas*

Tiernas (1948), and *El Rey del Barrio* (1949). Valdez combined some elements of Cantinflas's character with the *pachuco* styles of the border in the 1940s and even added the skills of a song and dance man. Yet as Cantinflas enjoyed imitators and the success that enabled him to build a mansion in the Lomas, his later films tended to settle into a more predictable pattern. Foreign audiences never saw a glimpse of his talent when he appeared as David Niven's servant in *Around the World in Eighty Days*. Perhaps his work became an example of self-censorship, for by the late 1940s he had developed a complex relationship with the governing party. As president of the union, he became enmeshed in politics. Alemán would use him for public relations exercises, to meet dignitaries, and at the odd political occasion; at one point, he sent him to San Antonio under considerable protest. Cantinflas made only the briefest appearance, much to Alemán's annoyance.[117] Cantinflas had become the politically connected *pelado*.

Another great star of the period was Dolores del Río, the "Spanish" Mexican from Hollywood. Born Dolores Asúnsolo y López Negrete, a child of the Porfirian aristocracy, she was the first major Mexican star in Hollywood, and she managed to make the transition from silent films to "talkies" more than a decade before making her first Mexican film in 1943. Her success in Hollywood was so great that, in the tradition of U.S. racism, she was referred to as Spanish. As in the later example of Antonio Rodolfo Oaxaca from Chihuahua (Anthony Quinn), many fans in the United States did not know that she was Mexican.[118] Her work in Hollywood, as Dolores del Río, convinced many Mexicans that she had abandoned them. However, her highly publicized relationship with Orson Welles generated considerable interest in Mexico, and the pair were active in pro-Allies rallies in Mexico City at the beginning of World War II.

Dolores del Río's success in *Flor Silvestre* and *María Candelaria* (1943) was recognized at the film festivals in Cannes in 1946 and in Locarno the next year, which seemed to increase her reputation as a major international star with her domestic audience. Her beauty combined with the inevitable suffering that was then viewed as a woman's lot established a genre that is still thriving in contemporary *telenovelas*.

At times, life seemed to struggle to keep up with film mythology, never more so than in the story of Miguel and María, the president and the actress. María Félix had emerged as another great star of the era in Fernando de Fuentes's *Doña Barbara* (1943). Far from playing the traditional subservient female, she developed a powerful, fiery presence on camera, and her personal lifestyle was assertive and flamboyant. She commanded media attention with her daily activities, and when she traveled it required several taxis to shift her luggage.

Perhaps María Félix's most notable role also represented the height of the union between film and politics. In *Río Escondido* (1947), by "El Indio" Fernández, María Félix plays a schoolteacher, Rosura Salazar, who is such a good teacher that she is invited personally by the president to take up a new assignment and bring education to the small town of Río Escondido. Least anyone miss the point, President Alemán even has a walk-on role in the picture and gives a long interview in which he explains the importance of education to her. Rosura's effort in the town inevitably leads to tragedy, as she clashes with the local villain, an ex-Villista cacique who eventually attacks her for refusing his advances and for challenging the social order in the village. On her deathbed she dictates a letter to the president, just as his message arrives telling her that Mexico is proud of her pedagogical effort; the film ends in a patriotic rush of blood.

María Félix recalled the spirit of the age in an interview with María Elena Rico for the magazine *Contenido*, in October 1976:

> Jorge [Pasquel, a prominent figure in the Alemán circle] was the most splendid man that I have ever known. When we filmed Maclova at Lake Pátzcuaro he left a hydro-plane at my disposal. One day the ice ran out in the hotel and within a few hours, the hydro-plane returned from Mexico City with an enormous refrigerator. He accompanied me to Pátzcuaro and we travelled by highway in six Cadillacs in Indian file [fila india]. The cars contained uniformed waiters, barbers, a cook, a valet, three servants, a masseur, and even the master of the armory. We ate at a picturesque spot along the way: the servants, in the blink of an eye, provided great canopies, a stand for Jorge to use for target shooting, and a long table with coverings where the cook served us a grand banquet.[119]

The image of a peasant from Michoacán watching this procession could serve as a metaphor for the 1940s. María Félix made the union between film and state explicit, and one might add, not only on the silver screen.

The closest to a critique of Alemanismo was probably a genre known as *cabareteras*. Set in down-market nightclubs, frequently using as their theme the plight of innocent young girls trapped into working initially as B-girls and then as prostitutes, films such as *Sensualidad* and *Siempre Tuya* (1950) and *Aventurera* (1952) made Rosa Carmena and Ninón Sevilla into stars. The girls always seemed to represent a higher ethic than their tormentors, who were above them in social rank. These films also benefited from a strong Afro-Cuban influence even as they provided a searing representation of recent changes in society. As Mora put it: "Thus if the *cabaretera* film was the 'cinema par excellence' of *alemanismo*, the genre managed at times to express a devastating indictment of Mexican life. It can even be said that the unabashed greed given full rein by Alemán's ambitious developmentalist regime created severe social stresses that found expression in some of the most interesting films ever made in Mexico before outright commercial 'packages' came to predominate in the late 1950s and 1960s."[120]

The other critically acclaimed film of the late Alemán era was Luis Buñuel's startling portrait of urban poverty, *Los Olvidados* (1950). This film earned more respect abroad than in Mexico, as did his later films. The gap between the dominant myth of the nobility of poverty and Buñuel's harsh treatment of the poor—where they became indistinguishable from their oppressors—was too shocking to earn him either commercial success or influence among his contemporaries. That bleak vision contrasted with a more dominant view of poverty, as expressed in the film that Carlos Monsiváis called the masterpiece of the decade, Ismael Rodríguez's *Nosotros los Pobres* (1947).[121]

Given the enormity of the changes that were taking place in Mexico in the 1940s, it is notable how few contemporary issues appeared in the cinema. The greatest filmmakers, Eisenstein and Buñuel, especially after the latter's financial failure with *Gran Casino*, did not find a congenial climate and quickly left for Europe. However, melodramas, the *comedia ranchera*, and a new group of movie stars—Jorge Negrete, María Félix, Cantinflas, "Tin Tan," Dolores del Río, Pedro Armendáriz, and Pedro Infante—provided many genuinely popular films. None of these stars decided to follow the example of United Artists, however, in which successful actors invested in a studio. Each of their genres tended to ossify after achieving differing degrees of initial success.[122]

Several powerful mechanisms of social control limited the creative potential of the Mexican cinema. First, private companies predominated in the early years of filmmaking, and none of them chose to make an adequate investment in a studio. Thus the "gloss gap" grew between Hollywood and Mexico City, a point that Dolores del Río made repeatedly. Without exception, these early producers of films dissented from the Cardenista version of the Mexican Revolution and were intolerant of alternative political views. Independent filmmakers could not break into the industry.

Then, in 1942, the government established the Banco Cinematográfico with its foundation capital coming from the Banco Nacional de México under Luis Legorreta. Under a financial reorganization in 1947, Nacional Financiera also financed films through this channel, but it was clear that the Mexican establishment—a combination of big business and the government—would control the purse strings of the industry and keep critical voices out of the new media. The institutional support, nevertheless, had an immediate impact. In 1943, some seventy films were produced and a market throughout Latin America emerged to help absorb Mexican films. The Banco Cinematográfico developed powerful techniques of influence by controlling the financing of the industry. What was clear was that the retreat from revolution after 1938 was not going to be a theme for the movies.

A third major mechanism of social control focused upon the distribution of films. Here a group including William Jenkins, Gabriel Alarcón Chargoy, and Manuel Espinosa Yglesias developed a stranglehold on distribution throughout most of the Republic. These men shared the most reactionary political views that existed in Mexico, and their close links with the presidents of the 1940s guaranteed that any films that were unwelcome to the governing party would not find channels of distribution. As distributors, they violated every standard of fair trade practices by bundling hit films with duds, thus denying hits to any outlets that opposed their prices or policies, and also by blacklisting independent competitors. Repeated complaints to the authorities about abusive trade practices fell on deaf ears.[123]

Thus at the levels of production, finance, and distribution the mechanisms of social control were well in place by the 1940s. There is little doubt that the broad alliance in support of the war effort also contributed to sewing up the cinema in the first half of the decade by imposing a high degree of self-censorship on the left. Numerous critics of the Mexican cinema of the era complained about the artificial gap between popular cinema and the reality of life in Mexico. As Carlos Martínez Assad put it, "The Mexican cinema of the 1940s resembled a house of mirrors where the figures appeared multiplied, repeating and fooling themselves until they created a new image."[124]

This political tutelage did not happen by chance. There were good structural reasons for this phenomenon. F. Gregorio del Castillo was the chief of Censura Cinematográfica de la Secretaría de Gobernación. He was known to have intervened to block segments of *Los Abandonados* (1944) by Emilio Fernández and *El Rayo del Sur* (1943) by Miguel Contreras Torres when he spotted fictitious scenes that he viewed as being critical of the military.[125] An atmosphere of censorship handicapped the industry and prevented many foreign films from being presented in Mexico. Even when the government decided to support the making of a film, such as Jaime Salvador's *Escuadrón 201*, the accomplishments were modest.

The same measures of social control that limited the creativity of Mexican filmmakers and protected the sensibilities of the governing party may indirectly explain the astonishing popularity of U.S. films in Mexico. Mexican audiences flocked to the latest release from Hollywood far more than to films from other parts of the Spanish-speaking world—even though the government forbade the dubbing of English-language films into Spanish as a protectionist measure. Just as *el pato Donald* and *el ratoncito Mickey* became part of Mexican children's childhood, Rita Hayworth occupied a deep and meaningful place in many young men's adolescence—and it did not go unnoticed in Mexico when Marilyn Monroe posed for that calendar in 1949.[126]

With the passing of the years, there has been inevitable growth in nostalgia and in the tendency to idealize the films of this era. The visual images of this first generation of Mexican movie stars evoke an already distant age. Certainly, the films' photographic record of what Mexico looked like in the 1940s is invaluable. Thus some call the 1940s a golden age of Mexican cinema.

Radio

The history of the battle for control of radio will be recounted in Chapter 6. At this point it is useful to remember that radio stations had been proliferating since El Buen Tono Tobacco Company discovered the benefits of having their own outlet in the 1920s. Stations combined into chains, following the lead of XEW, the "Voz de América Latina desde México." U.S. radio companies, NBC, and CBS were involved with the growth of radio from the beginning, and a U.S. technical mission had improved the quality of transmissions during the war.

The country was being brought together in a new way, as the music and commanding presence of Agustín Lara demonstrated. And what a presence Lara constructed as the *veracruzano profesional* who cultivated a legend from his early days playing piano in brothels to the spectacles he presented in cabarets: his very public marriage to María Félix; his boasting on air of his thousands of silk suits and of his even more numerous conquests; his recalling his "millions of kisses," or the three fortunes he had won and lost. "I want to die Catholic, but at the last possible moment," he shamelessly plagiarized from Saint Augustine. Some thought "Te vendes" worked as the anthem for the age. "Te vendes, quién pudiera comprarte, quién pudiera pagarte un minuto de amor."[127]

During the war, radio reports on military events brought news of battles in distant places home on a regular basis, and when a popular song came out called "Ya me voy a la guerra," it seemed to link Mexicans to the war effort in a new, more direct way. People could tune to national events such as the star-studded opening of a new Anderson Clayton factory in Monterrey in 1950, or, on a weekly basis, they could listen to Manuel Esperón or Everett Hoagland's orchestra "coming directly from the Hotel Reforma in the heart of Mexico City." It was a small step from radio to records.

Popular recordings sold in unheard of quantities. *Mariachis* played live on air from the Plaza Garibaldi, and ranchero musicians such as Lucha Reyes found unprecedented cash markets for their traditional music. Popular songwriters such as Pepe Guízar "Como México no hay dos" discovered that sentimentality sold. The mambos of Pérez Prado, the romantic boleros and tangos from Argentina, and the "son" music of Manuel "Punitillita" Licea from Cuba were extremely popular. Los Panchos brought traditional Mexican popular songs to new audiences. Treasured songs like "Por un amor" by Gilberto Parra were followed by new hits in the 1940s: the *huapango* "La cigarra" by Ray Pérez y Soto (1940) and the *canción ranchera* "Tu solo tu" (1949), written by Felipe Valdez Leal, and Chucho Martínez Gil's "Dos arbolitos"—both of which were sung by Pedro Infante. Minerva Elizondo's exuberant celebration of worldly pleasures, "Y andale," among many others, helped to crystallize the essential meaning of *"lo mexicano."* Perhaps popular songs best evoked a nostalgic view of the rural past that helped the millions who were losing that world forever by moving to the cities.

But the city offered new pleasures as well, such as the highly fashionable Club Smyrna at San Jerónimo #47, where the latest popular music was performed by singers such as the beautiful

Amparo Montes, who sang romantic boleros with Agustín Lara. The club was in a remodeled colonial building built over the grave of Sor Juana Inés de la Cruz that had evolved from a convent to a warehouse and finally to a nightclub.[128]

By contrast, the theater of the day was dry and excessively formal and of extremely limited appeal. It had boomed from 1920 to 1935. However, the critics seem to agree that the 1940s was a difficult time. "Theaters presented second-run plays in lackluster productions. Theater groups were imitative rather than imaginative, bringing little freshness to the theater scene. The terrain of the theater was, in the word of poet Octavio Paz, the 'desert.' "[129] The problem was, apparently, that the war, *carestía*, and the political environment had all added to cultural stagnation; moreover, the audiences were tiny.[130] Or, as Antonio Magaña Esquivel put it, "The shortcomings of the theater in Mexico are founded in the limitations and hereditary weaknesses of the old school of Spanish theater." Even the attempt to create a "Teatro de Ahora" that would deal with contemporary political and social issues and rescue "from anonymity some economic and social aspects of life for peasants, rural and urban workers" was forlorn.[131]

The state of the nation's high culture became a matter of concern to the extent that it elicited an institutional response. Additional resources were dedicated to the national university. The size of UNAM had doubled between 1940 and 1954, and the construction of the new university city was timed to coincide with the four hundredth anniversary of that great university in 1953. More directly, the Department of Fine Arts was reorganized in 1947 as the Instituto Nacional de Bellas Artes, and it provided immediate financial and institutional stimulus to a variety of fine arts, including drama, dance, music, painting, and the *poesía en voz alta* movement. The Ballet Folklórico was in many ways the crowning achievement, and it became the proud face of *indigenismo* to the world. Somewhat later, the Instituto Mexicano de Seguro Social (IMSS) would also dedicate resources to developing a popular base for theater.

Literature

The literature of the 1940s was also in a period of relative decline, at least from the perspective of making a mark on the wider society. There were a number of poets who were distinguished within a fairly narrow circle: Luis Castillo Ledón (he also wrote *Hidalgo:*

La vida del heroe, 1949), Joaquín Méndez Rivas, and Bernardo Ortíz de Montellano (*Cinco horas sin corazón*, 1940, and *El sombrerón*, 1946). Jaime Torres Bodet published *Sonetos* in 1949, one of the seven volumes he had published since 1927 while also maintaining a political and diplomatic career. Yet whatever the artistic merit of their work, these poets did not break out and communicate with a broad range of literate people in their society.

Among the novelists of the decade were Mariano Azuela (*El padre don Agustín Rivera*, 1942, and *Cien años de novela mexicana*, 1947), José Rubén Romero (*Rosenda*, 1946), Gregorio López y Fuentes (*Cuentos campesinos*, 1940), Rafael Muñoz (*Bachimba*, 1941), Miguel Angel Menéndez (*Nayar*, 1941, which was acknowledged as an *indigenista* novel), and Francisco Rojas González (*La negra angustias*, 1944, which explored for the first time the role of women in the revolution).[132] Perhaps the most audacious novel of the 1940s was José Revueltas's *El luto humano* (1943), in which Revueltas offered an alternative explanation for the peasant rebellion against the state, known as the Cristero rebellion, as a defense of peasant rights. He represented the rebellion, whose perpetrators the state viewed as feudal and backward, as an attempt by these rural people to own at least their culture—if not their land. It was not a perspective welcomed by official Mexico.

B. Traven's last major novel was *A General Comes from the Jungle* (Amsterdam, 1940); it already anticipated the shift in the revolution's course, perhaps because Traven had seen firsthand how little life had changed for the Indians of southern Mexico. As Heidi Zogbaum explained: "Although *Ein General kommat aus dem Dschungel* appears on the surface to be a successful story full of victory and optimism, underlying the book is a deeply pessimistic statement about how revolutionary goals deteriorate once military victory is complete. Traven's last novel bears clear signs of resignation and disillusionment, as well as a heightened understanding of the complex problems associated with the restructuring of a society along revolutionary lines."[133] Although he published a book, *Macario*, based on Mexican folk tales, in Zurich in 1950, none of his new work appeared in Mexico in the 1940s. His themes cut too close to the bone.

Agustín Yáñez, generally acknowledged as the best writer of the decade, wrote *Espejismo de Juchitán*, 1940; *Genio y figuras de Guadalajara*, 1941; *Flor de juegos antiguos*, 1940; and *Archipiélago de mujeres*, 1943. "The year 1947 marked the publication of the single most important work in the history of the Mexican novel," wrote

Walter M. Langford in 1971. With Yáñez's *Al filo del agua*, "the novel in Mexico took a quantum jump into a respected place in the main channel of world literature."[134] Although after Carlos Fuentes few would quite share Langford's enthusiasm; there is little doubt that Agustín Yáñez shifted the novel to a new level of individual introspection. By using inner monologue, a focus on the subconscious, a timeless interior landscape, and a multileveled story line, Yáñez undoubtedly brought new levels of art to his literature. Yet his work was also an escape from the social issues of the day—a not unwelcome accommodation from an official perspective in the 1940s. (Yáñez held a number of official positions with the government and was appointed an ambassador in 1946.) For many readers, his "magical realism" was more interesting—and certainly politically safer—than reacting directly to the culture or politics of the 1940s.

The work of Octavio Paz included *A la orilla del mundo* (1942), *Semillas para un himno* (1945), and *Libertad bajo palabra* (1949), although it would be difficult to argue today that these novels are passing the test of time. He accelerated Agustín Yáñez's shift from politics to psychology with the publication of *El labertino de la soledad* (1950). Paz followed the psychologist Samuel Ramos, *El perfíl de hombre y cultura en México* (edition after edition evolved through the 1930s and 1940s), and finalized this transition by shifting an analysis of Mexico's great national problems from the realm of politics and economics to that of psychopathology—not of an individual, but of the entire Mexican nation. Recently, Roger Bartra has offered a delightful critique of this tradition by focusing upon the images of peasants and the rural past, a kind of "paradise subverted" in relation to the evolution of national identity. It is a healthy corrective.[135] Like the cinematographers, few of the novelists of the day drew their work from the social reality of their country.

The most successful writer of the era was Luis Spota, "possibly Mexico's all-time best-selling novelist." Spota was just beginning his publishing career at the end of the 1940s. His highly popular novels included *El colonel fue echado al mar* (1947), about a hospital ship on which rations were generously increased after each patient died, and he wrote his own experience in trying to cross the river illegally to Texas in *Murieron a mitad del río* (1948). In general, though, however much the public bought his books, the critics were underwhelmed.[136] And Carlos Fuentes was still a young man enjoying Europe as the decade ended.

There was an extraordinarily rich tradition of popular music in Mexico. Manuel M. Ponce, the country's most celebrated classical

composer, based his music to a considerable degree on folk traditions. He was still active in the 1940s, producing the symphony
Ferial (1940); *Concierto del sur*, for guitar and symphony (1941); and
Concierto, for violin and orchestra (1943). Carlos Chávez wrote his
great *Concierto* for piano and orchestra in 1943. He also formed the
Orchestra Sinfónica de México in association with Silvestre
Revueltas and took symphonic music to new heights in *La coronela*
and in an adaptation of *Los de abajo*. Their use of traditional themes
and their subsequent association with INBA placed symphonic
music from Mexico on the world map.[137]

Finally, it is important to recognize that our contemporary cultural categories—film, art, theater, symphony, and literature—overlook the impact of the popular culture on the streets and in the
nation's folklore. On a regular basis, comedians in the tradition of
the *carpa* tents from which Cantinflas emerged would stop on the
streets and present their material. (Some tents, like the Carpa
Bombay, were evolving into permanent theaters in the late 1940s.)
Musicians would perform, or some would simply have a rave in
public, as crowds gathered quickly. This tradition of street theater
largely died out after the 1940s but revived after the economic crisis of the 1980s. What we now call "busking" was part of a vital
street life, although it is difficult to retrieve from this distance.

One source of popular culture that was ignored until recently
was the emergence by the 1940s of a major industry, the production of comic books. Armando Bartra and Anne Rubenstein, among
others, have demonstrated how historians can tap this source for
additional insights into popular culture to enrich our understanding of an era. The success of comics (*historietas*) was remarkable.[138]
The sales figures were stunning as comics first arrived with
rotographic presses in 1934. Some one hundred thousand readers
bought newspapers in the 1920s; by the 1930s, millions were reading comic books. The most popular, *Paquín*, *Pepín*, and *Chamaco*,
were printing sixty-four pages per day by 1940. *Pepín* by the late
1940s was selling two hundred thousand copies a day, and twice
that on Sunday. These comics had an amazing longevity. "Tarzán"
ran on the front page of *El Universal's* Sunday section from 1932 to
1978. In the 1940s, the price printed on the cover was 10 centavos.[139]

The early comics were in a sense naive; however, the combination of drawing and simple text engaged the largely proto-literate
audience. In 1940 some 58 percent of those responding to the census taker claimed to be illiterate. But that figure almost certainly
overstated the case for literacy. By 1957 one study claimed that only

one in four Mexicans could read a book. Comics filled a gap for new readers, although the success of the comics also related to their stories.

Comics were fun! In *Pepín* #891 the series "Adelita y las guerrillas" saw the heroine in a car falling off a cliff, with the hero stranded far away, unable to help her. The reader wondered how the heroine could be saved. In the next issue, the writers simply had Superman fly by, save the heroine, and ask if he was in the wrong comic strip. Anne Rubenstein's analysis of the success of these comics is worth emphasizing. The comics were connected with the readers' lives. The problems of the protagonists were understood by the reader, and the stories took place in recognizable places: ruins, towns, buildings, even restaurants. The promotional aspects of the comics made cartoonists into stars, and readers were urged to send in their own cartoons. Story lines always had simple morals. There was one failure: "Adventuras del espacio." This series relied on a story set on an imaginary planet. Apparently, audiences did not engage as "a giant fly carried off the heroine to be eaten by a giant snail." After a few months, the authors simply left the hero stranded on a meteorite, and few readers cared.[140]

While reading these recent studies of the phenomenon in Mexico, I was struck by the differences between the comics in the 1940s and those of my own childhood in the early 1950s. By the 1950s the extraneous material in comics was primarily advertisements of items for sale, but not in the 1940s. The comics focused on interactivity; readers were invited to submit material and to engage in such varied activities as playing games, entering contests, inventing advertising and patriotic slogans, submitting drawings, and playing lotteries. Readers were also asked to suggest story lines by sending in stories about their lives. Lonely hearts ads were popular. *El Universal* ran an annual contest for the best amateur cartoonist. There were stories about the authors of the comics, and readers were asked to write essays on why they read their favorite series. In addition, there were prizes (5 pesos for the first twenty readers who could name the second viceroy of New Spain) and money-earning schemes: sell to your friends, help the Mexico City District Attorney find criminals, decipher puzzles with complex rules, or submit a photo with a suggestion for a character in a comic. Pen pal pages were also very popular.

The Church heirarchy attacked the comics for engaging in the black arts by including columns with fortune telling, horoscopes, and astrology. Above all, readers mixed fantasy and empathy. In

"Cumbres de sueño" (Dreaming Heights), middle-class women faced the same problems that poor readers either confronted or hoped to encounter.[141] Thus their interactivity, simple moral lessons, and engagement with what modern urban/industrial lifestyles meant and required, all set in a familiar context, contributed to the huge success of these comics. As happened with the films of the era, a new technology (rotogravure) offered the individual an imaginary space in which to blend his or her individual dreams and experiences with stories set against the background of a rapidly changing and increasingly urbanized and industrial world.

Not only the landscape but also much of the fabric of daily life in the 1940s is already lost, so great have been the changes in recent decades. Sadly, the work of the chronicler of the City of Mexico, Salvador Novo, is virtually useless from this distance.[142] Novo's was not a description of the daily life of the great city. Rather, his was a self-indulgent prose that, even at the time, required inside knowledge of what was going on within the elite and the gay community in order to decipher his meaning. Although the historian can learn enough about the politics of the period to "get" the superb drawings of *Excélsior*'s cartoonist Freyre, Novo's writing remains impenetrable. As Carlos Monsiváis explained:

> Novo's city was the physical, psychological, social, cultural and (almost) moral space of the elite, this sector so refined and/or powerful that it has always characterized itself as "Everyone in the World" and that—with an understandable presumption—has felt that the part of the city that served it constituted the entire Federal District and the whole country. The Mexico that Novo described and directed, today magically dissolves in their megalomania. Today it cannot be traversed, now that its mythical geography has disintegrated in the face of mass society, and now that the notion of the nation as a "grand family" is no longer useable.[143]

Sports

Sports were not for the poor traditionally, indeed, they scarcely existed before the *porfiriato*. There was a point below which extremely poor children, especially those living in rural settings, scarcely had the luxury of play, much less of playing sports. Peasants did not play games, but cock fights were very popular at country markets and carnivals. Small ranchers loved to bet on their horses, and local races could be organized on a country lane. A whole network of horse races eventually brought the fastest horses from the country to the great city. The Jockey Club was established in Mexico City in 1881, and the great races became events for high society. The top track was located in Colonia Hipódromo, before the Hipódromo las Américas was built after the war. It is still possible to walk around the oval of the old track, which is now a circular city street, Calle Amsterdam. Then, for almost everyone, sports were to be watched, not played.

Today's highly organized and commercialized sports are vastly different from those at midcentury. Arenas are booked years ahead, and most of the world's popular sports are now played in Mexico; however, this took a while. In the 1880s baseball took root and became popular in some regions, and by 1904 leagues were formed. Many sports are more recent imports, however, having been introduced by reformers and moral improvers after the revolution as a secular crusade intended to tempt the poor away from what their "betters" viewed as their traditional vices—drink, dirt, disease, and the blood sports. The YMCA worked hard to introduce basketball and volleyball for this purpose. By the 1930s many of these new sports had become well established.[144] This began to change in 1941 as the García Valseca group brought out the first daily sports magazine, *Esto,* and as such films as *Campeon sin Corona* dealt with sports for the first time.[145] Before the marriage of sports with the electronic media there were only a few sports that were truly indigenous, and they afforded the opportunity for only a few to participate.

For people living in the country, and for many in the cities who maintained an emotional identification with their rural past, the tradition of *charrería* (the day's event is a *charreada*) represented the quintessential essence of the Mexican being. "Es y será gallarda expresión de mexicanismo," said Carlos González Peña, writing in 1940.[146] The *charros* had developed a striking mode of dress—the *traje de gala,* from which the *mariachi's* costume evolved—and specialized accessories that emerged over centuries. The *faenas charras,* the rural spectacle from which the U.S. rodeo evolved, served quite a different function in Mexico, even though there was a certain similarity. Not just the rural aristocracy found something fundamental in the sport. Daniel Cosío Villegas boasted to his biographer, Enrique Krauze, that the *charros* from his native Colima were even better than those from Jalisco.[147]

The *charreada* begins with a grand entrance, *el jaripeo,* in which the elegantly attired women enter the arena singing while riding sidesaddle, a true test for a singer. Then there are the events: *manganas*, roping a horse on foot or from horseback; *coleando*, throwing a bull by the tail; *jineteo de yeguas*, riding a wild horse, or wrestling a bull down as one leaps from a horse; *jineteo*, riding young *novillos* bulls; and the culmination of the spectacle, *paso de muerte*, in which the *charro* jumps from one racing horse to another. In his poem, Enríque Guerrero wrote:

> Charro gallardo gentil,
> eres bizarro y marcial,
> el tipo más varonil,
> y un emblema nacional.

The *charrería* was a bastion of the old rural aristocracy. After the revolution, Carlos Rincón Gallardo, scion of one of the oldest aristocratic families of hacendados, whose title of nobility went back to 1810, dedicated himself to preserving the tradition.[148] This was a conscious decision to fight back, since the sport had been ill received by French guests when it was presented in the Jockey Club in 1884 and had gone into decline, at least for the Porfirian elite.[149] A founding member of the Asociación Nacional de Charros, Rincón Gallardo received the high honor of "Gran Maestro de la Charrería." The class pretensions of the tradition, and Rincón Gallardo's extremely formal use of Spanish, were quite explicit. Even in 1977, when he published his book *El libro del charro Mexicano*, he used his family's crest and colonial title, "Duque de Regla, Marqués de Guadalupe y Marqués de Villahermosa."[150] For Rincón Gallardo the urgent need to preserve the *charrería* was not merely the love of a game or even of the spectacle, it was the preservation of a threatened social order.

Jorge Ramón Ballesteros was the son of the owner of Hacienda San Isabel in the state of Mexico. Born a decade before the Mexican Revolution, his longing for the Porfirian rural order also fueled his dedication to the sport. His book was dedicated to the children of his class who should be compelled to learn the rituals of the *charrería* so that they could learn to love his Mexico.[151] His extraordinarily candid chapter "Categorias Sociales y Culturales del Charro" can serve as a primer on the values of the rural aristocracy of old Mexico. The working vaquero was "this crude man . . . whose learning is merely his experience, which rings of illiteracy." The same traits were shared by the *caporal*, or foreman, and the *mozo de estribo*, the groom who cared for the horses. Moving up the rural hierarchy, approval was greater for the administrator "*hombre de bastante cultura"* and culminated in the hacendado: "By the nature of his position he has great knowledge and a high level of culture. In addition to being the master, he is the adviser and guide for all who work on the estate and on many occasions, he imparts moral instructions to his servants."[152]

Charros in front of a rustic bullring. *Courtesy Hermanos Mayo, Archivo General de la Nación, Mexico City*

Needless to say, the number of people able to participate in the *charrería* was extremely limited. (Rincón Gallardo ended his book arguing for the superiority of the traditional *charro* saddle, even though he admitted it was not too good for playing polo.) Even in the cities, the rings were small, and it was not a popular sport to watch. There was another traditional sport, however, that had a much broader following. Indeed, the bullfight was the first sport that attracted large numbers of spectators.

The bullfight was indisputably the quintessential Hispanic spectacle. Long before the animal liberation movement or the Walt Disney view of the animal kingdom, the bullfight evoked far more than the spirit of the hunt. The bullfight's pageantry, costumes, and tension produced a great spectacle. William Beezley points out that the bullfight was also a mirror of social divisions as people took their proper place in the ring, and social hierarchy was replicated as the authorities maintained control over the flow of events.[153] Fundamentally, it was a supreme test of masculine courage in which

style was everything. No one suggested, even as technology perfected the process of killing, that an upgrading of weapons was the
way to dispose of the bull. The idea was for a man to push his courage to the limits as he confronted a deadly beast. When Manolete,
the greatest Spanish bullfighter of the era, visited Mexico, it was a
major occasion, and crowds filled the bullring in Mexico City, which
seated twenty thousand and claimed to be the world's largest.

Some *aficionados* thought that the zenith of Mexican bullfighting occurred on January 31, 1943, as Silviero Pérez, the third son of
a great dynasty of bullfighters from Texcoco, alternated with others as bull after bull was brought into the main ring to test the limits of his courage. The fifth bull, "Tanguito," was especially *bravo*,
and Silviero produced an unrivaled *trasteo*, which is the most dangerous of the *muleta* passes.[154] It was still a world in which individual courage counted against the forces of nature. Even then,
some shared our contemporary sensibilities about the blood and
killing, but the spirit and mythology of the *corrida* defined one kind
of Mexican identity, and, as such, it complemented the *charrería*.
Today, many of us live in a world of committees, paperwork, and
numbers. In the 1940s, people were closer to rural life and that life
seemed related to danger, courage, and the force of nature.

At the other end of the social scale from the equestrian events
were boxing and *lucha libre*, which were genuinely popular sports,
although the wrestling—à la Santo—was rapidly shifting from a
sport to a bizarre spectacle. Although boxing was no longer a sport
of gentlemen, the success of Mexican boxers in the light-weight
categories in the United States created some authentic local heroes,
none greater than Julio César Chávez. Fans were not as squeamish
then about blood sports, and talented fighters who got their start
at local carnivals could move up into another subculture where, if
they were among the best, they could eventually perform in the
Arena Coliseo. For those who faltered, boxing inevitably tapered
off into the world of *pistoleros*, bodyguards, seedy nightclubs, and
red light districts where violence was just another commodity for
sale.

Attempts to introduce U.S. football into Mexico failed, and the
sport was widely rejected as barbaric by the 1890s. In contrast, the
power and eventual triumph of association football (soccer), first
introduced by English miners in Pachuca, may well have had something to do with its making play accessible to all. One only needed
to know someone who had a ball to join in the game, and a goal
could be improvised in a plaza or field.

Although both the Fédération Internationale de Football Association (FIFA, founded in 1904) and the first World Cup (1930) were organized by the French, soccer was a British game that took the world by storm, or "colonialism by consent," in William Murray's phrase. This great international sport came to Mexico during the *porfiriato*, and the first league was formed in 1903. It spread rapidly in the 1920s, with its first Football Association in 1927; Mexico joined FIFA in 1929. The sport became dominant in the 1930s.[155] In 1924 a general sporting body, CONCACAF, was formed for Central America and the Caribbean, and in 1941 a football spinoff comprising Mexico, Cuba, and the United States formed the North American Football Confederation.

The U.S. influence, especially in baseball and basketball, has kept the region's football organizations weak by world standards. Mexico suffers—but also benefits—from a problem of isolation, although domestic support for its clubs is quite strong, and teams such as América developed an impressive following from the earliest years. By contrast, cricket, from the islands of the Caribbean, never became established on the mainland. Even after soccer caught on, Mexico's distance from the great football powers of South America, not to mention Europe, was immense. Important matches were played in the Estadio Nacional; neither the Estadio Azteca nor the UNAM stadium had yet been built in the 1940s.

Mexico was eliminated early from the Olympics in Amsterdam in 1928, in the second World Cup in Rome in 1934, and again in Paris in 1938. Because of the war there was not another World Cup until 1950 in Rio de Janeiro, the second time the World Cup was played in South America. At the first, in Montevideo in 1930, only four teams came from Europe. Mexico has usually had a fairly easy run to qualify for international competition; it is the fourth most frequent qualifier for the World Cup, behind Brazil, Germany, and Italy. However, Mexico's regular lack of success may reflect its fairly self-contained circumstance by world standards. Only air travel in recent decades has brought international teams. But football is still a passion on every street.

All the world's sports eventually came to Mexico, and the country became known for its high standard of equestrian sport, polo, and fencing. For the *niño bien* of the late 1940s, however, nothing was more fashionable than a diversion from the Jockey Club at the Hipódromo de las Américas—owned by Ben Smith and Bruno Pagliai—to the jai alai, or *frontón*, just across from the monument to the revolution. Unless it was Easter in Acapulco!

Conclusion

For a foreigner writing about Mexico, it is fascinating to learn how long outsiders have been falling in love with one or more aspects of the country: its people and their art, crafts, archaeology, ethnography, landscape, and cultural life. Even the tragic aspects of Mexican politics and development strategies engage outsiders. For years, the culture of the Mexican Revolution merged with other political and cultural agendas. The visions of the muralists, new attitudes toward the Indians, and the Latin Americanists' concern for the region were influential abroad. Some on the political Left, such as the lawyer Robert Haberman, lived in Yucatán. While he worked for the Ministry of Education, Haberman "recruited" Frank Tannenbaum, Ernest Gruening, and Carlton Beales to the Mexican cause, even as he battled U.S. Ambassador James R. Sheffield over specific policies.[156]

Katherine Anne Porter, the novelist, stayed with the Catholic radical Dorothy Day in Xochimilco; later, they moved to Mixcoac where they had gardens and animals. Their experience in Mexico made them imagine a church more committed to the kinds of social issues they thought the Mexican Revolution, at its best moments, was addressing. Or again, Dwight Morrow, who generally is not treated with reverence in the Mexican historical literature, and his wife, Elizabeth, had an unexpectedly large impact on Mexican art and crafts. It was Morrow who paid Diego Rivera U.S.$12,000, enabling Rivera to paint the murals in the Palace of Cortés in Cuernavaca. The Morrows also had a significant influence in popularizing *artesenías*, even inspiring the businessmen William Spratling and Moisés Sáenz to finance the revival of silver craftsmanship in Taxco. Others, including Stuart Chase, in *Mexico: A Study of Two Americas*, and Carlton Beales, in *Mexican Maize*, found in the *indigenista* movement a new respect for Indians and peasants as a source of integrity and a parallel between the depression and the plight of the Indians and peasants.[157]

Mexico developed a high profile in the international community as large numbers of painters, writers, scholars, and students descended upon the country and as many tourists returned from their holidays in Mexico with a new respect for Mexican culture. It was curious that just as the world was discovering a new level of respect for the culture of the Mexican Revolution, the political and business leaders of the country were moving in the opposite direction. In reality, the 1940s was the era in which, as the journalist

Carlos Denegri put it, the revolution got down from its horse and got into a Cadillac. It is to the concrete political and economic mechanisms that enabled these changes to take place that we now turn.

Notes

1. Even when a leading Mexican demographer argued an extreme case for an exploding population in 1960, he understated the case by projecting 46.7 million for 1970 and 63 million by 1980. See Durán Ochoa, "La explosión demográfica," 23.

2. R. W. Wilkie, *Latin American Population and Urbanization Analysis*, 321–23.

3. In her study of emigration from Toxi and Dotejiare, in the state of Mexico, Lourdes Arizpe noted that only 4.9 percent of the emigrants (between 1940 and 1980) left Toxi in the 1940s. The figure was negligible for Dotejiare. Although far from conclusive, it is suggestive that studies based upon local data rather than on official statistics show a far less dramatic exodus from the countryside, by contrast with later decades, suggesting that the low statistical divide between urban and rural simply counted population growth as urbanization. See Arizpe, *Migración, etnicismo y cambio económico*, 88.

4. Jan Rus makes the point that even the most radical leaders and community structures in Chiapas were much more tightly harnessed to the state in the 1940s. See "The 'Comunidad Revolucionaria Institución al': The Subversion of Native Government in Highland Chiapas, 1936–1968," 267.

5. Jacobs, *Ranchero Revolt*, 134; Pansters, *Politics and Power in Puebla*, 40–43.

6. J. W. Wilkie, *The Mexican Revolution*, 32.

7. Memorandum of conversation between Dr. Josué Sáenz and U.S. economic diplomats: Whitney, W. A. Raferty, and H. R. Wellman, July 23, 1948, USNA, RG/59, 812.501/8-1848. His curious way of expressing percentages apparently meant that agriculture figures were too low by 66 2/3 percent and industry estimates were too low by 37.5 to 50 percent.

8. The phrase was the description of one U.S. statistical report that complained of poor analysis by the Dirección General de Estadística. Labor Report, December 8, 1950, USNA/59, 812.06/3-3152.

9. Ifigenia M. de Navarrete, "La distribución del ingreso," in *El perfil de México en 1980* (Mexico: Siglo Veintiuno, 1971), 37.

10. Ifigenia M. de Navarrete et al., *Bienestar campesino y desarrollo económino* (Mexico: Fondo de Cultura Económica, 1971), 53–58.

11. Alemán's private cost-of-living index may be found in Elmer H. Bourgerie to secretary of state, August 30, 1954, USNA/59, 812.061/8-3054.

12. Comments on the data from the Ministry of the Economy and the Ministry of Labor came from the report "Annual Indices from 1939 to 1953," USNA/59, 812.061/8-3054.

13. Bortz, "Wages and Economic Crisis in Mexico," 45.

14. These figures were based upon U.S. consular reports on daily wages for men without board. October 1949, USNA/59, 812.5041/12-3049.

15. González Navarro, *Raza y tierra: La guerra de castas y el henequén*, 266–67.

16. Spanish feudal assertions of common rights, such as fishing in lakes and rivers, *pesquería*, were still contested in many rural areas.

17. González, *Pueblo en vilo*, 244.

18. Arizpe, *Migración, etnicismo y cambio económico*, 91.

19. Lewis, *Life in a Mexican Village*, xii–xiii. His baseline was provided by Robert Redfield, *Tepotzlán—a Mexican Village*.

20. Lewis, *Life in a Mexican Village*, xv.

21. Pansters, *Politics and Power in Puebla*, 51–52.

22. Holland, *Medicina Maya en los altos de Chiapas*, 211.

23. Gledhill, *Casi Nada*, 117–41.

24. Arizpe, *Migración, etnicismo y cambio económico*, 78.

25. Wasserstrom, *Class and Society in Central Chiapas*, 172–78; Becker, *Setting the Virgin on Fire*, 105–32.

26. Friedrich, *The Princes of Naranja*, 153.

27. At one point, when Caso was wounded in retaliation for an assassination he had ordered, Cárdenas visited him in the hospital. Ibid., 155–72.

28. Pansters, *Politics and Power in Puebla*, 48–59.

29. Thurston to secretary of state, December 18, 1946, USNA/59, 812.51/12-1846.

30. In July 1946, Antonio Espinosa de los Monteros finally convinced the Federal Power Commission to authorize export of natural gas to Mexico through his company, the Compañía Mexicana de Gas, which gave him a monopoly over much of Northern Mexico. Antonio Espinosa de los Monteros to J. Jesús González Gallo, July 2, 1946, AGN, RPMAC, 577/180.

31. García Canclini et al., *La ciudad de los viajeros, travesías é imaginarios urbanos: México, 1940–2000*. When they showed photographs from the 1940s and 1950s to their subjects, they found a considerable degree of nostalgia.

32. Andrés Caso, "Las comunicaciones," in *México: 50 años de revolución: La vida Social*, ed. Julio Durán Ochoa (México, 1961), 449–50.

33. *El Nacional*, September 1, 1942.

34. González, *Pueblo en vilo*, 258–59.

35. Report on transportation and communications, September 20, 1950, USNA/59, 812.00/9-2050.

36. The normal route before the inauguration of the Pan American Airways service was to take one of the Ward Line steamships from New York to Veracruz via Havana and New Orleans, which took seven days, and then travel up the same camino real to Mexico City that had carried Spanish viceroys. Alternatively, one could take the Standard Fruit Line from New Orleans in three days.

37. The photographic record has been preserved in the National Archives of the United States, Photographic Records of the Office of War Information, Record Group 208.

38. Caso, "Las comunicaciones," 477–78.

39. González Navarro, *Raza y tierra*, 86–89.

40. Beezley, *Judas at the Jockey Club*, 67–76.

41. Lewis, *Life in a Mexican Village*, 174–76.

42. Arizpe, *Migración, etnicismo y cambio economico*, 74–75.

43. Monsiváis, *Amor perdido*, 21

44. Lewis, *Life in a Mexican Village*, 290.

45. For an analysis of the religious/gender basis of this, see Becker, *Setting the Virgin on Fire*, 10–38.

46. Kandt, "Fiesta en Cuetzalan," 49–74.

47. For a description of the brutality of life in a convent, see Franco, *Plotting Women*, 12–22.

48. Beezley, *Judas at the Jockey Club*, 89–97, 117.

49. González, *Pueblo en vilo*, 250.

50. Juan de Dios Boróquez to Alemán, February 23, 1951, and reports from the editors of the financial magazine *Bancos*, AGN, RP/MAV, 950/23652. See also Niblo, *War, Diplomacy, and Development*, 236–38, for a discussion of the organization of banking in the period.

51. Holland, *Medicina Maya en los altos de Chiapas*, 169–210.

52. For the meanings of "active" and "inactive," see the discussion of the evolution of national income statistics in Niblo, *War, Diplomacy, and Development*, chap. 1.

53. Rangel Contla, *La pequeña burguesía en la sociedad mexicana, 1895–1960*, 57.

54. The record, including photographs of the glass factory, can be found in Bursley to secretary of state, September 20, 1943, USNA/59, 812.5047/1.

55. Jorge Basurto could write an excellent book on the working class in the period without mentioning artisans, so completely did he identify the working class with the industrial union movement. See Jorge Basurto, *La clase obrera en la historia de México: Del avilacamachismo al alemanismo, 1940–1952*.

56. Abbey Schoen to the Department of State, October 5, 1950, USNA/59, 812.00/10-550.

57. Ortíz Garza, *México en guerra*, 53–56.

58. *South American Handbook*, 1940, 452.

59. Logan, *Haciendo Pueblo*, 14–18.

60. Arias, *Guadalajara: La gran ciudad de la pequeña industria*, 64.

61. Knight, *The Mexican Revolution: Counter-revolution and Reconstruction*, 2:42–44.

62. "Strictly Confidential Report on the Mexican Mining Industry," USNA/59, 812.00/12-2944.

63. Berger, "Under North American Eyes: Liberal Historiography and the Containment of Central America, 1898–1990," 105.

64. Pacheco, *Las batallas en el desierto*, 10.

65. Ibid., 11.

66. *El Automóvil Americano*, May 1949.

67. Camara Nacional de Industrias de Transformación (Sonora) to Alemán, October 1, 1948, AGN, RP/MAV, 527/84.

68. Embassy report to secretary of state, USNA/59, 912.51/5-2950

69. George Roper to the Department of State, June 5, 1950, USNA/59, 812.3331/6-550.

70. Carmen Toscano produced *Memorias de un Mexicano* from contemporaneous footage he shot during the revolution, between 1910 and 1923. The Archivo Historico Cinematográfico produced the film, and in 1967 the government officially declared it a "Historical Document of Mexico."

71. Lew B. Clark to secretary of state, "Report on 1948 Projected Budget," USNA/59, 812.50/12-3047.

72. As cited by García Canclini et al., *La ciudad de los viajeros, travesías e imaginarios urbanos: México, 1940–2000*, 16.

73. Raymond J. Barrett to the Department of State, January 25, 1951, USNA/59, 912.44/1-2551

74. Embassy to secretary of state, "Non-communist Press," April 7, 1954, USNA/59, 912.60/4-754.

75. *South American Handbook*, 1940, 424–29.

76. Major representatives of capital sat on the college's Board of Trustees: Jess N. Dalton, Manuel Espinosa Yglesias, Emmet K. Goodrich, Burton E. Grossman, Gulliermo Jenkins II, Manuel Sosa de la Vega, Joe Sharp, and Harry Steele.

77. In the 1930s, local authorities and the Bureau of Immigration had a program to deport Mexicans from the United States. See Nodín Valdés, "Mexican Revolutionary Nationalism and Repatriation during the Great Depression," 5–6.

78. Public Law 78 regularized the program in 1951 and allowed the issuance of 4.6 million labor contracts before the program lapsed in 1964. See Henry E. Cross and Jorge A. Sandos, *Across the Border*, 36–46.

79. Vicki L. Ruiz recalled how those who stayed in the United States tried to pass as Spanish; see " 'Star Struck': Acculturation, Adolescence, and the Mexican-American Woman," 130–31.

80. Cotter, "The Origins of the Green Revolution in Mexico," 224–47.

81. Hewett de Alcántara, *Modernizing Mexican Agriculture*, 149. By contrast to Cotter, Hewett de Alcántara focuses on the interaction of political forces and economic vested interests in the private sector.

82. Riva Rodríguez, "Salubridad y asistencia médico-social," in *México: 50 años de revolución: La vida social*, ed. Julio Durán Ochoa (México, 1961), 395–424.

83. Halberstam, *The Fifties*, 293.

84. *Fortune*, February 1959, 81–83.

85. Díaz-Guerrero, "Contemporary Psychology in Mexico," 83–112.

86. M. Bohan to secretary of state, August 6, 1947, USNA/59, 812.50/8-647.

87. Cabral, "The Mexican Reactions to the Hiroshima and Nagasaki Tragedies of 1945," 81–118, and "The Interaction of Science and Diplomacy: The United States, Latin America, and Nuclear Energy."

88. Manuel Gamio to Alemán, January 18, 1947, AGN, RP/MAV, 708.1/5.

89. Agustín Foque to Alemán, July 11, 1952, AGN, RRP/MAV, 45/(32)/3273.34.

90. Alejandro Carrillo Flores to Alemán, July 22, 1948, AGN, RP/MAV, 565.32/88.

91. Franco, *The Modern Culture of Latin America*, 14–20.

92. Jaime Torres Bodet et al., *México: 50 años de revolución: La cultura*, 1–240.

93. Cano, "Análisis de la acción educativa," 37.

94. Alemán placed a thirty-foot statue of himself at the entrance to the new university city. See Cockcroft, *Mexico: Class Formation, Capital Accumulation, and the State*, 152.

95. Muñoz Ledo, "La educación superior," 120–25.

96. W. K. Ailshie to secretary of state, December 27, 1944, USNA/59, 812.504/10-2744.

97. Krauze, *Daniel Cosío Villegas*, 115–22.

98. On Sunday evening, the government required every radio station in the country to suspend programming and present a heavy propaganda program highlighting the week's official accomplishments.

99. When Rockefeller forced Rivera to destroy the mural in New York City, Miguel Covarrubias responded by painting *Rockefeller Discovers the Rivera Murals*, in which he depicts a pained Nelson Rockefeller peeking under the cover to glimpse the portrait of Lenin. See Oles, *South of the Border*, 140.

100. The Radio City mural was reconstructed in the Palace of Fine Arts in Mexico City. See Wolfe, *The Fabulous Life of Diego Rivera*, 317–38. By contrast, the management of the Hotel del Prado simply placed a screen in front of the mural to protect devout sensibilities.

101. Philip Raine to the Department of State, February 24, 1950, USNA/ 59, 712.00/2-2450.

102. Knight, "Racism, Revolution, and *Indigenismo*," in Graham, ed., *The Idea of Race in Latin America, 1870–1940*, 71–113.

103. For a review of the relationship between theories of race and early anthropology, see Stepan, *The Idea of Race in Science*, 83–110.

104. The relationship between social Darwinism and eugenics is explored in Mass, *Population Target: The Political Economy of Population Control*, 19–34, and in Stepan, *The Idea of Race in Science*, 111–39. The Mexican Eugenics Society for the Improvement of the Race was started in 1931; Stepan, *The Hour of Eugenics*, 81, 145–53.

105. Wolfe, *Diego Rivera*, 370.

106. Keen, *The Aztec Image in Western Thought*, 464–69.

107. Mora, *Mexican Cinema: Reflections of a Society, 1896–1980*, 24.

108. Karetnikova in collaboration with Steinmetz, *Mexico According to Eisenstein*, 19–20.

109. Karetnikova has attempted to reconstruct the four episodes into which Eisenstein had planned to divide ¡*Que Viva México!*: *Sandunga*, dealing with life in the Tehuantepec tropics; *Maguey*, a study of the brutality of social relations on Hacienda de Tetlapayac in Hidalgo; *Fiesta*, about the bullfight and festivals; and *Soldadera*, tracing the women who followed the revolutionary soldiers. His footage also appeared in *Thunder over Mexico* and *Death Day* by Sol Lester and in Marie Seton's *Time in the Sun*, all of which Eisenstein disavowed. The one film he completed in Mexico, *Earthquake in Oaxaca*, is apparently lost. Ibid., 4–19.

110. Mora, *Mexican Cinema*, 45.

111. Ayala Blanco, *La condición del cine mexicano*, 171–254.

112. Mora, *Mexican Cinema*, 47.

113. In the 1940s he starred in twenty-four films, including *Historia de un Gran Amor, Así Se Quiere en Jalisco, Cuando Quiere un Mexicano, No Basta Ser Charro, Gran Casino, Alla en el Rancho Grande*, and *Jalisco Cante en Sevilla*. See Diana Negrete, *Jorge Negrete: An Authorized Biography* (México: Editorial Diana, 1987).

114. Mora, *Mexican Cinema*, 19.

115. Huer, *La industria cinematográfica mexicana*, 121–28, and Mora, *Mexican Cinema*, 69–70.

116. There is an alternative tradition of intellectuals, such as Samuel Ramos and Agustín Yáñez, who viewed the *pelado* as only vulgar, violent, and vicious. For a discussion, see Bartra, *The Cage of Melancholy*, 90–94 and 125–29.

117. Report to secretary of state, February–March 1945, USNA/59, 812.504/4-445.

118. Apparently, Quinn worked to keep his original name obscure. When he married Cecil B. DeMille's daughter in 1937, her family would not attend the wedding. See *Current Biography* (1957), 440–41.

119. Quoted by Monsiváis, *Amor perdido*, 35.

120. Mora, *Mexican Cinema*, 85–87.

121. Monsiváis, "Sociedad y cultura," 267.

122. Seth Fein notes how the editors of the trade publication *El Cine Grafico* worried that the attempt to mimic Hollywood worked against the quality of Mexican films. See Fein, "Hollywood, U.S. Relations, and the Devolution of the 'Golden Age' of Mexican Cinema," 110.

123. Lauro E. Doblado and Daniel Quirín to President Alemán, April 6, 1949, and the Asociación de Exhibidores Independientes de Monterrey to President Alemán, March 25, 1949, AGN, RP, MAV, 523.354. See also Pansters, *Politics and Power in Puebla*, 62–63.

124. Martínez Assad, "El cine como lo vi y como me contaron," in *Entre la guerra y la estabilidad política*, 343.

125. Ibid., 347–48.

126. Manuel Puig, *La traición de Rita Hayworth* (Barcelona: Seix Barral, 1976).

127. See Monsiváis's essay on Agustín Lara in *Amor perdido*, 61–86.

128. Miller, "Culture and State in Mexico in the Sexennium of Manuel Avila Camacho," 108.

129. Unger, *Poesía en Voz Alta in the Theater of Mexico*, 1.

130. The entire theater scene in 1940 was limited to six theaters in Mexico City: Arbeu, Bellas Artes, Ideal, Hidalgo, Fabregas, and Lirico.

131. Magaña Esquivel, *Medio siglo de teatro mexicano, 1900–1961*, 48.

132. Martínez, "La literatura," 335–41.

133. Zogbaum, *B. Traven: A Vision of Mexico*, 201.

134. Langford, *The Mexican Novel Comes of Age*, 71.

135. Bartra, *The Cage of Melancholy: Identity and Metamorphosis in the Mexican Character*, 13–24. This is a revised version of *La jaula de la melancholia*.

136. Langford, *The Mexican Novel Comes of Age*, 105–6.

137. Baqueiro Fóster, "La música," 439–49.

138. Armando Bartra points out that not only the publishing empire of García Valseca but also those of Novedades Editores and Publicaciones La Prensa were based on the profits of the "monito" magazines. See Bartra, "Seduction of the Innocents," 304–5.

139. Rubenstein, "Mexico 'sin vicios': Conservatives, Comic Books, Censorship, and the Mexican State, 1934–1976."

140. Ibid., 29.

141. Ibid., 19.

142. Novo, *La vida en México en el periodo de Miguel Alemán*, and *Nueva grandeza mexicana: Ensayo de la ciudad de México*.

143. Monsiváis, *Amor perdido*, 267.

144. Knight, "Popular Culture and the Revolutionary State in Mexico, 1910–1940," 410–11; Vaughn, "The Construction of the Patriotic Festival," 223–26.

145. Bartra, "Seduction of the Innocents," 308.

146. *El Universal*, February 1, 1940.

147. Krauze, *Daniel Cosío Villegas*, 13–14.
148. Ladd, *The Mexican Nobility at Independence*, 19.
149. Beezley, *Judas at the Jockey Club*, 6–7.
150. Rincón Gallardo and de Terreros, *El libro del charro mexicano*, i–xxvii.
151. Ballesteros, *Origen y evolución del charro mexicano*, 7.
152. Ibid., 166–70.
153. Beezley, *Judas at the Jockey Club*, 14–17.
154. Bonet et al., *Bulls and Bullfighting*, 67–70.
155. Murray, *Football: A History of the World Game*, 55, 84, 125.
156. Delpar, *The Enormous Vogue of Things Mexican*, 49–51.
157. Ibid., 61–68.

2

Avila Camacho's Moderation

"No hay que matar la gallina de los huevos de oro."

—Manuel Avila Camacho

From our perspective today the administration of Manuel Avila Camacho saw a dramatic shift to the right by which the Mexican Revolution abandoned much of the radical nationalism of the early Cárdenas era and moved toward the adoption of a far more orthodox development program. Whether one approves of that process or not, it is difficult to miss the phenomenon. The deemphasis of land and labor reform, the deterioration of real wages, the rapid increase in the concentration of income and wealth, and the taming of the unions are all part of a shift in policy that began after the petroleum expropriation under President Cárdenas and his economic advisers Eduardo Suárez, Luis Montes de Oca, and the private banker Luis Legorreta. After the 1940 election, Manuel Avila Camacho accelerated a process that reached landslide proportions under President Miguel Alemán.

It is striking, therefore, to delve into the historical record for the administration of President Avila Camacho and realize that his contemporaries frequently commented upon Avila Camacho's moderation as a dominant characteristic of Mexico's leadership between 1940 and 1946.[1] There are a few clues as to why the president enjoyed this comfortable reputation at the same time that his government began to reverse many of the reforms for which millions of Mexicans had given their best since 1910. This chapter will return to this problem from a number of different levels of analysis, for it was an uneven and at times contradictory process by which the Mexican Revolution changed course.

The Family and the Individual

On a personal level, Manuel Avila Camacho seems to have impressed his contemporaries with an aura of tranquillity and balance. The word that friendly commentators often used to describe
the president's countenance was "serene." The man was not vin-
dictive, and he was frequently credited with wanting to make democracy more effective, a rather remarkable observation given the
origins of his own administration in the election of 1940. He lived
in a premedia age and was able to maintain a distance from the
daily political battle. Much of the crush that surrounds a head of
state today had not yet emerged in Mexico in the 1940s. The man's
personal bearing and style certainly accounted for a large part of
his reputation for moderation and serenity.

Manuel Avila Camacho was born on April 24, 1897, in Teziutlán,
in the Sierra Norte de Puebla. Coincidence provided that Vicente
Lombardo Toledano, the first president of the CTM, and the future
president of Mexico were childhood friends. The father of Lombardo
Toledano was a wealthy copper magnate, whereas Avila Camacho's
father, Manuel Avila Castillo, was a small farmer and muleteer.
There was a generational class reversal as the son of the mining
entrepreneur became a labor leader and the farmer's lad emerged
to negotiate Mexico's place in the world with men who were at the
pinnacle of international capital.

The president's mother, Eufrosina Camacho Bello, in addition
to having eight children, took on the task of maintaining the family after the untimely death of her husband. Her success was notable in spite of the dislocation caused to the family by the arrival
of the railroad as the century began (the family had been, among
other things, mule drivers) and then by the revolution. She started
a store and later moved to Mexico City, where the Avila Camacho
family bought busses. After that they moved around the country
in pursuit of small entrepreneurial projects. Her emotional ties with
the Church were thought to be influential with her children.

Manuel Avila Camacho married Soledad Orozco, and they
adopted a boy, their only child. As the president's wife, Ana Soledad de Avila Camacho patronized the arts; however, she censored
works of art that she considered sexually suggestive—the statue
of the huntress Diana by the sculptor Olaguíbel, set for the Paseo
de la Reforma, and Frida Kahlo's painting *Still Life*, which used
watermelon and cassava to suggest the female reproductive anat-
omy. This tendency of the president's wife and her close ties to the

Church limited her appeal in cultural, revolutionary, and anticlerical circles.

The president's reputation for being quite a family man came from the prominence of his brothers. Maximino was the best known of the president's siblings, acting as the governor of Puebla from 1937 to 1941 and then as minister of transportation and communications in Manuel's government until his death in 1945. Emiliano Avila Camacho had also been a governor of Puebla, and Rafael was the head of the state PNR, mayor of the City of Puebla, and governor in the 1950s; another brother, Gabriel, after acting for a while as chief of police in Puebla, returned to Teziutlán and ran the family farm.

As a young man, Manuel became caught up in the events of the Mexican Revolution and he had the good fortune to have joined the winning faction. By 1918, as he reached his legal majority, his career was rapidly advancing. Avila Camacho rose in the ranks of the Third Division of the Constitutionalist Army, which was loyal to the leadership of Venustiano Carranza, becoming the paymaster for the Third Division in 1918. During the 1920s, Manuel was identified with the government faction, and he was rewarded for his effort at the Battle of Morelia in 1924. It was at that time that Alvaro Obregón promoted him to general. Later Avila Camacho fought against the Cristeros. A close friend of Lázaro Cárdenas since 1920, he rose with the Cardenistas in the 1930s.

A few hints exist as to the future president's early political inclinations. The Avila Camacho brothers had been tutored by a well-known figure associated with the land reform program of the 1917 constitution, Luis Cabrera. However, it would be an error to confuse Cabrera's identification with Article 27 with agrarian radicalism, for Cabrera had shifted to the right over the years. When Manuel received the PRM's selection in 1940, Luis Cabrera was enthusiastic over the likely "suppression of radicalism." Don Manuel's affection for Cabrera was untempered by the latter's opposition to the Cardenista land reform.[2]

General Avila Camacho seemed to want to preserve capitalism while trying to maintain some of the reforms of the Mexican Revolution, although his specific ideas remain vague. He had thought highly of Marquis W. Childs's book on Sweden called *The Middle Way*. He also translated a French Captain Lebaud's volume, *The Education of the Army in a Democracy*. He was obviously involved in trying to understand the way in which the military ought to relate to civil society in a democratic country. He eventually wrote a book on the topic entitled *El libro del soldado*.[3] In 1935, Cárdenas recognized Avila Camacho's concern for the way the military fit into civil society when he chose Avila Camacho to implement his *plan sexenio militar*, which urged young officers to join popular, labor, or peasant sectors of the governing party.[4]

Perhaps a small episode reveals the sense of order and hierarchy that appealed to President Avila Camacho. When George Messersmith arrived in Mexico to replace Josephus Daniels as the U.S. ambassador in 1942, he was immediately invited to spend a weekend at the president's home in Cuernavaca. The new ambassador immediately reported that the Mexican president had the most favorable view of the United States that could realistically be expected: "As you know, President Avila Camacho believes that we must live in the present and look forward into the future and forget, so far as possible, the past."[5]

Although Messersmith described the president's home as "unpretentious and simple," he did record that the grounds included a nine-hole golf course. Messersmith recounted that he was invited to play golf with the president, Foreign Minister Padilla, and Interior Minister Alemán. His initial concern about the quality of his game quickly receded as the ambassador realized that no one, except an aide, seemed to care about keeping score. The poor quality of the golf did not prevent the aide from reporting fictitious scores for eighteen holes in a revealing order of rank: Avila Camacho, 76; Messersmith, 77; Padilla, 78; and Alemán, 79.[6]

Within the Cárdenas administration, Avila Camacho had been a late developer. After a brief stint as the zone commander in Tabasco, he spent the remainder of the 1930s within the bureaucracy of the Ministry of National Defense, rising to be the minister from 1937 to 1939. The president used Avila Camacho in several sensitive positions, to negotiate first with dissident generals Román Yocupicio and Anacleto Guerra in Nuevo León and then with the semi-fascist leaders of the PRAC, Generals Pablo González and Marcelo Caravelo.[7] The rebellion in spring 1938 by Saturnino Cedillo finally catapulted him into prominence, as the president selected Avila Camacho to head the military campaign against Cedillo. As is frequently the case, the frontrunners for the 1940 selection faded, and the general and minister of national defense Manuel Avila Camacho emerged as a compromise candidate.

The Avila Camacho family, through Maximino, had established a political machine in Puebla. As a result of incredibly complex political battles in the late 1930s, generous applications of force against opponents, and his control of the *Diario de Puebla*, Maximino established domination over state politics, even requiring all members of the state legislature to sign a *pacto de honor* swearing unconditional personal support. Even though Maximino was acerbic in his treatment of Cárdenas and a bitter enemy of the CTM, the president supported Maximino's state machine against the CTM state affiliate, FROC, in part due to his brother Manuel's importance in repressing the Cedillo rebellion. Cárdenas's support for Maximino was doubly striking since the Puebla caudillo was open in his admiration for Italian fascism and even appointed military officers to administer the state university.[8]

Selection and Election

The politics of selection for the 1940 election was linked to the political shift of the final years of the Cárdenas administration. A political retreat from the more radical Cardenista reforms flowed from the alignment of factions within the PRM and responded to the conservative pressures opposed to Cardenismo. A financial crisis in 1937 was magnified by the indirect effects precipitated by the expropriation of petroleum. Together, these forces convinced President Cárdenas that the time had come to pull back to less radical ground. Eduardo Suárez was central to this process, and even the most radical of the Cardenistas, Francisco Múgica, began to adopt a position critical of labor by May 1938. Clearly, the swing to the right began near the end of the Cárdenas administration.[9]

There were genuine political mobilizations around a number of potential candidates leading up to the 1940 selection. Avila Camacho, Francisco Múgica, and General Juan Andreu Almazán were the three main contenders. President Cárdenas played a central role, mainly by distancing himself from Múgica, who many of the president's most fervent supporters thought of as his natural successor. As Ariel José Contreras put it, "It was evident then that as Cárdenas would not openly support Múgica, neither would he distance himself from Avila Camacho."[10] There was a desire within the PRM to move toward the center, and Lombardo Toledano's famous statement in announcing his support for Avila Camacho—that Avila Camacho was the man who could keep the military united—undoubtedly influenced many, especially given the widespread speculation about the possibility of a rebellion led by General Almazán.

One thing that tended to confuse people about Manuel Avila Camacho was the platform on which he campaigned for the presidency. The PRM had just unveiled a second Six Year Plan; it was adopted November 1–3, 1939, and published on January 25, 1940. Deeply committed to rapid industrialization, it envisioned governmental encouragement of programs in which the state had joint participation with the workers in the control and administration of industrial enterprises. (The fact that, by some estimates, as many as twenty thousand CTM members belonged to workers' militias made this vision of worker-controlled industries formidable.) Thus, on the surface, Manuel Avila Camacho appeared to be running for the presidency on a platform calling for continuation of the early radicalism of the Cardenista program, especially the workers' administration that existed in the railroads and the petroleum industry. Yet it is a researcher's folly to focus upon the six year plan because of its easy accessibility.[11]

Lombardo Toledano's influence over Avila Camacho's election program seems obvious; on at least one account it had been written by the labor leader even if his authorship was not acknowledged. In the campaign, the candidate continued to support, and promised to carry forward, the radical changes of the early Cardenista period. The plan called for a further increase in the participation of organized labor in the administration of the government, further collectivization of agriculture, and nationalization of heavy industry. The U.S. embassy thought that acceptance of this plan was the price that Avila Camacho had to pay to gain labor's support and the PRM nomination. But people who expected the candidate to make good on his electoral platform were in for a rude awakening.[12]

The candidacy of General Avila Camacho also enjoyed the genuine support of the CTM and the CNC at a mass level, not merely at the level of the high functionaries of those organizations. That mass support convinced many observers—including the U.S. and British embassies—that Avila Camacho represented a continuation of Cardenismo. An example of the conventional wisdom of the moment was expressed by the American consul in Mexicali, who reported: "It appears at this time that all local substantial Mexicans who are holders of property and real assets are realizing that a regime under General Camacho [*sic*] would prove contrary to their personal interests and be largely devoted to the application of purely socialistic philosophy."[13]

On the radical side, supporters of the early Cardenista version of the Mexican Revolution believed that they had no place to go given the military threat General Almazán represented in the 1940 campaign. Even *La Voz de México*, the organ of the PCM, called upon all workers to fight for Avila Camacho and his second Six Year Plan, and against those who seemed to be their greatest enemies: Emilio Portes Gil, a lawyer and caudillo of the CNC; Luis Montes de Oca, president of the Banco de México; and Foreign Minister Hay, Ezequiel Padilla, and Gonzalo N. Santos of the PRM.[14]

Appearances were deceptive. We now know that the selection of 1940 was an extension of the conservative pullback that had started in 1937–38 in the Cárdenas administration itself. Even from the early days of the campaign, there were occasional signals that things might change. Attentive followers of the campaign noted that on December 19, 1939, in a press interview, the candidate began to distance himself from Article 3 of the constitution.[15]

Josephus Daniels was correct in writing to Secretary Hull when he stated, "Without any necessity for doing so, he [Avila Camacho] has indicated that he is conservative, and has practically informed the CTM, and its leader Lombardo Toledano, either to accept his position or leave it."[16] Indeed, Daniels had received reports of conversations between staff members and General Luis Bobadilla, who had been the candidate's chief of staff when Avila Camacho was minister of defense. As early as March 6, 1939, he was told that "the General [Avila Camacho] is desirous of quieting down the present radical tendencies of labor, and states that Lombardo Toledano is agreeable to such a procedure, and that President Cárdenas has given his assent to this."[17]

In the end, political realists on the left like Lombardo Toledano of the CTM and Graciano Sanchez of the CNC used the negotiations leading to the election as a way to bargain for more seats in Congress and other immediate rewards. In retrospect, these rewards were often illusory.

1940 and the Monterrey Group

The official candidate began to forge alliances with people who had been the most unyielding opponents of the major reforms of the Mexican Revolution. The powerful Monterrey Group was surprisingly influential in the events leading up to the election of 1940. The founders of the group, men such as Patricio Milmo (né Patrick

Mullins), Isaac Garza, Francisco Sada, José Muguerza, and Valentín Rivero, had by this time been followed by a second generation that had come of age after the revolution of 1910. Combining deep opposition to the revolution with a close group affinity and ambivalence toward the United States, men such as Luis Garza (of the steel mill); Roberto G. Sada (head of the Vidriera); Luis G. Sada (of the Cervercería Cuauhtémoc); Joel Rocha (Salinas y Rocha department store); Manuel Barragán (initially, of the Topo Chico soda works, later of Coca-Cola, and, after 1928 editor of *Excélsior*); Pablo Salas y López (Cementos Hidalgo); Arturo Padilla (Casa Claderón); and a newcomer, Emilio Azcárraga (manager of the Ford distributorship in Monterrey) came to occupy the most extreme position on the right within the Mexican private sector.

The Monterrey Group had been through a long period of opposition and, for some members, of exile after Bernardo Reyes had been forced out of the governorship in 1909. They had tried for decades to find a political replacement for Reyes. For a while in the 1920s Aarón Sáenz appeared to be their man. Indeed, he had been a front-runner for the candidacy for president in 1929 when President Calles surprised the country and brought a virtual unknown, Pascual Ortíz Rubio, back from his ambassadorship in Brazil to be the official candidate of the PNR. Calles was confident that Sáenz would not join the González Escobar rebellion. One recent student of that political battle has characterized Aarón Sáenz as too weak, opportunistic, and grasping to take a chance on joining the rebellion.[18] Sáenz eventually made his peace with the official party—for which he gained state favors in the sugar and banking sectors—and the Monterrey Group lost its man at the center of the national political arena.

After the crisis following the assassination of Alvaro Obregón in 1928, the Monterrey Group founded COPARMEX—the Confederación Patronal de la República Mexicana—and the bosses from Monterrey were drawn further into the politics of opposition. COPARMEX adopted a laissez-faire attitude opposing governmental action in the economic sphere, a highly unusual position in Mexico. In large part, the autonomy of the brewers and steelmakers enabled this organization to take an antistatist position. It is important to recognize that a fundamental difference between the Monterrey Group and the rest of Mexican industry was that the Norteños developed industry without much aid from the state, save in the broadest protectionist sense. The extreme laissez-faire position of the group made alliances, even with PRM conservatives, quite difficult.

Even moderate leaders of the PRM were considered radical by the standards of the group, as Plutarco Elías Calles and Emilio Portes Gil became their bitter enemies by producing a labor code to implement Article 123 between 1929 and 1931. The Monterrey Group, through their front COPARMEX and using their new voice, *Excélsior*, adopted both a position of absolute intransigence against the government's reforms and the view that the state should not intervene in either their local elections or their factories. The Monterrey Group was also unusual in that its social program represented an extreme version of Catholicism, "Catolico, Romano y Apostolico," as the saying went. The anticlericalism of the Reforma and the revolution was foreign to the elders in Monterrey.

The other favorite son of the Monterrey Group as early as the 1920s had been General Juan Andreu Almazán, head of the Monterrey garrison in 1926. Having come to an understanding with the main figures in the group during his posting in Monterrey, Almazán gained a large number of favors from the group for his Anáhuac Construction Company. For a time he seemed to represent a great opportunity for the group in the 1940 election. But scarcely able to believe their good fortune, the leaders of the Monterrey Group discovered a far more amenable figure in the person of the new candidate of the PRM, General Manuel Avila Camacho. For the first time since 1910, the patriarchs of Monterrey viewed the approach of an election with considerable confidence. This did represent a change.

The Monterrey Group's domination of their region was based upon a paternalism that offered rewards for docile workers while keeping the CTM on the run, even during Cárdenas's term as president. However, before the accommodation with Avila Camacho, the group's problem had been that it viewed Calles as being as bad as Cárdenas. At the level of national politics the group's favorite sons—Aarón Sáenz and Almazán—had always failed to gain the top prize; now, during the 1940 election, the group hedged its bets by supporting both Avila Camacho and Almazán. The Monterrey Group's local base, unyielding commitment to prerevolutionary political and social values, and economic independence from state favors (especially in brewing) gave the group a high degree of independence from the government.

In 1935–36 an epic conflict took place between the Monterrey Group and the forces of President Cárdenas. Lombardo Toledano

of the CTM had supported, or perhaps inspired, an attempt to organize the workers in the Garza-Sada factories into a pro-
government union to replace the company union that the group
was using to dominate labor in its factories. The conflict focused
on the glass factory, the Vidriera. Between November 1935 and July
1936 there were pitched battles, shootouts, lockouts, strikes, and
much political manuevering by the two sides. President Cárdenas
had gone to Monterrey in the first half of February and his well-
known "14-Point Speech" of February 11, 1936, was a thrust aimed
at the Monterrey Group. Luis G. Sada (the tactician) and Joel Rocha
(the spokesman) led the opposition to President Cárdenas. On
March 16, the government backed off and effectively gave up trying to get the CTM into the group's factories.

By the spring, the terrain of battle had turned to the central
government's attempt to impose their candidate for governor,
Anacleto Guerrero, over the group's candidate, Fortunado Zuazua.
(Young Rodolfo Elías Calles quickly faded as a candidate after his
father was expelled from Mexico on April 11.) The height of conflict came on the night of July 29, 1936 when a pro-government
rally clashed with a pro-group rally; two CTM supporters were
killed, and six hundred of the Monterrey Group's Acción Civica
members were arrested, including Rocha and Virgilio Garza, Jr.[19]
The results of the conflict were mixed. The federal government lost
its bid to bring the CTM into Monterrey, and the group's economic
autonomy remained inviolable. However, the Cárdenas administration was able to impose its candidate as governor. Having sal-
vaged something in the political arena, the Cárdenas administration
then gave up the battle to bring the Monterrey Group's economic
activities to heel. The standoff between the political power of the
central government and the economic power of the Monterrey
Group continued, even as the Cárdenas administration began to
trim some of the more radical aspects of its programs.

Historians differ only slightly in dating Cárdenas's political
reversal. There is general agreement among those who have studied the documentary record that Cárdenas's retreat from radicalism occurred between the battle with the Monterrey Group and
the petroleum expropriation. Thus Saragoza relies on the comments
of the U.S. consul in Monterrey to date the pullback at June–July
1937. Consul Blocker reported that by then the PRM was supporting conservative candidates in local elections, having given up on
its plan to break the company unions in Monterrey.[20] Nora Hamilton
dates the pullback in the domestic political arena to the time of the

President Lázaro Cárdenas with his ambassador to Washington, DC, Francisco Castillo Nájera. *Courtesy Hermanos Mayo, Archivo General de la Nación, Mexico City*

petroleum nationalization in March 1938.[21] However, on the labor front the retreat was even earlier. Friedrich Schuller concludes that the flight of foreign capital in 1937 and the resulting discipline that Suárez exercised over the budget triggered the pullback.[22]

As World War II broke out in Europe, Manuel Avila Camacho was in Monterrey. Avila Camacho appears to have courted the Monterrey Group, or possibly it was the other way around. To this point no one has turned up any record of the negotiations between General Avila Camacho and the leading figures in the group. However, we do know that Avila Camacho was in Monterrey four times in October 1939. On October 8, he was given an opulent luncheon by the Cerverceria Cuauhtémoc. As world war loomed, the importance of an accommodation between the country's largest industrial group and the man who would be the wartime president could not have been underestimated.

This moment in October was the point at which, Luis Javier Garrido had argued, the existence of a candidate to the right of the official candidate had the effect of moderating the PRM in general and Avila Camacho specifically.[23] Saragoza also thinks that in these dealings, the group's support for the Acción Nacional further moderated positions taken by the PRM.[24] Ironically, the United States still opposed the influence of the Monterrey Group, thinking that the businessmen from Monterrey were soft on the Nazi threat, and, on the eve of World War II, this was a major issue for the United States.

From his earliest moments as the official candidate, General Avila Camacho moved to mend his fences with the most profoundly counterrevolutionary forces in Mexico. That political move became possible because there was a candidate to his right who was widely identified with the rise of European fascism and, as the plight of a growing number of refugees from Franco's Spain reminded most Mexicans, that was a fate to be avoided at all costs. Moreover, the candidate and the party had come to an agreement as to the relationship.

The PRM-Avila Camacho-U.S. Pact

One important diplomat of the period reported that in private conversation he had learned that an agreement had been formalized between General Avila Camacho and the PRM. The party required of the candidate that he not attack former President Cárdenas and, indeed, that he leave Lázaro Cárdenas' legislative innovations intact, or at least on the books. The agreement also required the new government to respect Vicente Lombardo Toledano's tenancy as head of the CTM. Also, the new president must allow neither his brother Maximino nor moderates into the cabinet. In the words of one British diplomat, "These demands were communicated by Avila Camacho to the Department of State in Washington which accepted them always on the basis that the Cardenista party would not oppose the granting by Mexico of military bases to the United States and in the case of necessity would make a Military Agreement and would accept a commercial treaty."[25]

This threeway agreement—between Avila Camacho, the Cardenista wing of the PRM, and the U.S. State Department—which was passed on to London by U.S. diplomats, cleared the way for wartime cooperation between the United States and Mexico. It meant that Manuel Avila Camacho would be the winner of the election, the people's choice. It also gave the radical Cardenistas a false sense of security, as many of their number believed that their victory over the party's center and right wing was complete. The agreement inadvertently cleared the way for the new government to follow its own policies by tying the Cardenistas to the war effort. Anticipating a bonanza of wartime construction contracts, the president's brother, General Maximino Avila Camacho, formed a construction company in association with General Rodrigo M. Quevedo Moreno and the banker Carlos Trouyet. The election of 1940 was one of the most controversial elections in the country's history, at least until 1988. Considerable violence surrounded the voting, as Almazán's supporters pursued the tactic of trying to hold voting booths. The main Mexico City newspapers announced Almazán's victory the day after the voting. Portes Gil reported that Cárdenas wavered immediately after the voting.[26] Many Mexicans were convinced that support for General Almazán was so great that the PRM had to steal the election, and when the official election results showed the PRM candidate gaining 2,476,641 as opposed to 151,101 for Almazán and 9,840 for Sánchez Tapia even the credulity of the faithful was tested. Supporters of General Almazán wore green ribbons on election day, and in many urban electorates observers reported that green was omnipresent. Almost certainly, however, urban backers of Almazán had underestimated rural support for the governing party.

Political speculation centered on the likelihood that General Almazán would rebel if and when the count went against him. Imaginations ran wild. Some thought the candidacy of General Avila Camacho was part of a Byzantine government plot by which Almazán would be provoked into rebellion after being robbed of the victory and would thus inadvertently play into General Cárdenas's hands by providing a pretext for Cárdenas to stay in office for another term. Other versions predicted that the defeat of General Almazán would set off a military rebellion in support of the cheated candidate. However, General Almazán was not exactly fighting fit in 1940, and it quickly became clear that he wanted no part of a military rebellion.

Today we know that the Saturnino Cedillo rebellion of 1938 was the last military uprising, or *pronunciamiento* by a governor, in Mexican history. But in 1940 politically sophisticated people took the threat of rebellion quite seriously. One interesting FBI evaluation of the 1940 election casts some light on events. The FBI, always worried about disorder, saw the situation in Mexico as chaotic. The bureau understood that General Avila Camacho would win the election, "regardless of the vote." As the FBI put it, "According to information confidentially obtained from members of the Permanent [Electoral] Commission, the Commission has been hand picked and is 100% pledged to declare General Camacho [*sic*] elected."

The FBI, through its contacts, did have it right when it asserted that General Almazán would not risk his substantial business interests in such firms as Cía. Constructora Anáhuac, Impulsora de Acapulco S.A., Credito Industrial de Monterrey S.A., Cía. Petrolera Independiente, and Augusto Flores S.A. by rebelling. Intelligence officials risked little in making this prediction since much of the general's property and most of his construction interests were dependent upon government contracts. Hence by July the attraction of overseas travel was irresistible to General Almazán.

The FBI, however, misread President Cárdenas's intentions. The bureau asserted that the president would declare a state of siege and extend his term "for at least two years," basing this opinion on conversations with Manuel Avila Camacho's brother, Emiliano, who was then governor of Veracruz. Emiliano spoke to the FBI about the possibility of Cárdenas's group and Avila Camacho's supporters falling out. In this version of events, Avila Camacho was cooperating with the CTM in order to keep them from being totally committed to President Cárdenas alone.[27]

The trick in accessing the Almazán phenomenon is to separate the man from the movement. There were important social forces on the extreme right in Mexico that made the movement significant. Recently, Friedrich Schuller has also made a strong case that, despite the cool attitude toward Almazán on the part of the German embassy, ex-president Calles—from his exile in Los Angeles—was making a major effort to attract both funds and overseas fascist support for Almazán.[28] Thus almost in spite of himself, Almazán represented powerful international movements in Mexico. When his supporters continued their effort after the election, Almazán left them in the lurch. Moreover, the fear that fascism might find political leadership within this sector made the remainder of the political spectrum in the country rally around the more moderate figure of Avila Camacho.

As a result of the peculiarities of the election of 1940, rumors abounded about the restrictions to which Avila Camacho had had to agree in order to be selected as the official candidate in the first place. Some observers came fairly close to the mark. One anonymous member of the Mexican Senate, in his discussions with U.S. embassy personnel, even spelled out, ministry by ministry, which PRM caudillos—Lázaro Cárdenas, Emilio Portes Gil, Aarón Sáenz, and Abelardo Rodríguez—had the right to name ministers to the first cabinet. (Avila Camacho himself, according to this version, had the right to name only the ministers of agriculture and the interior.)[29]

First Moves

Avila Camacho continued to pursue the politics of centralism by reducing independent political machines. Cárdenas had overseen the humbling or destruction of local caudillos by the central government in the 1930s, including Saturnino Cedillo in San Luis Potosí, Tomás Garrido in Tabasco, Adalberto Tejeda in Veracruz, and Fidencio Osornio in Querétaro.[30] Similarly, Avila Camacho oversaw the final demise of the Figueroa machine in Guerrero by making certain that the PRM's candidate for governor, Rafael Catalán Calvo, prevailed.[31] Yet that centralizing project was nearly completed by the 1940s, although there would be a perpetual struggle between local movements and the national machine. It was to the central use of state power that the Avila Camacho administration turned.

In contrast to initial public statements and the Six Year Plan, early remarks by the candidate gave some indication of the orientation of the new president. In one postelection interview he signaled a more pro-business attitude, characterizing his government's orientation as "ample guarantees to capital; help to the worker and to the peasant; development of industry; improvement of justice; better diplomatic and commercial relations with the other countries of the world; democracy; absolute freedom of the press and of thought."[32]

There was a continuing attempt to attract foreign capital to Mexico. In one example, H. L. Scott developed a business relationship with Pascual Ortíz Rubio to create a consortium with $37 million to invest at 3 percent in "the financing of Highways, Oil Pipe Lines, Gas Pipelines, Oil Refineries, or any other projects that would be self liquidating over a period of thirty years."[33] Public statements and these early entrepreneurial initiatives signaled a new direction.

More than press statements can offer, the first cabinet of a president often provides a gauge of the balance of forces within the party, not in the new administration, rather, of the relative strengths of the internal factions within the governing party at the time that the negotiations took place leading to the selection of the candidate, the *tapado*. Avila Camacho's first cabinet was a case in point.

A number of figures in the first cabinet were seen to be Cardenistas, close associates and partisans of the faction and the philosophy of the previous president. According to one British intelligence estimate, Ignacio García Tellez, the minister of labor, General Heriberto Jara, the minister of the navy, Ing. Fernando Foglio Miramontes, the minister of agriculture, and Antonio Villalobos, the president of the PRM formed the Cardenista bloc within the cabinet. They were joined by three other Cardenista high officials who were, strictly speaking, outside of the cabinet: Efraín Buenrostro, the head of PEMEX, Eduardo Villaseñor, the president of the Banco de México, and Francisco Castillo Najera, the Mexican ambassador to Washington. Apart from the fact that Lázaro Cárdenas was out of power, the Cardenistas were also badly handicapped by the growing coolness between Vicente Lombardo Toledano of the CTM and former president Cárdenas.

According to the FBI's assessment of the new cabinet, Miguel Alemán and Marte R. Gómez were moderate opportunists:

> Alemán . . . plays ball first with the leftists and then with the rightists . . . and Gómez was difficult to place since each side thought him with the other. The Cardenistas included: Pablo Macías, Defense; Eduardo Suárez, Hacienda y Credito Publico; General Heriberto Jara, Navy. The main figures on the right consisted of Ezequiel Padilla, Foreign Relations; Francisco Javier Gaxiola, Economy; and Dr. Gustavo Baz—who the FBI called the ". . . closest thing to being pro-nazi as anyone in the cabinet"—in the Ministry of Health and Public Assistance.[34]

The Cardenistas faced the bitter opposition of a conservative group within the high echelons of the party that included the former presidents Abelardo Rodríquez, Emilio Portes Gil, and Plutarco Elías Calles (in order of their importance in the 1940s). Maximino Avila Camacho, although technically still out of the cabinet, nevertheless carried the full fury of the battle against Cardenismo. No one was ever quite certain of the degree to which Maximino, as the president's brother, expressed the views of the president. At one point he went so far as to try to buy newspaper space to use in attacking former president Cárdenas, until his brother stopped him. When that effort failed, Maximino embarked upon a campaign to try to gain a foothold in the control of several of the country's newspapers and magazines. Eventually, Maximino became the minister of transportation and communications, a position from which he enjoyed substantial benefits of office.

Not surprisingly, some of the men who were to emerge as the winners in the long run were viewed as moderates, occupying an intermediate position between the Cardenistas and the right wing at the time of the first cabinet. Perhaps Miguel Alemán was the most successful at keeping his positions hidden. He had emerged out of the Cerdán family political machine in Veracruz, and he was actively engaged in the in-fighting between Governor Cerdán and the CTM. Yet his elevation to the cabinet had come through his success in the Cárdenas administration. Under the new Avila Camacho government, he appeared to have cut his personal links to Maximino and shifted his allegiance to the new president. As one British intelligence report put it perceptively: "I am inclined to believe that Lic. Alemán may prove to be a somewhat reliable gauge as to the political trend in Mexico. He undoubtedly has presidential aspirations and I believe he would not hesitate to transfer his allegiance back to General Cárdenas if he thought that these aspirations would be furthered by his doing so."[35]

The foreign minister, Ezequiel Padilla, formerly a supporter of Calles, was also against Cárdenas and the Cardenista tendencies in the party. He soon became the favorite of the U.S. government and especially close to the wartime American ambassador, George Messersmith. Like Alemán, Padilla kept his views to himself in the early stages of the new administration. Padilla, who would inadvertently play an important role in the selection of Alemán as the new president at the end of the war, was hurt domestically by becoming the most visible Mexican symbol of close cooperation with the United States in World War II. When he was in Rio for the Pan American Conference, the international press was very impressed with his performance, as well as with his support for the allied cause. He was frequently referred to in the United States as a future president of Mexico. This hurt him badly, as every other member of the cabinet with aspirations for 1946 sharpened his political dagger.

As always, President Avila Camacho placed himself between the two groups, and only gradually did observers realize that a new group of "avilacamachistas" was emerging between the right wing and the Cárdenas faction within the PRM. It was not long before the message was out that cabinet members should moderate their positions, from either right or left, or face the slow erosion of their powers. The men quick to learn this lesson were Miguel Alemán, Eduardo Suárez, and Ramón Beteta. For a while, it became the national sport to try to figure out where the government really stood.

The Shift to the Right

President Avila Camacho rapidly began to distance himself ideologically from the radical nationalism of the Cárdenas presidency. In the first few months after the accession to power, a number of clear indications emerged suggesting that the government was changing its course. The most obvious indications initially were in the president's own statements. The new president declared that he was neither a Communist nor a socialist. Separating himself from the Cardenista tradition and a series of projects that were referred to loosely as socialism, he placed his top priority on his relationship with the business community, arguing, "It is necessary to create confidence in the investors: first in the Mexican investors; then in the foreigners."[36]

President Avila Camacho moved to make foreign investors welcome, in a manner that stood out in contrast to his predecessor. The British representative in Mexico reported, "The President has thrown out hints to capitalists and foreigners that he is prepared to co-operate with them."[37] Since even the British representatives—who still pursued large claims against Mexico stemming from the petroleum nationalization—received these pro-business feelers from the new administration, the word was well and truly out.[38]

As Avila Camacho's term began, Antonio Ruiz Galindo faced a strike in his factory, Distribuidora Mexicana S.A. On February 14, 1941, he asked for an audience, which was quickly granted by J. Jesús González Gallo, the president's private secretary. The secretary reassured Ruiz Galindo: "Now all the administrative functionaries have instructions from the president himself on how to attend to matters pertaining to their respective positions with efficiency." The strike was quickly settled, as Ruiz Galindo expressed it, "thanks to your generous intervention."[39]

Another example of the tilt away from labor emerged when Evaristo Araiza of the Compañía Fundidora de Fierro y Acero de Monterrey wrote to the president. The steel foundry began to expand its plant in 1943; the following year it added a fifth semicontinuous steel mill worth 13 million pesos. Claiming it would make the industry more price competitive and self-sufficient, the managing director explained to the president that the investment would make 130 workers redundant and asked for his approval. In contrast to Cardenás's 1936 battle with the Monterrey Group, Avila Camacho's support for Araiza in the subsequent labor dispute reveals the changing values of the government in the 1940s.[40]

President Avila Camacho receiving labor leaders, including Vicente Lombardo Toledano, on May Day, 1942. *Courtesy Hermanos Mayo, Archivo General de la Nación, Mexico City*

The Avila Camacho administration also backed away from radical Cardenista reforms in other important ways. The Supreme Court was immediately changed by the administration, and the new composition of the court was widely seen to have been expressed in the Sabino Gordo case. In that spectacular case, the court ignored the views of the Cárdenas administration on the ownership of minerals and agreed to a weakening of the state's claim to subsoil rights. Mexico's claim of subsoil rights had been expanding ever since the 1917 Constitutional Assembly adopted the famous Article 27; it was also the legal foundation on which the expropriation of the Mexican petroleum was based.

Top appointments reflected the new political direction. The first states in which governorships were open, Jalisco and Coahuila, saw the new government move to install governors who were opposed to the Cardenista tradition of the recent past. The hand of the president's private secretary, González Gallo, was seen as obvious in the process of selecting more conservative governors.[41]

Also separating itself at once from the agrarian reform movement, the Avila Camacho administration returned a number of henequen, or hemp, plantations in Yucatán to their previous owners on the grounds that the former state governor had not had the right to order an act of expropriation.[42] That decision at least opened up the possibility that the land granted to ejidos *colectivos* under President Cárdenas could be open to legal challenge. Although it did not quite come to that, agrarian reform was largely over. Official government statistics continued to report significant amounts of land being turned over to ejidos, 5.9 million hectares under Avila Camacho and 4.8 million under Alemán.[43] Nevertheless, as Arturo Warman would report for Morelos, "By 1942, the peasants of Morelos had received practically all the land that the revolution was going to give them, on which, like the Biblical curse, they had to grow and reproduce themselves from the sweat of their brow."[44]

All these early signals were minor compared to the stunning move to change one of the most fundamental social aspects of the Mexican Revolution. President Avila Camacho immediately bought into what was probably the longest-running symbolic topic in Mexican politics, the religious issue. Always before, leaders of the Mexican Revolution had maintained positions of guarded or open hostility toward the Catholic Church. As a symbol for revolutionaries of all that was backward in Mexico's colonial heritage, the Church had been engaged in conflict with the government that at times had merged into open warfare. Anticlericalism had been written into the constitution of 1917, and the depth of bitterness in the Church-state struggle in the 1920s is still striking. Even the most conservative of the leaders in the official party had maintained strictly anticlerical positions. It was therefore really quite extraordinary when the Mexican president openly stated *"soy creyente"* (I am a believer).[45]

Opposing the anticlerical tradition in Mexico was something new for the leader of the Mexican Revolution. Today we frequently forget how central the battle against the worldly powers of the Church had been since independence. Friends of the administration within the revolutionary tradition blamed Avila Camacho's lapse upon the influence of his wife, who was quite devout in the tradition of many Mexican women of her class. At the very minimum, the president's profession of religious faith heralded a major change of course for the Mexican Revolution. Throughout his administration he continued to support and subsidize religious activities that previous presidents would have opposed. And

Mexicans understood that this position had serious implications for the social program of the Mexican Revolution.

As his presidency proceeded, the Avila Camacho administration became bolder in its support of the Church. It was, for example, fairly obvious that the extra magnificence of the festivities in honor of the Virgin of Tepeyac from January 5 to 12, 1944, represented an official subsidy. The right-wing magazine *Mañana* could scarcely contain its enthusiasm over the government's new line. Reinforcing this gesture to the right, Foreign Minister Padilla announced, in a speech at Atlixco, that the Sinarquistas and Acción Nacional would not be dissolved despite Mexico's wartime cooperation with the Allies.

Conflict quickly emerged between the president and some formerly prominent figures within the PRM. To many of the staunch followers of the early reforms of former president Cárdenas, these early moves by the new president seemed to be a profound betrayal. On September 1, 1941, at the end of his first annual report to the Congress, President Avila Camacho had to endure the extraordinary experience of hearing Alejandro Carrillo—the close associate of Lombardo Toledano in the CTM and now the president of the Chamber of Deputies—immediately take the podium in the Congress to refute directly and energetically the president's speech. Offering an overt rebuttal to a State of the Union message was unprecedented. The president was furious, and Carrillo's political days were numbered.

Many supporters of former president Cárdenas desperately tried to block these new presidential initiatives; the battle focused upon changes in the cabinet. It was, therefore, a major reversal for the Cardenistas when, on September 12, 1941, the president removed two men who had been the most active proponents of socialist education under the previous administration, the minister of education, Luis Sánchez Pontón, and his undersecretary, Enrique Arreguín. Héctor Aguilar Camín points out that Avila Camacho shifted the emphasis in education toward "a civic tone, a nationalistic exhortation, the ideology of the Fatherland, the stability, serenity and the defense of the spiritual patrimony of Mexico." In addition, emphasis was placed on the provision of technical skills for the new factories.[46] The forced resignation of the minister and his subsequent replacement by Octavio Vejar Vásquez initiated a purge of the left within the Ministry of Education, a purge that generated great bitterness within circles that had provided some of the most dedicated supporters of President Cárdenas's program.

Octavio Vejar Vázquez pushed a hard anti-Communist line during the first years of the Avila Camacho administration. More than simply to ensure that conservatives received promotions within the education ministry, he hoped to convince the president to view these stunning changes in the Mexican education department as a model for the rest of society. Vejar Vázquez wanted the state to concentrate on primary education and leave secondary education for private initiatives. He wanted coeducational schooling eliminated after kindergarten, and he thought that only one official teachers' union should be tolerated. Once in power, he quickly cut funding to the Colegio de México, as did the Banco de México in 1944. More controversial still was his belief that as many army officers as possible should be placed in the schools to impart compulsory military training to students and teachers.[47]

Vejar Vázquez wanted the president to support the expulsion of all Communist teachers from the schools. He wore a pistol on his belt and headed a paramilitary gang that went around closing schools that he thought were controlled by Communists. The issue came to a head during the last days of 1943 as Vejar Vázquez gave the president an ultimatum to the effect that Avila Camacho should support him in his plan to sack Communists, or he would resign. The matter became public when *Excélsior* openly blamed the president for failing to support Vejar Vázquez's plan. The president was not willing to go that far, and the ultimatum ill-served the minister. Nevertheless, Vejar Vázquez had shifted the political fulcrum substantially to the right before his departure from the cabinet.

In another symbolic move that distanced his administration from that of his predecessor, the president acted against the Partido Comunista Mexicana (PCM) early in his first term. Even though the PCM was a small party, light years away from being able to enter the contest for control of the state apparatus, Avila Camacho's campaign against the PCM ranked with Vejar Vázquez's purge of the Ministry of Education as a central ideological battle of the day. Anti-Communism was a position with which the new president deeply agreed.

It did not take the new administration long to make its position on the PCM clear. On the night of Friday, November 29, 1940, regular army personnel under the command of Major Guillermo García Gallegos raided the PCM headquarters at Calle Brazil #10. Police entered the building over the rooftop of the Hotel Lido next door, much to the discomfort of the hotel's guests. Major García

Gallegos was shot and killed, and some fifty PCM members were detained, although many others escaped.

Excélsior, El Universal, and *La Prensa* all reported that the PCM had been plotting to overthrow the established government in Mexico. They indulged in the most amusing fantasies about the means that the PCM was going to apply in this rather ambitious project. The newspapers asserted that the plan was to sabotage petroleum and electrical supplies and, in the darkness, burn public buildings, foreign legations, and the homes of government officials. There was also, they asserted, a plan to assassinate President Avila Camacho and former president Cárdenas. Somehow these acts were supposed to precipitate the collapse of the Mexican government rather than an authoritarian backlash.[48]

The response of the Mexican Communist Party and forces sympathetic to the Left is revealing. The Left was unwilling to break openly even with a government that was using armed force against it. In a pathetic rationalization, *El Popular* asserted that the raid was done without the authorization of the government, but with the backing of Avila Camacho's organization.[49] In the days following the raid Dionisio Encina, the head of the PCM, denied that any such plan was under consideration, and in fact the government's own action on the matter seems to have downplayed the episode. All but three PCM members were released. Those detained in jail were members of STERM and employed by the Ministry of Education. According to the information available to the U.S. consul general in Mexico City, Morris Hughes, both the president and the president of the Senate, Alfonso Gutíerrez Gurria, opposed this kind of police action on the grounds that it was undemocratic.[50] Whether the president was or was not behind the events of the night of November 29–30 (and this is the kind of episode for which the contemporary press is a worthless source), the anti-Communist orientation of the government was clear.

The appointment of the president's brother, Maximino Avila Camacho, was another signal of a shift in political stance by the administration; it was also a major affront to many honest Mexicans of various political persuasions. Maximino was a reactionary figure, possibly the most recalcitrant figure to sit in a national cabinet since Victoriano Huerta. Not only was he anti-PCM, which was anything but rare, but he was deeply antagonistic toward the CTM as well. His entire career was surrounded by scandal. While he was governor of Puebla, he had been an important member of the

William Jenkins's clique, and he had used his power at the state level to defy President Cárdenas's pro-CTM policy in Puebla. Maximino's appointment as minister of transportation and communications augured ill for labor.

The CTM came under considerable pressure with the change of government. Not only did they lose their founding leader, Vicente Lombardo Toledano, in 1941, but they faced strong pressure to

moderate their position on a wide range of topics. Whereas today we tend to learn first lessons about the PRI and its component parts—the CTM, the CNC, and the CNOP—as though these groups were naturally and always had been the agents of the state, that was not the case. The government of the day was involved in a massive effort to tame the labor movement. Early signs of this effort emerged at once.

The CTM congress that opened on February 24, 1941, was a new low for the political career of the CTM's founding president, Vicente Lombardo Toledano. Avila Camacho had made it clear that he was not keen on labor, yet Lombardo

Maximino Avila Camacho in the bullring. *Courtesy Hermanos Mayo, Archivo General de la Nación, Mexico City*

Toledano had been unreserved in his support for the PRM candidate. Lombardo's keynote speech was in substance anti-Avila Camacho, in that he was critical of the new political agenda of the government. However, in his somewhat precious political logic, Lombardo Toledano concluded that since the CTM had nominated Avila Camacho for the presidency, the labor organization should support his policies, even when they took a position inimical to working people. The unpopularity of Lombardo's political position was clear; he had to be escorted to the speaker's podium by a CTM guard of militiamen, so hostile was the CTM's congress. Lombardo Toledano's reliance upon the workers' militia for his personal protection was all the more poignant since as recently as two months earlier he had condemned the existence of the CTM militia.[51]

Labor leaders Vicente Lombardo Toledano with U.S. Ambassador George Messersmith. *Courtesy Hermanos Mayo, Archivo General de la Nación, Mexico City*

The CTM congress chose as its leader Fidel Velázquez, the man who would remain in that position, with only a brief exception, until his death in 1997, As irony would have it, the first leader of the CTM, Vicente Lombardo Toledano, had resigned in order to be faithful to the principle of "no reelection," which has become such a proud icon of the governing party—but not of the CTM. At least that was his public reasoning. In the understated comment by one British diplomat, "he [Fidel Velázquez] is believed to be somewhat less fanatical and less of a visionary than Toledano."[52] Velázquez also made every effort to augment the level of bureaucracy within the CTM as a way of taming radicals.[53]

A secret report based upon discussions between unnamed British commercial contacts and the new president perhaps best captured the essence of Avila Camacho's labor stance. After having flirted with the possibility of firing all of the Cardenistas in the cabinet, the president was quoted as saying, "You know, I could easily crush these labour leaders with a strong hand, but I don't wish to use force unnecessarily."[54] Instead, the president played the divide-and-rule card. Indeed, the CTM was only one of five national labor confederations (CTM, CNP, COCM, CROM, and the CGT). As Barry Carr noted, "Never in its entire history would the CTM be so weak and divided as it was in the war years."[55]

The new president did stress his desire to welcome foreign capital back to Mexico. He also called Cárdenas's support of collective ejidos his "cardinal sin," and he committed himself to granting freeholds to small peasants in order to reverse the momentum favoring collectivization. Avila Camacho also was already claiming credit for taking the railways away from the control of the railroad workers' union and placing General Enrique Estrada in charge of running the railways.[56]

The CTM took the easy way out. In the ancient tradition of blaming the king's advisers rather than the monarch directly, the CTM focused its campaign against the president's extraordinary brother, Maximino. The CTM organized a massive demonstration as early as October 23, 1941, in which participants denounced Maximino for his antilabor stance and his support for the proto-fascist group the *camisas doradas.* The organization took some risk in naming and attacking the president's brother directly; however, no sooner did the CTM act than it apologized. The CTM stated in its public pronouncements, "The working class knows how to distinguish between the errors of the President's aides and the conduct of the head of the government."[57] On the very day that the public demonstration was taking place, the leadership of the CTM was visiting the president to assure him of their support.

The same month that President Avila Camacho was maneuvring successfully to remove Lombardo Toledano from the presidency of the CTM, the Mexican Senate hosted a banquet for General Abelardo Rodríguez. A wealthy businessman in his own right, former president Rodríguez spent the day before the banquet in consultation with President Avila Camacho. (Rodríguez had been treated well even in the heyday of the Cárdenas administration.) At the banquet, the ex-president strongly condemned the ideology of the Cárdenas administration and called for national unity—to be achieved by dropping the Cárdenista reforms and by adopting business methods in government. The CTM and its journalistic voice, *El Popular,* attacked Abelardo Rodríguez openly, recognizing his pro-business orientation.

In the state of Veracruz, the CTM was engaged in an intense struggle against the antilabor position being taken by Governor Giorgio Cerdán. The same conflict had happened in Puebla, the president's home state, a few years earlier, when Maximino Avila Camacho had led an antilabor government. In that case, however, Maximino had been bucking a trend that President Cárdenas had set nationally. Now, Manuel Avila Camacho was supporting Governor Cerdán in ways that were understood to be clear political statements.

The long-discredited Confederación Regional Obrera Mexicana (CROM) was unexpectedly resurrected under Avila Camacho's administration. In a classic divide-and-rule ploy, there was an incident in which amazing signals were sent out from the new administration to the labor front. The 15th National Convention of the CROM took place at the end of July. The minister of the interior, Miguel Alemán, addressed the convention as the representative of the new president. He talked of the high esteem in which the new chief executive held the CROM. No one could miss the message that the CTM would no longer be the government's only labor organization. Miguel Alemán was the highest government official to address the CROM in years. The intimate links between foreign and domestic issues were on display. Roberto Haberman, the representative of the CROM in the United States, warned the delegates not to denounce Yankee imperialism, since that was what the Nazis wanted. Luis Morones, long-term head of the CROM, declared his undying support for the president; and even the American Federation of Labor in the United States sent its third vice president, Matthew Wall, to address the delegates.

The CROM had not had it so good since its split with President Calles back in 1928. Avila Camacho was giving notice that the CTM could be reduced to a level comparable with that of the CROM. In addition, there was also the threat that continued emphasis on such touchy issues as U.S. imperialism could be used against the CTM as the war clouds in Europe continued to roll closer. Not only had the CROM supported Franklin D. Roosevelt's Good Neighbor Policy and symbolically wrapped itself in the U.S. flag, it even displayed that flag on the speaker's platform during the 15th Congress. It was also at this time that the Ministry of Labor denied the use of the name CROM to an anti-Morones group that had been challenging the old *patrón*'s dominance.[58]

A meeting of the International Labor Office was planned for the autumn of 1941. It had been taken for granted that Fidel Velázquez, as the new head of the CTM, would be Mexico's representative to the meeting in New York and that Lombardo Toledano, as president of the CTAL, would also be a delegate. However, President Avila Camacho personally intervened to ask the aged head of the CROM, Luis Morones, to attend in Mexico's name. This labor leader, who patterned his personal style on the U.S. gangster Al Capone, created an unexpected tone for the new government as the country's representative to a major international labor conference.[59]

The minister of labor, Ignacio García Tellez, tried to block the granting of such a major favor to the CROM when he learned of it, but the president persevered. Eventually, three representatives were named: Luis Morones (head of the delegation) of the CROM; Elías Hurtado, a relative unknown, representing the CTM; and Mario Suárez for the tiny Bloque de Obreros y Campesinos. In addition to directing expected plums away from the CTM, and giving quite a warning to the leadership, the new administration temporarily demoted the largest labor confederation to a secondary political role. The net impact was to leave Morones as the only well-known figure in the delegation. Lombardo Toledano had to attend the conference merely as an observer and not as an official delegate. By the next conference of the CTM, September 11–13, the Avila Camacho administration did not even send an official representative to the meeting. Signals had been sent.

In November 1941, Lombardo Toledano tried to boost his standing as a supporter of the Allied war effort by releasing a list of Nazi agents who were active in Mexico. The conservative press had a field day charging "Detective Toledano" with having just discovered the German Club and the German School. More seriously, the new Mexican president used the incident to distance his administration from the CTAL with which Lombardo was identified; instead, the president chose to identify with the far more conservative Pan American Confederation of Labor, an organization linked to the pro-U.S. Pan American Union.

In the president's view, not only the Church but also the CROM regained favor. Other institutions of the right that had been losing ground during the Mexican Revolution also found their stars on the rise. In these early days of the new administration there was also a bill before the Congress to allow ten thousand Sinarquistas to establish a colony, similar to the old military colonies of the colonial period but this time in Baja California. U.S. diplomats thought this very dangerous given the reactionary nature of Sinarquismo and the possibility that the Japanese might link up with the group. They feared that these colonists would welcome Axis forces in the remote northwest of Mexico.[60]

It should also be remembered that these attempts to divide the labor movement were accompanied at the local level by a high degree of violence. The regular use of *pistoleros* to intimidate workers who bucked the official union leadership left a record of constant complaints. Oddly, the victims of these attacks frequently wrote to the president about their plight, as in the dispute at the Casa Clemente Jacques in 1943 in which the workers claimed to have been attacked by the union leader Jesús Yurén and a group of gunmen.[61] Although it is impossible to evaluate these and many other accusations at this distance, there did seem to be the systematic use of violence in labor disputes. At the worst moments, as at William Jenkins's sugar refinery in Atencingo, the government ignored the violence even when Jenkins's *sindicato blanco* used machine guns against independent workers.[62] In the most extreme cases, the president's brother Maximino, Colonel Serrano, certain governors, and the police were frequently singled out as having been party to these practices.

Finally, the growing unpopularity of the official labor leaders opened an additional opportunity for the government to regain control of the CTM by the late 1940s. Kevin Middlebrook has demonstrated that not only did political and judicial support for compliant leaders help to defeat more independent-minded labor leaders, but declining financial support from angry and alienated members was matched by "unspecified" (almost certainly government) funds that represented 62.2 percent of monthly CTM income by 1950.[63]

Undermining Agrarian Reform

In the final stages of the Cárdenas presidency a brake was applied to the land reform process by the Supreme Court. The president of the Supreme Court of Justice, Daniel V. Valencia, argued that once the president had protected a small private property under the doctrine of *inafectabilidad* other agrarian authorities could not touch this property.[64] Given the extreme dependence of the judiciary upon the executive, this decision was further evidence of President Cárdenas's retreat from his own program.

A further revision of the Agrarian Code was presented to the Chamber of Deputies in August 1940, and it also insisted on respect for small properties. The doctrine of *inafectabilidad* became the central mechanism by which private property was protected from the possibility of land reform, and this protection quickly went beyond small properties. In Tlaxcala, for example, Mario Ramírez Rancaño reported that Cárdenas had apparently decided to issue *concesiones de inafectabilidad ganadera* for thirteen large cattle estates, although the decrees were not promulgated until the time of

Avila Camacho. The result was that "the demands for the division of land have crashed, time and again, against an indestructible wall since the 1940s: legally, great haciendas or *latifundia* do not exist."[65] What is astonishing is how quickly the word got out that the spirit of the age had changed. George Collier, in examining petitions from twenty-three municipalities for land in Chiapas, found that the number of petitions initiated and awarded dropped off from nearly thirty to zero between 1938 and 1941.[66]

To reform rural finance, the Avila Camacho administration moved quickly to place the Banco Ejidal and the Banco Agricola under the Ministry of Agriculture. According to an official at the ministry, Ing. Bernardo Avilez, "[this] will change the banking policy from one of social advancement to one of banking." Administration officials privately acknowledged that the Ejidal Bank in the Laguna, a Cardenista showpiece, employed twelve hundred people to do a job that fifty private-sector employees could accomplish.[67]

When Avila Camacho came to power, he stressed that the criteria for those who governed ejidos should be that of efficient production rather than concern for the peasants' needs. New powers to carve private titles out of ejido lands were established, based upon the need of production for domestic consumption and export markets.[68] Legal changes were complemented by new administrative practices: no new communities were to be registered unless unprotected land was to be tapped; all petitions were to be handled in chronological order, thus ensuring long delays; any agrarian activists who occupied lands would be expelled; and no provisional awards would be forthcoming. Those changes applied legal brakes on land reform; a few years later the governments of the 1940s would go even further and modify the legal definition of small property.

The new administration was sympathetic to pressures emanating from the private farmers, in a reversal of the sympathy that the ejidatarios enjoyed under the Cárdenas administration. Government backing for the organizations representing *pequeña propiedad* had the effect of pitting the small farmers against the ejiditarios, and by ignoring the role of the large private farmers, the administration revealed its sympathy for private land owners.[69]

Specific episodes showed the most extreme face of the administration's shift to the right on land reform. In at least one dramatic case it appeared that the central government was using the army to reverse the political momentum favoring land reform. In the Huasteca, the mountainous region that overlaps parts of several eastcentral states and roughly corresponded to the 8th Military Zone, there was a series of atrocities. Now that Cardenismo was over, the zone commander, General Anacleto Guerrero, from his headquarters in Tampico, vowed to discipline what he called "the agrarian element" in the state. In his attempt to combat the CNC radicals, who in his view had been protected because of Portes Gil's dual positions as regional caudillo and as the original head of the CNC nationally, the army committed eighteen summary executions against agrarian activists. The American consul in Tampico reported that General Guerrero had been acting to protect U.S. farmers in the agricultural settlement at the Chamal colony against *campesinos'* demands for land. The intervention by the army in the political process seemed clear since even the governor, a close follower of Portes Gil named Magdaleno Aguilar, opposed General Guerrero's antiagrarian policy. The American consul reported that Governor Aguilar's frustration flowed from the fact that Guerrero's instructions to act against those who were demanding land reform were coming from Mexico City. This may have been so; the pro-Portes Gil newspaper in Tampico, *El Mundo*, was also complaining about the authorities' action as the newspaper covered the trial generated by the events at Xicotencatl, Tamaulipas.[70]

In fact, efficiency was not the main criterion. We now have a significant number of local studies demonstrating that efficient ejidos *colectivos* were systematically undermined as the rules of the game were shifted against them. Capital became scarce, even when funds were generated by efficient local operations. As Cynthia Hewett de Alcántara demonstrated for Sonora, ejidos such as El Yaqui, Morelos, and Quechehueca set aside five percent of their gross sales in a special social fund with which they built schools and offices and drilled wells—in addition to purchasing hundreds of mechanized pieces of modern equipment. A political attack by the state and private landholders had doomed even the most efficient projects. "Unfortunately, these considerable resources were soon to be destroyed, or sold, as the cooperatives were torn apart and their assets concentrated in the hands of a few."[71]

Small incidents hinted of the new, more conservative orientation of the government. Conservative governments in many countries have sought ways to deemphasize the moments at which workers celebrate their victories and lament their losses. In the United States, for example, the evolution of May 1 from May Day to Law Day has accompanied a massive swing to the right. More commonly, sport and carnivals seem to have been the favorite devices for turning mass attention from more serious matters of class and politics. Such, at least, was the attempt in Mexico. On May Day in 1942 the workers' celebrations were held without incident or much official support. To compete with the traditional May Day celebrations, the government began to schedule bullfights and even a polo match, although it was doubtful how much polo would divert the attention of working Mexicans.

The government's shift to the right scarcely went unnoticed, even in the most conservative circles in Mexico and abroad. There is a fascinating report, obtained from a "most secret source" within the Vatican, in the U.S. archives. It was written by Luis M. Martínez, archbishop of Mexico and the apostolic chargé d'affaires in Mexico to Cardinal Luigi Maglione, secretary of state to the pope. In this report, Archbishop Martínez could barely contain his enthusiasm for the new president: "As I have already suggested to Your Eminence, lately the President of the Republic has given proof of his energy in the repression of Communism."[72]

The new administration was coming to terms with the Mexican Church at the same time that it was acting against radicals in several areas. Simultaneously, it reduced the patronage enjoyed by the Left. The astonishing thing is that the administration was not simply seen as having initiated a period of counterrevolution. Indeed, there was no major break between the government and the Mexican Left. Enumerating the ways in which the government shifted to the right makes one wonder how President Avila Camacho was able to manage such a change without causing a massive split in his party. To understand this historic phenomenon, the intricacies of political patronage and the politics of the war must be set against the broader context of Mexican politics.

The Meaning of Moderation

An incident at the beginning of President Avila Camacho's term of office could easily have become the hallmark of the era in more normal times. The workers at the government munitions factory had been in conflict with the manager, General Bobadilla, over the terms of their contract. The general wanted to militarize the workers, thus subjecting them to military discipline and breaking their union. On September 23, 1941, a crowd of about two thousand members and supporters of the Union of Workers of War Materials marched upon the president's residence to deliver a petition of grievances in the form of an open letter to the president. The government had just tightened its control over the production of munitions, and the rights of workers that were taken for granted in other industries were suspended in the munitions trade.

As reported in the conservative press, a large number of the workers demanded to be allowed to present their petition to the president in person. The officer in charge of the Forty-Seventh Battalion, a Colonel Ochoa, stated that his men had been marching by the presidential residence and that they had tried to persuade the workers to form a small delegation to deliver the petition to the president, rather than for so many people to see the president in person. According to the press accounts, some workers were armed and shots were fired. In response, the commander of the Forty-seventh Battalion fired warning shots, followed by shots into the crowd as the workers tried to climb over the fence surrounding the presidential residence.[73] Official reports suggested that seven people were killed; the number of wounded was variously reported as between fifteen and sixty. One problem with this version of events is that we are required to believe that the soldiers of the Forty-seventh were just passing the president's residence at the vital moment. It also asks us to imagine workers assaulting troops in the face of fire from the soldiers' weapons.

A version in *El Popular* rather lamely blamed Nazi agents provocateurs for whipping up the crowd. There was also an account in which the episode was seen as a reaction against the dismissal of the minister of education, Sánchez Pontón. Since no moves were made specifically against any Axis diplomats or citizens, this account seems pat and is difficult to believe.[74] That it was a political missile aimed indirectly against the Cardenista faction is also incredible, given the lack of peripheral evidence or subsequent developments to support this idea. It could have been so, but there is little to back up such an interpretation of these events.

A report on the incident by the U.S. vice consul in Mexico City, William K. Ailshie, may have been closer to the mark. Having informally inquired into the episode, he expressed doubt that the incident had been part of a broader design. The officer in charge, in this version, was described as pro-Axis and "an officer of the most rigid type, bordering on barbarity." U.S. figures estimated between nine and thirty-three demonstrators killed and from fifteen to sixty wounded, although the exact figures were difficult to ascertain. He argued that the incident may well have been committed by soldiers who "lost their tempers and went to extremes."[75]

A British diplomat reported confidentially that the troops were inside the residence and, therefore, implied that the story of passing troops was spurious. The workers tried to climb the wall, and the army significantly overreacted. He asserted that the true number of workers killed was twenty-one.[76] His account is similar to Valentín Campa's recollections, which were that the soldiers fired upon the workers, who were demanding higher wages.[77] The personal tragedy in the shooting was great, and the political implications of the episode for government-labor relations were also ominous.

Yet the most interesting aspect of the armaments massacre is that both the government and the labor movement worked hard to defuse the potential for further violence, even at the victims' funeral, indirect evidence that the incident had been spontaneous and in the interest of neither the labor movement nor the government. The president did not attend the workers' funeral, but he did assign several cabinet ministers and Lombardo Toledano to represent him. As the coffins carrying the slain workers were lowered into the ground, angry voices cried out: "Listen to the voice of protest!" and "Now give a speech, Lombardo!" or "Speak up, Alemán!" As the workers pressed in against the leaders, Alemán and the others were rushed into their cars as the crowd continued to press in, trying to overturn the automobiles.[78]

Colonel Ochoa asked for and received a leave of absence, and the episode quickly died down in Mexico, although it was reported more widely overseas. What is politically fascinating about this tragic incident is the way that both sides—labor and the government—played it down. Only by understanding the broader dynamics of Mexican politics can we begin to make sense out of the way in which people who had formerly been demanding sweeping change in many areas came to acquiesce to the government's shift to the right, even in the face of such dramatic events as the killing of striking workers in front of the presidential residence.

Politics in the 1940s

Mexican politics during the 1940s took place at a number of levels. The most obvious locus of political activity may have been the contest between the various political parties. At the level of the parties, the PRM had a claim on the middle ground under President Avila Camacho.

The parties of the Right, many of which were open in their admiration of the Spanish Falange, were taken quite seriously as representing a threat to the revolution, although today it may be tempting to view such groups as the Sinarquistas, the Dorados, the Confederación Patronal de la República Mexicana, the Partido Antireeleccionista Acción, the Vanguardia Nacionalista Mexicana, and the Juventudes Nacionalistas as little more than fringe groups that were attracted to fascism. Many viewed the Partido de Acción Nacional (PAN) as tainted by its sympathy for Almazán, Franco, and fascist theories of corporativism.[79] Not until the end of the decade did it become the main party around which protest votes could be organized. However, tainted by their nostalgia for the *porfiriato* and by their evident clericalism, the parties of the Right carried a terrible burden of history and were never able to challenge the government effectively.

Almost in spite of themselves, the leaders of the right-wing political groups found events in Europe casting them into greater and more serious issues associated with the rise of fascism. The Dorados, after all, got their name from the color of their shirts, and the political meaning of creating paramilitary forces wearing the same shirt colors in the 1930s was not lost on many. In addition, the events in Europe gave added intensity to the battles in the *zócolo* in Mexico City between the Dorados on their horses and the taxi unionists. (The film footage of these events in 1938–39 is really quite remarkable.)

The growing number of Spanish refugees in Mexico by 1939 also served as a continual reminder that even an inept minor party of the Right, given the right conditions, could deliver its nation into the tragedy that was represented by fascism. Thus during the war people were not quite so quick to dismiss the small parties of the Far Right as we may be today. Certainly, the British and American diplomats in Mexico during the war joined in expressing concern over these right-wing groups, although the Mexican government expressed somewhat less concern. Issues like the existence of hidden German radio transmitters in Mexico played a much larger symbolic role in public discussions than one might imagine. In short, the splinter groups of the Far Right were feared, and since they had links to powerful industrialists—the Monterrey Group being the most ominous—they were not underestimated.

The Left, which had taken heart from the establishment of the first Communist state, the USSR, also placed support for the war effort at the top of its list of priorities. This position went well beyond the tiny PCM and was held by Lombardo Toledano and many in the CTM. The parties of the Left, especially the PCM, also played a role that was disproportionate to their numerical importance in the political life of the country. They were very far from trying to take over the government in Mexico, and their numbers plummeted from a high of about eleven thousand in 1939 to a mere forty-five hundred after the Comintern's purge of Valentín Campa and other leaders at the Extraordinary Congress of 1940. The FBI believed that the true figure was more like two thousand by 1943.[80] Almost by weight of their name alone, the PCM seemed to be the local inheritor of the version of socialism that was represented by the Russian Revolution. Before the terrible side of Stalin's purges and forced collectivization became generally known, the Russian Revolution enjoyed a great moral position among working people in Mexico. On the other side, the propertied class had also heard of these events from the East.

All political movements did not fit neatly into a Left-Right political schema. Prieto Laurens's Partido Socialdemócrata (PSD) may be viewed as an attempt to create a political voice for the rural middle class. Small ranchers from the north tended to support the Frente Constitucional Democrático Mexicana (FCDM), associated with General Ramón Iturbide and Bolívar Sierra. And there were many local movements that did achieve national significance.[81]

Nevertheless, within the context of the formal political parties of the day, Avila Camacho's PRM enjoyed a middle ground between the parties of the Left and the Right. Yet by no means was interparty rivalry the most important level of politics. The real political life of Mexico rarely goes on between parties; it is within the umbrella party of the revolution—and only occasionally between the government and the masses of the population—that the real political machinations associated with the exercise of state power transpires. Apart from the struggle for political ideology, where the small parties of the Right and the Left do participate, the day-to-day battles are fought among the factions of the governing party.

On the left of the PRM was the larger-than-life figure of former president Cárdenas. A man untouched by scandal, a former president whose breadth of vision had included no less than the political reorganization of Mexican society, Lázaro Cárdenas was someone to be reckoned with. The ex-president enjoyed an enormous following and an intensity of support among his followers that had been unknown for a very long time, and possibly never, at the level of national political life in the country. The former president basked in the glow of land reform, petroleum expropriation, the nationalization of the railroads, support for labor and peasants, the political reorganization of the country, socialist education, experiments in workers' control, and a renewal of national pride. For many of his supporters during the period he was the Mexican Revolution. For the remainder of his life—even during the traumatic events of 1968—Lázaro Cárdenas could by a mere hint, by the nuance of his words, dominate the left wing of his nation. (Today, a younger generation of historians has raised serious questions about the Cardenista era, and it is clear that Cárdenas's administration was more contradictory than many realized at the time; nevertheless, in the 1940s his memory seemed synonymous with the Mexican Revolution.)

President Lázaro Cárdenas taking the oath of office with U.S. Ambassador Josephus Daniels at his side. *Courtesy Hermanos Mayo, Archivo General de la Nación, Mexico City*

It was a hard act to follow. Manuel Avila Camacho entered his presidency not only under the enormous shadow of his predecessor but also through the most questionable election since the *porfiriato*. This background scarcely seemed a likely requisite for someone who was setting out to reverse the trajectory of the Mexican Revolution.

Cárdenas's was not the only wing of the governing party. On the right of the PRM were several other figures, each of whom played a slightly different role and dominated a different constituency. The expulsion of the old king, Plutarco Elías Calles, by

Cárdenas in 1936 had created something of a vacuum on the right wing of the PNR (soon to be renamed the PRM by Cárdenas). Although Calles continued to plot from his exile in California, his influence inevitably waned, even within the right wing of the PRM. The two caudillos who emerged to contest for control of the right wing of the governing party were Abelardo Rodríguez and Emilio Portes Gil.

Abelardo Rodríguez has too frequently been dismissed as merely one of the presidents of the *maximato*, the period of President Calles's indirect rule from 1929 to 1934. Often belittled for his style (sort of a Mexican parallel to LBJ) or for his origins as a baseball player, Rodríguez nevertheless became enormously powerful in the private sector in Mexico. The caudillo of the northwest, he became arguably the richest man in the country. In a stunning interview in *Novedades* in 1943, he claimed to have personally founded forty industries in Mexico.[82] Yet his pretensions went beyond the accumulation of money. He was rabidly anti-Communist; indeed, he had a lot to lose. But he also wanted to play a dominant role in the political life of the PRM, and he even dabbled in writings that his friends viewed as political theory (based upon a short holiday in the USSR, he had written a tirade on the Soviet revolution). He was the caudillo of Sonora and also of a segment of the right wing of the PRM. He was, in short, a power to be reckoned with. It is revealing that, after naming General Lázaro Cárdenas commander of the Pacific Coast Zone as World War II started, Avila Camacho restored a semblance of political balance by naming General Abelardo Rodríguez the commander of the Caribbean Zone. This was as much a political move as a military act, although it was presented as part and parcel of the preparation for war. Abelardo Rodríguez was not popular, but he was rich and powerful.

Emilio Portes Gil also headed up a faction on the right (or perhaps we could say the center-right) of the party from his regional base in Tamaulipas. His strength as the caudillo of the CNC, as well as his positions in law, business, and journalism, made him the head of another faction of his party. The author of many books on Mexican politics, Portes Gil was the owner of the newspaper *Candil*, which the Allies subsidized during the war. The Allies may have overestimated Portes Gil's degree of commitment to the reactionary cause of Almazán during the 1940 campaign. One British agent, H. Blake-Taylor, even went so far as to report back to the Foreign Office that "Portesgil [*sic*] . . . had received the shipments of arms and that . . . he will attempt armed revolt" if his negotiations with Avila Camacho go poorly after the election.[83] Emilio Portes Gil was a caudillo who expanded his base beyond the regional *patria chica*. To that geographical base of power, he added a political base through the CNC as well as the influence generated from his activities in law, business, and journalism.

So it was that within the circles of the governing party, as well as between parties, General Avila Camacho came to occupy that which the other participants viewed as the center ground. Since he was personally amiable and did not seem too threatening, the president was low on everyone's list of enemies. Indeed, he may have been systematically underestimated. But there was much more to it than his personality. People on the left realized that if they went too far in opposing the president, they risked inadvertently playing into the hands (within the party) of Rodríguez or Portes Gil, and they risked (beyond the party) the catastrophe of strengthening the hands of the pro-clerical and/or semi-Fascist political forces within the country. This was a major restraining factor on Lombardo Toledano and the left wing of the CTM, even as "their" government abandoned labor in the 1940s.

Avila Camacho also found that holding the center ground was as useful in dominating the right wing of his party as the Left. For the Right, the years of Cardenismo had been terrifying. Land reform, the mass organization of workers and peasants, socialist education, and experiments with workers' militias and workers' control had been more revolution than they had wanted. The fact that the core economic policies were set by quite orthodox economists— even at the most radical moments of the Cardenista project—was frequently overlooked. Therefore, the flirtation with the cause of Almazán faded quickly, and Avila Camacho became, for the Right, the first bulwark against the resurgence of Cardenismo. Beyond Cárdenas was Vicente Lombardo Toledano, who at the height of his rhetorical excess could sound like a veritable reincarnation of Lenin himself. His combative rhetoric and support for the Soviet revolution terrified the Right, never mind that his actions rarely left the opportunistic sphere. Such a man as the heir apparent for the first years of the Cárdenas administration had been frightening. Lombardo Toledano seems to have frightened the conservative forces with the dangers of radical reform without being able to demonstrate to the country's workers the benefits they would have received from his programs. He was an opportunist of the first rank. As if this were not enough from the perspective of the Right, the specter of the PCM was added to their nightmare. So, for these people it seemed like a miracle when Avila Camacho said "*soy creyente.*" He was in their view doing quite a job in holding back the masses and the forces of the Left.

Of course, there is no pat formula by which one always succeeds in politics by occupying the middle ground, but in this instance each side of the political spectrum viewed the other with such profound consternation that they all seemed to settle for the mild-mannered and somewhat innocuous-appearing president. He was very far from being the worst alternative that anyone could imagine.

Moreover, Mexico joined in the Allied cause during World War II, making the general-president the wartime leader of his nation, with all of the additional leverage that this implied. The Left was keen to support the war effort, even if its traditional interests had to be put aside for the duration. The United States was eager to have Mexico's support, and a marriage of convenience ultimately emerged linking the United States and the Mexican Left. The most obvious evidence of this is the large number of memorandums to be found in the National Archives of conversations between U.S. diplomats and important leaders on the left. There was a small right wing that favored the Axis forces, but even on the right, anti-U.S. spokesmen became nationalized as the war generated business opportunities.

Sra. Avila Camacho and Eleanor Roosevelt in Texas during their visit to Houston.
Courtesy Hermanos Mayo, Archivo General de la Nación, Mexico City

The War Lover

Mexico's participation in World War II became absolutely critical in the process of shifting the revolution away from Cárdenas's populism and onto a more conservative course. It was the convergence of the war effort with the general passion for a program of industrial modernization that enabled Mexico's leaders in the 1940s to shift the trajectory of the Mexican Revolution. But politics is not all a matter of grand themes and interests. The role of the well-placed individual also counts.

There was an indication that, in spite of his calm demeanor, General Avila Camacho was really quite fond of war, at least from a distance. Although his military origins had been as a paymaster in the army of Venustiano Carranza, he fought in his party's military battles in the 1920s and 1930s; as a result, he became enraptured with military strategy, and thus World War II intrigued him. There is a fascinating description of the Mexican president, written by the U.S. ambassador, relating that General Avila Camacho had several rooms set aside as war rooms in Los Pinos, the presidential residence. In these rooms he had constructed elaborate maps and battlefields on which he relived the excitement of the various engagements of World War II. He would not allow any of his aides to move his little soldiers around his war map; he preferred to do this by himself. Ambassador Messersmith wrote to Franklin D. Roosevelt urging the U.S. commander in chief to listen to General Avila Camacho's strategic suggestions regarding Allied strategy, and the ambassador sent the general's wartime suggestions on to President Roosevelt.[84] The U.S. president actually found time to respond, thanking Avila Camacho for his suggestions. The Mexican president was also willing to send troops to the war, but this was politically impossible given the climate of the day. (At the very end of the war, a Mexican air squadron did see some service in the Philippines.)

Political Windfall

From a political perspective, the war provided General Avila Camacho with a political windfall of the first magnitude. The war enabled Manuel Avila Camacho to escape from the great shadow of his predecessor. Moreover, the immediate events that precipitated the country's formal declaration of war were the sinking of several Mexican merchant ships by German submarines. So the

threat to Mexico was credible enough to justify war measures. Politically, the call to arms was issued in resounding terms. The
thought that war might come to Mexico caused a number of prominent figures to volunteer their services to their country.[85] Many top
politicians were also generals, and Avila Camacho was astute
enough to spot a political bonanza when it came his way. He jumped
at the offer from the general and ex-president Cárdenas to defend
the country, and he appointed General Cárdenas as the zone commander for a newly organized and expanded Military Zone of the
Northwest.

General Cárdenas was not only activated as a general of the
army, and thereby subjected to military discipline, but he was also
sent to the northwest to organize Mexico's coastal defenses in case
the Japanese tried to invade Mexico. (As the war planners were
aware, the U.S. defenses along the Pacific Coast and the southwest-
ern border were virtually nonexistent.) Besides responding to a
possible wartime need, the move had the additional political advantage of sending General Cárdenas into the heart of Abelardo
Rodríguez's territory. The Japanese threat may not have been entirely a matter of lively imaginations. Recently, Friedrich Schuller
has discovered that the Japanese embassy in Mexico had been
working on a plan to send a fleet and ten thousand men to conquer
Acapulco, sever its links with the rest of Mexico, and establish a
base there.[86] It will require research in the Japanese records to
establish whether this was a serious plan. At least we may conclude that concern about the security of the northwest was taken
seriously.

General Rodríguez was not amused to find General Cárdenas
setting up shop to defend Mexico's Pacific Coast in Rodríguez's
home ground at Hermosillo. The president responded by generating an equal appointment (in rank) for General Rodríguez and sending him as the zone commander to Mexico's Caribbean Coast.
Again, this move was quite credible since there was actually a sub-
marine campaign of some importance going on in the Caribbean
during 1942.

It was a political masterstroke by Avila Camacho. His two most
important rivals were now working for the president and he was
in a far better position to arbitrate disputes as well as to distribute
the fruits of wartime cooperation through a military-political structure that was clearly under his control. In addition, both Generals
Cárdenas and Rodríguez had been pried away from their base political constituencies. The ploy, while effective, was quite obvious.

In its enthusiasm, *Excélsior* published an interview with the president's brother Maximino in August 1942 in which it was revealed that Cárdenas would "almost certainly" become the minister of defense.[87] In a subsequent conversation between U.S. diplomats and sources close to President Avila Camacho, the president admitted that the best way "to limit the political activities of General Cárdenas" was to put him in the cabinet and under military discipline. The president also admitted that his only disappointment with the *Excélsior* articles was that they "showed his hand too early."[88]

As World War II started, the desire to come to the country's aid spread rapidly. Even General Plutarco Elías Calles, now back in Mexico, volunteered his military services. President Avila Camacho accepted Callas's offer and reinstated him in the army as a general of division, but without command. So again another important figure—albeit by now one who was a spent force—was integrated into the structure of military discipline. Since President Avila Camacho was simply following the lead of his predecessor in committing Mexico to the Allied side in World War II, there could be no question of conflict between the two figures. In the name of the patriotic crusade, the shadow of Cardenismo began to fade.

The broad political support for the war effort also aided the government in another sense. When conscription was introduced, it tapped old sentiments against forced labor and the *leva*, as well as those against the draft. Guerrilla action erupted in Zacatecas, Guerrero, Puebla, and Morelos and in the state of Mexico. In the most significant case, in 1942–43 in Morelos, the brothers Barreto and Rubén Jaramillo led armed groups against the draft, as did several figures close to the Partido Nacionalista, including José Inclán and Magdalena Contreras. In these examples, as in the resistance to the *aftosa* campaigns after 1946, the opposition from nominally pro-peasant groups on the national scene led to their political isolation.[89]

There were additional ways in which the war provided a political windfall for the Avila Camacho administration. Mexico used the war to negotiate a highly beneficial settlement of its foreign debt and force the registration and vesting of some $60 million to $70 million of bonds held in Switzerland and the occupied countries.[90] German, Japanese, and Italian businesses had been important in Mexico before 1941. After Mexico entered World War II, the government seized all firms that were controlled by Axis citizens and corporations. In total the Junta de Administración y Vigilencia de la Propiedad Extranjera vested 346 firms, of which they divested 59 and sold or disposed of 38. This left 249 enterprises subject to direct control. The Junta ran these companies at a profit of 16.55 percent in 1945–46. Since these firms included many in the chemical, pharmaceutical, hardware, and manufacturing industries, they gave the government a considerable amount of largess to spread around, which meant political muscle for the administration.[91]

The treatment of Axis nationals in Mexico by the Avila Camacho administration is an uneven story. German and Italian nationals were vulnerable to pressures generated by the United States' creation of the "Black List," and, as just noted, some 346 properties were seized. The fate of individual Axis citizens rested in the hands of the minister of the interior. U.S. diplomats concluded that businessmen frequently "bought their way out."[92] The worst moments for individuals with Axis citizenship were probably experienced by some five hundred German and Italian seamen who had the misfortune to be in Mexican waters as the war began. They were sent to a desolate detention camp set up at Perote, Veracruz.

The fate of the Japanese citizens in Mexico appears to have been quite different. They were treated as a group more than were the Europeans; however, their treatment was possibly less severe.[93] The number of Japanese in Mexico was very small. Japanese emigration to Mexico had been a trickle until the first decade of the twentieth century when, between 1904 and 1907, some 10,497 left Japan for Mexico; this figure plummeted to zero by 1908 and rarely reached three figures after that. Some Japanese viewed Mexico as a stepping stone to the United States and moved on. The experience of those who stayed varied considerably. Contract laborers arrived, and by 1907 it was estimated that 8,706 Japanese worked in mines and on plantations and railroads, mainly in northern Mexico. Conditions were difficult, as one group found that went to work on plantations in Oaxaca, where there were many deaths and a strike in 1906. By contrast, one small group settled in Chiapas and made a place for themselves. Indeed, their success—based on socialist ideals—and their contributions to Chiapas were recognized by the state government during World War II.

Although a 1907 gentlemen's agreement between Japan and the United States to discourage Japanese emigration had some effect, by 1925 a Japanese legation was established at Mazatlán. After the revolution, many Japanese started families and settled into the community, and the percentage of Japanese business and professional people increased significantly by the 1930s. Estimates for the number of Japanese in Mexico in 1936 were that 4,691 living in northern Mexico and 602 in the D.F. In addition, 3,634 Japanese lived in the territory of Baja California.[94]

The community in the territory became significant as another war approached. The cotton boom of World War I had attracted many Japanese to Baja California, where they formed the largest concentration of Japanese in Mexico by the eve of World War II. It was the existence of this relatively large Japanese community that fueled fears that Japan might use Baja California as a launching pad for an attack on the large and undefended naval base at San Diego. This Japanese community worried U.S. and Mexican leaders because it was "the largest concentration of unacculturated Japanese" in the country.[95]

As World War II came to North America, the territory's Japanese—unlike the German and Italian nationals—were ordered to relocate to Mexico City or Guadalajara. The idea was that it would be easier for the authorities to keep tabs on them in those cities. The evacuation of Baja California was completed by January 14, 1942, and it was "the most massive, hasty, and strictly enforced in Mexico."[96] By contrast, the Japanese in Chiapas were not relocated until 1944, and then only for two months, whereas in other states the relocation order had come in the winter of 1941–42. In Chiapas Governor Rafael Gamboa had negotiated a deal whereby the state government guaranteed their loyalty, and the Japanese were left alone.

The Mexican authorities made no preparations for the displaced Japanese who had been ordered to go to Mexico City or Guadalajara —much less did they create detention camps, as happened in the United States. The Japanese were allowed to continue their own economic activities in the two cities. Only a few individuals who did not surrender were arrested, and only four were sent to the prison at either Isla Maria Madre or some other high security prison. In Mexico City, U.S. authorities monitored Axis citizens from the OSS headquarters in the Hotel Maria Cristina, where two hundred "G-men" worked under the diplomat Raleigh Gibson and the FBI chief Gus T. Jones throughout the war.

Mexican authorities were surprisingly sympathetic to the Japanese. Ex-presidents Ortíz Rubio and Cárdenas intervened with the president to protect them, and Maximino Avila Camacho was friendly to them, even becoming a godfather to the sons of several community leaders. Also, their schools were allowed to remain open throughout the war. President Avila Camacho's secretary and the future governor of Jalisco, González Gallo, took twenty-five Japanese families onto his estate, as did the director of the lottery.

Realizing that they were on their own in Mexico City and Guadalajara, the Japanese organized a Committee of Mutual Aid and quickly gained access to a large building to house some nine hundred new arrivals from the provinces. In addition, a wealthy member of the community turned over a ranch near Batán, which was near Contreras. Community leaders met with the president who agreed to their establishing farms at Temixco, Morelos, so that they could support another three hundred fifty people.

Undoubtedly, some Japanese individuals suffered difficult times, facing personal hostilities and swindlers, but there appears to be no record of violence against them. As Watanabe put it, "the government's treatment of the Japanese was considerably milder and more benevolent than in other American countries."[97] Certainly, nothing that occurred in Mexico resembled the U.S. internment of 110,000 individuals. Sending the Japanese to the D.F. probably protected them. At one point, the government even acted to protect the Japanese farm at Temixco against peasant demands under the provisions of the land reform to occupy their land, as frequently happened to Spanish nationals.

Fundamentally, the Japanese were viewed as harmless, even as a curiosity. "Many *Issei*, who have lived in Mexico over half a century, testify that Mexico is a pro-Japanese country and that they have been well received."[98] This is strikingly different from the anti-Chinese pogroms during the revolution that Alan Knight has examined.[99]

After the war, a majority of the Japanese stayed in the D.F. and Guadalajara, and the Japanese community grew to 12,545 by 1980. Although the Japanese maintained a strong sense of self-esteem and a separate identity, and retained their own educational system, they also merged with the broader Mexican community; some married Mexicans and adopted such local customs as the *compadrazgo*. For its part, the government felt certain it had neutralized any threat from Axis nationals for the duration of the war.

The Terms of Sacrifice

President Avila Camacho was able to make stirring speeches about the defense of the national territory and to appeal to his compatriots to give patriotism precedence over politics. That may sound well and good to the politically uninitiated, but the advantages to wartime leaders are enormous since the leaders are the ones who set the terms of collaboration in the name of the war effort. The real and imagined threat of war was enough to justify the creation of a state of siege in Mexico. Congress granted President Avila Camacho extraordinary powers for the duration of the war. The president did not use these powers, but their existence gave the government considerable leverage, especially in dealing with its opponents.

The labor movement provides a case in point. In June 1942, as Mexico was entering World War II, the president and the minister of labor, García Tellez, presided over the formation of the National Labor Unity Pact. This tripartite pact, between government, business, and labor, prohibited strikes on the grounds that they might impede the war effort. Labor vowed to avoid interunion conflicts, strikes, and slowdowns. Business agreed to maintain living standards, and the government provided a national conciliation framework for settling disputes. The agreement was signed by the CTM, the CROM, the CGT, the CPN, and many smaller labor groups and then was forwarded to the U.S. embassy for its reaction to the pact.[100]

Several points are clear. No party lived up to the agreement. Strikes continued, living standards fell, profits increased for business, and the government did not work to maintain past labor victories. Furthermore, the relative sacrifices were anything but even. Business gained from falling real wages, and speculators had a tremendous run; labor found that national strikes were impossible, and national labor leaders frequently spent their time arguing against the workers' grievances. Strikes degenerated into spontaneous or fragmented exercises in which union leaders were effectively converted into frontline fighters for management against the legitimate objections of workers in their forlorn struggle to arrest the rapid decline in their real wages. All this took place in the name of the war effort.

The first major strike after the enactment of the National Labor Unity Pact was against the Compañía Mexicana de Luz y Fuerza Motriz; the use of the company's reserve fund was at issue. The workers alleged that the reserve fund for distribution of profits to the stockholders had grown to 20 million pesos, not to the 11 million pesos that the company announced, at the very time that the cost of electricity was increasing. The conservative press charged that the workers were using the National Tri-party Council to try to take over postwar control of the enterprise and not merely to work for a wage raise. The strike showed how close to the surface the battle over control of public utilities was, wartime rhetoric not-withstanding.[101]

Great pressure was placed on workers to join in the patriotic pursuit of the war effort. In August 1942 there was a campaign in favor of President Avila Camacho's policy of wartime cooperation. In one mass meeting held in the Electrical Workers Union hall, Vicente Lombardo Toledano and his close aide Alejandro Carrillo presided over a polyglot gathering that saw an astonishing group of celebrities call for wartime cooperation. Pablo Neruda, the great poet who was then the Chilean consul in Mexico City, sat on the same platform with representatives of the CTM such as Fidel Velázquez and Senator Vidal Díaz Muñoz and with Angel Olivo of the PCM, as well as with the leaders of many individual unions. Midway through the rally the U.S. actor and filmmaker Orson Welles and his *compañera* of the moment, the actress Dolores del Río, entered the hall and spoke to the enraptured audience. Cantinflas was a regular at such rallies. Only the war effort could bring such disparate figures onto the same stage.[102] Yet on a daily basis a pro-war rally scarcely placated the labor movement, which was suffering under acute pressures.

During the Avila Camacho years workers still won some important battles. In May 1942, at the Third National Ordinary Congress of the miners' union, the Sindicato Industrial de Trabajadores Mineros, Metalúrgicos y Similares (SITMMSRM), Minister of Labor Ignacio García Tellez refused to recognize several members of the executive committee, including Secretary General Juan Manuel Elizondo, since they were members of the PCM. In response, the union raised the issue of the right to strike. This was a particularly sensitive subject since the majority of the SITMMSRM workers were employed by foreign firms (especially the ASARCO), whose production was vital for the war effort. The first declaration of a strike was in September, in Fresnillo, Zacatecas. After a month with the miners on strike the president intervened to conciliate, and the union held a congress in October to raise the question of falling real wages. The union's pressure was only temporarily successful in 1943. By the following year the erosion of real wages had intensified. For the first time during the war the union served notice of the workers' intention to strike all companies simultaneously, on June 10, 1944. Ignoring the Camera de Minera Nacional as a mouthpiece for the ASARCO, the union launched a strike that lasted forty days.[103] Not only did the union win this critical strike, but it also extended the strike to cover 105 firms, including the most important producers of silver, copper, iron, and other strategic minerals for the war effort. Foundries in Monterrey, Piedras Negras, and Torreón closed their doors as thirty-five thousand workers struck. And they won most of their demands.[104] They also addressed the broader issue of the deterioration of the living standards of the community.

The ability of the government to discipline those with whom they disagreed extended to the issuing of contracts. Economic activity increased significantly during the war years, and there were more "carrots" to distribute. Contracts were often lucrative, and resources were allotted in ways that favored friends and penalized enemies. The standard of living for Mexican workers fell without a major political backlash. World War II had tamed many revolutionaries. However, there was a safety valve in the belief that corruption, and not the war effort, was behind the crisis of want, or *carestía*, as it was called in Mexico. It enabled people to focus upon corrupt functionaries and not to question Mexico's contribution to the war effort. The allegation in the July 1944 issue of the magazine *Mañana* that everything was becoming dear because the *gringos* were taking so much production for the war effort may have had considerable merit, but the government, labor, the Left, and the United States all worked hard to deny the obvious.[105] In spite of this concerted effort, however, the Mexican president was bombarded by constant complaints linking domestic difficulties to the war effort.[106]

In the last instance, the government could rely upon special wartime measures to enforce its will. In February 1942, for example, the workers at Du Pont's munitions factory at Dinamita, Durango, went on strike. The government immediately sent in troops to keep the production of explosives uninterrupted, and the workers relented.[107]

A convention of U.S. women's clubs revealed the labor conditions for some Mexican workers during the period. The clubs held a convention in Mexico City in 1943. During their stay, they visited a glass factory at Calle Carretones #5. To their horror, the women discovered that more than half the people working there were young children. They took photographs and complained to their embassy that since the children's labor was related to products imported by the United States for the war effort, and since these Dickensian conditions contravened the child labor laws in that country, action was required. The U.S. embassy sent an investigator who established that of the thirty to thirty-seven workers who were normally employed, fifteen were under fourteen years of age.

They worked from 7:00 A.M. to 5:00 P.M. under very poor conditions. Children frequently were injured since many worked barefoot, and 90 percent of them contracted tuberculosis. The production was bought by a company named Raymor de Mexico S.A., which was owned by Mrs. Elizabeth Curtiss Cervantes. Fully 20 percent of the glass was exported to fashionable department stores such as Lord and Taylor in New York City. The U.S. Treasury official in Mexico acknowledged that importing this material violated child labor laws and unfair competition legislation; however, he noted, action in this kind of case required a presidential decree. Moreover, as the counselor of the embassy put it, to act in this case would "serve to cause considerable ill feeling in official circles."[108]

The Gaxiola Affair

As the impact of wartime austerity bit harder, especially after the crop failures of 1943, there was a stronger tendency on the part of many to blame the government for conditions generated by the war.[109] Popular bitterness focused on the wartime regulatory agency Nacional Distribuidora y Reguladora S.A. (N.D. & R.), which was under the direction of Amado J. Trejo and the Ministry of the National Economy headed by Francisco Javier Gaxiola.[110]

On July 24, 1943, the popular magazine *Hoy* charged Minister Gaxiola with disloyalty to the president. Manuel Suárez, the publisher of *Hoy* and a close friend of the president, even added a special editorial calling on President Avila Camacho to dismiss Gaxiola, who responded to these accusations by going to the attorney general and pressing charges against the editor of *Hoy*, Alfredo Kawage Ramia.[111] Most of the best-known journalists in the country, including José Natividad Macías, José Vasconcelos, Rafael Zubarán, Pepe Elguero, and Alejandro Carrillo, quickly chose sides in the matter. The Gaxiola affair became a cause célèbre.

Specifically, the charges against Gaxiola were that he had been party to the manipulation of the prices of grain and meat and that he had been aiding his mentor, General Abelardo Rodríguez, in monopolizing the fishing industry. He was also charged with manipulating the price of rayon—a new luxury item in considerable shortage—and, in coalition with his brother-in-law, of speculating in the price of leather through the National Chamber of Tanneries. *Hoy* went on to allege that Gaxiola had profited with his friends in the manipulation of the price of corn in 1941 and that the four had earned 40 million pesos for their efforts. Gaxiola was also accused of impeding the purchase of Canadian wheat—even over the president's instruction—in order to sustain high prices from which he benefited.[112]

Press comments initially reflected the political positions of the various newspapers and magazines of the day. *La Prensa* took the line that Gaxiola was close to President Avila Camacho and was keeping him informed. The president's private secretary tried to play down the issue by saying that President Avila Camacho would not comment on matters that were before the courts. *El Universal,* on August 7, 1943, reported the issue under the headline "Yellow Journalism." It pointed out that *Hoy* had recently changed owner-ship and was now under the effective control of the rival industrial and commercial magnate Manuel Suárez. *La Nación,* the voice of the Acción Nacional, said that these were the sins not merely of one man, but of the revolutionary party. *El Popular,* of the CTM, and *La Voz de México,* of the PCM, quickly focused on Gaxiola as being responsible for the dramatic increases in the cost of living for the country's workers. The railroad union demonstrated against Gaxiola on August 5, and the CTM planned a demonstration for August 11 and included a speech against corruption by Fidel Velázquez. In contrast, *Excélsior,* on August 7, defended Gaxiola and claimed that Kawage Ramia's evidence was "flimsy" and based on newspaper reports that were already discredited. So far these positions were fairly predictable, given the political predilections of these publications.

Then, on August 10, *La Prensa* reported that the attorney gen-eral had ruled that Mexican law required that the Chamber of Depu-ties sit as a grand jury and hear the evidence against Gaxiola; however, Kawage Ramia had not brought formal charges against Gaxiola. Instead, Gaxiola had brought defamation charges against *Hoy's* editor. This was not as potent as it may sound because there was a provision in the penal code relating to defamation that made guilt virtually dependent upon the ability of a defendant to prove that the journalist in question had acted with the idea of exposing the plaintiff to public contempt. The issue thus rested upon one's ability to prove one's motivation, a nearly impossible task in this situation.

Sophisticated observers in Mexico soon wondered who was behind these developments. A popular version in circulation viewed the Left in general, and especially General Cárdenas, as being be-hind *Hoy's* attack on Lic. Gaxiola. The reasoning was impeccable: since the poor were hardest hit by the combination of low wages

and rapidly rising prices, and since some on the Left had been making the cost of living their primary domestic issue, it followed that
the Cardenistas were behind the attack on Gaxiola.[113] But such tight
a priori reasoning does not always hold up in history. Certainly,
the political officer of the U.S. embassy had not picked up any such
hints in making his rounds of governmental contacts. Harold D.
Finley, the first secretary of the embassy, believed that "General
Cárdenas is not participating in politics and is devoting his whole
attention to his duties as Secretary of War."[114]

The attack on Gaxiola in Hoy was seen to be a convenient way
to get at Abelardo Rodríguez. Since Gaxiola had been Rodríguez's
private secretary, it was widely believed that Gaxiola was still serving his mentor's interests, especially since Rodríguez's position in
the private sector insulated him from public scrutiny more than
any other leader of a faction within the PRM. The Left found it
tempting to link the already unpopular Gaxiola with the rising cost
of living. Two of Mexico's most independent critics of the shift in
the Mexican Revolution, Narciso Bassols and Víctor Manuel
Villaseñor, worked under the slogan "contra los funcionarios
ladrones" during 1943. It was not empty rhetoric.[115]

Regional rivalry may also have spilled over into the Gaxiola
affair. Abelardo Rodríguez, the strongman of Sonora, was not the
only Sonorense in a high position. Alejandro Carrillo had been a
central figure in the CTM under President Cárdenas, although it
had also been Carrillo who had quickly criticized the president's
address of September 1, 1941, on the grounds that he was moving
away from the revolution's program. Criticism is one thing, but at
the time Carrillo was the speaker of the Chamber of Deputies. By
1943, Carrillo was out of these two vital political positions, although
he was still the editor of the CTM's newspaper *El Popular* and the
close collaborator of Vicente Lombardo Toledano. In a recent election for the position of governor of Sonora, both Rodríguez and
Carrillo had planned to run for that office. (Rodríguez won the
PRM's nod and the election.) This rivalry between the two sons of
Sonora made the plot thicker.

There was a point of confusion, however. The ownership of the
magazine *Hoy*—ownership always being a vital element in understanding the politics of journalism of the day—was split between
the Spanish entrepreneur Manuel Suárez and the president's elder
brother, Maximino Avila Camacho. Theories proliferated as Maximino's hand was seen to have been behind the attack on Gaxiola
in *Hoy*. The immediate confusion stemmed from the fact that both

Maximino and Gaxiola were politically on the right. So the question leaped off the page: Why would General and Minister Maximino be attacking someone in his own faction, and indeed someone who could issue contracts at that?

Another version had the attack on Gaxiola as a way to take the heat off Maximino. This theory's Byzantine logic had it that if the charges of corruption were more widely distributed among cabinet officers, Maximino might be seen to have benefited from Gaxiola's discomfort, and the light of day might stay away from his own controversial business practices. Even if that does not seem a terribly convincing explanation, one still has the problem of accounting for the presence of the president's brother behind the attack on Gaxiola.

It was also rumored that the attack had been ordered by the president as a way of discrediting Gaxiola and, by extension, General Rodríguez.[116] This version, in some formulations, had the president discrediting Gaxiola in order to get rid of him. It might seem ridiculous to imagine a president discrediting a key minister when he could simply sack him without discrediting his own government. There is, however, a political scenario in which this maneuver might make sense. President Avila Camacho could afford the risk of attacking his own minister only if he was certain that the charges against Gaxiola would not hold up to legal and public examination. This attack, however, could bring to light the names of other speculators against whom the president might want to move, and such a ploy could give the appearance that the government was trying to do something about the corruption associated with high prices in the public mind. After the Gaxiola affair it became more difficult to blame the president for inflation, and such a result could account for the president's brother being behind the attack.

Daniel Cosío Villegas once explained how Porfirio Díaz had used a similar maneuver against former president Manuel González during Díaz's second term. Díaz had simultaneously urged young Turks in the Congress to attack González for corruption while he posed—behind the scenes—as González's protector. The move cleverly tarnished González as a rival in the election in 1888 at the same time that it made González dependent upon Díaz for protection from the consequence of his misdeeds.[117] Using the same ploy, President Avila Camacho may have discredited Gaxiola and Rodríguez—and their wing of the PRM—in the public eye while privately assuring them of his protection.

The trouble with political analysis is that without inside information the degree of certainty that one can have in any of these hypotheses is low. There is little evidence thus far uncovered in Mexican archives on the episode, so one tends to rely upon the remarks of foreign diplomats who may have tapped into solid information on the cocktail party circuit. Harold D. Finley, first secretary of the U.S. embassy, thought that General Cárdenas was not behind the move and that although the Left took advantage of Gaxiola's discomfort, it could not have precipitated the attack in *Hoy*. Finley did not see it primarily as an attack on the leader of the faction, Abelardo Rodríguez, and he thought that if the president was aware of the move beforehand Gaxiola would be exonerated, which was eventually the case. Finley did not discard the possibility that *Hoy* had attacked Gaxiola simply to boost its circulation, although there is a degree of naivety in thinking that a magazine controlled by the president's brother might move against the very administration in which the two brothers were serving. In his report of August 11, Finley admitted that the politics behind the episode was obscure and speculative.[118]

There was a considerable element of an intra-agency battle associated with the Gaxiola affair. N.D. & R. was headed by Nazario S. Ortíz Garza. Even by the end of the war, he had not implemented the presidential directive of October 28, 1941, ordering the Ferrocarriles Nacionales de México to grant the highest priority to N.D. & R. for the transportation of articles of basic needs. At the end of March 1943, Ortíz Garza sent an urgent request to Lic. J. Jesús Gallo, the personal secretary to the president, asking for the use of troops to force the National Railways to release cars to his agency.[119] (Similarly, Efrain Buenrostro also had to petition the president on a daily basis to get railroad cars for PEMEX.[120])

Eventually, the Gaxiola case ended with more of a whimper than a bang, which was characteristic of the Avila Camacho administration. The editor Alfredo Kawage Ramia and Minister Gaxiola exchanged charges of graft and liability, and the attorney general accordingly instructed his Department of Primary Investigations to conduct an inquiry to see if these charges had substance. The inquiry concluded that Kawage Ramia had not produced the proof, and Gaxiola declined to bring charges against the editor for criminal liability. The minister rather lamely stated to the press that he had pressed his accusations only to gain a fair hearing in the public eye. His letter to the attorney general of August 23, 1943, was made public. The resolution smacked of a political solution from on high.

Amado J. Trejo was dismissed as chief of Nacional Distribuidora y Reguladora S.A. de C.V., apparently for blocking the Canadian wheat purchases to sustain high prices, which had been a central allegation in *Hoy's* attack. Gaxiola would follow Trejo into the political wilderness. Gaxiola was unhappy with the lack of support from the president's private secretary, Lic. J. Jesús González Gallo. Gaxiola became a victim of *carestía*, albeit at a rather more opulent level than Mexico's workers, as he was widely believed to have been involved in the manipulation of grain scarcities for private gain. Thus despite the support from his "great friend," Attorney General José Aguilar y Maya, Gaxiola had to go. Certainly, the government took some pressure off itself by dismissing Trejo and Gaxiola; it was finally seen to be doing something about the problem.[121]

Finley eventually proposed a suggestive explanation for the events of the summer of 1943. He concluded that President Avila Camacho had not been behind the events from the beginning and raised the intriguing possibility that the pressures against Gaxiola may have come from the nationalist business sector in Mexico. One of the most profound divisions in Mexican politics during the period was that between the nationalist and internationalist tendencies in the business community. Finley thought he saw the hand of the economic nationalists behind the dismissal of Gaxiola, which alarmed him. As he put it, "If big business pressures succeeded, moreover, cabinet changes might produce an atmosphere in which American interests would not prosper as at present."[122]

This assessment puts rather a different light on the affair. In this version, the Mexican nationalists, smarting under wartime regulations, blamed Gaxiola for the restrictions at the very time that he appeared to have delayed the Canadian wheat purchases. The uneven impact of wartime regulations was also signaled by a British observer: "The small fry among the speculators have been forced to toe the line, but a sterner policy will be needed to discourage the large racketeers, among whom may be counted Governors of States, generals, and labour leaders, whose habitual exploitation of their weaker brethren it will need more than decrees of the government to extricate."[123] Not popular pressure for lower prices, but private sector frustration over not being able to also take advantage of a bull market—and the knowledge that Gaxiola's own circle was cashing in on war-induced shortages—

accounted for the presence of economic nationalists behind the attack on Gaxiola.

At the public level there was another of those symbolic moves through which the PRM closed ranks to offer a solid front to informed political observers. Minister of War Lázaro Cárdenas and Minister of the National Economy Francisco Javier Gaxiola traveled in the same automobile from Mexico City to Hermosillo, Sonora, in order to represent the federal government at the inauguration of General Abelardo Rodríguez as governor of Sonora on September 1, 1943. General Cárdenas was the president's official representative at the ceremony. In the words of the first secretary of the U.S. embassy: "The display, at any rate, of friendship between the three men was rather dazzling. The administration, Secretary Gaxiola, General Cárdenas and General Rodríguez emerged unharmed, and the political forecasters have now retired to await the next incident."[124] Clearly, the factions of the governing party had worked out the problem, and the affair was over.

The Gaxiola affair was an escape valve through which the political pressures generated by falling standards of living were eased. The dismissal of two visible figures who were seen to have been responsible for wartime shortages and were personally benefiting from those shortages was a form of relief to the long-suffering population. Constant rumors of cabinet changes also tended to serve the same function of diminishing pressures on the system.

Today, it may be difficult to believe that workers would have acquiesced to the reduction of their standard of living without having questioned Mexico's participation in the war effort. Yet labor's most prominent figures repeatedly passed up opportunities to draw a link between shortages, high prices, and Mexico's contribution to the war effort (although Eduardo Villaseñor, director of the Banco de México, drew this conclusion on April 6, 1943). At the Third Congress of the CTM in 1943, Vicente Lombardo Toledano, never one to allow precision to stand in the way of rhetoric, blamed speculators for high prices and denied that the export of food to the United States was behind the country's hardships. As one U.S. diplomat reported to Washington, "It would have been an easy course for Lombardo to lay blame on the United States, as so many people are doing; but in all fairness to him, it must be said that he firmly rejected this popular explanation and laid blame on the speculators."[125]

Allied diplomats feared that the United States would be blamed for Mexico's hardships. George Messersmith thought that the war effort would be hurt if the flow of Mexican minerals and agricultural products was interrupted. One of his assistants mused about the ease with which General Cárdenas could interrupt the wartime cooperation if he wanted: "The suffering of the lower economic strata in Mexico because of the increased living costs has recently offered General Cárdenas an unsurpassed opportunity to undermine the administration and to fan the discontent of the masses. Neither he nor his leftist supporters have done so. On the contrary, they have urged the proletariat to support the President."[126]

Clearly, this attitude of the "natural spokesmen for the poor" is a key to understanding how the war interacted with the move to the right during the Avila Camacho years. The leaders on the left of the PRM, and in the CTM as well, were not happy about the falling real wages, the restrictions on the right to strike, and the pro-business policies of the government; however, they made the assessment that it would be parochial and wrong to do anything that would hurt the war effort. Especially after the German invasion of the USSR, the further to the left one was, the more fervent one's support of the Allied cause. The Gaxiola affair was as far as the Left would go in indulging their consternation with the rapidly rising level of corruption for fear of hurting the war effort. Whatever General Cárdenas's true position was—and he would maintain a sphinxlike silence for the remainder of his life—he would not serve as a public rallying point to oppose the shift to the right by the Avila Camacho administration. This posture had a deeply debilitating impact upon his supporters.

A similar self-discipline was exercised by others on the left. Andre Simon, a Czech refugee from fascism, was a writer on the CTM's newspaper *El Popular*. In discussions with U.S. embassy officials, Simon acknowledged that the pro-Allied position of Vicente Lombardo Toledano and Alejandro Carrillo was influenced by Soviet policy. According to this account, which may well have been tailored to please the U.S. officials, Lombardo Toledano and Carrillo realized that Mexico was far from being able to move toward socialism, much less toward communism, so they were being "realistic." These labor leaders desperately wanted industrialization programs, and they were keen to have U.S. capital and U.S. technicians to help Mexico industrialize.[127]

The Role of the State

When historians look back upon the twentieth century, it will be surprising if they do not view the increasing role of the state as a fundamental characteristic of the century. Regardless of the political system, and political rhetoric not withstanding, governments grew exponentially in virtually every corner of the globe. Whether we should have large or small government seems to be a false issue. Even the most ardent advocates of small government have been unable to reduce the state sector. The more useful question is why the role of the government increased so rapidly, and several factors together suggest a reason for the phenomenon.

Certainly, in Mexico, the state sector grew rapidly, not only as the defender of the nation during World War II but also as the overseer of the economy. The desire to industrialize merged inexorably with the need to regulate the economy for the war effort. Wartime regulations gave the government the ability to influence the development process in ways that were more pronounced than or at least different from those of the past. Many war regulations formed part of the postwar development program. Rather than try to trace the myriad of regulatory changes that took place because of wartime cooperation, it might be more worthwhile to look at some of the more important spin-offs that emerged as the indirect and unintended results of wartime cooperation, especially the ones that were critical to the Avila Camacho administration in affecting the change from radical national development to orthodox policies.

First, there were special favors. People who had good relations with the political authorities enjoyed generous treatment. Antonio Ruiz Galindo began his career as a businessman in Veracruz. He began to receive special favors from the state government when Alemán and Jorge Cerdán were governors. When he built the beautiful Hotel Ruiz Galindo at Fortín de los Flores, he received a 90 percent exemption from state taxes, as he did for his other enterprises: the Cía. Urbanizadora y Fraccionadora, Calhidra Veracruzana S.A., the Banco Veracruzano S.A., and the Fraccionamiento y Hotel del Río Metlac S.A. When the tax office started sending him bills, he simply wrote to Governor Ruíz Cortines asking the governor to solve his tax problems on the grounds that his enterprises would help the state.[128] No claims of taxation for purposes of social justice were going to limit private accumulation.

Capital

A second issue high on the political agenda which affected capital was taxes. Opponents of taxes concentrated upon the excess-profits tax that Cárdenas had placed on the agenda and the degree to which tax evasion would be punished. In addition, during the war it was tempting to combat inflationary pressures by raising taxes to soak up demand. The United States urged Mexico to adopt this course in the face of *carestía*, and the Ministry of Finance tended to support it as a way of furthering the government's interests. The financier Julio Lacaud, by contrast, organized a running campaign among businessmen to convince the president that these policies would drive away capital and put a brake on the industrialization program.[129]

Still another important area of business policy, albeit one that rarely is discussed, is that of trade practices. Culturally and historically there was a deeply anticompetitive tradition in Mexico. Not only did both the formal doctrine of industrial saturation and the colonial heritage favor restrictive trade practices, but also the *palancas é influencias* of the strong—as the saying went—led to monopoly and oligopoly on a massive scale. The economic nationalists were acutely aware of this. Ruiz Galindo explained to the president how this worked in the cement industry in Veracruz. The state had traditionally suffered, in his view, from a dependent relationship with manufacturers in Puebla. Cementos Atoyac had had its own way by dictating price and supply to its advantage. The weight and bulk of this product precluded competition over long distances. With this factor in mind, a group of Veracruz industrialists founded the Banco Veracruzano S.A., with thirty branches, to challenge restrictive trade practices and raise capital. They attracted interest from the Portland Cement Company, which entered into a franchising arrangement to found the Compañía Oriental de Cemento Portland S.A. and thus bring a degree of competition to the industry.[130]

There was a battle for control of the Banco Nacional de México that engulfed the entire banking sector between 1941 and 1943. Luis Legorreta had frozen a number of independent directors out of the decision making process. Jorge Vera Estañol, a lawyer who represented Anderson, Clayton and Company among his many other corporate clients, led the dissenting group. He accused Legorreta and Finance Minister Eduardo Suárez of having conducted illegal corporate elections and of ignoring legitimate directors: "We haven't been able to gain access to the offices of the bank, to its books, or to the accounting, just because the Director General has wanted to keep the business of the institution arbitrarily with his directors, who are only his servants." He went on to allege that "the present director continues to manage the business *as if it were his own and that of his assistants* [underlined in the original]." Although the surviving record does not go into further detail, it is clear that the president supported the Legorreta interests.[131] This was the background to a more public conflict that involved the entire banking community.

The meeting of the Tenth Mexican National Convention of Bankers, held in Monterrey, from April 17 to 19, 1944, gave a number of indications of the depth of change in the government's policies. Prominent among the Mexican figures from the government who attended were Minister of Finance Eduardo Suárez and Octavio Vejar Vázquez, the former minister of education, who had wanted the purge of leftists to spread beyond the Ministry of Education. From the private sector, the top figures who attended included Evaristo Araiza, director of the Fundidora y Acero de Monterrey S.A. and a member of the U.S.-Mexican Commission, Luis G. Legorreta of BANAMEX, and Salvador Ugarte, president of the Banco de Comercio.

Notable among the topics discussed at the convention was the effect of the wartime boom on price levels and credit policies. More broadly, there was an attack on the agrarian reform program of the revolution. Ing. José F. Ortíz of the Banco de la Laguna, recognized that private bankers would not support agrarian reform, especially in light of Supreme Court rulings denying private-property holders protection against invasions by peasants demanding land for their ejidos. Ing. Felix Palavicini, one of the *constituyentes* of 1917, also asserted that the reformers had not meant to damage private property by means of the division of large estates in 1917. The bankers applauded energetically as José Lino Cortéz of the Banco de Michoacán attributed food shortages to the agrarian reform projects of the government. At that point, Eduardo Villaseñor, director of the Banco de México, spoke. He avoided the controversy by limiting his talk to technical banking considerations. By doing so, he in effect refused to support the existing agrarian reform projects. When Eduardo Suárez spoke he also distanced himself from the land-reform program. He mentioned that some thirty-two million hectares of land had been distributed and that this made him wonder how much more land could be distributed. He also said he favored some arrangement to protect private property in land. Thus two of the top economic ministers in the Avila Camacho government failed to defend the tradition of land reform in front of Mexican and U.S. bankers.[132]

It is widely argued today that Cárdenas's efforts were oriented around the effort to reorganize the state sector based upon mass organizations and to modernize the capitalist sector of industry. Yet it is also important to remember that there were a number of specific reforms that promised to bring rather major changes to the lives of many Mexicans. One profoundly radical requirement was to make employers provide housing for their workers. The momentum for this proposal within the Congress was such that on December 19, 1941, a change in Section 3 of Article 3 of the labor law had actually gone so far as to require employers to provide "comfortable, hygienic dwellings" for their workers. This major reform was on the agenda as the law gave employers only thirty days to file a study showing how they planned to implement this law. Workers were to have the right of legal redress to force compliance by their employers.

Political will was vital for the success of land reform and the housing program. Once in office the Avila Camacho government instructed the courts to turn a blind eye to this provision to provide housing. Instead, a mechanism emerged by which the denial of that reform would take place. Land owners and employers could apply to the courts for an *amparo*—a writ by which the courts protect the petitioner from the action of the executive—to exempt them from the impact of the law. The British chargé d'affaires reported that his contacts with the business community indicated that the courts were flooded with these requests for protection against the Mexican law.[133]

The government's attitude toward land reform was becoming ever less favorable. Many of the Cardenistas who strongly favored the land reform program of the Cardenista era were becoming disenchanted. One such figure was General Miguel Flores Villar. The Mexico City press, led by *El Nacional*, carried stunning allegations by Flores Villar at the end of February 1946. He charged that Mexican sovereignty was endangered in that between 200,000 and 300,000 hectares were being held by U.S. and British citizens in Chihuahua and Coahuila. His allegations claimed that Emeterio de la Garza had received 4,384,475 hectares in a series of land grants from Porfirio Díaz after 1881; some of this land had been seized by the Galan, Zambrano, and other Mexican families during the revolution; and, in turn, those lands were sold to U.S. and British citizens in direct contravention to the provision of the 1917 constitution prohibiting foreigners from owning land within 100 kilometers of the border or 50 kilometers of the coast.[134] General Flores Villar was in a position to know. As commander of the Eighth Cavalry Regiment, he had military jurisdiction over 1,300 square kilometers, including Reynosa, Villa Acuña, Piedras Negras, and Torreón. The Ministry of Foreign Affairs responded by denying the charges. In an official statement, it claimed that only people who had inherited land might hold it for up to five years before being forced to sell it. Even Mexican companies with foreign partners were prohibited from holding this land.[135]

Ambassador George Messersmith was in the office of Foreign Minister Castillo Nájera when these allegations were breaking. The U.S. minister reported that Castillo Nájera dismissed the allegations as a play for publicity on the part of General Flores. On March 3, Flores again went to the press, reaffirming his claims that he had maps from the Ministry of Agriculture substantiating his allegations. He went public after having been barred from presenting his evidence at the attorney general's office. His charges focused upon the Magnum property in the municipalities of Ocampo and Múzquiz; the Mayer estate in Acuña, known as the Hacienda de San Miguel de Zaragoza; the Mackou hacienda in Ocampo and Múzquiz; the cattle ranches Santo Domingo and Piedra Blanca; and the Hacienda Cloete y Mineral de Agujitas, a property alleged to be owned by the British monarch and administered by a Mr. Riser. The U.S. citizens named as absentee land owners were Hall Magnum, George Mayer, Wander Stafford, Whitehead N. Stafford, and L. Tyne.[136]

These accusations set off a spate of additional claims. Press allegations proliferated as charges that the New Sabinas Company Pty., the Hacienda La Babia, the Hacienda La Huerfana—allegedly owned by Charles Lindbergh—the El Boleo properties in Baja California, and some twenty other properties were all in violation of the constitution. Ambassador Messersmith searched his files and admitted that the Palomas Land and Cattle Company and the Santo Domingo Ranch in Villa Ahumada in Chihuahua were U.S. owned. He thought that General Flores had it wrong in including General Miguel S. González's 280,000-hectare ranch in Chihuahua and Coahuila since González was "a very pro-American Mexican national" who, although a U.S. resident with a wife who was a U.S. citizen and a son who was a cadet at the Texas Military Academy, had remained a Mexican citizen. More seriously, Ambassador Messersmith gave away the reason why General Flores's charges, however accurate and in line with the constitution, would not be investigated:

> While the sensational allegations made by General Flores received a good press for several days, it is not believed that any study of the question that may be made by the Mexican government will reveal facts concerning properties along the border that have to date been unknown to the Government. American financial interests in some of these properties, which yield considerable tax revenue, has been established for many years, for example, The Cananea Cattle Company at Cananea and Naco, Sonora, which is legally a Mexican company.[137]

A senator from Guerrero, Nabor Ojeda, brought the matter to the popular attention again in April by promising to reveal a list of foreigners who owned land along the Pacific Coast within the prohibited zone.[138] However, the matter died down after a few days. In short, there was no political will to implement the constitution when the provisions of the fundamental charter clashed with powerful U.S. interests. The relationships between the U.S. and Mexican elites clearly provided political cover against the passions of economic nationalism.

Cases in which publicity shone upon foreign landowners and flagrant violations of the constitution were rare. It was far more common for poor rural supplicants to file their petitions for land under the land reform provisions and then wait for an eternity. The PCM claimed that by 1944 there were fifteen thousand petitions for land awaiting attention in the Ministry of Agriculture.[139] These fundamental changes in core economic policies were paralleled by a new political tone that touched many aspects of life.

Beyond the politics of the land reform, the effort to build an industrial base made considerable headway during the Avila Camacho presidency. By 1945 more than five hundred new industries were established in Mexico, representing an estimated $41 million. Fully half that amount was concentrated in eight plants, and the largest number of new industries could be found in the areas of rayon, cement, and industrial chemistry.[140]

The electricity industry offers a case in point as to how industrial development worked. Westinghouse wanted to expand into Mexico. However, by this time it was clear that the company could not act alone. Based upon U.S. technology, a new firm, Industria Electrica de México, was formed with a foundation capital of 111 million pesos. Shares not taken up by the group around Legorreta and the Banco Nacional de México were sold in New York. Thus Westinghouse, Kuhn Loeb, Legorreta, and BANAMEX controlled most of the stock.[141] In addition, Antonio Carillo Flores, the new head of NAFISA, subscribed five million dollars of public funds to help the project get off the ground, arguing that this would help the balance of payments picture.[142] Each year, similar new industries were given tax-exempt status: 71 in 1944, and 97 in 1945, including such major corporations as Kraft, Westinghouse, Reynolds, and Celanese.[143]

Finally, there was room for special projects, and none was as important in the 1940s as the development of Acapulco. The president entrusted Ramón Beteta to reorganize the Juntas Federales de Mejoras Materiales and the Jefatura de la Aduana Marítima and place them under the iron hand of Melchor Perusquía. With that structure in place, the president and his successor systematically worked to alienate ejido lands in the port and attract foreign investment. The pleasures of Acapulco were used to attract foreign investment, and the drive for tourism was clearly seen as an adjunct to that broader effort.[144]

Symbols and Siblings: The Church and the Brother

From his early statement *"soy creyente,"* Avila Camacho oversaw a process by which the Church in Mexico was reintegrated into the nation's life. Representing a basic change from the Calles years, Avila Camacho allowed the Church to regain a degree of national prominence. Although the president played down the relationship, it was generally believed that the president's wife was a close friend of the archbishop. When plans were being made in 1945 to celebrate the fifteenth anniversary of the beatification of the Virgin of Guadalupe, Mexico was treated to an outburst of religiosity. In the first weeks of October 1945, the four principal daily newspapers in the D.F., *Excélsior, Novedades, El Universal,* and *La Prensa,* all rejoiced daily on their front pages over the impending celebrations and the visit of foreign churchmen, most prominently Cardinal Villeneuve of Canada. The government's toleration of this religious celebration was striking in contrast to the recent past. Yet many wondered whether this represented a change of government policy or a personal peculiarity of the president.

In the 1946 election the position on the Church of likely candidates, especially of Miguel Alemán, was less well known. His father had been politically Catholic, a protector of the young Avila

Camacho and a member of a losing faction during the 1920s. But Miguel Alemán, Jr., was less public in his views. The U.S. embassy viewed Miguel Alemán as a leftist, close to and deriving his support from the CTM. The situation was further clouded by the fact that Gómez Morín, the national head of the Acción Nacional, and González Luna, the head of the party in Guadalajara, were both openly anti-United States. They frequently asserted their unwillingness to surrender the benefits and accomplishments of Hispanic culture for economic advantages that might flow from cooperation with the United States. The Catholic Right also blamed the United States for Mexico's moral degeneration. *Novedades,* for example, in an editorial of October 13, 1945, alleged that U.S. motion pictures were subverting Mexican morals. Thus, a public celebration of Catholic religion in Mexico, as welcomed by the Avila Camacho government, represented a complex blending of traditional conservativism, anti-U.S. sentiments, and an apparent victory over the Calles policy of anticlericalism. Nearly a century had passed since a government in Mexico had been so openly associated with a celebration of Catholic religiosity. It was a striking symbol of change.

The president's shift in favor of international capital did have its rewards. After leaving office, Manuel Avila Camacho several times traveled to the United States. On one trip, for example, he was feted by Louis B. Mayer, of MGM, and later he was a guest at the opulent Hearst estate at San Simeon, California.[145] For even the most vulnerable points of his administration, the passing of time seems to have smoothed over embarrassing problems. Maximino Avila Camacho, the president's brother, however, remained a great embarrassment to the administration. He was crude, violent, dishonest, and a member of the nouveaux riches. He was fond of dressing in a singular style and would wear every item of apparel the same color, selected to match the automobile he would drive that day. He was known as "the man of a thousand silk suits" in the press. Friends of the administration gave up apologizing for him after a while and lamely argued that it was the president's sense of family that protected Maximino in the cabinet. Although he had obvious symptoms of megalomania, Maximino was also useful to the president because he was both hostile to the Cardenista tradition and extremely antilabor. As head of the Ministry of Transportation and Communications, the agency of the government that issued contracts for telecommunications, road building, and other public works, Maximino's personal greed was boundless. He became known as "Mr. 15 Percent." His business associates included Axel Wenner-Gren, who was on the blacklist during the war, and William Jenkins, the former American consul in Puebla, who had become extremely wealthy from his interests in sugar, land, film distribution and exhibition, and banking. Maximino handled the political cover for Jenkins in the face of bitter opposition from workers and ejiditarios. He was not bothered by any fine line between sharp business practices and outright crime. Maximino's corruption knew no bounds.

To the relief of many supporters in the official party, Maximino's time on center stage was limited. The circumstances of his demise were consonant with the man's style: "He died of a heart attack brought on by ignoring medical advice [he was diabetic] during a vigorous party on his estate in Puebla on February 17, 1945, that honored Fulgencio Batista of Cuba. Even the best face that *Excélsior* could put on the matter was to state rather lamely that, in spite of his excesses, he did provide a counter balance to the leftists in the Avila Camacho cabinet!"[146]

Political Legacy

By the end of his term, Avila Camacho's place in the middle ground seemed to be secure, at least in the sense that both the Far Right and the Far Left felt that his regime had been considerably better than the likely alternative would have been. Events of the second half of the *sexenio* seemed to confirm this analysis. The Left took heart from the decree of June 29, 1944, limiting foreign ownership of major industries to 49 percent and also from the law of June 23, 1944, formally abolishing the Sinarquistas and prohibiting further issues of their publication *El Sinarquista*. Torres Bueno and his associates did not make much of a fight of it, and the group receded into oblivion. The Acción Nacional was more durable, if only because of the sociological basis of the group, which was urban and middle class. Closer to the hierarchy of the Church, they concerned themselves with private-sector politics and matters associated with Spanish culture. They tended to work more as professionals and consequently to be more affluent than the Sinarquistas, whose movement had smacked of a more parochial version of lower-class radicalism on the Right. Times had changed so much that by the end of 1944, Dr. Brito Foucher resigned from his position as the rector of the National University under criticism from the UNAM community for being too sympathetic to fascists and Nazis.

Similarly, on the left, the PCM was on the decline. It claimed only 3,913 members by 1945, and most of those members were *campesinos*; the party's strategic base with railroad and petroleum workers had been destroyed by the purges associated with the 9th Congress.[147] In addition, Dionicio Encina, the secretary general of the PCM, was far less effective as a popular leader than Vicente Lombardo Toledano had been. Few called him a charismatic figure. Even the *Saturday Evening Post*, in the United States, deemphasized the importance of the PCM in Mexico. In an article on USSR Ambassador Constantin Oumansky, the *Post* stated: "Soviet propaganda in Mexico is limited largely to the publication of an information bulletin every two weeks and the presentation of a daily radio commentary over a small local station."[148]

Thus, President Avila Camacho appeared well established in the middle of the political spectrum, even within the governing party, and the center of political life had shifted considerably. Lázaro Cárdenas had absolutely resisted the temptation to serve as a focal point for those revolutionaries who felt betrayed by recent developments. And the group on the right, associated with Abelardo Rodríguez and Portes Gil, had settled for business opportunities rather than political prominence.

President Avila Camacho's term appeared to be ending with less controversy than in the crisis year of 1942–43. Even an unsuccessful attempt to assassinate the president on April 11, 1944, created sympathy for him as it was seen as an isolated act. The president's controversial brother, Maximino, was no longer in the picture, and the sacrifice of Gaxiola had helped to diminish the aura of scandal around the administration. In addition, the U.S. success in supplying Mexico with corn and wheat by 1945 seemed to cool criticism of the cooperation between the two nations.

As the war was coming to an end, Mexico sent a fighter squadron into battle in the Philippines, and the country took considerable pride in having contributed to the successful Allied war effort. Without exception—and in striking contrast to similar news in 1940—banner headlines celebrated the successful election of Franklin D. Roosevelt for a fourth term in 1944. In marked contrast to the lack of public support for the war in 1941, the policy of wartime cooperation with the United States had taken root by the end of the war. Revelations of German atrocities in the concentration camps further confirmed the correctness of having supported the Allies in the war, and the country's industrial program of development seemed to be progressing as a result of the wartime cooperation.

Notes

1. Luis González sees Avila Camacho primarily as a force for conciliation. González, *Pueblo en vilo*, 255.

2. Cosío Villegas ridiculed Cabrera's attempt to free the peasant without abolishing the hacienda as being as absurd as the concept of *blanco negro*. Krauze, *Daniel Cosío Villegas*, 88.

3. This biographical sketch comes from *Mexican-American Review*, January 1, 1941; and Camp, *Mexican Political Biographies, 1935–1975*, 23.

4. Miller, *Culture and State in Mexico in the Sexennium of Manuel Avila Camacho*, 37.

5. George Messersmith to Franklin D. Roosevelt, October 2, 1943, George S. Messersmith Papers, University of Delaware (hereafter cited as GSM Papers).

6. Messersmith, "Memoirs," vol. 2, no. 8, GSM Papers.

7. Miller, *Culture and State in Mexico in the Sexennium of Manuel Avila Camacho*, 38.

8. Pansters, *Politics and Power in Puebla*, 50–75. The Avila Camacho machine survived under Gonzalo Bautista Castillo (1941–1945), Carlos I. Betancourt (1945–1951), and Rafael Avila Camacho (1951–1957).

9. Schuller, "Cardenismo Revisited: The International Dimensions of the Post-Reform Cárdenas Era," 279–80.

10. Contreras, *México 1940: Industrialización y crisis política*, 46.

11. Ruth Adler, "Experiments in Worker Participation in the Administration of Industry in Mexico during the Presidency of Lázaro Cárdenas."

12. James B. Stewart to secretary of state, "Political Report for February," March 8, 1939, USNA/59, 812.00/30700.

13. Horatio Mooers, American consul in Mexicali, to secretary of state, January 16, 1940, USNA/59, 812.00/30918.

14. *La Voz de México*, February 2, 1940.

15. See Avila Camacho's interview in *Hoy*, December 19, 1939.

16. Daniels to Hull, February 2, 1940, USNA/59, 812.00/30927.

17. Daniels to secretary of state, March 6, 1939, USNA/59, 812.00/30704.

18. This section relies upon Saragoza, *The Monterrey Elite and the Mexican State*, 192–97, and William P. Blocker, U.S. consul in Monterrey, to secretary of state, July 29, 1937, USNA/59, 800/145

19. Saragoza, *The Monterrey Elite and the Mexican State*, 179–91.

20. William P. Blocker, U.S. consul in Monterrey, to secretary of state, July 29, 1937, USNA/59, 800/145.

21. Hamilton, *The Limits of State Autonomy*, 237–39.

22. Schuller, "Cardenismo Revisited," 251–53.

23. Garrido, *El partido de la revolución institucionalizada*, 227.

24. Saragoza, *The Monterrey Elite and the Mexican State*, 197.

25. Secret report to the Foreign Office, March 3, 1941, PRO/FO, 371/26074.

26. Contreras, *México 1940*, 194–95.

27. J. Edgar Hoover to Adolph Berle, "Mexican Matters: Political, Radical, Nazi, and Revolutionary Activities," May 27, 1940, USNA/59, 812.00/31065 1/2.

28. Schuller, "Cardenismo Revisited," 217–18 and 230–34.

29. Anonymous memorandum of conversation, September 4, 1941, USNA/59, 812.00/731762. See also "Report from the American Consul General in Mexico City," George P. Shaw, June 28, 1941, USNA/59, 812.00/31715.

30. Pansters, *Politics and Power in Puebla*, 40–43.

31. Jacobs, *Ranchero Revolt: The Mexican Revolution in Guerrero*, 134–37.

32. *El Universal*, September 20, 1940.

33. H. L. Scott to Walso Romo Castro, oficial mayor de la presidencia, August 24, 1942, AGN, RP/MAC, 565.1/21.

34. "Biographies of the Members of Cabinet of the Mexican Government," December 16, 1941, USNA/59, 812.00/31845 .

35. Intercepted letter from the Asiatic Petroleum Corporation to Mr. Leigh-Jones of St. Helen's Court, London, August 9, 1942, PRO/FO, 371/30517.

36. *La Prensa*, September 19, 1940.

37. T. Ifor Rees to the Foreign Office, January 7,1942, PRO/FO, 371/30571.

38. Rees to the Foreign Office, January 7, 1942, PRO/FO, 371/30571.

39. Ruiz Galindo to Avila Camacho, February 14, 15, and 18, 1941, with the resolution from J. Jesús González Gallo to Ruiz Galindo, February 17, 1941, AGN, RP/MAC, 432.2/18.

40. Evaristo Araiza to the president, September 1945, AGN, RP/MAC, 432/205. For a similar attitude on the brewing industry, see the complaints that Fidel Velázquez had had opposition brewery workers beaten in his offices. Saturnina R. Ralia to the president, December 30, 1945, AGN, RP/MAC, 432/300.

41. Guy Ray to secretary of state, "Report . . . on Political Activities . . .," January 10, 1944, USNA/59, 812.504/2255.

42. Secret report received from the commercial relations division of the Ministry of Information, February 24, 1942, PRO/FO, 371/30571.

43. J. W. Wilkie, *The Mexican Revolution*, 188.

44. Warman, " . . . *y venimos a contradecir*," 213.

45. *La Prensa*, September 19, 1940.

46. Aguilar Camín, *Saldos de la revolución*, 124–25.

47. Interview in *Hoy*, October 4, 1941.

48. *Excélsior, El Universal*, and *La Prensa*, December 1, 1940.

49. *El Popular*, December 1, 1940.

50. Hughes to secretary of state, December 2, 1940, USNA/59, 812.00B/648.

51. *El Popular*, February 25, 1941.

52. Letter to the Foreign Office from the British consulate, March 4, 1941, PRO/FO, 371/26067.

53. Chassen de López, *Lombardo Toledano y el movimiento obrero mexicano (1917–1940)*, 272–73; Yañez Reyes, *Genesis de la burocracia sindical cetemista*, 194–216.

54. Secret report to the Foreign Office, based on unnamed British business contacts with President Avila Camacho, March 3, 1941, PRO/FO, 371/26067.

55. Carr, *Marxism and Communism in Twentieth-Century Mexico*, 116.

56. Ibid.

57. *El Nacional*, October 24, 1941.

58. Report from the U.S. consul in Mexico City, Morris H. Hughes, to secretary of state, "Transmitting Final Report on the XV National Convention of the CROM," July 30, 1941, USNA/59, 812.504/2020.

59. Carr, *El movimiento obrero y la política en México, 1910–1920*, 160–67.

60. George P. Shaw, U.S. consul in Mexico City, to secretary of state, "Bimonthly Report on Communist Activities, September 1 to November 1, 1941," October 31, 1941, USNA/59, 812.00B/729.

61. Emeterio Arochi to the president, January 14, 1943, AGN, RP/MAC, 432.3/59.

62. Martín Rivera to the president and accompanying petition, January 30, 1945, AGN, RP/MAC, 761(18)/3.

63. Middlebrook, *The Paradox of Revolution*, 100–101.

64. *El Universal*, December 23, 1939.

65. Ramírez Rancaño, *El sistema de haciendas en Tlaxcala*, 116–19.

66. Collier, "Peasant Politics and the Mexican State," 293.

67. Memorandum of conversation between L. D. Mallory, agricultural attaché, and Bernardo Avilez, September 25, 1940, USNA/59, 812.61/110.

68. *Excélsior*, December 12, 1940. The executive order was dated December 11, and further technical limitations were announced in the *Diario Oficial*, January 25, 1941.

69. Félix C. Ramírez, president of La Union de Fomento y Defensa de la Pequeña Propiedad, to Avila Camacho, October 4, 1943, AGN, RP/MAC, 545.3/51.

70. Thomas McEnelly, American consul in Tampico, to Messersmith, April 16, 1942. *El Mundo* of Tampico, April 14, 1942, USNA/ 59, 812.00/ 31936.

71. Hewett de Alcántara, *Modernizing Mexican Agriculture*, 191–92. It is the same pattern that Eckstein found in *El ejido colectivo en México* and *El marco macro-económico del problema agrario en México*.

72. Archbishop Martínez to Cardinal Maglione, report entitled "Mexican Government's Successful Fight against Communism," October 2, 1941, USNA/59, 812.00B/744.

73. *Excélsior*, September 24, 1941.

74. *El Popular*, September 24, 1941.

75. Report from Vice Consul William K. Ailshie to secretary of state entitled "Labor Riot in Front of the Presidential Residence; Workers Killed by Troops," October 2, 1941, USNA/59, 812.504/2039.

76. Legation report to the Foreign Office, September 27, 1941, PRO/ FO, 371/26068.

77. Valentín Campa, *Mi testimonio: Memorias de un militante comunista* (México, D.F.: Ediciones de Cultura Popular, 1980), 169.

78. The narrative comes from Ariza, *Historia del movimiento obrero mexicano*, 237, as cited in Basurto, *La clase obrera en la historia de México*, 29.

79. Founded in 1939, it was not until 1946 that the government gave the PAN its first four federal deputy seats; it won its first municipal council seat in 1947. Mabry, *Mexico's Acción Nacional*, 37–49.

80. Carr, "Crisis in Mexican Communism: The Extraordinary Congress of the Mexican Communist Party," 61–62. See also Raleigh Gibson to secretary of state, August 17, 1944, USNA/226 (Records of the OSS) 90921.

81. Contreras, *México 1940*, 18–19.

82. *Novedades*, November 2, 1943.

83. Letter from H. Blake-Taylor to Bateman, March 6, 1942, PRO/FO, 371/30571.

84. Messersmith to FDR, July 10, 1942, USNA/59, 812.00/32007.

85. For the support from Narciso Bassols, who later tried to resist Alemán's swing to the right, see Bassols to Avila Camacho, December 15, 1941, AGN, RP/MAC, 550/44-16-8.

86. Schuller, "Cardenismo Revisited," 241–42.

87. *Excélsior*, August 30 and 31, 1942.

88. Guy W. Ray to secretary of state, "Report of a private conversation with source close to Manuel Avila Camacho over the *Excélsior* article of 30 August," August 31, 1942, USNA/59, 812.00/32035.

89. Bartra, *Los herederos de Zapata*, 73–74.

90. Memorandum of conversation, Thomas H. Lockett and Eduardo Suárez, August 31, 1943, USNA 812.51/2703.

91. Luis Cabrera to the president, AGN, RP/MAC, 432.2/42, and July 24, 1944, AGN, RP/MAC, 564.5/355; "Economic Report," July 14, 1946, USNA/59, 812,50/7-2446. As late as 1950 the drug companies were still struggling with the government over the ownership and control of these industries. "Economic Developments in Mexico," February 10, 1950, USNA/59, 812.00/2-1050.

92. Niblo, *War, Diplomacy, and Development*, 101–4.

93. This account of the Japanese in Mexico comes from Watanabe, "The Japanese Immigrant Community in Mexico: Its History and Present."

94. Watanabe, "The Japanese Immigrant Community in Mexico," 48, cites figures from the Japanese Ministry of Foreign Affairs in 1936 that updated a survey conducted by the Japanese Legation in 1927.

95. Ibid., 189.

96. Ibid., 65.

97. Ibid., 77.

98. Ibid., 82.

99. Knight, *The Mexican Revolution*, 331, 416.

100. Harold D. Finley to secretary of state, "Unification of Mexican Labor," June 26, 1942, USNA/59, 812.504/2087.

101. *Excélsior*, June 26, 1942.

102. *El Popular*, August 19, 1942.

103. Giménez Cacho, "La constitución del sindicato industrial de trabajadores mineros"; Elizondo, "El periodo 1942–1946," 87–90.

104. Elizondo, "El periodo 1942–1946," 189–90.

105. *Mañana*, July 1, 1944.

106. See the numerous complaints and petitions, especially the articulate petition from the Cruz Azul Cooperative to the president, June 30, 1943, AGN, RP/MAC, 545.22/133.

107. Hoover to Berle, February 18, 1942, USNA/59, 812.5045/985.

108. Bursley to secretary of state, September 20, 1943, USNA/59, 812.5047/1.

109. For a detailed discussion of the economic impact of World War II upon Mexico, see Niblo, *The Impact of War: Mexico and World War II* (Bundoora: La Trobe University, Institute of Latin American Studies, 1988), and "Decoding Mexican Politics: The Resignation of Francisco Javier Gaxiola," 23–39.

110. See, for example, the petition with some four hundred signatures from the *Comité de lucha contra la carestía* to the president, August 18, 1943, AGN, RP/MAC, 545.22/160-1-8.

111. *Hoy*, July 24, 1943.

112. Ibid., July 31, 1943.

113. This was the line of explanation taken by Medina and Torres, *Historia de la revolución mexicana, periodo 1940–1952: Del Cardenismo al avilacamachismo*, 196–98, and also by Blanca Torres, *Historia de la revolución mexicana, periodo 1940–1952: Mexico en la Segunda Guerra Mundial*, 355.

114. Report from Harold D. Finley to secretary of state, "Further Developments in the Matter of Attacks by *Hoy* Magazine against Secretary of National Economy Lic. Francisco Javier Gaxiola," USNA/59, 812.00/32183.

115. V. M. Villaseñor, *Memorias de un hombre de izquierda*, Vol. 2, *De Avila Camacho a Echeverría*, 33. Bassols, *Obras*. Bassols was out of power by this time so his memoirs are less helpful on matters of internal divisions within the PRM than one might hope. After the closure of *Combate*, he was even more isolated and demoralized. He left Mexico for South America in November 1944, not to return for two years.

116. Gaxiola and Rodríguez organized a chocolate company, La Suiza, in 1943, and in 1944, after his resignation, they also started the company Petrolera del Noroeste. In addition, they owned Peñafiel Mineral Water Company together. See Miller, *Culture and State in Mexico in the Sexennium of Manuel Avila Camacho*, 60.

117. Cosío Villegas, *Historia moderna de México: El porfiriato, la vida politica interior, parte segunda*, 275–305.

118. Finley to secretary of state, August 11, 1943, USNA/59, 812.00/32183.

119. Telegram from Nazario S. Ortíz Garza to J. Jesús Gallo, March 31, 1943, AGN, RP/MAC, 545.22/160-1.

120. Efraín Buenrostro to Avila Camacho, May 7, 1946, AGN, RP/MAC, 545.22/160-1.

121. Gaxiola, *Memorias*, 303.

122. Harold D. Finley to secretary of state, "Developments in the Case of the Attacks by *Hoy* Magazine against Secretary of National Economy Lic. Francisco Javier Gaxiola," August 24, 1943, USNA/ 59, 812.00/32188.

123. T. Ifor Rees to the Foreign Office, November 26, 1941, PRO/FO, 371/26087.

124. Harold D. Finley to secretary of state, "The Mexican Political Situation," September 23, 1943, USNA/59, 812.00/32196.

125. W. K. Ailshie to secretary of state, "Third Congress of the CTM," April 2, 1943, USNA/59, 812.504/2196.

126. Harold D. Finley to secretary of state, "The Mexican Political Situation," September 23, 1943, USNA/59, 812.00/32196.

127. Guy W. Ray to secretary of state, "Memorandum of conversation with Andre Simon," November 17, 1944, USNA/59, 812.00/11-1744.

128. Antonio Ruiz Galindo to Adolfo Ruíz Cortines, November 23, 1945, AGN, RP/MAC, 4321/11.

129. Julio Lacaud to the president, November 13, 1943, AGN, RP/MAC, 564.2/214.

130. Ruiz Galindo to the president, December 13, 1943, ANG, RP/MAC, 564.2/214.

131. Jorge Vera Estañol to Avila Camacho, July 22, 1942, AGN, RP/MAC, 565.1/49.

132. For accounts of the meeting, see *El Porvenir* and *El Norte*, of Monterrey, April 18–20, 1944.

133. Report of December 19, 1941, PRO/FO, 371/30584; letter from Bateman to the Foreign Office, March 23, 1942, PRO/FO, 371/30571.

134. *El Nacional*, February 28, 1946.

135. *Excélsior* and *El Universal*, March 2, 1946.

136. All of the Mexico City press covered the allegations on March 2–8, 1946.

137. Messersmith to secretary of state, March 5, 1946, USNA/59, 812.00/4-1346.

138. *Novedades*, April 3, 1946.

139. Dionisio Encina, general secretary of the PCM, to the Comisión Nacional de Planeación para la Paz, November 22, 1944, AGN, RP/MAC, 433/310.

140. Messersmith to secretary of state, January 10, 1946, USNA/59, 812.5034/1-1046.

141. Thomas Lockett to William MacLean, September 19, 1945, USNA/59, 812.5034/9-1945.

142. *El Universal*, October 12, 1945.

143. Bateman to Bevin, "Annual Report for Mexico for 1945," January 15, 1946, PRO/371, 51592.

144. Alejandro Gómez Maganda, *Acapulco en mi vida y en el tiempo*, 220–21.

145. Report, December 12, 1949, USNA/59, 812.00/Avila Camacho/12-1249.

146. Ibid.

147. Carr, *Marxism and Communism in Twentieth-Century Mexico*, 137–40.

148. *Saturday Evening Post*, December 23, 1944.

3

The 1946 Selection

By 1945, President Avila Camacho thought that he was holding the prenomination maneuvers within acceptable bounds. The early candidates for president had emerged: General Henríquez Guzmán was again widely believed to be the choice of General Cárdenas, and Miguel Alemán, from his platform as minister of the interior, was working hard to win over the governors and those with influence within the party. *El Universal* was already pro-Alemán. It was also taken for granted that Avila Camacho supported his minister of the interior, since General Alemán, Miguel's father, had been his protector and patron in the early stages of the president's career. Young Miguel had continued his father's friendship with Manuel Avila Camacho after the elder Alemán's death. In 1939, Miguel Alemán resigned his position as governor of Veracruz in order to run General Avila Camacho's presidential campaign, and there had been no breakdown of relations between the two men during the administration. In addition, Mrs. Alemán and Mrs. Avila Camacho were close friends. There was really never any doubt about the president's support for his minister of the interior, and this backing provided Alemán with a considerable advantage.

Today we tend to forget that the early leader in the 1946 presidential stakes was Foreign Minister Ezequiel Padilla. Although many thought of Padilla as the front-runner, he was also the most hated of the various candidates. The Left viewed him as the favorite of the U.S. embassy in Mexico City, which was true. (George Messersmith's dispatches to Washington were full of effusive praise for the foreign minister's cooperation in the war effort.) And he had received high praise in the international media at the time of the Rio conference and was frequently honored in the international arena. Neither the approval of the U.S. government nor that of the international media helped Padilla domestically. The Right hated him for quite different reasons. At the time of the assassination of General Obregón, he had been the attorney general. He led the prosecution of José de León Toral and Concepción Acevedo de la Llata (Madre Conchita), who were accused and ultimately convicted of the assassination. As such, Padilla was anything but the favorite of the Catholic Right. His international standing ran far ahead of his domestic political base.

As the selection approached, President Avila Camacho seemed to be firmly in control, and serenity appeared to be on the ascent. Little did anyone anticipate that such a major crisis was going to be unleashed on the government in the final hours of the Avila Camacho administration that the legitimacy of the governing party would be profoundly discredited.

The Endgame Crisis

The meaning of democracy had always been problematic in Mexico. Historically, the regime based its legitimacy on its identification with nationalism and the revolutionary process, especially as those forces merged with the great goal of industrial modernization. Few would argue that the success that the revolutionary family has enjoyed in Mexico has been based upon a scrupulous respect for the electoral process. Electoral honesty has frequently been sacrificed in the interest of nation, progress, party, or personal advantage. Emphasis on electoral practices, either by Mexicans or by foreign observers, often led to serious doubts about Mexican democracy. Manipulation and falsification of elections were common, especially when large numbers of the people wanted to register their dissent against a local government. Yet many who complained about fraudulent electoral practices focused upon that issue because they were unwilling to oppose openly the reforms of the Mexican Revolution. This was especially true for the Acción Nacional and the Monterrey Group, whose leaders dreamed of a return to the regimes of Porfirio Díaz and of his governor of Nuevo León, Bernardo Reyes.

The heart of the problem of implementing democracy in Mexico was that such acute class divisions existed that any "democratic opening," as President Luis Echeverría so poignantly phrased it in the 1970s, would inevitably challenge the privileges of the rich. And rich men normally held the dominant positions in all political parties, even those of a revolutionary hue. Laurens Perry has provided an excellent discussion of the limitations of liberalism in the nineteenth century, and many of the shady electoral devices he identified and documented in the era of the restored republic, 1867–1876, still prevailed.[1]

Questionable electoral practices survived the violent phase of the Mexican Revolution. In many localities, charges of the imposition of official candidates were valid and to a degree were accepted as the prerogative of the dominant party. Especially in Monterrey, the imbalance between political and economic clout was so great that the powerful local oligarchy—known as the Monterrey Group—clashed stunningly with the revolutionary elite. The municipal elections of December 2, 1945, is a classic example of a political elite, the PRM in the capital, clashing with a powerful, but local, economic oligarchy. The PRM and Gobernación decided to allow the state governor to impose his brother-in-law, Felix González Salinas, in the municipal elections. The Monterrey Group opposed González Salinas with Manuel L. Barragán, who they ran as a "good government" candidate. Negotiations between the two elites broke down, and the PRM installed its candidate, González Salinas, on January 1, 1945. As the U.S. consul in Monterrey described the installation ceremony, "We were both struck with the attendance as there was not a single man of substance in the community there, no representative of capital, industry, or commerce, no representative of the real working class, only labor leaders and political hangers-on of the state and municipal governments."[2] In spite of President Avila Camacho's close relationship with the Monterrey industrialists during his own candidacy and administration, the Monterrey Group and the PRM still clashed profoundly over local elections.

Similar battles occurred during these years in such diverse states as Yucatán and Oaxaca. In Puebla, constant gang warfare, in which political gunmen—*pistoleros*—were freely utilized, gave a vicious taint to state politics. Usually, however, the political machinations involved one political group, or *camarilla*, battling another group for the nomination of the official party. It was unusual for the private sector to contest a formal political office.

At times, political violence went beyond electoral fraud. In the west, a political murder occurred that badly discredited the Avila Camacho administration. While attending a dance in Mazatlán, Governor and Colonel Rodolfo T. Loaiza of Sinaloa was assassinated in February 1944. Governor Loaiza was succeeded by General Macías Valenzuela, who was a close friend of President Avila Camacho and had served briefly as his minister of defense in 1942.

A year after the murder, a notorious criminal known as "El Gitano" was arrested. He was alleged to have been involved in many murders. Brought under guard to Mexico City, he accused Macías Valenzuela of having ordered the crime. Governor Macías Valenzuela went to Mexico City to contest the right of the central government to charge him with the murder on the grounds that whether a governor or not, he should be tried only in a military court. After a fortnight, he returned to Sinaloa, claiming that his leave of absence had expired. In the words of one British diplomat, "He had however said enough, before his departure, to disclose a sordid picture of dealings in high places with professional criminals, of paid assassinations, and, generally, of just the sort of thing that the opposition wanted to appear in print."[3]

As bad as the Loaiza murder was, it was in León, Guanajuato, that the political violence increased to the point that it generated a serious challenge to the legitimacy of the PRM. The government performed so badly that, for a time, the established patterns of control seemed threatened. The civil attaché at the U.S. embassy obtained a secret copy of the Mexican government's chronology of events at León from an investigator who accompanied the minister of the interior, Primo Villa Michel, in his investigation. (Miguel Alemán had by this time resigned to run his campaign.)

Events in León began in July 1944 when a local group of industrial leaders and the former Sinarquista, José Trueba Olivares, organized a party called the Unión Civica Leonesa (UCL), under the leadership of Ricardo Hernández Sorcini, to oppose the PRM in local elections. The group planned what the government investigator admitted was an intelligent campaign in support of Carlos Obregón for mayor of León against the PRM candidate, Ignacio Quiróz. The investigator also admitted that the election of December 16, 1945, would have resulted in a victory for Obregón had the vote count been truthful. By 10:00 A.M. election officials, sensing the depth of opposition, closed the polls. When the government announced the victory of Quiróz a delegation of local political figures went to Mexico City to confront the president, who refused to see them.

Mayor-designate Quiróz was scheduled to be installed on January 1, 1946, and as that date approached tension grew. The dynamics of the struggle became more complex when, on December 31, the government brought into León numerous truckloads of *agraristas*, many of whom were actually reservists attached to the army. The questionable electoral imposition thus became overlaid with class conflict as rural *agraristas* with links to the PRM through the CNC came to town and clashed with the more urban and middle-class supporters of the UCL. Clearly, two mutually exclusive visions of political legitimacy collided in León.

With the installation of Mayor Quiróz on New Year's Day of 1946, tensions ran high. The UCL held a protest rally, not in the *zócalo*, but in Hidalgo Park, some three kilometers away from the central square. About two thousand people, primarily from the town, attended the rally. Colonel Pablo Cano Martínez, chief of the General Staff of the military forces in Guanajuato, personally led a force of about one hundred soldiers into Hidalgo Park. With a machine gun in hand, Cano Martínez led his troops with fixed bayonets into the crowd and broke up the demonstration; many people were beaten and wounded. In the latter stages, others were run over by the cavalry. What the government's own investigator privately described as a "scandalous show of force" resulted in the death of a pregnant woman a few days later.

That such force had been used against unarmed civilians, in defense of an illegitimate election—and against urban people at that—convinced shopkeepers to close virtually all of the town's businesses by noon on January 2. As crowds milled around the square, leaders of the Unión Civica Leonesa tried to negotiate with the government. Pressure was also great on Dr. Quiróz to resign his post. By evening the crowd had returned, and a group of young boys, between ages twelve and sixteen, carried a coffin around the plaza with the twin signs saying "Quiróz" and "PRM." Their initiative was received warmly by the crowd.

The Mexican government's account then said that, at about 9:00 P.M., a stray stone "hit or fell close to" Colonel Emilio Olivera Barrón, the ranking military officer, who then gave the order to fire upon the crowd. After three warning shots, twenty soldiers filed out of the Municipal Palace and took up formation, with ten troops standing and the others lying prone. They fired into the civilian crowd, which by this time had reached an estimated five thousand people. Two machine guns on the palace roof also opened fire. As the crowd panicked, the troops divided into two groups, flanking left and right as the machine guns fired, thus catching the crowd in the crossfire. After a stretcher-bearer was killed, the Red Cross withdrew.

The police chief asserted that the troops were answering fire, but no evidence was forthcoming to support that allegation and no officials were killed or wounded. The official body count was that thirty had died, but the Red Cross reported that the accurate figure was seventy-four dead. Unofficial estimates, accepted by the government's internal investigator, put the number at roughly two hundred wounded. Officials had dressed some victims in uniforms to make it appear that soldiers had been fired upon; however, Red Cross officials pointed out that the bullets that had entered those bodies had not passed through the uniforms. In León, PRM leaders Delfino Carranza, Manuel Carmona, and Felipe Hernández Segura convinced Colonel Olivera Barrón that the disturbance was an opening move by Sinarquistas trying to start a general revolt.[4]

The shock produced by the events at León was great. After the president received the investigator's report from Gobernación, the government reported its version to the Permanent Committee of the Congress, and in the process President Avila Camacho declared vacant the office of governor and also ruled that the municipal elections were null and void. In consultation with the Permanent Committee, an associate justice of the Supreme Court, Lic. Nicéforo Guerrero, was named interim governor of Guanajuato. At the same time, the provost general of the Mexican army, General Roberto Bonilla, went to the state to investigate the army's responsibility. The unique nature of these events in contemporary Mexico is clear when one looks, in vain, for other examples of the official party nullifying the results in their own spurious victories.

The press reacted to the events in León with consternation. *Excélsior, Novedades,* and *La Prensa* all treated the episode as the disgrace of the decade. And indeed, the combination of a political imposition; a broadly based, if divided, popular response; and the outrage of troops firing upon an unarmed crowd was a scandal of major importance, and manna from heaven for the conservative press. By mid-January, banks and businesses throughout the republic were being closed in mourning and protest. Disgraceful attempts by *El Popular* to treat the protest over the killings as sedition and the effort by *El Nacional* to downplay the incident rang false. In its first report on the incident, on January 3, *El Popular* confused the events in León with those in Monterrey. The next day the paper settled upon the line that U.S. imperialists were arming the Sinarquistas, thus provoking the troops. This a priori reasoning, without evidence, set up the CTM's journal for a counterattack by the conservative press. *Excélsior* responded by noting that it was a working-class crowd into which the soldiers had fired, thus further embarrassing *El Popular.*

Ambassador Messersmith also confirmed the outline of these events. He wrote to Assistant Secretary of State Spruille Braden (son of the founder of Braden Copper Company in Chile) that after President Avila Camacho had removed the governor of Guanajuato, the Supreme Court, citing Article 97 of the constitution, sent two of its members—Roque Estrada and Carlos Angeles—to León to investigate events leading up to the massacre. The report was not made public, but the findings failed to support the governor's version of what had happened. The president then removed the governor and declared the election invalid. The episode was finally closed in February, when the new governor turned the municipal government over to Carlos A. Obregón, who had been the original candidate of the Unión Civica Leonesa and in whose support the demonstration had been organized.

The two Supreme Court justices gave their report on the incident. They found that all of the bullets were fired at, not from, the crowd and that the military had acted in an irresponsible way. Following this report the press again placed the incident at the top of the national agenda. *El Popular* continued to blame the matter on the Sinarquistas, and *El Nacional* tried to minimize the negative impact of the report. International attention fell upon the events at León, and the story grew with the telling. U.S. diplomat George Kennan related from Moscow that *Pravda* was reporting that the Sinarquistas were trying to overthrow the government of Mexico.[5]

At first the president tried to dismiss the incident as being entirely local in significance.[6] However, the episode was rapidly expanding in the national consciousness. Rumor had it that the Permanent Committee of the Congress might investigate and that the PAN was already petitioning the Supreme Court to do so. The Mexican Bar Association called for justice. By coincidence, Ambassador Messersmith dined with President Avila Camacho on the very evening, January 7, on which the president implicitly accepted the illegitimate nature of the imposition in León by declaring the governorship to be vacant. Messersmith described the president as greatly relieved that he was doing the right thing in condemning his own political machine. By removing the governor and two military commanders and also by allowing the Supreme Court to send a delegation to investigate, President Avila Camacho was reining in the PRM and effectively admitting official culpability. Indeed, by January 15–16, *Ultimas Noticias, Excélsior, Novedades,* and *El Universal* all reported rumors that the party's public relations specialists were mooting a name change for the governing PRM in an attempt to divert public rage away from candidate Alemán.

The military's attempt to whitewash events proved to be ineffective. Rumors leaked that the provost marshal, Roberto Bonilla, was about to submit a report asserting that bullets of different calibers than those used by the army had been involved in the shooting. González Tejada, writing in *La Prensa*, ridiculed this version by asserting that 100,000 witnesses must have had it wrong.[7] This line was subsequently dropped, and the military eventually charged Colonel Cano Martínez and Colonel Olivera Barrón with misdemeanors, thus leaving them answerable only to military tribunals. More serious charges, carrying penal implications, were dropped, and the minor charges were dismissed on November 3 at a court martial in Guadalajara.

The Supreme Court justices released their findings on the last day of January. In a rare act of defiance of executive authorities, the justices found no sign of damage to the Municipal Palace, thus eliminating the possibility that troops were firing in self-defense. They also reported that some 80 percent of the wounded were shot in the back, hands, or feet, a finding that further discredited the federal forces. By Mexican standards, this was virtually a judicial insurrection.

Another source of pressure on the Mexican government was the United States. The close links between the military establishments of the two countries added another dimension to the events at León. The U.S. embassy sent an agent to León following the earliest reports of the massacre. As Messersmith described the interest of the United States in these events, "The incident at León had sent shivers up and down the spines of our people in Washington at the thought of sending down [military] materials of the kind mentioned in the interim agreement."[8]

It was clear that the massacre at León had cast a pall over the PRM convention scheduled for January 18–19, 1946, in Mexico City. Miguel Alemán, by then the leading contender for the party's nomination, was clearly discredited since he had remained silent over the affair. The events in León and Monterrey had so compromised the ruling party that its leaders reportedly considered delaying the convention. Nevertheless, the convention went ahead as scheduled and nominated Miguel Alemán as its presidential candidate on January 19. It is interesting to note that in his acceptance speech on January 20, Alemán made no mention of the political upheavals of recent months and instead discussed almost exclusively his plans for industrial and agricultural development. For some time, candidate Alemán was extremely subdued in his campaign efforts.

Perhaps even more than that of the governing party's candidate, the credibility of Vicente Lombardo Toledano was damaged by the massacre at León. He tried to argue the fairly convoluted position that the PRM leadership in León had been asleep and had missed the clever machinations of reactionary agents who had planned the entire massacre in order to discredit the PRM. Both Miguel Alemán and his campaign manager, Ramón Beteta, were already telling the U.S. embassy's first secretary, Guy Ray, that whereas Lombardo Toledano's help was useful in delivering the labor vote, neither he nor his close aides would have a place in the new Alemán administration. Ray, however, did not believe that Lombardo Toledano would campaign so hard for Alemán without a better agreement than that.

Lombardo's allegations, that the United States was smuggling arms to the Sinarquistas, were without substance and were an embarrassment to the Alemán campaign. It is noteworthy that by this stage Beteta was arguing in private correspondence with U.S. diplomats that the election of Padilla would mean "the elimination of 35 years of the Mexican Revolution." This written correspondence also provided the first word to the U.S. diplomats that the events at León were behind the PRM's decision to change its name to the Partido Revolucionario Institucional (PRI). Guy also believed that the impact of inflation had been a real factor behind the events in León.[9] He was not the only U.S. official to have difficulty accepting that such a fundamental shift in the policies of the state was likely.[10]

Further investigations of the events at León only seemed to make matters worse from the government's perspective. The Supreme Court justices investigating the incident reported no sign of any damage done by the masses of protesters except for a couple of broken windows. Many bullets were found in the trees and benches of the plaza across from the Municipal Palace, thus proving that the shots had come from the troops located in the Palace and not from the protesters. Those in the crowd denied they had been armed, even with sticks and stones. Moreover, there was no evidence that the events had been precipitated by the excessive use of alcohol. The justices reported that all the evidence was "unfavorable to the federal forces." Many rank-and-file CTM members had protested locally against the line argued by the CTM's national leadership that the demonstration had been staged by reactionaries in order to discredit the revolution. The "mass provocation" consisted of youths carrying a casket around the plaza with the name of Dr. Quíróz—the imposed victor of the election—on it, and nothing more. There was also evidence, the justices reported, that the troops had thrown a hand grenade into the unarmed crowd. The justices also noted that they had been unable to interview the troops who had been involved because those soldiers were immediately shifted to Irapuato after the incident. All of the press gave these findings great prominence.[11]

Clearly the government troops had acted with inexcusable violence when faced with a peaceful protest against the imposition of the official candidate over the real victor in León. There was not much of a case to be made in defense of the government, and even CTM members on the scene in León were appalled. Labor leaders like Lombardo Toledano hurt their credibility enormously by trying to rationalize away the government's behavior. So great had been the public consternation over these events that it had nearly become necessary for the government to postpone the PRM convention at which Miguel Alemán was selected to be the next president of the republic.

It is notable that the massacre in León, which approached in scale the Tlaltelolco massacre of 1968, has been forgotten to history. The taint of association with the Sinarquista tradition converted the fallen into unworthy victims. The view from the ground, in which local grievances predominated, was quickly lost in the face of official amnesia from the governing party and its media allies. It is little wonder that the PRM decided that it was a fitting moment to change its name.

Trying to take advantage of the unprecedented nature of the Supreme Court's intervention after the massacre at León, the Acción Nacional immediately petitioned the Supreme Court to intervene also in the case of the recent imposition in Monterrey in which the governor of Nuevo León had installed his brother-in-law as head of the municipal government despite the probable victory of the candidate backed by the employers' group. That election was complicated by the long-standing conflict between the PRM and the Monterrey Group.

The central government decided that the threat of judicial independence was contagious. Operating on its rotation system, the Supreme Court sent Antonio Islas Bravo—the only justice to vote against the removal of the governor of Guanajuato—to Monterrey to investigate the Acción Nacional's charge. It was generally understood in Monterrey that the judge was in the government's pocket. Therefore, it was all the more surprising when, on January 21, 1946, in an unprecedented procedure, Islas Bravo openly announced his judgment against the imposition in Monterrey to the press. However, on the following day the Supreme Court held a long session and voted 13 to 6 against a judicial intervention in Monterrey. The conservative press, especially *Excélsior* and *Novedades*, noted cynically that to have opened the case of Monterrey would also have to apply to "5,000 other situations of a like sort." *La Prensa* and *El Universal* also applauded the Supreme Court's independent position in León, if not in Monterrey. The American ambassador viewed these events as evidence that the PRM/PRI had "lost the respect of a great part of the most respectable elements in Mexico."[12] The court then also refused to intervene in two parallel incidents in Tamaulipas, and it became clear that the Supreme Court's position in the face of events in León represented an exceptional moment of judicial opposition to executive absolutism. It also put a profound stain on the administration's final months.

The Avila Camacho years were important in the history of contemporary Mexico. The war had provided the Mexican president with the means to dominate the more powerful factions to the right and to the left of his own group, and the war also had created a situation in which the United States reentered the Mexican political and industrial scene to a depth of penetration that was unprecedented. Even during periods of direct U.S. intervention, such as the occupation of Veracruz, Mexico's northern neighbor had not been able to change the rules of the game so profoundly. President Avila Camacho had unleashed a conservative assault upon the program of the Mexican Revolution that would continue to intensify until it became a veritable counterrevolution under his successor. Thus, it is somehow appropriate that a government that set out to change the program of the Mexican Revolution so dramatically would end its term of office by changing the name of its own party. Whatever an institutionalized revolution might be, it was clear that it would be profoundly different from the dominant currents of Cardenismo.

The man selected to next hold the highest office went to ground during these dramatic events. Miguel Alemán was in an invidious position. He generally tried to keep a low profile while simultaneously remaining loyal to the administration and distancing himself from its official abuses of power. Once it became apparent that the governing party would weather the storm, the country turned its attention to the new president.

The Next President

Miguel Alemán was known as a playboy. As a young man he had been particularly fond of making frequent visits to Hollywood. His dalliances with the starlets of the silver screen became the raw material for pulp journalism of the day.[13] Indeed, his well-publicized activities in Hollywood may have been a major factor in gaining him the acceptance in governing party circles that enabled him to overcome his father's reputation. After all, having a father who had died in battle for an unsuccessful faction during the Mexican Revolution was scarcely a job qualification for a future president. By contrast, the son's somewhat lighter image as a playboy seemed less threatening. And for a young, flashy politician, the ability to operate in the heart of Hollywood did not hurt his reputation at all.

Miguel Alemán Valdez, like his father General Miguel Alemán, was born in Sayula, Veracruz. The senior Alemán ran a village store before joining the uprising against Porfirio Díaz and becoming an active military figure during the Madero and Constitutionalist periods. General Alemán was a Carranzista in the epic struggle, until Carranza's flight from Mexico in 1920. Later, he was involved in the June 1922 uprising of Francisco Murguía and Lindoro Hernández, known by the victors in the governing party as the "treason of Tlaxcalantongo." Although chance spared the elder Alemán the fate of many of his co-conspirators, his opposition to presidents Obregón and Calles was a constant for the remainder of the decade, and he eventually joined the Gonzalo Escobar rebellion. General Alemán was killed by government forces on March 19, 1929; by then his son was twenty-nine. General Alemán's memory was so reviled by the governing party that, as a boy, young Miguel was not allowed to attend the schools in Sayula.

Personal links already mattered a great deal within the revolutionary family. In an early crisis in his career the elder Alemán had protected Carranza's son-in-law, General Cándido Aguilar, and in later years Aguilar returned the favor by helping young Miguel to gain his first political appointment—as a judge of the Superior Court in Mexico City. Miguel received this position in spite of a lack of distinction in his education, first in Orizaba and Jalapa, then at the National Preparatory School in Mexico City, and eventually in law at UNAM. He did, however, found a school newspaper, *Eureka*, while at the "Prepa." The future president married Beatríz Velasco of Celaya, and they had two children, a son, also named Miguel, and a daughter, Beatríz. Friends and acquaintances generally viewed Miguel, Jr. as highly personable, even charming.

Sra. Beatríz Velasco de Alemán and the president's nephew, Fernando Casas Alemán (head of the Departamento del Districto Federal). *Courtesy Hermanos Mayo, Archivo General de la Nación, Mexico City*

The future president's first real break came as an inadvertent result of a political stalemate between would-be caudillos in the state of Veracruz. During the Emilio Portes Gil administration, there were two factions contesting dominance in the state; one was led by Manlio Fabio Altamirano, a former manager of *El Nacional,* and the other by the former secretary of Ortiz Rubio, Eduardo Hernández Cházaro. After Altamirano was assassinated in Veracruz in June 1936, Portes Gil—upon the recommendation of a mutual friend, Manuel Ramírez Vázquez—supported Alemán in order to try to generate a third force, one that would be more attentive to his direction. Alemán fought long and hard for the control of the state political machine, a battle in which, if the FBI's information is to be believed, Alemán ordered the "liquidation" of some forty-five opponents.[14] This is the first of many indications in the public record that there was a hidden, darker side to Miguel Alemán.

Since Miguel Sr. was a member of the Cándido Aguilar circle, and had a long association with ex-president Carranza, the younger Alemán had only modest luck during the *maximato.* But once "the old king," Plutarco Elías Calles, was out of the scene, Alemán's luck improved. When Lázaro Cárdenas became president, Miguel Alemán became first a senator from Veracruz, 1934–1936, and then the governor of Veracruz, 1936–1939. At the time, J. W. F. Dulles believed that Miguel Jr. was attractive to President Cárdenas because he "was recommended by a large number of labor and peasant groups, particularly those of his native state, Veracruz."[15]

When Manuel Avila Camacho ran for president in the controversial 1940 election, Alemán was his campaign manager. This was widely understood to be a move that signaled an agreement between the PRM factions led by Portes Gil and Cárdenas. As Avila Camacho's campaign manager, Alemán traveled to the United States to reassure important figures in the Roosevelt administration that the official candidate was going to follow policies acceptable to Washington. It was at this time that he cemented his business relationship with John A. Hastings, a former New York state senator. Through George Creel, Alemán also met many influential American business figures. At this stage in his career Alemán was described by J. Edgar Hoover: "He accommodates himself readily to whatever situations arise and apparently has few fixed political opinions, but governs himself more according to the expediency of the situation. . . . He plays ball first with the leftists and then with the rightists, as the exigencies of the situation may dictate, with the greatest benefit to himself."[16]

Alemán did not appear to be Washington's man, and his relationship with U.S. diplomats further deteriorated after he became minister of the interior under Avila Camacho. U.S. diplomats viewed him with considerable consternation. There was a dramatic gap in lifestyles between the diplomats of the 1940s and Alemán, as was driven home in 1941, when Alemán organized a tour by "Movie Stars from Hollywood" to promote the war effort. However, Alemán's reputation soon grew beyond that of a mere playboy; as minister of the interior during World War II, he also became known as a protector of Axis businessmen. Jorge Viesca Palma was Alemán's longtime private secretary, and he was "instrumental in arranging visas for Axis nationals prior to the Mexican declaration of war."[17] This placed both men on Washington's list of least-favorite people. Ambassador Messersmith concluded that Alemán continued to accept bribes to protect Axis nationals and remove them from the blacklist—even after the war began. It was not that Alemán was pro-Nazi, it was simply that he cashed in on the precarious situation of citizens of Axis countries in Mexico during

World War II.[18] Beyond that, there was another reason why Alemán had poor relations with the representatives of the United States.

Ambassador Messersmith was so close to Foreign Minister Padilla during the Avila Camacho years that Padilla would at times give the U.S. ambassador secret documents that his government had no intention of revealing.[19] For his part, Messersmith adopted a public stance that emphasized his neutrality with regard to the political contest within Mexico. However, his reports back to Washington make it abundantly clear that he found Ezequiel Padilla to be the most congenial politician of the day. Padilla took an extremely pro-U.S. position on matters of foreign relations, and, more than any other figure, he was associated with the policy of intimate wartime cooperation with the United States. He also favored increased rights of private property for foreigners in Mexico, including unregulated foreign investment. His pro-U.S. position was widely understood in Mexico. Padilla also developed an international reputation as an able diplomat during the war; he performed well at the Inter-American Conference in Rio de Janeiro in 1945, and he was widely reported in the U.S. press to be the likely successor to President Avila Camacho, a view that did not endear him to other political figures.

The Selection

Although it is difficult to penetrate the balance of forces that came together within the governing party as the next president was selected, some general tendencies were clear by the end of the Avila Camacho administration. The war and his years in office had enabled the president to gain considerable ground over the factions of the party that were loyal to former President Cárdenas or the old Right. Whereas Cárdenas still enjoyed great popular support with workers, peasants, and many within the army, it was doubtful that he still influenced one-third of the Congress as he had a few years before. Calles's influence was minimal, and Portes Gil was increasingly limited to a significant say over matters only in Tamaulipas. The CNC was drastically diminished as an autonomous force, and Portes Gil suffered from that decline; however, he had a niche within circles of power within the party, and his law practice benefited greatly from the influence that he was able to exert for his important clients. Former President Abelardo Rodríguez continued to wield strong influence within the business community, in the northwest of Mexico, and in deliberations within the party. However, he was not popular.

Alemán was also aided in his relationship with the right wing of the PRM by the death of Maximino Avila Camacho on February 15, 1945. Alemán benefited from the removal of the president's brother from his regional power base in Puebla and in his home state of Veracruz. Maximino also had had great influence within—some said control over—the Unión de Camioneros (truck owners' guild) by the end of his life. His power to dispense patronage and contracts while minister of transportation and communications in his brother's administration had created a natural rival on the right wing of the official party. No one could replace General Maximino, and that worked to Miguel Alemán's advantage.

The Cardenistas had been reduced to fewer than a third of the members of Congress, a number of zone commanders, and numerous officials in the army. Moreover, regional figures were again losing considerable autonomy in their battle with the central authorities. Therefore, the CTM with its million members—perhaps 1.5 million if one includes all of its sympathetic associate unions—was the most significant force on the left. Lombardo Toledano had lost much influence during the Avila Camacho years, but he still had many followers within the organization. By comparison, the CROM, with its alleged sixty thousand members, was important primarily as a lever with which the government could keep the CTM in line. In spite of his diminishing status, Vicente Lombardo Toledano's influence was critical in the 1946 selection.

Momentum in the international arena initially appeared to favor Padilla as the likely candidate for 1946. Mexico had been honored at the Bretton Woods Conference in 1944, and Foreign Minister Padilla operated at the pinnacle of international diplomacy as the postwar settlement was being formulated. At the Inter-American conference at Rio de Janeiro the next year he had played a star role in convincing other Latin Americans to allow the United States greater latitude to intervene against communism. Finally, his position as the head of the Mexican delegation at the postwar conference in San Francisco in 1945, where the United Nations was established, seemed to add momentum to his candidature.

Lombardo Toledano's standing with the government had fallen so low that he was denied a place in the official delegation that attend the conference in San Francisco. He traveled there on his own and tried in vain to play a role in the formation of the United Nations. Not only did he fail in his effort to create a regional Latin

American bloc, but he also earned the antipathy of the United States, which was fiercely opposed to the creation of exclusive regional groups. There is little doubt that Lombardo Toledano blamed his troubles on Padilla. Alarmed at his rival's string of successes, he returned to Mexico after the conference and immediately spoke with both Cárdenas and Alemán to convince them that Padilla was generating dangerous momentum. As the U.S. ambassador described the situation: "Cárdenas does not particularly love Alemán, and as Lombardo has no particular use for Alemán and vice versa, it was a strange bargain which was arrived at, and undoubtedly Lombardo made a very hard bargain with Alemán for his support."[20]

Still speaking for the CTM, Lombardo Toledano blocked Padilla by swinging his support to Alemán; however, he was playing his last card at the zenith of Mexican politics. When Miguel Alemán was able to announce his candidacy on June 6, 1945, with Lombardo Toledano's support, it made the position of other candidates on the Cardenista left impossible. General Henríquez Guzmán, a close associate of Cárdenas, and Rojo Gómez, head of the DDF, bitterly announced that they would not run against Alemán. Lombardo

Toledano's initiative had neutralized the left wing of the revolutionary coalition. Concerns within the party about the swing to the right during the Avila Camacho years were not going to find expression in the 1946 selection of the official candidate. After this, the bandwagon effect became irresistible. Years later, Alemán provided additional support for this reading of events when he boasted to Guy Ray that he and Beteta had beaten Cárdenas by getting the approval of the CTM—as a result of Lombar-

Labor leader Vicente Lombardo Toledano throwing his support behind Miguel Alemán. *Courtesy Hermanos Mayo, Archivo General de la Nación, Mexico City*

do Toledano's effort—before Cárdenas had decided whom to support in 1946. In his view, Cárdenas had "missed the boat" by being slow to make his decision.[21]

Padilla returned to Mexico a few days later and resigned from the government in protest over the selection. He bitterly stated that he had expected a more democratic procedure from President Avila Camacho. Padilla retired to his home in Cuernavaca, where he served as a center of opposition to what he called the "imposition" of Miguel Alemán. In November he announced his own candidacy; however, he had little money and few prospects as he faced the official party's machine. Moreover, his identification with U.S. interests and the fact than many Mexicans blamed wartime cooperation with the United States for the suffering (*carestía*) of the war years doomed his cause.

The political situation was tense as a result of a series of electoral impositions—most significantly in Monterrey—and the massacre at León on January 2, 1946. The legitimacy of the PRM was being questioned more seriously than at any moment since the election of 1940. President Avila Camacho saw the spirit of wartime collaboration dissipating as his powers inevitably slipped away. Based upon his intimate daily contact with the president, Ambassador Messersmith concluded that "perhaps one of the unhappiest men in Mexico in the last half of the year has been the President of Mexico, who is really a very fine and serene, wise and constructive man."[22] In Messersmith's view, Avila Camacho had been led into supporting Alemán's candidacy by former president Cárdenas and by his wife "whose closest personal friend probably is Mrs. Alemán." It was a candidacy that Messersmith hated since, even as the campaign began, he still feared that Alemán would be dominated by Lombardo Toledano: "The most serious danger in the election of Alemán is that if he is elected, Lombardo and the extreme left elements in Mexico will claim credit for this being so and, as they are the strongest and most resourceful and vociferous elements, it is easy to foresee who would be guiding Mexico's internal and external policies."[23] But Messersmith had it wrong. However logical Alemán's deal with Lombardo made it appear at the time, Lombardo Toledano was a rapidly diminishing force. The U.S. ambassador might have noticed in his own embassy's reports that the official candidate had spent the unprecedented sum of 16 million pesos on the campaign, much of which had come from Alemán's close friends and business associates including A. C. Blumenthal, Ben Smith, Bruno Pagliai, and Samuel R. Rosoff.

Alemán's Initial Orientation

The results of the 1946 election were never in doubt. President Alemán won by 1,800,829 votes to 431,847 for Padilla, or so the official count claimed. Alemán almost certainly won since Padilla's base was small and, furthermore, he had made a serious mistake in

Miguel Alemán campaigns for the presidency in Acapulco, September 1945. *Courtesy Hermanos Mayo, Archivo General de la Nación, Mexico City*

Miguel Alemán is sworn in as president. *Courtesy Hermanos Mayo, Archivo General de la Nación, Mexico City*

the final days that hurt his campaign. In an interview with the *New York Times*, Padilla stated that the United States should not recognize just anyone as president of Mexico. There was an outcry when this remark was reported back in Mexico; many denounced the statement, claiming that it came close to inviting U.S. intervention in the domestic political process.[24]

Alemán's campaign committee was headed by his nephew, Fernando Casas Alemán, with Ramón Beteta acting as the secretary general of the campaign and Aarón Sáenz heading the finance committee. The conductor Carlos Chávez was in charge of a cultural committee, and the philosopher Alfonso Caso headed the education committee. The campaign was orchestrated in a fairly businesslike way. The party organized campaign rallies for which they bussed in people, paying them from two to five pesos to attend.[25] Alemán brought a tight inner circle with him when he assumed the presidency. Jorge Viesca Palma, whose sister was married to a U.S. foreign service officer, was his long-serving private secretary, and Enríque Parra was his personal lawyer. Parra had worked exclusively for Alemán since he was governor of Veracruz. Many considered him Alemán's closest friend.[26]

In the next circle, Alemán chose to spend his time with pals from the world of business, the racetrack, films, and nightclubs. Campaign contributions provide a glimpse of Alemán's inner circle of friends. Financiers Raúl Baillerés and Rosoff, who built the Valsequillo irrigation project in Puebla and other public works projects, contributed 2 million pesos to the Alemán campaign, and Pagliai, of the Hipódromo de las Américas, gave 1 million pesos. Smith, also of the racetrack, and Blumenthal, a nightclub owner, contributed significant sums as well. Leading figures in the Alemán campaign reported these and other contributions to U.S. diplomats to convince them that they would be as friendly to the United States as the Avila Camacho administration had been. Aware that Alemán was viewed as having "too much sympathy for the Germans and Japanese" in Mexico, they thought that by informing the U.S. diplomats of these deals they would demonstrate their pro-business orientation. Instead, revealing these deals to them only made the diplomats conclude: "Judging by all indications that can be observed, the graft and corruption which now exists would pale into insignificance compared with what Alemán and his supporters could demonstrate. American capital would apparently be welcome in Mexico, provided, of course, that it 'treated Alemán right.' "[27]

Miguel Alemán was the first civilian president of Mexico since the *maximato*, 1929–1934. Avila Camacho and Cárdenas had been generals, and it was widely believed that Cárdenas was the one man who could potentially organize a military rebellion. Alemán believed he faced a problem of keeping the military on his side. Mexico is divided not only into states but also into military zones that do not line up with state borders. This arrangement had emerged to combat the power of regional caudillos. Zone commanders are always generals, and many who are knowledgeable about Mexican politics think that the zone commanders are far more powerful than the state governors, certainly in times of turmoil.[28]

Since he was not a military man, the new president decided to rely upon money to retain the loyalty of the army. Zone commanders "received fat secret allowances for their personal use. . . . Under Alemán, this money was drawn from the secret funds of the *Presidencia* which, as we know, were not subject to audit."[29] Moreover, military men frequently head civilian institutions for which they receive additional salaries although they have nothing to do with their administration. In this way, generals are drawn toward the governing party and given a stake in the system, even after their retirement. These practices make a simple calculation of the importance of the military based upon the ratio of military expenditures to the total budget—which dropped from 21 percent in 1940 to 10 percent in 1950—utterly misleading.[30] This is the Mexican solution to the problem of military insurrection that has so plagued Latin America since independence. With the loyalty of the military thus assured, the president was ready to use his power.

President Alemán's first acts were a public relations exercise aimed at placating the general public over doubtful electoral practices. He announced an anticorruption campaign as was becoming de rigueur at the start of every presidential term, or *sexeño*. His early effort gave Juan Gutíerrez, secretary general of the Liga de Pequeños Industriales del D.F., hope that the president would move against excessive paperwork and corrupt government officials and union leaders.[31] He initiated a campaign against the *mordida*—the system of semiofficial bribes; ordered the arrest of beggars on the streets of Mexico City; and targeted the *coyotes*, the legal sharks who prey upon the innocent in the *zócolo* by promising to get them help from the appropriate government functionary. These were rather ephemeral initiatives, clearly aimed at creating a good opening impression on public opinion.

Alemán's central motivating concept was to pursue industrial modernization as rapidly as possible. In a poor country it seemed self-evident that the immediate goal should be to start industries that would provide products that the country was lacking. This fundamental proposition served to galvanize Alemán's team around a central program at the same time as it offered them immediate projects to support. The archival record is replete with letters from Alemán's acquaintances writing to the president asking for his support for one project or another. Private industrial projects were usually justified in terms of helping the nation to modernize, even as they benefited the petitioner. Members of the government team had no worries about a possible conflict of interests between these private business ventures and the administration of the public's business.

To pursue his goal of industrial modernization, Miguel Alemán ran a pro-business administration. He began to consult regularly with Abelardo Rodríguez and immediately froze out the Cardenistas.[32] When he was preparing to take power, Alemán had approached the Confederación de Camaras Nacionales de Comercio asking them to help identify and invite "prominent businessmen from Detroit and New York" to make contact with his administration. The Mexican Chamber of Commerce was happy to oblige.[33] Once Alemán had been elected he was quickly wooed by U.S. officials who began to negotiate the terms of their future relationship, which shifted away from wartime cooperation and toward loans for industrial projects. In the words of one participant: "For months administrative committees have burned the midnight oil and consumed grosses of pencils working out projects which would stand the scrutiny of keen [U.S.] appraisers of Mexico's economic situation, both financial and economic."[34]

Accusations of imperialism against foreign companies operating in Mexico made no impression on Alemán. George Messersmith, the wartime ambassador, returned to Mexico in 1947, after an absence in Argentina, to head MEXLIGHT, the largest foreign firm in Mexico, upon George Conway's retirement. Mexican Light and Power was owned by Sofina, a European holding company registered in Canada. Dannie Heineman, the chairman of the board, had approached Messersmith because the company was a favorite target of anti-imperialists in Mexico. Messersmith said that he would take up the post only if both the United States and the Mexican government approved. U.S. approval was a certainty. When Messersmith approached the new Mexican president about the prospect, he was apprehensive given their wartime conflicts:

President Alemán, who had received me very warmly, said that on the contrary he and the government were sure all concerned with the electricity situation would only be too happy for me to come and head this private company, which was the most important electricity business in the country. [Messersmith then urged better treatment for MEXLIGHT.] The President said that he thoroughly understood the situation and that it was the desire of the government that private companies should get on a firmer basis, and he could give me assurances that his government would do the necessary things.[35]

Messersmith concluded that Alemán was signaling his belief in the superiority of MEXLIGHT over the CFE, which Cárdenas had established in 1937. This was especially symbolic since MEXLIGHT only recently had been forced to cede back to the CFE the power-generating plant already known as the Miguel Alemán system. This facilitated a World Bank loan of another $26 million which enabled the company to pay interest on its capital and earn 13.97 percent profit, or 9 percent after taxes, in 1954.[36]

The Alemán administration approached the United States with a plan for ten major public works projects and a plan for industrial development, both of which were to be financed through the International Bank for Reconstruction and Development (the World Bank) and the Export-Import Bank. U.S. Treasury Secretary John W. Snyder went to Mexico in the first fortnight of December 1946 and immediately entered into detailed discussions with Ramón Beteta, Torres Bodet, and other high officials of the new administration. At an important meeting between Snyder and Beteta on December 5, Mexico agreed to continue to meet its financial obligations, to come to a rapid agreement on the repayment of Lend Lease loans, to allow free movement of investment, and to defend the fixed exchange rate; in return, the new administration was invited to submit possible projects to the U.S. embassy for evaluation. The Mexican account of the meeting mentions a "verbal offer" and an agreement in principle by Secretary Snyder to finance pet projects to last through Alemán's term of office. The issue of foreign finance was pressing because in the last eight months of the Avila Camacho administration the gold and foreign exchange holdings of the Banco de México had decreased from $372 million to $256 million.

The Alemán administration approached the United States for 1.7 billion pesos for the National Irrigation Commission for construction of the Alvaro Obregón Dam on the Yaqui River in Sonora,

the El Marquez Dam in Tehuantepec, and the Falcón Dam on the
Rio Bravo. The plan was for these projects to irrigate 3.7 million
acres of new farmland. Another 119 million pesos would build hydroelectric plants. Mexico would match these funds with 1.5 billion pesos of its own funds. One and one-half million hectares of
new land would be brought under cultivation. The engineer J. L.
Savage, formerly with the U.S. Bureau of Reclamation, served as
the consulting engineer on these projects.

There was an important change in Alemán's irrigation plan.
The old way of building irrigation systems was based upon a 1926
law that shifted the cost of irrigation projects to the landholders
over a relatively short period, thus increasing land taxes and water
revenues to help pay for construction. President Alemán's approach
stressed the role of the state in funding these projects, issuing the
contracts for them, and underwriting the necessary loans. Thus the
cost of the projects was shifted away from the immediate benefi-
ciary in the private sector to the tax base. Since it was widely believed that this would increase production and lead to a decrease
in the cost of food for the domestic consumer, the entire community was thought to benefit. Since the minister of hydraulic resources was a friend of the private landowners, the new law was a
windfall to the private sector and a setback to the ejidos.

The plan for a complex of irrigation projects for the northwest
was consciously based upon the success of the Tennessee Valley
Authority during the New Deal. The projects consisted of a dam
on the Fuerte River in Sinaloa, the completion of the Chihuahua-
Pacific Railway, and port works in Topolobampo, Manzanillo, and
Tampico. Further improvements were planned for the Isthmus of
Tehuantepec, including a transisthmian highway, as well as for port
works at Salina Cruz and Puerto México. There was also a plan for
an oil pipeline between Minatitlán and Salina Cruz. Industrial
projects included a gas pipeline between Poza Rica and Mexico City,
which would—according to the U.S. engineering firm E. Jolly Poe
and Associates—capture natural gas that was being wasted. This
project was particularly important to Mexican Light and Power for
the generation of electricity in thermal plants for the capital. There
was a proposal by the Chemical Construction Corporation for a
sulfate of ammonia plant. A coking plant with fifty-one ovens for
ASARCO was also included as a Mexican project.

NAFISA had been running the Nueva Compañía de Chapala's
Colimilla Dam since 1938, and there was a proposal to increase its
generating capacity. In addition, seventeen important enterprises

in Monterrey—operating through Gas Industrial—wanted a gas pipeline from Reynosa to Monterrey to bring U.S. natural gas to that industrial city. At the time, it was not known that Mexico was rich in this resource. There was also a proposal to upgrade the textile industry. The total cost of these projects initially was estimated at $180 million, soon to be increased to $240 million, to be financed over twenty years at 4 percent interest. The U.S. diplomats acknowledged that the overall figure could be reached only over many years.[37]

As U.S. Ambassador Walter Thurston and Beteta approached these discussions, Beteta revealed a degree of lingering economic nationalism by linking the question of the exchange rate and exchange controls to the loan. Beteta noted that the drain on the Banco de México's reserves was so rapid, especially for "expensive luxury goods" such as automobiles, consumer durables, and furs, that Mexico would have to look at exchange controls. Ambassador Thurston leaped to the attack: "I stated that in my opinion the new Mexican regime had gotten off to a brilliant start." The ambassador complimented President Alemán on his inauguration speech and on his new policies toward labor and capital. However, in the ambassador's view, the threat of exchange controls to preserve foreign exchange for industrial investment rather than opulent consumption was intolerable: "I stated that I would venture to urge that the greatest care be taken not to nullify the good start and that if the slightest doubt existed as to the propriety or the advisability of any such action as that which he mentioned, my advice would be to abandon the projected action instantly." The point was not lost upon Beteta. According to the U.S. account, "Licenciado Beteta stated that my remarks were approximately what he had expected, that they had clarified his own thinking, and that he would abandon completely the idea of tampering with the tariff or Trade Agreement."[38]

The proposals reached President Truman's desk by the middle of December, and the prospective loans became tied into complex negotiations over PEMEX; the project was then submitted to the Export-Import Bank on February 26, 1947, for $175 million even though the Export-Import Bank had indicated their willingness to loan only $50 million when President Alemán had visited Washington.[39] Mexico was financing these projects through dollar loans that Nacional Financiera would underwrite and administer.

At the heart of this agreement with Washington was Mexico's rapidly deteriorating international account. The country had been on a roller coaster ride in the international arena. The average accrued net increase on the Banco de México's reserves had been about $9 million per annum. The reserves then jumped to an average of $46 million between 1943 and 1946. This forced savings was a result of Mexico's contracts to sell a long list of products to the United States at fixed prices under conditions of wartime rationing. As conditions returned to normal, Mexico's reserves fell by $85 million in 1946 alone. Mexico also faced an outflow of about $20 million per annum in servicing its $447 million in international obligations.[40] The situation was not critical at the moment since the Banco de México held $262 million in gold, silver, and foreign exchange by the end of 1946. Indeed, income tax receipts had increased by 600 percent during World War II. However, it was easy to see that the servicing requirements would consume the nation's reserves in the near future.

Basing the Mexican desire for postwar development projects upon financing from the United States meant that U.S. rules had to be followed. Therefore, even after the period of wartime controls, the U.S. embassy continued to play a determining role in accessing the viability of projects in Mexico since the IMF, the World Bank, the Export-Import Bank, and private U.S. banks all required the embassy's imprimatur before considering specific loans. The minister of hydraulic resources, Adolfo Orive de Alba, cooperated closely with Merwin L. Bohan, counsellor for economic affairs, Lew B. Clark, commercial attaché, and Horace H. Braun, economic analyst, in evaluating all loan proposals.[41] Detailed U.S. involvement in the assessment of Mexican development projects, which had started as an aid to importers in finding their way through the maze of wartime regulations, was rapidly becoming a normal part of the postwar period. And at one level it worked. In addition to the first wave of loans at the beginning of the Alemán administration, President Truman wrote to President Alemán in 1950 telling him that the Export-Import Bank would extend to Mexico another $150 million in loans.[42]

The Alemán administration, however, did not rely exclusively upon official channels to attract foreign capital to Mexico. Alemán put one of his closest friends and business partners, Francisco Buch de Parada, in charge of attracting private U.S. business to Mexico. Together they made a brilliant selection as they looked to U.S. business. Donald Nelson was a former Sears, Roebuck executive who had organized the War Production Board (WPB) to boost production for the war effort without offending vested interests in the various industries involved. By 1943, Nelson had staffed the WPB with some eight hundred "dollar-a-year-men" who looked after their industries' interests even as they organized production for the war effort.[43] Nelson was not as open to labor: Stanley Hillman of the CIO was pushed out, and the Truman committee's criticism of pro-business attitudes was ignored. This, however, was not a disadvantage in postwar Mexico.

President Alemán and Buch de Parada recruited Donald Nelson to come to Mexico to organize a study of the country's industrialization program. Nelson urged the Mexicans to think not only of official sources of capital such as the Export-Import Bank or the World Bank but also of private sources of capital, a point that Under Secretary of State Will Clayton and S. Braden had also been making to the Mexicans. Guy Ray attacked the inadequate performance of the transport sector and also that of PEMEX. "They only produced 45,000,000 bls. per day when they should be able to produce 200,000,000 bls." It was at this point that the two countries' officials agreed that Mexico's standard of living could be increased only if production could generate exports to cover the cost of imports and not by restricting imports. Nelson was able to tell the Mexicans that if they moved in this direction, as they agreed, he "was going from the [State] Department to the White House, where he had an engagement with the President at noon."[44]

At the same time, the new administration was following leads in the private sector. At the end of January 1947 a conference was held in the offices of Turner Construction Company in New York. Representatives of the largest civil engineering and construction companies in the United States were present: in addition to Turner, the heads of Spencer, White and Prentis; Morrison, Knudsen Company (which had just built the Boulder Dam and the Grand Coulee Dam and was building the Sanalona Dam in Sonora); and Raymond Concrete Pile Company. These firms had built many of the most important engineering projects during the war.[45] Thus support for the new projects went to the top of the two administrations and was topped off by personal meetings.

Presidential Visits

President Truman visited Mexico City from March 3 to 6, 1947. Ed Pauley, a close friend of Truman and a man that Miguel Alemán's confidant Miguel Ordorica referred to as *el gran financiero demó-crato*, served as an informal contact between the two presidents in establishing the groundwork for the visit.[46] In preparation for the visit, President Alemán made such an effort to clean up the city that *Ultimas Noticias* suggested that similar care be forthcoming, "just as though Mr Truman always lived among us." The visit was a success. Apparently, the two presidents took a liking to each other. Upon his arrival, Truman gamely tried to pronounce "Tenochtitlán," and his effort served to break the ice with his audience at the airport. A series of state occasions and receptions was topped off by the U.S. president's dramatic gesture of laying a wreath at the monument to the Niños Heroes, the child martyrs of the U.S. invasion of Mexico in 1847. As Foreign Minister Torres Bodet put it, President Truman "threw a bridge across the chasm of the past."[47] Clearly, the Good Neighbor policy had created a considerable residue of good will among the Mexican population.

When the Mexican president returned the visit to the United States, he was treated very well. On May Day, 1947, President Alemán had a meeting with George Marshall aboard the presidential yacht. Miguel Jr. got to meet with Babe Ruth, the famous baseball player. The elder Alemán received honorary degrees from the University of Missouri at Kansas City and Columbia University in New York. He reviewed the army cadets at West Point, meeting there a man who would eventually become one of the United States' most successful political generals, Maxwell Taylor. There was even a parade for the Mexican president in New York City.[48] President Truman attended a reception for him at the Mexican embassy in Washington.[49] President Alemán also had a private meeting with the "F Street Forum," described by his aides as "the best people in Washington."[50] While in New York City, he met with William Oldenburger, director of the National City Bank, who invited him to the University Club of New York.[51]

This VIP treatment demonstrated that an understanding between the United States and the Alemán administration had been achieved. Most importantly, at a banquet for the private sector in New York City, given by Thomas W. Palmer and Jerome S. Hess, and again in a talk to the Pan American Union at the Waldorf-Astoria Hotel, President Alemán stressed collective security and Mexico's openness to foreign investors: "American capital that really means to share in the life of Mexico; that is, willing to observe its laws and be satisfied with a fair profit, without selfish greed or the illusion of becoming a law unto itself, shall be welcome to Mexico and will derive all of the advantages that American citizens who are cooperating with us in the economic development of my country are actually enjoying."[52]

The U.S. trip may have helped President Alemán gain increased political legitimacy within Mexico. As the first civilian president of Mexico in decades, he was something of an unknown quantity. He had been a loyal follower of both Presidents Cárdenas and Avila Camacho; however, his selection had taken place under the cloud of events at León. His preinauguration statements had been fairly bland, stressing simply his desire to modernize the country and increase production as a way of reducing costs, especially in the agricultural sector.[53] Very soon, however, the plans he had in mind for Mexico emerged.

The Rise of the Entrepreneurs and Technocrats

Former president Cárdenas did not attend the Alemán inauguration, although he paid a courtesy call on the new president a few days later. No cabinet posts went to Cardenistas, if one accepts that both Ramón Beteta and Nazario Ortíz Garza had shifted their loyalties and ideology significantly away from Cardenismo since 1940. Alemán kept his cabinet appointments to himself until the last moment. Some appointees, such as Carlos Novoa, the new director of the Banco de México, apparently did not know of their luck before the announcements.

Labor and left-wing PRI members were forced out, with only two exceptions: Mario Souza of the agrarian department and Adolfo Orive de Alba, of hydraulic resources.[54] Orive de Alba was an engineer from Mexico City who had been a member of the National Irrigation Commission. Almost at once, workers and labor leaders found that their unsolicited views on matters touching the economic life of the country were unwelcome.[55] Things had changed considerably from the 1930s when ambassadors complained about being kept waiting while President Cárdenas interviewed Indians and workers. Lombardo Toledano and his associates were denied a presidential audience, much less a job.

The next surprise was that President Alemán appointed a number of people from business, law, and academia to top posts, thus avoiding the Left-labor people within the governing party. Many of the appointees were either wealthy in their own right or had been working for those who were. Alemán brought his long-term lieutenant from Veracruz, Adolfo Ruíz Cortines, into the powerful Ministry of the Interior. Ruíz Cortines's loyalty had been unquestioned since 1935. Carlos I. Serrano headed the other sensitive unit at the center of power in Mexico, the Dirección Federal de Seguridad. As one CIA report described the "political police organization" and its leader, "Serrano, an unscrupulous man, is actively engaged in various illegal enterprises such as the narcotics traffic. He is considered astute, intelligent and personable, although his methods violate every principle of established government administration."[56]

Former president and General Abelardo Rodríguez returned as head of Teléfonos de México (in 1948). Alemán turned to Antonio J. Bermudez to head PEMEX; the owner of substantial cattle interests, movie houses, and properties, Bermudez was close to General Guerrero and Sr. Ballina, who were leading capitalists in Chihuahua. His political career had been short: mayor of Ciudad Juárez, 1941–1944, and treasurer of Chihuahua, 1944–1946. Agustín García López was a surprise choice as minister of transportation and communications. For the previous sixteen years he had been a lawyer representing the employers in labor disputes for the foreign electric power interests. After George Messersmith retired from the U.S. Foreign Service, he went back to Mexico as director of the Mexican Light and Power Company, and García López worked for him in that capacity. As one diplomat succinctly put it, "He is certainly not a pro labor man."

The new head of the country's educational system, Manuel Gual Vidal, was a professor of law at UNAM who had been a manager of the Mexican Bankers Association, a trustee of Monte de Piedad, and a legal representative of the "José de la Mora interests," which consisted of the Banco de Discuento, the Atoyac Textile Company, and the Mexican Northwest Railway. His income from the de la Mora interests alone amounted to more than 100,000 pesos per year. A central economic portfolio, Finance, went to the former Cardenista Ramón Beteta. He earned a bachelor's degree at the University of Texas (Phi Beta Kappa) in 1923; he was viewed by U.S. diplomats as anti-U.S., in part because of the racism he experienced as a student in Austin. Married at the time to a citizen of the United States who took an anti-imperialist position, and speaking English with a Texas accent, he was something of a problem for U.S. diplomats. Another appointee, Antonio Ruiz Galindo, was a prominent businessman with interests in finance, manufacturing, the hotel industry, and property. He was also believed to be financially overextended as he took up his new post as minister of the national economy.[57]

By naming Josué Sáenz as director of credit within the Ministry of Finance, Alemán was moving an heir apparent to the Sáenz interests into a central position, one in which he would have considerable influence in the financial arena. Similarly, the appointment of F. Jimenez O'Farrill as ambassador to the United Kingdom linked the government to the powerful family of Romulo O'Farrill.[58] The new ambassador to the United States was Antonio Espinosa de los Monteros. Born in the Federal District in 1903, he attended Gettysburg College in Pennsylvania and then Harvard University. His English was excellent, and his experience as the head of Nacional Financiera was also important. He was known as a cool and aloof banker in Mexico, and his antipathy toward former President Cárdenas was ill concealed; someone with similar views in the United States would have belonged to the Republican Party, if not to the National Association of Manufacturers.[59] It is therefore surprising to learn of his warm reception by the Truman administration. As the U.S. secretary of state explained to the president, "Because [of] his friendly attitude and understanding of the United States and his deep desire to collaborate with us, Ambassador Messersmith has recommended him very highly."[60] The tone of his correspondence with U.S. officials was positively gushy. In one letter to President Truman's private secretary, Charles G. Ross, he began: "My dear Charlie (that's what you are to me)."[61] Clearly the tone of the administration was changing, in spite of the appointment of former PCM member Professor Germán Parra as undersecretary of the national economy.

The most impressive appointments of the Alemán government were, not unexpectedly, in the area of foreign relations. Manuel Tello was a respected professional diplomat who headed the Ministry of Foreign Affairs. Already a seasoned diplomat with experience in Antwerp, in Geneva, at the ILO, and at San Francisco in 1945 when the United Nations was founded, he took the office for the first of three times. Jaime Torres Bodet, another professional diplomat of high quality and a writer, became director-general of UNESCO. With his team in place, and his overall agreement with the United States explicit, Miguel Alemán was ready to unleash his domestic program on Mexico.

Notes

1. Perry, *Juárez and Díaz*, 12–17.

2. Henry S. Watterman to secretary of state, January 4, 1946, USNA/59, 812.00/1-446.

3. *Novedades*, April 10, 1946. S. Walter Washington to secretary of state, "Murder of Ex-Governor Rodolfo T. Loaiza of Sinaloa," April 13, 1946, USNA/59, 812.00/4-1346; C. H. Bateman to Neville Butler, March 14, 1945, PRO/FO, 371/44478.

4. "Memorandum from the Civil Attaché [Kenneth M. Crosby] Regarding Unfortunate Shooting of Participants in a Popular Meeting of Protest in the City of León, Guanajuato," January 8, 1946, USNA/59, 812.00/1-846.

5. George Kennan to secretary of state, January 7, 1946, USNA/59, 812.00/1-74.

6. *Novedades*, January 4, 1945.

7. *La Prensa*, January 16, 1946.

8. Messersmith to Carrigan, January 16, 1946, GSM Papers.

9. Guy W. Ray to secretary of state, "The Present Campaign and the Political Situation in Mexico," January 15, 1946, USNA /59, 812.00/1-1546.

10. J. Edgar Hoover was circulating the same State Department report on the events of January 2, 1946, in León, Guanajuato, under the letterhead of the FBI, thereby giving the impression that the FBI was on top of events in that provincial Mexican city. J. Edgar Hoover to Fredrick B. Lyon, chief, Division of Foreign Activity Correlation, Department of State, report entitled "Political Riot in León, Guanajuato, Mexico, January 2, 1946," January 21, 1946, USNA/59, 812.00/1-2146.

11. Messersmith to secretary of state, February 1, 1946, USNA/59, 812.00/2-146.

12. Messersmith to Braden, January 26, 1946, USNA/59, 812.00/1-2646. *Excélsior, Novedades, El Universal*, and *La Prensa*, January 23, 1946.

13. Even in campaign, U.S. diplomats recorded "President elect Alemán visits the United States regularly every few months, especially Hollywood." Guy W. Ray to Briggs, Braden, and Woodward, July 30, 1946, Truman Library, HST Official File, 146.

14. These biographical data come from an anonymous official biography prepared for the Mexican president, AGN, RP/MAV, 131/2; an FBI report, Hoover to Berle, "Biographies of the Members of the Cabinet of the Mexican Government," December 16, 1941, USNA/59, 812.00/31845; and Camp, *Mexican Political Biographies, 1935–1975*, 13–14.

15. John W. F. Dulles, *Yesterday in Mexico*, 607.

16. Hoover to Berle, "Biographies of the Members of the Cabinet of the Mexican Government," December 16, 1941, USNA/59, 812.00/31845.

17. Thurston to secretary of state, April 24, 1947, USNA/59, 812.001Aleman, Miguel/4-2447.

18. George Messersmith to Nelson Rockefeller, April 27, 1945, USNA/59, 812.00/4-2745.

19. This secret document revealed the reasons behind the Mexican economic strategy as the two countries entered into negotiations in the Mexican-American Committee for Economic Cooperation. Messersmith to Philip W. Bonsal, May 14, 1943, USNA/59, 812.50/562.

20. Messersmith to Acheson, January 12, 1946, USNA/59, 812.00/1-1246.

21. Guy W. Ray to secretary of state, April 25, 1950, 712.00/4-2550.

22. Ibid.

23. Ibid.

24. *New York Times*, June 1, 1946.

25. Guy Ray to secretary of state, October 3, 1945, USNA/59, 812.00/10-345; *Novedades*, October 3, 1945.

26. Thurston to secretary of state, April 24, 1947, USNA/59, 812.001 Aleman, Miguel/4-2447.

27. Guy Ray to secretary of state, November 6, 1945, USNA/59, 812.00/11-645, and November 7, 1945, USNA/59, 812.00/11-745.

28. U.S. officials used their contacts to assess the loyalties of zone commanders on the eve of the selection in 1945. They judged that nine of the thirty-one governors and seven of the thirty-three zone commanders still maintained primary loyalty to Cárdenas. See Raleigh A. Gibson to secretary of state, March 24, 1945, USNA/59. 812.00/3-2445.

29. Franklin C. Gowen to secretary of state, June 30, 1953, USNA/59, 712.00-6-3053. Ruíz Cortines ended these payments.

30. See, for example, Edwin Lieuwen, "Depoliticization of the Mexican Revolutionary Army, 1915–1940," in Ronfeldt, ed., *The Modern Mexican Military*, 61.

31. Juan Gutíerrez to President Alemán, January 3, 1947, AGN, RP/MAV, 523/12.

32. Bateman to Bevin, December 9, 1946, PRO/371, 51590.

33. President Alemán to the Confederación de Camaras Nacionales de Comercio, AGN, RP/MAV, 523/5.

34. Lew B. Clark, commercial attaché, to secretary of state, May 9, 1947, USNA/59, 812.50/5-947.

35. Messersmith, unpublished manuscript, GSM Papers.

36. "Notes on the improvement of the earnings situation of the Mexican Light and Power Company, Limited," Box 27, item #131, GSM Papers.

37. Ambassador Thurston to secretary of state, "Foreign Office note #2542 of December 16, 1946 and Ministry of Finance memorandum of December 14, 1946," December 18, 1946. USNA/59, 812.51/12-1846.

38. Thurston to secretary of state, December 30, 1946, USNA/59, 812.51/12-1846.

39. Foreign Office note, December 18, 1946, and D. R. Bell to Herman W. Braun, July 14, 1947, Truman Library, PSF #130.

40. The 1941 claims commission still had 21 million outstanding; 100 million was owed on the European petroleum settlement; 120 million was owed to the Export-Import Bank and another 76 million was in the pipeline; interest on these amounted to 60 million over the period; another 50 million was in direct external debt and interest; and the railroad debt was still 50 million. Banco de México, *Transacciones internacionales de México*; Secretaría de Gobernación, *Seis años de actividad nacional*.

41. "Analysis and Comment upon the Mexican Government's Six Year External Financing Program," January 8, 1947, USNA/59, 812.51/1-847.

42. Truman to Alemán, September 1, 1950, AGN, RP/MAV, 530/5295.

43. Brody, "The New Deal and World War II," 289.

44. Memorandum of conversation between Donald Nelson, Francisco Buch de Parada, Guy Ray, and William G. MacLean; the latter two were of the State Department's Division of Mexican Affairs, April 29, 1947, USNA/ 59, 812.50/4-2947.

45. Eduardo Hidalgo of the law firm Curtis Mallet-Prevost, Colt and Mosle to President Alemán, March 7, 1947, AGN, RP/MAV.

46. Miguel Ordorica appeared to act as a personal channel between these key figures. See his reports on the September 1949 meeting between R. Beteta and Eugene Black, president of the IBRD, AGN, RP/MAV, 606.3/ 247.

47. Bohan to secretary of state, March 9, 1947, USNA/59, 812.50-3-1347.

48. The favor was returned in 1948 when General Taylor visited Mexico and was awarded the Order of Merit, 1st Class, at the Military College of Mexico.

49. The photographic record of the visit may be seen in the USNA/ RG 208, Photographic Records of the Office of War Information.

50. The text of the president's speech at the banquet was reported in *El Nacional*, March 5, 1947. Notes on the president's assurances to foreign investors—a theme he stressed even at West Point—are located in Morris L. Cooke to the president, April 30, 1947, AGN, RP/MAV, 135.2/ 37-2.

51. William Oldenburger, director of the National City Bank of New York City, to President Alemán, March 2, 1947, AGN, RP/MAV, 135.2/5-6.

52. Morris L. Cooke to Alemán, April 30, 1947, AGN, RP/MAV, 135.2/ 37-5.

53. See the "Fourteen Point Program" of the president-elect, *El Universal*, November 17, 1946.

54. The president's immediate staff consisted of Rogerio de la Selva, secretario de la presidencia; Roberto Amoros G., sub-secretario de la presidencia; Luis G. Larrañaga, oficial mayor de la secretaría de la presidencia; and Arnulfo Torres y González, secretario particular.

55. One such example was when the workers of the Julio Albert y Cía. asked for an interview in May to discuss economic matters; it took a month before they were told that the president was too busy to see them. Petition to Alemán, May 27, 1941, AGN, RP/MAV, 432/174; Alemán to the union, June 11, 1947.

56. CIA, *Situation Report: Mexico*, January 24, 1951, 66.

57. Horace Brown to secretary of state, December 4, 1946, USNA/59, 812.00/12-1246.

58. In addition to controlling the *Novedades* newspapers, the O'Farrill family controlled automobile distributorships and other interests. Romulo O'Farrill to the president, June 1, 1949, AGN, RP/MAV, 606.3/235; Rodolfo Sánchez Taboada to the president, February 2, 1950, AGN, RP/MAV, 437.3/ 224.

59. Acheson to Truman, September 10, 1945, Truman Library, Official File, #146.

60. Secretary of State James Byrnes to President Truman, November 2, 1945, Truman Library, File 146.

61. Antonio Espinosa de los Monteros to Charles G. Ross, March 25, 1947, Truman Library, File 146.

4

Alemán's Counterrevolution

The Winds of December:
The Legislative Program

President Alemán used the early days of his administration to unleash a legislative program that represented a profound reversal of many central reforms of the Mexican Revolution. So deep were some of those innovations that it is difficult not to accept that the Mexican Thermidor had arrived. December 1946 saw both houses of the Mexican Congress engaged in a frenzy of activity. Thirty-nine laws were passed before adjournment on the last day of the year. All of the laws were drafted in the executive branch, and stories abounded that legislators voted, in many cases, without having had the opportunity to read the bills upon which they were passing judgment. Among the more important bills were the reform of Article 27, the reorganization of the executive branch, the extension of the vote to women, reform of the social security law, reorganization of the charters of PEMEX and Bellas Artes, an agricultural credit program, and a commission on colonization and military structure. In addition, there were new budget regulations. The frenzy of legislative effort continued for some time. A major newspaper claimed "a new world record" as twenty-four laws were passed in only six hours.[1]

The Land and Article 27

The business and financial communities were against the Cárdenas land reform program in general and the *ejido colectivo* in particular. This sector has argued—with absolute consistency from the 1930s to the present day—that such semicollective farms, really the continuation of the age-old tradition of village agriculture, were terribly inefficient. Although there have been some very interesting rebuttals to this business perspective, in the main, economists and business analysts have tended to agree that the accountants' logic doomed the *ejidos colectivos*. Attempts to destroy the land reform program were frequently based upon partial measurements of efficiency relating immediate inputs to outputs without reference to broader social measurements of misery in the countryside or of the overall social cost of pushing millions of peasants off the land and into urban slums.[2]

The Avila Camacho administration had already withdrawn considerable practical support from land reform, as had President Cárdenas by the end of his term. However, popular enthusiasm still placed severe limitations upon counterreform projects. For example, Eduardo Villaseñor set off storms of protest when, at the 1945 bankers' convention at Guadalajara, he publicly called for changes to Article 27. Although his government backed off in the face of the opposition that his statement precipitated, the situation quickly changed after President Alemán's inauguration.

Only two days after the inauguration, changes to the agrarian code were proposed by the new administration as amendments to Article 27, and they became law in February. The very first provision was that landholders could receive certificates of exemption, thus allowing them to apply for a writ (*amparo*) protecting their property from the land reform. Alemán's reform did not go as far as the Acción Nacional (AN) had been demanding; the AN wanted all private land holdings to carry automatic injunctions, a proposal tantamount to the repeal of Article 27.

Under Alemán's proposal, the size of individual ejido grants was increased from 6 to 10 hectares of irrigated land and from 12 to 20 hectares of arable land. Private landowners could now increase their holdings to 100 hectares of irrigated land or 200 hectares of arable land. Up to 300 hectares of sugarcane land, or land dedicated to perennial crops, could be protected, and special concessions were granted to protect forestry projects and cattle stations to 50,000 hectares. Additionally, 5,000 hectares could be removed from the land reform if doing so would be useful for industry.[3] Improvements to land provided a basis for the exemption certificates. Although these changes were justified by arguing that the parcelization of land into very small plots was unproductive, they appeared to many to be a reversal of land reform by administrative decree.

It was unclear how far Miguel Alemán wanted to go with these changes. When General Cándido Aguilar, the head of the Comisión Coordinadora de Asuntos Campesinos, stated on July 21, 1947, that ejiditarios who did not cultivate their land would have it taken away from them, it created another storm of protest. Since Cándido Aguilar—Carranza's son-in-law—had protected Alemán the elder, many feared that he was expressing the president's candid opinion.[4] When General Rodolfo Sánchez Taboada, president of the PRI, tried to reassure the country, his words were somewhat unfortunate: "Not even the President of the Republic will make a backward step in agrarian policy, nor is there any thought of taking lands away because of the charges that they are not being worked. The president of the ruling party clearly conceded that peasants often are unable to cultivate their lands because of the lack of credit facilities."[5]

As late as December 15, 1949, the Partido Popular and its union, the UGOCM, under Juan Manuel Elizondo, tried to use his position as acting president of the Senate to take exception to the land reform; these provisions were debated, at times rejected, but usually approved. By contrast, the Confederación Nacional de Campesinos president, Roberto Barrios, argued the syllogism that since the PRI could never do anything against the interests of the peasants, and since the authorities wanted these innovations, the changes must be supported.

The president shifted the terms of the debate considerably as he changed Article 27. He claimed that his innovations were aimed at protecting the small farmer against the ejiditario, calling farmers and ranchers "the most unprotected social class in Mexico." He asserted that high prices were the result of corruption and inertia in the ejido sector.[6] To aid private farmers would increase supply and reduce the cost of living. At this point even the language began to differentiate between the *reforma agraria* of the past and Alemán's technologically driven *reforma agrícola*. The president glossed over the fact that the prices of basic food products were controlled and, therefore, that artificially low commodity prices reflected a conscious government decision to have the countryside subsidize the urban-industrial development program. He also refused to recognize that ample credit together with agricultural extension work—and not merely the creation of agricultural bureaucracies in urban office buildings—were essential in order to increase rural production.

Again in November 1949, several PRI deputies proposed bills further limiting the land reform by exempting land for the development of lumbering, livestock, mining, and quarrying. The Partido Popular and the UGOCM immediately attacked the proposal. The CNC worked within the Congress to limit some of these changes, which it accomplished behind the scenes when the bill emerged for reading on December 15. Still, the government's opposition to the land reform meant that there would be little enforcement of existing statutes.

Perhaps just as important as these fundamental legal restrictions on the land reform program was the attitude that the Alemán administration brought with it to power. The new president knew which side he wanted to be on in the perpetual struggle between the landowners and the landless. It is very clear from the administration's attentive treatment of complaints against *paracaidistas* (those who carry out de facto occupations of underutilized land) that such grassroots demands received no sympathy from the Alemán administration.[7]

In the countryside, the struggle over land reform was frequently brutal. In Yucatán, on January 17, 1949, one conflict came to a head. A group called the Frente de Defensa de la Industria Henequenera was locked in battle with the government monopoly, the Henequeneros de Yucatán. The state governor, José González Beytia, and the manager of the Henequeneros, Santiago Leal Acero, were not able to control the local newspaper, the *Diario de Yucatán*. On January 10, 1949, the Frente had been able to publish an open letter to President Alemán from the ejidatarios in Hoctun in which it charged the Henequeneros with working against the interests of the ejidatarios, whose leader, José Vallejos Polanco, had been kidnapped and was being held without charges in Merida. The henequen workers alleged that the manager and his relatives had become millionaires, while they were working for a pittance. Their hopelessness was sealed by the fact that they were allowed to sell only to the government monopoly. They complained that they had no homes, no bread, and that their children died from hunger. Moreover, the hospital maintained by the Henequeneros refused to admit them unless they paid, even though the employers were legally bound to treat the henequen workers.[8] By January 18, the Frente reported that the police had barred entrance to Merida by the ejidatarios and that José Vallejos Polanco had been kidnapped on January 16 to prevent a planned demonstration for the following day. Two days later, the *Diario de Yucatán* reported that an additional nine workers had been kidnapped and tortured by the state police. Petitions from the workers were directed to Mario Souza, the chief of the agrarian department, for transmission to the president. The Partido Socialista del Sureste, by now totally submissive to the PRI, worked to discount the impact of the charges made by the Hoctun ejidatarios. The U.S. consul in Merida reported, "It is the opinion of certain well informed persons in Merida, that Souza will probably return to Mexico City richer by several thousand pesos, and that he will do nothing to interfere with the local officials."[9] The central government found nothing objectionable in this situation.

Changes were more forthcoming on the business side of agriculture. Immediately after his inauguration, President Alemán was faced with a campaign against the Nacional Distribuidora y Reguladora S.A. (N.D.&R.). The Confederación de Camaras Nacionales de Comercio (CCNC), with Ernesto J. Amescua as president, launched a campaign to disband the N.D.&R. Arguing that the organization was monopolistic and sustained higher than market prices, the CCNC saw no reason for the N.D.&R. to exist, and it coordinated its campaign with Abelardo Rodríguez's anti-Communist campaign of 1946. The CCNC published pamphlets such as *El Reto Comunista al Mundo Cristiano* and *La Intervención de Estado en el Proceso Económico*, written by the extremely conservative U.S. politician Claire Boothe Luce, as well as their own *Carta Semanal*.[10] The president supported the CCNC initiative.

The most important battleground over land reform was agricultural finance. One Mexican innovation for financing development was the requirement that banks invest half of their demand deposits on productive development projects instead of simply finance the purchase of existing property. Rather than merely bidding up the price of existing assets, the idea was to create something new. This had been one of the most effective devices to support development programs during the economic nationalist phase of the Mexican Revolution. The policy was undercut in several ways in 1950. The reserve level for productive investments in the future— which had already been cut from 50 percent—was further reduced from 30 to 20 percent, even though, at the time, 60 percent of the existing loan portfolios were still dedicated to productive investments. Devastatingly, loans for agriculture were then removed from the category of productive investment, forcing the banks to loan even less to small agriculture. Thus the decapitalization of small agriculture was state policy.[11] The new administration clearly favored agribusiness over small farmers, and still less ejiditarios. Credit was reduced for the ejido sector, especially for the Banco Nacional de Crédito Ejidal, and funds were shifted to finance modern items such as tractors and irrigation systems for private farmers. Still, about 40 percent of the agricultural subsidies were linked to a strategy of having the rural sector produce cheap food for the cities. Between 1947 and 1950 there was also a significant shifting of funds to finance agribusiness for export.[12] The gap between the ejido sector and the agribusiness sector rapidly became a chasm as the impact of these policies spread.

The financial records of *ejidos colectivos* that have survived from the period show how the system worked. The Unión de Sociedades Locales de Crédito Colectivo Ejidal Eldorado in Sinaloa was comprised of one thousand growers. They owed the Banco Nacional de Credito Ejidal 4.5 million pesos in 1949. Luis G. Legorreta, the director of the private Banco Nacional de México, did a study of the operation of the ejido for the president. He concluded that by the standards of agribusiness the ejido should be able to produce 40 percent more sugar than it was producing. His study was an analysis of productivity based on optimum utilization of inputs: seeds, fertilizers, and planting and harvesting technology. It glossed over the fact that the government expected the ejido to pay for water, for new equipment, and for drainage ditches to increase production even as these costs were being removed for the private cultivator. Finally, the government dictated the price the ejido would receive for production. Not surprisingly, Legorreta indicated that the Banco Nacional de México would finance the mill (*centrál*), but not the producers' ejido, as was normal banking policy. These policies meant that, in spite of the recent harvest, the ejido was bereft of funds by the time of the next planting.[13]

As in the case of the workers' administration of the railroads or of PEMEX a few years before, "economic reality" was an odd mixture of government pricing policies that limited the ejido's income—by refusing to let prices rise to reflect demand—yet allowed the market to force full payment on the expenditures side. By contrast, the government was giving grants of money freely to a wide variety of private industries and individual entrepreneurs. Furthermore, the government used the most hostile accounting and billing practices where the collective ejidos were involved. All the while, business analysts characterized the ejidos simply as inefficient.

Pro-business Orientation

The Alemán government quickly set a tone that favored business. The president was fond of saying that there was no point in talking about distribution until there was something to distribute. Poverty was so great in Mexico that few disagreed with the need to industrialize and that this meant policies that favored business enterprises. Nothing so irritated business as the previous close association between President Cárdenas and labor leaders. Therefore, one of Alemán's first changes was to absolutely freeze Lombardo Toledano out of the presidential circle. Whereas Avila Camacho would usually see him, Alemán wanted nothing to do with Lombardo. The only sop to the old labor establishment was to name his old assistant, Alejandro Carrillo, as head of the municipal government of Mexico City, the DDF.

The attitude of the new government toward business clearly had changed. "British businessmen are unanimous in their testimony to a visible change in the tone of public offices. This is especially true of the labour boards, the Ministry of the National Economy and the National Railroads. Employees are now punctual, attentive and courteous. Matters which normally took months to settle are now promptly dealt with and where reference to higher authority is required, the lapse of time is noticeably shortened."[14]

The implementation of administrative policies also became more favorable to business. The federal system of conciliation and arbitration was a battleground between labor and capital. There had been a tilt toward labor under Cárdenas when the boards were set up with representatives of three parties: labor, business, and government. In the early years, the government representatives had tended to vote with labor. This changed after 1946. The same pattern could be seen in taxation courts. The Confederación de Camaras de Comercio boasted that of the 527 cases they had defended before the Tribunal Fiscal de la Federación in 1947, only 26 had been resolved against their interests.[15]

Alemán made a systematic effort to welcome foreign businessmen to Mexico and to extend to important prospective investors every amenity during their stay. A steady stream of captains of industry took advantage of this hospitality; the presidential files contain many effusive letters of gratitude from such figures as R. S. Kersh, vice president of Westinghouse; Clyde E. Weed, vice president of Anaconda Copper; Donald Gilles of Republic Steel; R. R.

Cole, Monsanto Chemical Company; G. C. Wipple, Quaker Oats; Amos B. Foy, Chemical Bank and Trust of New York; Marsden Blos, Bank of America; and William Kuhns, editor of *Banking*, the journal of the American Bankers Association.[16] Acapulco played an increasingly useful role in entertaining visiting dignitaries in order to attract foreign investment.

Some of the most important business executives in the country occupied crucial roles in the public banks and economic agencies. For example, board members on Nacional Financiera in 1951 included Eduardo Suárez of Hardin, Hess and Suárez; Luis Legorreta of BANAMEX; Antonio Arendáriz of Seguros la Provincial; José and Josué Sáenz, the next generation of that powerful family; and Juan Gallardo Moreno of Aseguradora Mexicana S.A.[17] The line between the economic decision makers in the private sector and those in the public sector was indistinct.

Curbing Labor

President Alemán openly avoided attending the CTM's meetings, rallies, and celebrations, even on the day commemorating the expropriation of the petroleum industry. He pursued traditional policies of divide and rule by making rival union leaders—such as Enrique Rangel, secretary general of the CPN, and even Luis Morones of the CROM—welcome in the president's office. After the split developed within the CTM, when the CUT was founded, the president did nothing to prevent the division. The government was quite pleased to see the CTM diminished in strength. U.S. diplomats confirmed this impression in conversations (at the British Boat Club at Xochimilco) with José Barros, an officer in the presidential secretariat, and also in private discussions with Jorge Viesca Palma, secretary to President Alemán.[18]

Almost at once after coming to power, Miguel Alemán moved against people on the left who held official positions. A former Supreme Court justice, Xavier Icasa, told U.S. diplomats that "all of the experienced leftist leaders are being ousted from their former positions." Although displeased with Alemán, he related, they continued to support the president because there was no alternative: "Many of them hope, at least, to obtain posts in the Government which will provide them with a living. He added that he himself expects to have a post in the Presidency soon."[19]

The old problem of *empleomania*—the frantic search for government jobs in an economy bereft of opportunity—had returned with a vengeance after the war as many of the former supporters of Cárdenas and Lombardo Toledano scurried to adapt to the change. As postwar exports declined, leading to a crisis in the current account, the problem of unemployment grew. The role of personal rewards in this process was fundamental. *Pan ó palo* still worked remarkably well in taming labor, as the first strike of the Alemán era demonstrated.

The president selected the petroleum workers as a target in the first moments of his administration. Provocatively by contemporary standards, he announced publicly that strikes or stoppages would not be tolerated. He took this step both because he was already confronted by a work stoppage by petroleum workers and because the petroleum industry was at the vortex of the ideological struggles of the day. Not only had the nationalization of the petroleum resources distressed the president, but also that industry had been at the heart of President Cárdenas's experiments in workers' administration, policies with which President Alemán deeply disagreed. On April 27, 1947, the new president ended the last of those experiments from the Cárdenas era. The public slaughterhouses in the D.F. were removed from the *administración obrera*. They had been administered by workers' committees since 1939. The president blamed the exigencies associated with the hoof-and-mouth disease campaign for the change. The conservative press, however, argued that poor management practices were to blame. All agreed that workers' administration had ended definitively.

The Petroleum Strike

In his inaugural speech, Alemán warned labor that its independence would not be tolerated. Senator Bermúdez was rumored to have accepted the position as head of PEMEX only on the condition that he could clean house. That both he and Ruiz Galindo, the minister of the economy, were businessmen inclined them to have little sympathy for the union movement. Events quickly came to a head. Seventeen days after taking power, Alemán was faced with a work stoppage (*paro*) by the petroleum workers. (A *paro* was less formal than a strike [*huelga*]. Workers called for a *paro* as an intermediate form of bargaining pressure. A strike, however, implied a long legal process by which the company, government, and labor agreed upon a formal conciliation and arbitration.)

The president struck fiercely at the workers. When, on December 19, the petroleum workers' union broke off talks in a dispute over wages, working hours, and the classification of workers, the workers found that the government was waiting for them. Federal troops immediately took over the refineries, pipelines, and oil wells. Troops even began to distribute petroleum products. PEMEX canceled fifty labor contracts, and the press was alerted to support Alemán's moves. Union leaders found that their attempts to gain support from the CTM were fruitless. Lombardo Toledano's astonishing support for the government was crucial in isolating the petroleum workers. Coming just two weeks before the long-touted "Roundtable Conference," the impact upon the labor left was devastating.[20] All of this was Alemán's response to the workers' call for a twenty-four-hour strike. It was also Lombardo Toledano's swan song.

Alemán was adamant in his opposition to the PEMEX workers' demands, and soon he stopped attending even the most innocuous independent labor gatherings. He began to cultivate a far more compliant brand of union leaders, men who came to be known as *charros*, or labor cowboys, after their cavalier attitude toward their members. On January 24, 1947, the president convened a meeting of these more compliant leaders, calling them a Consejo Obrero Nacional. The rules of the game were spelled out. Under the rubric of working for the "economic recuperation of the country" workers were to join forces with the government and not pursue their own interests. The cryptic comment by the president that no sector would be favored under his administration in reality meant that labor would lose official support. President Alemán ignored a deluge of objections to *charrismo* that descended upon his office from disgruntled unionists who thought the government should tolerate independent unionism.[21] (The term *"charro"* for pro-government labor leaders came from the favorite sport of the railroad leader Jesús Díaz de León, who was imposed in 1948.) *El Popular* and especially Lombardo Toledano indulged in a high degree of sophistry by arguing that labor must curb its independence in order to join with other sectors in defending the economy from the forces of imperialism.[22]

The campaign against the petroleum workers' union finally came to fruition when, on December 1, 1949, at its Fourth Ordinary National Congress, the union expelled its left-wing leadership. U.S. diplomats were gleeful as they observed "one of the most significant developments of the year." They viewed the expulsion of Eulalio Ibañez, José Luis H. Andrade, Jesús Chiñas Corón, and Pedro Durán on December 3 as the culmination of the anti-

Oil workers on hunger strike, Mexico City. *Courtesy Hermanos Mayo, Archivo General de la Nación, Mexico City*

Communist campaign that Alemán had initiated just after coming to power. The new CTM leadership immediately severed its ties with the UGOCM, the CTAL, and the WFTU. This victory for the government confirmed a general pattern of strong opposition to wage demands. The U.S. embassy understood the entire official union movement to be moving closer to the moderate program of its favorite union, the Confederación Proletaria Nacional (the Mexican affiliate of the CIT), which had split with the CTM in 1943.[23]

The defeat of the petroleum workers convinced the government to broaden its antilabor efforts. It also precipitated a union reaction that set up an intense period of labor struggle. It was what Kevin Middlebrook called "a defining moment in the evolution of postrevolutionary state-labor relations."[24] On June 17, 1947, the president announced changes to the country's labor laws. Measures were introduced to apply criminal sanctions to those who would strike or failed to live up to a collective labor contract. The business community took heart from this newfound sympathy for their position within the government. The terms of the debate shifted so rapidly that by the summer of 1947 the conservative press was seriously discussing whether the Taft-Hartley law, which outlawed the closed shop in the United States, could be implemented in

Mexico. Business groups, the Acción Nacional, and even foreign investors were pushing for changes to the country's labor laws to favor management.[25] Independent labor leaders such as Juan José Rivera Rojas, the secretary general of the Electrical Power Workers Union, tried to fight against the wave of antiunion sentiment; however, red-baiting undercut their strength. In short, Miguel Alemán set out to dominate the labor leadership and to ensure that labor leaders were accountable to the central government rather than to their members.

The following year, the government felt strong enough to reduce wages for workers in the Atzcapotzalco petroleum refinery. This was a heavy blow to the heart of the union movement, and it was followed by an attack on conditions of health and safety in the refinery. In the 1940s working conditions had been appalling, and, in those days, unions had not accepted a general obligation to oppose unsafe work practices. Yet there had been a few minor victories in this area. Extra wages had been paid to employees in the unhealthy alkaline and isomerization sections of the refinery. Earlier moderate victories had provided that free medicines would be distributed to sick workers. Under the new labor policies, these benefits, including the free medicines, were eliminated.[26] Even middle management lost the bonuses that had been awarded to *empleados de confianza*. The government blamed the Communist influences in Section 35 of the STPRM for precipitating these cuts.[27]

After the defeat of the petroleum workers, the other major unions backed off in shock. An intense period of reassessment followed, and by early 1948 a number of important unions had decided that they had to try to assert their interests. The mining, railroad, and petroleum unions joined together to form the Coalition of Industrial Unions. Astonishingly, they moved toward Lombardo Toledano's CTAL as an alternative to the CTM despite the stance he had taken during the recent petroleum conflict. These independent unions were particularly offended by the government's attempt in February to implement the "Corona thesis," named after the Supreme Court justice who had held that it was illegal to strike if a labor contract was in effect.

In June the miners' union initiated a series of *paros* at the Altos Hornos plant in Monclova. The president backed management by declaring the strike nonexistent. The government decided to go all out against the three unions. The secretary general of the railroad workers' union joined with the president against the majority of the union's radical leadership. Luis Gómez Z., secretary general of the CUT, was jailed on fraud charges. Miners' petitions were also opposed by the Board of Conciliation and Arbitration. Two strikes followed in the telephone industry, one against Telefonos de México S.A. and the other against the Compañía Telefónica y Telegráfica de México, in which the government granted wage increases but applied the principle of not allowing *paros*. The CUT fought for the right to strike. A narrow interpretation of Article 260 of the labor law also emerged to insist upon the principle of "economic equilibrium" thus preventing a union from trying to use the expiration of a strike to improve conditions.

The political climate, violence in organizational disputes, corruption, and the general fragmentation of the union movement all took their toll as unionists became increasingly isolated. Fragmentaton increased beyorid the old split between the CTM and the CROM. In general, unions divided in multiple combinations along two poles: pro- versus anti-*charro* and pro- versus anti-Lombardo. Thus the Confederación Proletaria Nacional (CPN) broke off from the CTM in 1942 in opposition to Lombardo Toledano; at the same time, the Confederación de Obreros y Campesinos de México (COCM) broke away from the CROM. The Confederación Nacional de Trabajadores (CNT) split in 1944 from the CROM, and the Confederación Unica de Trabajadores (CUT) formed in 1947 as the railroad workers and telephonists opposed the *charros* of the CTM. A loose anti-CTM alliance called the Coalición de Organizaciones Obreras y Campesinas (COOC) claimed a large following: CUT (400,000), STFRM (90,000), SITMMSRM (85,000), STPRM (35,000), AOCM (180,000), and the CNE (40,000).[28] In 1948 the Alianza de Obreros y Campesinos de México (AOCM) left the CTM. Finally, in 1949 additional groups left the CUT and the Coalición de Sindicatos Industriales to form the pro-Lombardo UGOCM. The majority of these challenges were against the CTM.[29]

The Split in the CTM

As a result of Alemán's suppression of the PEMEX workers in his first month in office, a split developed in the CTM. Valentín Campa led a dissident group out of the CTM and formed the CUT, which was in reality little more than the railroad workers' union. Deeply opposed to Alemán's repudiation of labor, Campa became one of the government's most outspoken critics. Having been driven out of the PCM in 1940, Campa then departed the CTM into the wilderness of the fragmented Left from where he resisted *charrismo* with great personal courage for decades.

Workers' theater, Mexico City. *Courtesy Hermanos Mayo, Archivo General de la Nación, Mexico City*

The government responded by organizing official demonstrations of workers who supported the Alemán administration in the name of anticommunism. To cite one example, Carlos Romero Sagaón wrote a long and detailed report of a demonstration of some thirty thousand workers who rallied under the banners *"No somos comunistas: Estamos con Alemán"* and *"Mueran los Hambreadores"* ("We are not Communists: We are with Alemán" and "Death to the purveyors of hunger") among others. The idea was to create a counterbalance to the older radical traditions of labor in order to further divide and neutralize the labor movement. This was accompanied by an effort to create a counterorganization in each union to oppose anti-Alemán sentiments and support the government's labor policies.[30]

The moral bankruptcy of the mainstream labor movement was best illustrated by Vicente Lombardo Toledano as he continued to support Alemán's initiatives; he even went so far as to condemn the *petroleros* for having had the audacity to try to improve their working conditions. Never was Lombardo's position more pathetic. Having been central to the politics of Alemán's selection he continued to argue, as he had throughout the Avila Camacho administration, that labor owed the government its loyalty—no matter what the administration did—since the president had been labor's candidate. This abandonment of independent labor organizations at their most vulnerable moment was terribly destructive to the old Cardenista constituency. Facing a whirlwind of opposition, Lombardo made his position even less tenable by attempting yet another backflip. He helped organize the Roundtable Conference, at which time he announced that he would begin forming an alternative to the official party, presumably one based on the independent unionists he had just helped to destroy. After a long period of gestation, this alternative became the Partido Popular.

The antilabor tone of the administration was utterly clear. Some workers continued the tradition of petitioning the president, even as they were enduring the deprivation that a strike implied. The workers at the Mexican Silk Mill, for example, petitioned the president for an audience to explain their side in a long-running dispute. Presidential secretaries repeatedly denied these and many other requests for a meeting with Alemán.[31] Or again, workers at Julio Albert y Cía. also found that the president was too busy when they tried to see him about their dispute.[32] By contrast, the employers' organizations were welcomed when they complained to the president about the "abuse of the right to strike" and asked the president to impose "economic order."[33]

At the Fundidora in Monterrey semiskilled workers began to demand higher wage rates as their contract came to an end in August 1948. Management, under Evaristo Araiza, refused to enter into discussions with the unions and kept the president informed of events in detail. In response to a slowdown, management fired twelve workers. The union retaliated by extending the slowdown, and management dismissed another dozen workers. For the first time, the government openly took the side of the Monterrey Group against striking workers. The contrast with Cárdenas's attempt to use a similar strike in 1936 to reduce the power of the bosses in Monterrey was dramatic.[34]

Even when the unions faced extreme demands from employers the government was still unsympathetic to labor. A dispute in Monterrey at the Cía. Mexicana del Amparo S.A. began when management decided to cut the miners' wages by 50 percent. The government backed management, as they did when the management of the Nash automotive factory moved to reduce their workforce, or again, when the Ford Motor Company fired 426 workers. In these and many other cases, the government was unmoved.[35] It is accurate to say that the Alemán administration supported labor initiative only when it was from their own *charro* union or when it was an attempt to divide and rule an independent union.

In spite of the growing hostility to labor, the main body of the CTM did not follow Lombardo Toledano out of the PRI and into the Partido Popular. Fernando Amilpa, then the secretary general of the CTM, spelled out to one U.S. diplomat the attitude of established labor toward the new party: "Amilpa and Velázquez are what we would call in American politics 'Organization Men' and [are] interested further, in practical considerations such as their own political prestige and private incomes. . . . But they would not care to risk their own standing with the Government or their own hold over the CTM membership for the sake of Lombardo."³⁶

Perhaps the most objectionable tactic of the Alemán government was to give tacit approval to using violence to divide the labor movement. The idea was, surreptitiously but officially, to condone the use of violence by a *charro* faction against an independent union or an employer. The state of Puebla saw the most frequent use of this tactic, especially in the city of Puebla, in Atlixco, and in the Jenkins-controlled sugar country around the mill at Atencingo. Dr. Ezequiel Teyssier, director of *El Sol de Puebla*—of the García Valseca chain of newspapers—maintained a campaign against the officially supported faction of the CTM that had used violence against his enterprise, an accusation that Governor Betancourt regularly denied.³⁷ Similarly, the head of an independent faction of the CTM in Puebla wrote to the president denouncing an attack by two hundred members of the CROM at the Fabrica La Oruga.³⁸

In Guadalajara the pattern was the same although the cast was different. In its struggles against the railroad union (STFRM) the government used the Confederación Unica de Trabajadores (CUT) as *charros* in a campaign that saw considerable violence, including the sabotage of railroad lines.³⁹ Or again, the head of the railroad workers' union in Tampico, Cristobal Alvarado Muñoz, wrote to the president accusing Fidel Velázquez and Manuel Moreno not only of dividing the union movement but also of being behind the assassination of the railroad worker Rodolfo Labastida by *pistoleros*. Fidel Velázquez responded to the president by accusing Guillermo Guajardo Davis, president of the Confederación de Cámeras Industriales, of "having instigated the violence in order to defend the interests of the capitalists."⁴⁰

Some unions did try to fight back. The taxi drivers of the UGOCM went on strike at the beginning of 1950. Their complaints related to immediate grievances: taxi meters they had paid for but not received, the high price of gasoline, and the increased number of licenses being issued. However, there was also a strong undercurrent of anger against a government that the workers felt had turned against them. The Alemán government lashed back at the striking taxi drivers. On January 3 the police dispersed a meeting of the drivers, leaving two dead and numerous wounded. They followed this up with a raid at night on the UGOCM headquarters. Government officials condemned the drivers for harboring sympathy for the petroleum workers. Before they went back to work, the drivers organized demonstrations in front of the homes of President Alemán and his nephew, Fernando Casas Alemán, who had replaced Alejandro Carrillo as head of the DDF.[41]

Even great icons of the Mexican Revolution did not deter Alemán from his antilabor policies. The government took a pro-management position in a strike at the famous copper mine at Cananea, Sonora. Manuel Morales, the manager of the mine, wrote to the president praising him for "not having accepted the [legality] of the strike at Cananea."[42] The old complaint against Porfirio Díaz of allowing differential wage rates between foreigners and Mexicans doing the same work still had currency. Drillers for PEMEX retained a lawyer to fight the company's practice of paying foreign drillers more for the same work.[43] There were even complaints that forced labor policies, in the tradition of the Porfirian *enganche*, were still being used in the construction of the highways between Xalapa and Perote and the project linking Córdova and Veracruz.[44]

Army intervention in strike by workers on Rio Lerma project. *Courtesy Hermanos Mayo, Archivo General de la Nación, Mexico City*

Perhaps the overall tone of the era is best revealed by the out-
pouring of petitions to the president by 1950, begging the government not to revoke Article 123 of the 1917 constitution and thus
eliminate the right to strike.[45] The political agenda had clearly
shifted.

Anticommunism

The Alemán administration was under increasing pressure from
the United States to take a hard line against Mexican Communists,
as the Truman administration intensified the Cold War. Although
the PCM was small and had just been through a purge, the international agenda played into the government's hands. An episode at
the beginning of the Alemán administration demonstrated this
when a Mexican diplomat in the United States inadvertently gave
support to the fervent anti-Communists in Mexico, especially to
the former president and industrialist Abelardo Rodríguez.

Luis Quintanilla, Mexico's ambassador to the Organization of
American States, published a response in the *Washington Post* to
Winston Churchill's famous March 6, 1946, Iron Curtain speech at
Fulton, Missouri. Quintanilla objected strongly to Churchill's call
for a special relationship—the merging of interests and possible
common citizenship—between the two English-speaking countries.
Quintanilla argued that this relationship would corrupt the growing ties of Pan-Americanism that linked Latin American countries
to U.S. policy. The Cold War, he argued, meant that Latin America
might become simply an extension of the anti-Comintern Axis that
the Allies had defeated in World War II. Quintanilla thought that
the USSR had improved the lot in life of its two hundred million
people and that if the West wanted to defeat communism it had
better do something about poverty in Latin America. Ending poverty, rather than heeding Churchill's call to repress parties of the
Left, would do the job. Sensitive to the historical erosion of Latin
American sovereignty by the United States, Quintanilla went on to
say: "If Pan Americanism means, among other things, that whatever affects Latin America also directly or indirectly affects the
United States, then I believe it should work both ways: anything
that affects the international position of the United States also affects Latin America." Quintanilla drew a parallel between Winston
Churchill's anticommunism and that of Francisco Franco. He ended
his article by quoting from a speech Churchill had delivered in
Rome on January 20, 1927, in which he praised Mussolini, saying

that if he [Churchill] were an Italian he would have "wholeheartedly been with the Fascists from the start to the finish in your triumphant struggle against the bestial appetites and passions of Leninism."[46]

Quintanilla's argument was out of touch with the spirit of the Cold War, however valid a commentary on Churchill's politics it may have been. U.S. diplomats hated his analysis, and Alemán responded with a series of initiatives aimed at reassuring the United States that Mexico would toe the line. In response to the *Washington Post* article, which appeared on March 16, Alemán and Beteta met with Messersmith on March 26. The president noted that he understood the United States' disquiet over Quintanilla's association with Lombardo Toledano and the independent labor movement, with whom he associated this line of analysis. Alemán assured Ray that he would "take care of" Lombardo Toledano and his friends. "It was obvious that he [Alemán] was anxious to get a message to the United States that he would not side with Russia."

In addition to disassociating himself from Quintanilla's position, the president introduced an interesting linkage by admitting that the petroleum and railroad industries were in such bad shape that they would require U.S. assistance at both the financial and technical levels. On the following day, Ray and Beteta continued their meetings at the home of a mutual friend. Since Ray was about to leave for Washington to head the Mexican desk at the State Department, Alemán used the opportunity to make some fundamental points. Alemán assured Ray of Mexico's support in the event "of a war or even a struggle of ideologies" against the USSR. When Ray pressed Alemán for what he meant, he said that "the comparison he had in mind was, first, that Mexico would declare war immediately against Russia in the case of hostilities between the United States and Russia, and second, that this time Mexico would be better prepared to render effective military aid."

On the petroleum issue, Alemán admitted that the nationalization was a "headache" and that PEMEX was a drain on the treasury. Although the return of the oil to its former owners was inconceivable, Alemán had indicated:

> American technical help would be required and that a way would have to be found to put the petroleum industry on its feet. He said that he deliberately referred to American technical knowledge rather than foreign technical knowledge because he was greatly interested in the industrialization of Mexico which could not take place without improvement in the railroad and

petroleum situation and that help in the industrialization of
Mexico would have to come from the United States, not from Great
Britain and much less from Russia. He said that the petroleum
question would have to drag along until after the elections were
over since it was "dynamite" at present.[47]

Alemán's comments went a long way toward reassuring the United
States that Quintanilla did not speak for the government of Mexico.
His desire to distance his government from any position that could
be considered even remotely sympathetic to the USSR merged
neatly with his desire to defeat independent labor voices.

The CROM was waging a campaign for the government to take
a much more repressive line against the Mexican Left. Anticommunism was becoming an obsession in the United States; however,
in Mexico many wondered what the fuss was all about. The PCM
had declined precipitously in both its membership and the vigor
of its program since the purge of 1940. Therefore, the Communist
party itself provided a very small target, and the broad Left merged,
degree by degree, with the left wing of the governing party. Thus,
the U.S. embassy worked with Morones of the CROM in trying to
handle the tricky question of defining communism in Mexico.

The CROM wanted the government to revoke Vicente Lombardo Toledano's citizenship. In this, they came close to anticipating the national security doctrines of the 1970s, so beloved by
military dictators throughout Latin America. The CROM provided
two lists to U.S. diplomats: the first was of fellow travelers, and
the second contained—in Luis Morones's phrase—real Communists. In the former category were Manuel Tello (acting minister of
foreign affairs), Francisco Castillo Najera (former ambassador to
the United States), Luis Quintanilla (former ambassador to the USSR
and now ambassador to the OAS), Luis Padilla Nervo (Mexico's
ambassador to the UN), and Isidro Fabela (diplomat and legal historian). On the latter list were Valentín Campa (purged from the
PCM in 1940), Diego Rivera (who changed his position with great
frequency but at the moment was rabidly anti-PCM), and Alejandro
Carrillo (editor of *El Popular* and close collaborator of Lombardo
Toledano), as well as the secretary of hydraulic resources, Adolfo
Orive Alba. Even the industrialists José Domingo Lavín and
Federico Sánchez Fogarty made the CROM's hit list. Staff in the
U.S. embassy admitted that these lists were "sweeping"; however,
Ambassador Thurston thought these lists would "smoke out some
of the more conspicuous fellow travellers."[48]

President Alemán did not go quite as far as Morones wanted, although by the end of 1949 the government's anticommunist campaign was in high gear. A particularly harsh blow was directed at the railway workers' union. In the early hours of July 16, 1949, passenger train #94 coming from Manzanillo crashed spectacularly with two locomotives in the station in Guadalajara. The accident was clearly the fault of poor maintenance on the part of the Compañía de Cementos de Guadalajara, the owner of the locomotives; neither that firm nor Ferrocarriles Nacionales had repaired a safety regulator. However, the local press jumped to the conclusion that the workers were at fault. Jesús Topete, the head of the local union, and other officials were arrested; some were tortured, including José Martínez Rodríguez, who died during the ordeal. The official claim was that Communists had ordered the sabotage.[49] The government's anti-Communist campaign was aimed at pleasing the United States and simultaneously proving to the Mexican Left that there was no future in bucking the PRI.

Official demonstrations were also choreographed in support of Mexico's integration into the Pan-American system of hemispheric defense. This meant that historically well-justified doubts about future U.S. intervention in Latin America had to be laid to rest. Alemán reiterated that in case of war Mexico would provide raw materials to the United States. This was a particularly interesting statement. On the surface it seemed to be a replay of Mexico's role in World War II, except that now there was no question of who the next enemy would be. Thus the broad anti-Axis coalition became a narrow version of anticommunism. When the PCM attacked these statements, on November 23, noting the degree to which Mexico's national interests were being subordinated to those of the United States, the government reacted by arresting a number of people who were participating at an unauthorized demonstration. Four important PCM leaders were arrested and held incommunicado and without charges for twelve days. On December 13 the prosecutor of the D.F., Carlos Franco Sodi, announced to the press that the government had found documents in Valentín Campa's home showing that Campa had been provoking a "seditious movement of extremist ideology." Yet U.S. diplomats admitted in private, "Actually, the documents, as described by Sodi, seem to be what one would expect the routine correspondence of a Communist Labor leader to be. They recorded a more or less continuous conspiracy but showed little evidence of a well developed plot to overthrow the Mexican government in the foreseeable future."[50] The sensational charges and press reaction together with the unexceptional documents showed that the government was making a political rather than a national security move. Taken together with the detention of the four PCM officials and the campaign against the Left within the petroleum workers' union, the government's position was increasingly clear.

The head of the Dirección Federal de Seguridad, Colonel Marcelino Inurreta, kept the presidential secretary, Rogelio de la Selva, closely informed about the involvement of Narciso Bassols and other prominent figures on the left in producing antigovernment literature. The PCM was under close surveillance.[51] The police kept tabs on the movements of PCM members, even at the state level, as when Manuel Terrazas was arrested in Monterrey.[52] The police reports make boring reading. They are usually long lists of license plate numbers—Communists without automobiles attracted less attention—as investigators recorded party members' visits to well-known figures. The Henríqistas were easier to follow since more of them owned automobiles.

To put pressure on the petroleum union to expel its left-wing members was a fundamental goal of the Alemán program. The task became easier for the president as the internal problems of the PCM multiplied. By 1947 the party's newspaper, *La Voz de México*, had started to miss publishing deadlines due to financial constraints. The U.S. embassy understood that the USSR no longer supported the PCM in any material way. The Soviets were disbanding their news agency, ANLA, leaving only *El Popular* and the *Buletín* of the Soviet embassy as major voices on the left.[53] The lack of a credible threat from the Soviet headquarters on Avenida Revolución, however, did not persuade the administration to relent.

The decision to build a new university city far to the south of Mexico City should be read within this context of reducing the influence of the left and labor. It was widely understood at the time that the close proximity of the National Palace to UNAM enabled students to congregate easily in the *zócalo* and bring the pressure of their numbers to bear on the government through demonstrations. The students' ability to tie up traffic and, occasionally, to locate ministers was intolerable to the administration. By building the new campus at the end of Ave. Insurgentes Sur, the administration would also be removing the students from the central government area. Thus, the students, like workers and people on the left, lost some of their influence. Pressure was applied against people on the left who were employed by the government. For example,

Statue of Miguel Alemán in academic robes at the entrance to the National Autonomous University of Mexico. *Courtesy Hermanos Mayo, Archivo General de la Nación, Mexico City*

Dr. Ester Chapa was forced to leave her post as director of health services within Mexico City's penitentiary. Guadencio Paraza, secretary general of the SNTE, was prosecuted with a righteous fervor for financial irregularities in a way that was rare during the Alemán years.

One small incident encapsulated the degree of change that had occurred in Mexico, especially since what took place could easily have been represented as an attack on Mexican territory by the United States. In 1947 the U.S. Army launched a V-2 rocket from a base in Texas; the missile went off course and landed near Ciudad Juárez. Rather than responding in terms of the history of U.S. filibustering in Mexico, or even faulting the competence of the rocket scientists who missed their target, the Mexican press and government were most understanding.

Over the years the pressure from Washington to battle communism did filter down to the local level. The Junior Chamber of Commerce in Laredo, Texas, helped their counterparts in Nuevo Laredo organize a "Combined American and Anti-Communist Week" ending February 17, 1951. Among the highlights of the festivities, ministers and priests were urged to adopt the theme "America" as their sermon subject on Sunday. Free copies of the Declaration of Independence were translated and distributed. Festival organizers expressed anger at Mayor Hugh Cluck, who apparently harbored doubts about the value of the project. In an ecumenical spirit, they urged their followers to burn effigies of Catholic, Protestant, and Jewish leaders as a warning against the dangers of communism. The Cold War had come to the border.[54]

Taming the Economic Nationalists

Upon coming to office, President Alemán continued to work to bring the economic nationalists to heel. One immediate issue was the trade agreement with the United States. As industrialists José R. Colín and José Domingo Lavín met with the new economic ministers of the Alemán administration they began to temper their opposition to the trade agreement that the United States wanted. It was clear to them that Alemán would not oppose the powerful neighbor, even to protect infant industries in Mexico. As Merwin L. Bohan, the counselor for economic affairs of the U.S. embassy, wrote, "It is all right to have hope and faith in a broad international trade authority, but until such an authority is a reality, the reciprocal trade agreements must be our main reliance in holding the line against an almost universal trend towards trade and economic selfishness [i.e., Mexican protectionism]." Bohan understood that Mexico's dependence upon the United States for "allocations, as well as export and import controls" forced the Alemán administration to deny the claims for industrial protectionism from such economic nationalists as Lavín and Colín. Very quickly, the Centro Patronal del Districto Federal realized that it had the open support of the new president in its decade-long battle with the Cámara Nacional de Industrias de Transformación over which group would speak for manufacturing. By Alemán's second month in office the Centro Patronal del D.F. was issuing circulars that were effusive in their praise of Alemán.[55]

Although the government had made clear its opposition to the economic nationalists of the CNIT by the middle of the Avila Camacho administration, Alemán's embrace of this most recalcitrant employers' group—who would have nothing to do with the underconsumptionist arguments of the CNIT—was new. Still, there were selected moments when aspects of the old economic nationalism, however eroded, were useful. In 1952, Alemán decided to apply the 51 percent ownership rule to regulate the content of television. In an attempt to protect his own interests and those of several close associates, Alemán declared that the new medium could not be totally exposed to U.S. material. U.S. diplomats opposed the plan without effect, calling it "very undesirable and dangerous."[56] These rules, along with a prohibition on dubbing films in Spanish, preserved a high level of Mexican content in the mass media. This was a rare instance when the legacy of economic nationalism was compatible with the pecuniary interests of the governing circle.

The most characteristic achievement of the Alemán political reforms may well have been at the beginning of 1950. At the national assembly of the PRI, in February 1950, the official party changed its system of selecting candidates. Dropping the pretense of primary elections, the party moved to simply name official candidates at a nominating convention. As one diplomat put it, "In practice, the change in party election procedure seems likely to result in closer and more centralized party control."[57] That, too, was an essential feature of Alemanismo.

Alemán and Business

Alemán was on good terms with international business. The defeat of the economic nationalists was so complete that by 1949 even top international industrialists were delighted. When F. B. Rhuherry, general manager of Ford Motors, announced a 50 percent increase in production, he stated that "Mexico is the American country which gives the most facilities and guarantees to private investment."[58] As the Alemán years passed, this became ever more evident. By 1950 the president was employing a consultant to make a study for the Comisión Intersecretarial Sobre Inversión de Capital Extranjero that would bring together all foreign investment policies and regulations. The final report explicitly stated that such nationalist provisions as the 51 percent decree were not to be implemented, "one should not demand that 51 percent of the capital in Mexican corporations should be Mexican." Other regulations, such as cabotage, were similarly set aside, although it was clear that because of its unique political symbolism PEMEX would have to limit its efforts to indirect ways of dealing with foreign investors.[59]

The United States continued to play a central role in the Mexican industrializaton program, even after wartime regulations were lifted. The desire to borrow capital from U.S. organizations meant that wartime patterns of influence over major projects of industrialization would remain in place. For example, in 1951, President Alemán put forth a plan to build a steel mill at Puerto Márquez, near Acapulco. He proposed building a gigantic enterprise that would use iron from Las Truchas, Michoacán, and coal from Oaxaca and be based on improved rail and port facilities. The Export-Import Bank and the U.S. embassy carried out technical studies of the plan and decided that the idea of making steel at Acapulco was "unrealistic and economically unsound."[60] No one commented upon the contradiction of developing Acapulco for both tourism and steel making.

In 1947, *Fortune* magazine ran a series of articles on the Alemán industrialization program written by Charles Koons, who was also president of an export company in New York City that traded with

Mexico. This series pleased Ruiz Galindo and the president a great deal.[61] The thrust of these articles was to convince the readers of the financial press in the United States that Mexico had changed from its revolutionary days and was now a safe and profitable place in which to invest. The president was less pleased a few years later when the same magazine included him on its list of the world's richest men.

The president had also developed close personal relationships with major corporate executives. Judging from the enthusiastic letters thanking the president for his hospitality, President Alemán found Mexico's superb tourist attractions very helpful in developing close links with large international corporations.[62] Presidential hospitality was legendary. Just in April and May 1952 alone the president entertained top executives from Anaconda Copper, Industrial Rayon, Monsanto Chemical, Chemical Bank and Trust of New York, B. F. Goodrich, the Bank of America, Sears, Roebuck, Mercantile Trust of Saint Louis, American Zinc, Lead, and Smelting, and the magazine the *Nation's Business*.[63] The flow of top corporate executives through the presidential office to the various tourist attractions, especially in Acapulco, seemed endless.

Little wonder, therefore, that one finds in a secret report from a Wall Street bank, the following assessment of the Mexican situation: "Mexico's long history of political instability acts as a deterrent to investment. But recent political experience is reassuring and there is reason for confidence that in an environment of economic expansion the fiscal, political and labor problems which were so pressing in the decade of the thirties are not likely to block the road to economic progress."[64] It is within this context that Alemán's effort to run a pro-business administration and attract foreign capital to Mexico and his political initiatives to that end should be read.

Clearly, the Mexican president adjusted the rules of the game for the domestic business scene. Antonio Ruiz Galindo, as secretary of the national economy, presented a further series of tax and financial concessions to business in April 1947. These focused on changes in the commercial code and valuation techniques for borrowing, as well as on a variety of tax breaks. In an attempt to convince the governors to join in the national effort to have 80 percent of profits invested in new industries, he suggested a press campaign. He also recommended such immediate measures as the increase of industrial credit, elimination of the 15 percent ad valorem tax on exports, and elimination of transport fees and taxes. Investment and lending policies by Nacional Financiera were at the heart of this effort.[65]

It is also important to recognize that there was a high, if frequently favorable, level of regulation for business. Requests for price increases for many industrial, chemical, and pharmaceutical products went to the Commission for the Control of Prices, which regularly checked with the Oficial Mayor de la Secretaría Particular de la Presidencia. This process gave the president a great deal of control over day-to-day business, making it imperative for executives to have good relations with the administration; company directors needed to keep in touch with national decision makers on a daily basis.[66] It also made it imperative for foreign business leaders to have good relationships with the governing circle.

The government refused to crack down on unpopular entrepreneurs, as one notorious case illustrates. Two film distributors in Reynosa wrote to the president complaining about the monopolistic trade practices that a major distributor, William Jenkins, was using in the film industry. By forcing cinemas to take only his packages of films—upon threat of future boycott—Jenkins was committing a clear abuse of trade practice legislation. Film exhibitors in Monterrey made a similar complaint at the same time.[67] These petitions fell on deaf ears; nothing was done to slow the growth of Jenkins's control over the distribution of films in Mexico. Similarly, complaints about his treatment of peasants in Puebla were also ignored.

Members of the inner political circle did well. Marte Gómez, who had been Avila Camacho's minister of agriculture, became the president of the affiliate of the U.S. irrigation pump manufacturer, Worthington de México S.A. de C.V. Gómez's contacts helped his new company obtain a million-peso credit from Nacional Financiera, and he approached Alemán in 1952 for help in obtaining government purchasing contracts over his competitor, Peerless Pumps. Political favoritism guaranteed success, given the importance of pumps in the irrigation projects under planning and construction.[68]

The mining industry also showed how unconcerned about foreign ownership the governments of the 1940s had become. By the end of 1950 total foreign investment in Mexico was $566,600,000, of which fully 20 percent was in the mining industry. Mexico was one of the world's richest storehouses of nonferrous metals, and virtually all of the mining companies were owned by either ASARCO, Phelps-Dodge, American Metals Company, or National

Lead Company. About 90 percent of the silver, lead, zinc, copper, antimony, molybdenum, cadmium, and bismuth mined was exported to the United States, and remittances were, in reality, intracompany transfers. The revenue thus generated from mineral exports amounted to $180 million, about 36 percent of total "Mexican" exports.[69] Even the supposedly high taxes on the industry, up to 70 percent based on a surface reading of the tax code, were systematically avoided in practice. As one OSS analysis confided, "However, the low income on corporation taxes and the rapid instrument amortization allowances to some extent ameliorate the confiscatory aspects of the mining and export taxes." Mining taxes were based on the volume of production, not on the cost of production, and this enabled the industry to pay low taxes by exploiting only high-grade ore. "Foreign investors tend to object as much to the method of levying the tax as to the burden itself."[70] Whereas Cárdenas had intended to increase Mexico's stake in mining before the expropriation of petroleum, any attempt to dominate this most important sector of the "Mexican" economy was off the political agenda by the 1940s.

One area in which conflict between government and business did exist was the investment-making process. There was a fairly open confrontation between Ramón Beteta and the country's highest bankers at the 15th Meeting of the Bankers Association in Veracruz in May 1949 over the investment priorities of NAFISA. Because Beteta had just stated in his introductory remarks that NAFISA was going to invest only in industries that were "of fundamental interest to the country," many bankers queried the decision to support the bailout of Tecate Brewery. The Banco de México provided 18 million pesos to rescue the business, with NAFISA providing another 15 million pesos. It was commonly understood in the private banking community that "inevitable links of friendship and mutual assistance" between the government and the Banco Nacional de México had been behind the Tecate deal. In addition, it was an open secret that the bank had just received another 11 million pesos for damages incurred decades earlier during the military phase of the Mexican Revolution. Finally, BANAMEX was the only clearinghouse dealing with the extremely lucrative property conflicts that resulted from the Mexican policy against Franco in Spain. (Much of the land reform of the Cárdenas era had been at the expense of Spanish landowners in Mexico.) All of these policies favored the Banco Nacional de México and were based upon the close personal relationship among Luis Legorreta, Alemán, and

Beteta. This favoritism so angered the other private bankers that they actually expelled the Banco Nacional de México from the Bankers Association. When Alemán entered the hall at the Villa del Mar at the height of the crisis the atmosphere was frigid; his main demand of the nation's private bankers was that they allow the Banco Nacional de México back in the association.[71]

This episode at the meeting of the Bankers Association is interesting not only because divisions within the elite frequently cast light upon matters that would normally be conducted in secret but because these events also reveal a peculiarity of the Mexican political system. There is nothing particularly unique in a head of state directing favors to political cronies in the business community: for example, the relationship between Lyndon Johnson and Brown and Root or Ronald Reagan and the Bechtel Corporation. Indeed, Alemán's and Beteta's relationship with Legorreta was a subtle one. In contrast, dictator Anastasio Somoza, in Nicaragua, used state power to take over the businesses of his rivals.

Unique about this episode at the 1949 bankers' convention was the lingering influence of the economic nationalism of the early Cardenista period. There was still a proposal on the table to implement an excess profits tax. Luis Montes de Oca carried the battle against Beteta over this plan. He argued that there is no such thing as excessive profit, and he was supported in this position by the presidents elect, Alfonso Díaz Garza of the Banco Internacional. Although an excess profits tax was never implemented, its proposal had the effect of blurring the target for Alemán's opponents. Many who disapproved of the deals between the nation's leaders and the Legorretas had to calculate whether their support of the aggrieved bankers would undercut implementation of an excess profits tax.

One area that mattered enormously in an age of falling real wages was rent control. Rents had been frozen in Mexico in 1942 as part of a package of wartime price and wage controls. As real wages fell dramatically during the 1940s, the government found it difficult to act on rents based on its liberal economic principles. Ramón Beteta drafted several proposals to end rent controls, or at least to increase protected rents. A proposal was introduced to the Congress on November 11, 1949, to increase rents up of to 150 pesos by 10 percent and to 300 pesos by 50 percent. In spite of great popular opposition to his proposals, Beteta tried again the next year.[72] Although the government desired to return to an unregulated rental market, it was never able to eliminate rent protection. Similarly, despite Nacional Distribuidora y Reguladora's scandal-ridden

recent past, the agency still had a role after the war in supplying
price-regulated basic commodities. This policy was the first of many
postwar efforts to subsidize articles of popular consumption in order to hold down wages.[73]

In the end, it was far safer to stick with the political agenda, as
set by Alemán's "Twenty-three Point Program," than to deal with
the issues of excess profits or rent control. Revolutionary rhetoric
and the odd proposal from the economic nationalist period still
served to obscure the nature of Alemán's reforms. Some of his early
political changes also reinforced this pattern. What was only partially obscured, however, was the president's own involvement in
the business life of the country.

Alemán's Business

Although it is doubtful that researchers will ever unravel the lion's
share of President Alemán's business interests, a number of approaches are useful. The fundamental problem is Alemán's systematic use of *prestanombres* and / or partners to mask his business deals.
The president's private secretary, Jorge Viesca Palma, and his personal lawyer, Enríque Parra, were among his closest collaborators.
Moreover, it was widely believed at the time that such associates
as A. C. Blumenthal, Ben Smith, Bruno Pagliai, Samuel Rosoff, and
possibly Carlos I. Serrano of the Dirección Federal de Seguridad
were also operating in association with Alemán. Ambassador
Messersmith referred to Jorge Pasquel as a "partner of Alemán."[74]

Beyond these individuals were many other well-known businessmen of the period who were also close to the president: Luis
and Agustín Legorreta, Antonio Ruiz Galindo, Aarón Sáenz and
his son Josue, Manuel Gual Vidal, Manuel Suárez, Raúl Baillerés,
and Fernando Buch de Parada. A few men in the government, like
Ramón Beteta, were eventually allowed into the inner circle. Finally, there was the old Maximino group, including former senator
John Hastings of New York and Axel Wenner-Gren; Alemán cooperated closely with them.

Possibly the most difficult level to penetrate are the arrangements that linked these Mexican political and business figures to
the return of foreign corporations to Mexico. If we accept that many
of the president's business interests were at least partially fronted
by these figures, then the public record reveals some of the
president's private interests. Firms in which the president appears
to have had a major stake through these associates included

Tubos de Acero de México, Siderúrgica Tamsa, Metalever, D.M. Nacional, Herramiento de Acero, Ferro Enamel de México, and Automagnetico S.A.[75]

The public record does reveal an insatiable interest in material acquisition. Press coverage refers to rural properties in most states as belonging to Alemán. The presidential archives reveal the locations of some of his properties, such as the ranchos Tepecuaco and Ixtacapa between Perote and Teziutlán.[76] José Navarro Elizondo wrote to the president from San Diego bringing him up to date on the state of his rancho "El Florido." Navarro Elizondo apparently served as an intermediary between Alemán's business interests in southern California and his ranching and fishing interests in Ensenada. He reported on the efforts of one Thomas Robertson, a grower in the San Fernando Valley (it was then rural), to select fruit trees for El Florido, a property in the Valley of Matanuce, near Tijuana. The orchard property was being planted with 3,000 olive trees, 5,000 almond trees, 200 fruit trees, and a vineyard. In addition, beans and oats and other grains were grown on the property. Colonel Serrano and Alemán supervised the ranch personally when they were in the area, and a Captain Luna of the local Recursos Hidráulicos organized irrigation (1,000 liters per minute) for the ranch after an initial effort to dig wells failed. Navarro Elizondo did complain that the manager, a Señor Barbachane, would suspend work as soon as Colonel Serrano or Alemán left the ranch.[77]

Alemán also owned a large seaside property, which extended from the entrance to the federal highway to the city of Veracruz and included the large Hotel Mocambo. In addition, he had fishing interests as well as land, plantations, and other rural properties throughout his native state. It was also widely understood at the time that President Alemán had a considerable stake in the new Hotel del Prado across from Alameda Park. As strong evidence for this interest, Roberto Chellet Osante, head of the company Inmuebles y Edificios S.A., sent the bill for furnishing the elegant hotel (1,078,677 pesos) to the president via the management company Operadora de Hoteles S.A. run by Aarón Sáenz.[78]

With Alemán's accession to political power, new possibilities emerged for him, as the Veracruz pineapple project demonstrates. Alemán approached the USDA for technical assistance in developing the pineapple industry in Veracruz. Alemán's group was headed by Manuel Nieto, the Ford dealer in Veracruz, and included Ruíz Cortines. They wanted advice in the preparation, fertilizing, planting, chemical analysis, packaging, and marketing of the product.

Their plan was to spend 3 million pesos to acquire 890 hectares of land in the region of los Robles, midway between Veracruz and Alvarado. The land was located near a projected highway, and 120 million pesos were pledged for paving to allow a fleet of as many as twenty semitrailers to bring the pineapples to Alvarado, where Alemán also intended major port improvements. Ultimately, the group planned to establish its own distribution network in the United States. Equally important, the Papaloapan River hydroelectric project would also serve the pineapple enterprise. U.S. officials were told that capital was no problem.[79] Eventually, the Truman administration organized a Point Four technical aid program to assist, believing that doing so would cement relationships with President Alemán.

The Export-Import Bank was approached by another group surrounding Alemán for a $2 million loan to build a hotel at the corner of the Paseo de la Reforma and Avenida de los Insurgentes. Headed by Manuel Suárez, the group included Alemán, Avila Camacho, and Beteta. The plan was to build the hotel and lease it to the Hilton hotel chain. Again capital was no problem since NAFISA guaranteed the project "for political reasons."[80] This pattern also applied to the Hotel Alemeda. The embassy actually opposed the use of U.S. funds on these projects on the grounds that basic development was more important than additional luxury hotels. Alemán also had major stakes in a number of property developments in Acapulco and Mexico City, including the U.S.-style suburb Ciudad Satélite. His interests in construction and sewer pipe companies complemented his direct proprietary interests in these projects.

Axel Wenner-Gren survived the war years on the Allies' blacklist. After the war, he was more closely tied into Alemán's business efforts. In 1949 he and Bruno Pagliai were in Sweden negotiating the merger between Teléfonos de México, the ITT-controlled Mexican Telephone Company, and the Ericsson interests. To bring the deal to fruition, a rate increase for the prospective buyers was imperative. At the same time Wenner-Gren was involved in private "oil deals," as well as in pushing "our dairy interests [and those in] the Banco Continental." He also worked to increase the marketing of Mexican bananas and pineapples in northern Europe.[81]

The development of television flowed from a number of initiatives, all of which were closely linked to the business interests of the presidents of the 1940s. Two individuals are usually associated with the growth of the industry: Emilio Azcárraga and Alonso Sordo Noriega. Azcárraga was born in Tampico and educated in Texas.

He had started radio stations XEW and XEQ in association with Charles W. Horn, a former member of the RCA-NBC radio organizations. Knowledgeable reports of the day agree that Azcárraga was even then extremely wealthy. The close link between politics and the media was reinforced in the Avila Camacho years. Alonso Sordo Noriega was a member of the governing party, and he acted as Avila Camacho's radio director during the 1940 campaign. After the election, he became the director of radio station XEX, and the U.S. embassy assigned a radio expert, Bill Ray, to help the group with technical problems; the relationship provided advanced equipment to the group for years. By 1947 his network had grown to eighty-four radio stations.[82]

By the time of Alemán, the PRI-Azcárraga relationship provided a foundation television license (XEW-TV). The importance of the new medium can be seen in that by 1951 Televicentro already represented a 3-million-peso investment. The other initial license went to Romulo O'Farrill, who had a long-standing relationship with the president centering on motor vehicle distributorships and media interests. His new television station—which was actually the first on the air—complemented both his radio station and *Novedades*. Alemán's son, Miguel Jr., maintained a lifelong association with Televicentro, which probably reflects the initial agreements.[83] The media battles of the 1940s will be examined in Chapter 6; however, it is clear that the president found it to be to his advantage to maintain close links with persons in the film and television industries.

Funny Business

Miguel Alemán enjoyed female company. On the eve of his election, "an intimate friend of Lic. Alemán brought Miss Lenora Amar to see an officer of this Embassy and requested his assistance in obtaining a visa for Miss Amar to go to the United States." When it became clear that he was talking to the wrong embassy official, Alemán's friend confided, "We simply must get this woman out of Mexico. . . . Unfortunately Miguel has been playing around with her and she is going around saying that she is the mistress of the next president of Mexico." Brazil joined the United States in denying her a visa, and this report concluded that the Alemán camp married her off to someone "vaguely connected with the motion pictures industry."[84]

A bizarre episode involving the president's well-publicized love life became known when the head of the secret police, Colonel

Serrano, approached the U.S. embassy in 1948. Serrano, stung by articles by the columnist Drew Pearson alleging his involvement in narcotics smuggling into the United States, stated that he and the president had had a falling out. The story he told was that Mrs. Alemán had caught the president *en flagrante* in their home in Acapulco with the actress María Félix. Apparently quite a scene occurred before the First Lady left for Mexico City and eventually the United States. Somehow Serrano thought it would help his standing with the U.S. embassy when he explained: "It is not Colonel Serrano, but Lic. Enrique Parra, who controls the house where the President goes for the opposite sex, and therefore it does not seem probable that Sra. Alemán's feelings about Col. Serrano has to do with this question."[85]

Miguel Alemán and Adolfo Ruiz Cortines at a banquet for Cuban President and Sra. Carlos Prío Socarrás held in the National Palace. *Courtesy Hermanos Mayo, Archivo General de la Nación, Mexico City*

Alemán's Political Reform

The government's main problem was no longer to defeat the Left. That had been essentially accomplished. The government's central problem was that its effort to run a pro-business administration encountered the deep opposition of considerable segments of the national business community. Although the PAN was seriously compromised by its support of Almazán in 1940, thus frightening off many important figures in business and finance who needed good relations with the governing party, many others in small business eventually coalesced around the PAN and its focus upon a never-ending stream of electoral abuses and interventions.[86] And as we have seen, there was also a nationalist line among some of the new industrialists. Some of these individuals like Ruiz Galindo and Ramón Beteta simply trimmed their nationalism to the new internationalist line as required. Nevertheless, among the middle classes the government faced opposition from precisely the groups that Alemán wanted to attract. Big business was another matter. The administration had its closest relationship with major capitalists, frequently as silent partners in lucrative enterprises. But that was usually out of sight. In the public arena the common perception was still that business and the PRI were antagonists, a view that was reinforced by lingering strains of revolutionary rhetoric from some lower-ranked party cadres.

To appeal to the small middle-class groups, Alemán initiated a spate of structural political reforms aimed at convincing Mexicans that the electoral abuses that had been so egregious in the final stages of the Avila Camacho administration were going to end. There had been an electoral reform law presented as a solution to impositions in December 1945, as the Avila Camacho administration came under great pressure. Some viewed this "reform" as cynical. A Federal Commission of Electoral Supervision was established to oversee the electoral process; however, the commission consisted of the minister of the interior, one cabinet member, one senator, one deputy, and two members of the Supreme Court—all appointed by the president.[87] The net effect of the reform was to diminish the role of the Supreme Court in the electoral process.[88]

In a striking initiative, women were given the vote. Yet it was an odd reform in that, to a degree, it had come out of the blue. Although popular campaigns had demanded the vote in the 1930s, early divisions between radical and moderate reformers were destructive, and the suffrage movement faded. President Cárdenas's effort to include women in the corporatist political project stimulated the formation of the Frente Unico Pro Derechos de la Mujer (FUPDM). The initiative merged easily with other aspects of mass organization. However, the push for the vote that Cárdenas had sparked with his 1935 presidential message and the proposal to modify the constitution—which was passed by Congress and ratified by the states—were killed at the last moment in Congress in 1939.[89] Insiders understood that Almazán's influence and the battle for the 1940 selection were central to that defeat, although admittedly many on the left also opposed the reform, fearing the influence of the Church on women's voting patterns. Historian Anna Macías believes that it was the diffusing of the religious issue during the Avila Camacho years that cleared the way for the extension of the vote to women in 1946.[90] The Alemán campaign raised the issue of equal political rights for women as its own initiative during the 1946 campaign, and General Sánchez Taboada, president of the PRI, frequently used the rhetoric of women's rights at that time.

At the beginning of 1947 the PRI organized a conference of distinguished women that emphasized the need to discuss a wide range of women's issues—equal civil and legal rights, social programs to support women and children, the fight against high prices, literacy campaigns, programs of health and hygiene, and even reforms to the statutes of the PRI. The most interesting aspect of this conference was the prominence that it gave to many distinguished women who normally received little public attention: Dr. Ester Chapa, on the medical faculty at UNAM; Nelly Campobello, a novelist and ballerina; Esperanza Oteo Figueroa, a surgeon; María Arriola, a member of the association (*gremio*) of lottery ticket sellers; Carmen Parra Vda. de Alanis, a veteran of the Revolution who was recognized as a full colonel by the defense ministry; Consuelo Maldonaldo, a model and the leader of the restaurant workers' union; Adelina Zendejas, a journalist; and a sampling of less famous women—including an obligatory *campesina*.[91]

There was another political reform aimed, at least on the surface, at reducing the alienation that voters frequently felt when their local candidates—some of whom residents had never heard of—were revealed. Candidates were expected to live in the district they represented. Official statements against corruption also abounded, and a few opposition candidates were allowed to hold local seats. Initially, therefore, the new president appeared to be combining a political move to the right with reforms that could plausibly be represented as a move toward cleaner politics. Yet, sadly, the gap between theory and practice remained constant.

On the final day of 1946, in Tapachula, Chiapas, the local PRM authorities pressed forward with an unpopular imposition for the head of the municipal council. When the populace organized a protest, the authorities fired upon a large and unarmed group of demonstrators, killing between nine and twelve and wounding more than forty people, including women. Gobernación stepped in and brought the crisis to an end; the governor requested, and was granted, an indefinite leave of absence, and a new governor was appointed.[92] Much the same thing had happened in Oaxaca, although without the loss of life. These episodes suggested that the new administration was willing to remove officials who had abused their power to the consternation of the people.

There was a notorious murder of a journalist in Ciudad Victoria. The murder of the editor of *El Mundo* led to the trial of the chief of police in April 1947. Because the editor, Angel Raúl Villasana, was a member of the PAN and had stood for office in 1946, his murder had political implications. President Alemán removed the governor for failing to arrest the culprit sooner, although government sources tried to represent this case as an example of clean politics, there was another aspect to the affair. Ciudad Victoria, Tamaulipas, was the territory of the Portes Gil machine, and it is clear that the move to correct an obvious abuse of power also had the effect of dealing a blow to a rival within the governing party, a development that pleased the president.

More surprisingly, the new Alemán administration allowed the participation of opposition members of the Chamber of Deputies for the first time. The PAN had four deputies, and the Partido de la Fuerza Popular had one, its first deputy. That party had been formed in 1946 by the remnants of the Sinarquista movement. To some degree the PAN was involved in the events in Oaxaca, and on the basis of this success, they decided to contest other municipal elections. Observers were tempted to conclude that the new administration was going to maintain higher standards of electoral politics than had its predecessors.[93] Thus Alemán's moves to the right were accompanied by these attempts to make it look as if a process of reform was underway. The laws implementing these reforms were passed through Congress, and women did receive the vote, although they were not allowed to vote in national elections until 1958. Still, suspicions and cynicism abounded. It soon became clear that even with the recent reforms vote counts could still be rigged. Perhaps the spirit of the age was best revealed as political wags asked when men would also get the vote.

Postwar Economic Downturn

By the end of 1947 there were a number of adverse economic signs. The wartime boom was coming to an end as the United States reduced its purchases in Mexico. Currency reserves were rapidly eroded in the wake of postwar imports. President Alemán's Six-

Year Plan initially had contained a proposal for the investment of $241 million in infrastructure and industrial investments that was in addition to funds generated in Mexico. U.S. diplomats immediately concluded that some $772 million would be required to meet Mexico's existing debt commitments. The poor supply of food production for the domestic market continued to be a problem; 1947 was the driest year since the agricultural crisis of 1943. Although Mexico could once again import foodstuffs, the drain on its currency reserves was acute in a world that was desperately short of food. The lack of rains produced power shortages, and electricity was rationed in the Federal District. Another outbreak of hoof-and-mouth disease further reduced agricultural output as many infected oxen were sacrificed.

By 1948, Mexico's strategy of trying to please the United States in order to gain capital and technology for the drive for industrialization received a cruel blow. At a conference in Bogotá in April 1948, Secretary of State George Marshall told Latin American diplomats that the United States would not include their region in the Marshall Plan.[94] After that declaration, the devaluation of July 21 was inevitable. Although the financial ministers managed to "sting" Citibank by converting Mexico's currency reserves into gold on the eve of the devaluation—a move that was challenged in the courts for years—it was an ephemeral victory. When Secretary of the Treasury John W. Snyder agreed with President Alemán to provide a $10-million fund to back the new peso-to-dollar exchange rate, he linked the money to discussions of how much foreign companies would be able to participate with PEMEX in the Mexican oil industry.[95] From that point on, Washington told Mexico to look to the private investor for the capital and expertise it needed to pursue its goal of industrial modernization.

On April 26 and 28, 1947 the Banco de México issued two circulars that ordered banks to restrict credits that financed luxury imports such as automobiles, refrigerators, radios, phonographs, furs, and jewelry. Underlying the problem was a shocking deterioration of the country's terms of trade; the foreign trade deficit increased from 177 million pesos in 1946 to 400 million in 1947. The Banco de México's effort was the kind of response the United States saw as a threat to its exports; however, U.S. economic diplomats viewed this as preferable to exchange controls or currency depreciation. As one economic diplomat wrote in 1947, "While the risks are great, the Embassy is willing to assume the responsibility for directing the battle against unreasonable tariffs and unfair and discriminatory import restrictions."[96] In years to come they would work against these restrictions.

The Alemán model of development rested solidly on the shoulders of the poor. By contrast to conditions during the war years, there was near self-sufficiency in food production during President Alemán's term of office (apart from regular shortages of wheat and lard). However, food was becoming less affordable, and the standard of living was under great pressure. According to one unpublished report, "No reliable index on wages is available but the Banco de México calculates that the purchasing power of the peso for consumer goods in terms of 1929 as 100 declined from 24.47 in June 1950 to 18.28 in June 1951 and 17.67 in June 1952, a decline of 25 and 4 percent respectively."[97]

Workers and even labor leaders did not need to have access to a truthful price index to know that the standard of living was falling. By the spring of 1950 some PRI labor leaders were arguing that in the current round of wage settlements the government had essentially gone over to management's side by supporting—many said dictating—settlements, as wages fell another 12 to 20 percent behind the cost of living. Government policies, like a 58 percent increase in telephone charges, reinforced that pressure.[98]

A reduction in public works projects followed a downturn in sales and rise in the cost of living. One U.S. diplomat concluded that it was in the United States' interest to work to strengthen the Mexican economy. As he put it in his remarkably inaccurate forecast, "The task of strengthening and stimulating a comparatively underdeveloped economy like that of Mexico's should be much less expensive than and much simpler than was the task of 'priming the pump' in our own country ten or fifteen years ago."[99] Juan de Zengotita was one of the most acute analysts in the U.S. embassy; however, his optimism about the battle against underdevelopment—shared by such renowned economists as Simon Kuznits and Paul Samuelson in the same period—should be viewed as evidence of his generation's outlook rather than as an accurate prediction.

At the same time that the standard of living was dropping, there were attacks on the social wage. The social security program faced decreased funding, and it was widely suspected that the government was cool in its support for the popular gains in the social wage that had been achieved during the Mexican Revolution, limited as they were in such a poor country. The Confederación de Cámaras Nacionales de Comercio petitioned strongly against an extension of the IMSS program to broader segments of the community. Even the Cámara Nacional de Industrias de Transformación was supporting that effort by the end of 1947.[100] Within the context of the massive entry of foreign private capital, minor political reform, a significant shift by the governing party away from support for the labor movement, and policies of economic nationalism, there emerged a major effort to change the tone of many important social institutions in Mexico.

Alemán's Social Program

There were a number of proposed social and political changes in the Alemán era that were intended to modify Mexican culture in fundamental ways. Essentially, the new administration attempted to strengthen the social hierarchy and to undercut any sources of power other than the government or the marketplace. These initiatives revealed something less than a total dedication to the preservation of liberties for individual Mexicans.

In January 1948 the government tried to pass an Authors' Rights Law. The law gave the authorities the right to restrict or prohibit publication of any written work that was—in the view of the government—contrary to "morality or public peace."[101] Clearly, the Alemán administration wanted the right to censor any publication in the country. A veritable storm of protest gathered around what critics dubbed the "gag law" or the "super-padlock law." Constitutional experts argued that the law violated Articles 6 and 7 of the constitution of 1917. Considered especially pernicious was Article 11 of the proposed law, which stated that documents in official archives could not be published without the consent of the authorities. This provision promised to reduce the already slight degree of public accountability that officials faced whatever their activities had been. The law threatened "whistle-blowers" with up to two years in prison. The veracity of an allegation was not to be allowed as a defense against prosecution under the Authors' Rights Law. This proposal was tantamount to creating a total dictatorship. In this case, public opposition forced the administration to let the proposal lapse. Soon, however, the government tried again.

Education has been an ideological battleground in Mexico since independence. From the old battles against the Church's monopoly of the civil register and education, to the anticlerical innovations of the 1920s, to President Cárdenas's attempt to bring socialist education to the young, ideological struggles frequently focused upon the classroom. At one level, debates over education could be seen

as a symbolic battle for the hearts and minds of the next generation, frequently based upon the most simple assumptions about
the replication of culture. Yet in a society with extremely low levels
of literacy and a high degree of class differentiation, the ability to
command the politics of education also represented control over
access to positions of power and privilege.

During the Alemán presidency education was demoted as an
item on the national agenda, usually receiving only a few para-
graphs in the annual presidential messages. According to Héctor
Aguilar Camín, "The utilitarian stripping that put education at the
service of the captains of industry, continued throughout the suc-
ceeding presidential terms as a norm in the educational policy of
the nation. Essentially, from that point the prolongation, increase
and multiplication of nationalistic education was distilled, to the
point of patriotic delirium, as the civic and spiritual accumulation
of nationalism in Mexico."[102]

The focal point of the ideological struggle over education was
the Alemán Doctrine. In the first instance, it was an attempt to control the teachers union (SNTE), the largest union in Mexico. In February 1951 the Department of Public Education produced a
pamphlet entitled *Pro-México*. Alemán's educational principles were
issued in a form that closely resembled a secular catechism—twelve
points that became known, in the phrase of General Sánchez
Taboada, head of the PRI, as the Alemán Doctrine. *Pro-México* was
distributed to all public and private schools in Mexico. Instructions
accompanying the pamphlet ordered all teachers to incorporate it
immediately into their teaching, under pain of dismissal if they
refused. The SNTE organized a series of roundtable conferences to
start the process of disseminating the material through the ranks
of the nation's teachers. Those who objected—and the teachers had
been among the most radical workers under the Cárdenas administration—were threatened with dismissal. The Alemán administration reaped a storm of protest from teachers and members of the
general public, not only because of the authoritarian manner in
which the doctrine was implemented but also because of the hypocrisy of the effort.

The Alemán Doctrine consisted of a dozen propositions: (1) the
Mexican Revolution inspires the Alemán administration, (2) the
government is and must be considered "essentially democratic,"
(3) the government is one of law, (4) the government is and must
be considered honest, (5) hard work must be carried out by Mexicans, (6) the nation's resources must be used for the good of the

nation, (7) workers are the basis of the country's well being, (8) human resources are the most valuable resource, (9) the moral greatness of the nation is fundamental, (10) youth must recognize its responsibilities, (11) patriotism must be encouraged, and (12) "invariable dignity" must be maintained in international affairs. The government had fallen victim to psychological projection. The Right and the Left had been attacking the government for years on points 2 and 3. Point 4 generated a great deal of comment, and the historical record adds considerable fuel to contemporary allegations of corruption. Points 5 and 6 seemed contradictory within the context of falling standards of living and an onslaught of foreign capital; and finally, point 10 invited comparisons between the youth and their powerful elders.

The impression that the government was attacking any alternatives to its own point of view was reinforced by two specific actions. Both the Universidad Obrera and the newspaper *El Popular* had their budgets reduced significantly. These were two major institutions that employed people associated with Lombardo Toledano. There was even a degree of black humor in the treatment of those who lost their jobs. When workers were dismissed in the early days of the administration, they were sent to Lombardo Toledano's long-term colleague, Alejandro Carrillo, who was then head of the DDF. The head of the municipal government in Mexico City was a position that had traditionally dispensed considerable amounts of patronage. Carrillo was quoted as telling the unemployed that "although there are many posts which he has the right to fill . . . none of the people whom he has recommended have been given jobs."[103]

In short, the social initiatives of the Alemán administration attacked its political opponents, working-class organs of expression, and the individual's right to criticize the government. An attempt to bring the educational system under close ideological control of the government grew into a general assault on the freedoms of individual Mexicans. Rich and diverse pluralism would not be tolerated if the president had his way.

Alemán and the Church

Early in his career, Miguel Alemán had been inclined to take an anticlerical position. This viewpoint changed in the 1940s when, as minister of the interior, he reined in the anticlerical activities and tendencies within the governing party on the occasion of the fiftieth anniversary of the beatification of the Virgin of Guadalupe. Alemán opposed such party figures as Ramón Beteta and Alejandro Carrillo, who were well known for their anticlerical positions.

Once in power, Alemán played it both ways. Accommodation with the Church continued to gain momentum, as the government provided aid in the construction of churches and of roads to them. In 1948 the government decided to hold a Eucharistic Congress in Mexico City and offered the cooperation of police during processions. This offer was also extended when a piece of "the True Cross" was brought to the host city, thereby causing great congestion in 1950 as the devout pressed forward to see the relic. This offer was in direct contradiction of the constitution of 1917, which prohibited religious processions in public. The Salesian Order was allowed to return and reclaim its old buildings, which had recently been used as vocational schools. Perhaps the most symbolic deed in the reconciliation between Church and state during the Alemán years was the construction of a boulevard connecting Mexico City with the shrine to the Virgin of Guadalupe. Archbishop Luis María Martínez, on the eve of his departure to Rome in 1950, observed, "They are magnificent works that satisfy the heart of the majority of the Mexican nation which is Catholic, *por excelencia.*"

Yet the old strains of anticlericalism frequently reappeared. Luis Cataño Morlet, president of the Superior Court of Justice for the Federal District, publicly opposed these developments on the grounds that Articles 3 and 130 of the constitution were being violated. Some important figures, such as Martín Luis Guzmán, editor of *Tiempo* and head of the Partido Nacional Liberal Mexicano (founded on March 17, 1946), were deeply opposed to the resurgence of the Church.[104] Guzmán had to walk a fine line. Although his party had been moribund since he backed Alemán in 1946, and even though *Tiempo* received a state subsidy, he still felt free to attack the government over the accommodation.[105] His magazine was bitter in October 1947 when the Church carried out its coronation of the Virgin of Guadalupe.

Alemán had supported financially the founding of the PNLM on March 17, 1946. With Guzmán as president and Raúl Carranza, magistrate of the Superior Court, and General Esteban Calderón as vice presidents, the party attracted some distinguished figures, including Daniel Cosío Villegas as secretary, Antonio Pozzi of CONCAMIN, and Jesús Reyes Heroles, then a law professor at UNAM.[106] In spite of their opposition to him, Alemán had supported *Tiempo* and the PNLM financially for years, as had Raúl Noriega, the editor of the official newspaper *El Nacional*. Lombardo Toledano and the Mexican Left could take some encouragement from Guzmán's efforts, in contrast to the long list of battles that the Cardenistas were losing. The president calculated that it was in his interest to let the two sides vent their energy on the relatively innocuous issue of anticlericalism.

For its part, the Church hierarchy was so pleased with its accommodation with the authorities that it maintained a discreet silence on such delicate matters as state violence and corruption. After the election of Ruíz Cortines, the archbishop and others praised the state of religious freedom in Mexico and instructed their members to work with the new administration.

The Varieties of Dissent

The changes to the political life of the country were so deep and rapid that many Mexicans, within and outside of the governing party, were in a state of shock. The spoils of office rather than political principles became the fundamental battleground after the shift away from economic nationalism in the 1940s. "Thus the fact that a plethora of political groups has sprung into being and that ostensibly they are operating outside the PRI and are engaged in various degrees of criticism of the PRI and the administration up to this date does not mean that all of them are in fact antagonistic to the PRI and the administration or are discounting the possibility of merging their forces into the PRI's political machinery at a suitable time on mutual acceptable terms."[107]

Nevertheless, it is useful to look at politics at two distinct levels: the use of state power on the one hand, and the battle for the hearts and minds of the people on the other. By the latter standard, there were still many people who believed that the Mexican Revolution should be a fundamental commitment to reducing the differences between the rich and the poor at the same time that it defended the national sovereignty and fostered industrial modernization. Even within the party there was opposition to Alemanismo, which maintained fidelity to only the third of these propositions.

A group of figures close to Avila Camacho began meeting at the former president's home to bring pressure to bear upon the government from within the circles of the revolutionary family. "There is a feeling of moral depression along with resentment over the situation, both economic and political, to which Alemán has brought the country. The fact that the President himself is conscious of the unpopularity from which he is now suffering and the inherent dangers in the situation is shown by the precautions which are now being taken for his security." The reference was to the president's increased use of the secret service and his obvious anxiety when dealing with the public. The president transferred troops of the First Division from Puebla to Mexico City, and he organized, trained, and armed to the hilt a paratroop division as presidential guards for his personal protection.

Specifically, the group that formed around Avila Camacho was concerned with increasing price levels; the spate of new laws, many of which had been poorly thought out and were even hurting business; fraud and corruption; and "especially the interests of a small group surrounding the president and perhaps the president himself." Above all, they objected to the way these objectionable practices were supported by "strong arm tactics and gangster methods." The murder of Senator Mauro Angulo topped off the whole process, in their view; they understood this murder to have been ordered by someone thought to be close to the president.[108]

Within labor circles, tensions over corruption fueled the bitter battle to fill the position of secretary general of the CTM in January 1950. His anticorruption position helped Fidel Velázquez regain that high office from Fernando Amilpa, and Velázquez held the post until his death in 1997. The congress was a bitter affair:

> Labor sources friendly to the Alemán Administration report a widespread dissatisfaction with the Administration, not so much on labor grounds—although the railwaymen, civil servants, and school teachers have complaints outstanding over the Government's refusal to increase their earnings—as on the grounds of widespread graft and corruption. This condition can hardly be reported as a novelty in Mexico but the fact that elements favorable to the Administration are commenting upon it seems worthy of recording.[109]

Dissent from the ranks of those who had formerly considered themselves to be firm supporters of the revolution led to numerous attempts to rectify the situation. Many thought of forming a true party of the Mexican Revolution.

The Formation of the Partido Popular

The formation of the Partido Popular coincided with the Mexican Roundtable, a summit of the Left held in the wake of Alemán's assault on labor. The new party straddled two worlds between the government and supporters of more radical versions of the Mexican Revolution. The party served as a genuine focus for those who felt that the PRI had moved so far to the right so quickly that it had left too much of the social program of the Mexican Revolution behind. Certainly, the hard rhetoric of the party reinforced this view. As seen through a Lombardista filter, the Partido Popular blamed all local opposition to the PRI either on the parties of the right or on U.S. influence—never on the policies of the governing party. The formation of the party began immediately after one of Lombardo's worse debacles—a speech on December 16, 1945, in which he asserted that U.S. firms were smuggling arms to the Sinarquistas; the next month he also blamed the PAN for the massacre in León.[110] These accusations were so outlandish that the entire politically aware community disowned them. Time and again Lombardo Toledano vastly overstated the case and ignored legitimate local anger over political impositions.

There was always something fishy about the Partido Popular, later known as the Partido Popular Socialista. Unhappy with independent socialists in the Acción Socialista Unificada (ASU), the party adopted a strident version of antiimperialistic rhetoric that blamed the United States for Mexico's every ill. At the same time, the party was extremely wary of confronting the government. Suspicions proliferated that the party was a government ploy, officially funded to provide an outlet for disaffected revolutionaries but under the ultimate control of the PRI. This view was reinforced by the fact that the government still subsidized *El Popular*, even if to a reduced degree.[111] Whether the party started out that way or merely evolved in that direction, the evidence for this suspicion comes from a number of directions. In spite of the party's extreme anti-U.S. stance, its leaders kept U.S. diplomats informed of their activities. The U.S. ambassador had superb intelligence on the Partido Popular, even in its formative stages. He boasted that he knew of the final formation of the party within two hours of the event. Moreover, as he told his boss in Washington, the inside information on Lombardo Toledano "doesn't cost us a cent."[112]

The opening session of the constituent assembly of the Partido Popular revealed many of the fundamental weaknesses of Lombardo Toledano's approach to politics. The six hundred delegates were treated to a two-hour speech by Lombardo in which he praised Miguel Alemán's attitude toward the formation of the new party, "to silence from the audience." Blaming the nation's problems on the clergy and on Abelardo Rodríguez, "as if the leadership of the PRI could in no way be held responsible for their actions," Lombardo repeatedly asked the audience to distinguish between President Alemán and the wicked men who ran the provinces.

The following day, after the leadership of the party had presented a bland platform, the artist Diego Rivera rose to demand that Article 27 of the 1917 constitution be returned to its original form. Lombardo was silent as delegates demanded that Deputy Victoriano Anguiano, who had voted for the emasculation of Article 27 in the first days of the Alemán administration, respond since he was present in the audience. Lombardo took refuge in procedural maneuvers to allow voting, for the first time, on a state-by-state basis rather than by individuals, thus allowing his new machine to defeat Rivera's proposal. The accusations apparently did not hurt Anguiano either since by 1949 he had become secretary general of the Partido Popular (later he was forced out for openly attacking former president Cárdenas).

At the end of the inaugural session—in an electoral process that mirrored the political culture of the PRI—Lombardo forced the acceptance by acclamation of an official slate of party officers. Unwilling to trust the majority view of the delegates, and in the total absence of any reflection upon the process of political decision making, this new party doomed itself to replicate many of the worst abuses of the PRI. Little wonder that by 1949 some of the party's most distinguished independent voices—Narciso Bassols, Víctor Manuel Villaseñor, and Diego Rivera—had resigned from it in disgust over the way the party's only successful candidate, Ignacio F. Pesquería, had broken his promises and collaborated with the PRI. It was quite a way to run an opposition party.[113]

More interesting still was the way Alemán dealt with the Partido Popular. After two years of publicly agonizing over the formation of the new party in the pages of *El Popular*, and having finally convinced himself that he had found a formula by which he could oppose the PRI without offending the government, Lombardo Toledano faced a reality check. President Alemán simply announced that anyone who joined the new party could not also be a member of the PRI. At this point, Mexico's best-known labor functionary explained his attitude to U.S. officials: "Fidel Velázquez told the Embassy's Labor Reporting Officer that there was no thought of opposition to the government behind the formation of the party. However, he added, because in many states the Governors are crooked, and corruption and the cost of living are disaffecting the people, it is necessary that a political force be organized to bring pressure on such governors to mend their ways and take steps to alleviate the distress and satisfy the complaints of the people."[114] This escape-valve theory for the Partido Popular probably offers the best explanation for the formation of the new party. Lombardo's unremitting—even forlorn—commitment to bring the Partido Popular into the president's good graces denied the party its natural constituency.

After Lombardo Toledano was expelled from the PRI and the CTM, he also tried to organize a new labor confederation, the UGOCM. By the time it tried to gain recognition from the World Federation of Trade Unions (WFTU) in 1949, it claimed to represent 711 collective ejidos, 18 agricultural colonies, 8 farmers' cooperatives, 4 agricultural cooperatives, 224 local unions, 7 regional confederations, 9 locals of the oil workers, and sugar workers.[115] Since there were an estimated ten thousand unions in Mexico, the UGOCM was a doomed effort. Resistance to Alemanismo from labor would remain fragmented and isolated, if frequently courageous.

The Judiciary and the Honey Murders

The remarkable independence of the judiciary in the face of the massacre at León raised the possibility that judicial independence might increase in Mexico. Certainly, opposition politicians quickly grasped at this straw. But it became clear that the Alemán administration would tolerate no such judicial autonomy. In the wake of the Supreme Court's unprecedented decision to send two justices to León to investigate the massacre, at least six other cases were aired in the press and pressure mounted on the court to investigate them under the authority granted it by Article 97 of the constitution. The most striking of these cases concerned the murder of five members of the deposed municipal council of Honey, Puebla, and their chauffeur. The factional and labor battles over control in that state were among the most ferocious in the country. Allegations of official lawlessness, caciquismo, and union violence abounded. The battle was especially fierce because this was the home base of Maximino Avila Camacho and William Jenkins.

The murder of the five deposed councillors generated several versions of the events. Killed were Municipal President Herminio Rodríguez, Chief of Police Elardo Neri, President of the Ejido Emilio Cruz, and two ejiditarios. In one account the murders were entirely local and personal, committed by an army lieutenant named Gayosso to settle an old score against his father. However, a more political version insisted that the slain men had been in conflict with the state governor, Carlos I. Betancourt. They had been denied an interview with him on July 14, 1947; on their way home, they were kidnapped fifty-seven kilometers from Puebla and subsequently killed. Since the crime occurred a few feet over the state border, it became a federal investigation.

It was probable that the incident was political because, on May 12, a mass meeting of some six thousand peasants in Puebla had initiated a campaign against what they called the imposition of the governor. He was accused of having increased taxes in the face of an absolute lack of public improvements in the state and of having looted 3.8 million pesos from the state treasury. As one diplomat noted, "Betancourt is reported to rest confidently on his 4- million peso contribution to Alemán's campaign fund, with which contribution he likewise explained the lack of money available for public improvements. He has sought no conciliation of the popular elements in the state. He has antagonized the Federal representatives of Puebla by refusing to consult or be consulted with them on any question whatsoever."[116]

Whether or not the Supreme Court should investigate the case quickly emerged as the central issue. Precedent held that if the case were classified as political, even if a common crime such as murder was involved, the Supreme Court would not interfere. Justice Fernando de la Fuente argued that the court should intervene to investigate the murders. At this point, Justice Islas Bravo left the room claiming that he was hungry, thus causing the suspension of the session. The conservative press had a field day in stressing the hunger of the people for justice in this case. *Excélsior's* cartoonist, Freyre, mercilessly characterized Islas Bravo as a glutton at his table watched by starved peasants from Puebla and the townsfolk of León. On July 29, by a vote of 17 to 2, the court decided not to investigate the Honey murders. Legal sophistry abounded in the argument, and cynics commented that the court would quickly run out of investigators if the León precedent was followed. Press demands for the resignation of Justice Islas Bravo proliferated. Minister of the Interior Héctor Pérez Martínez responded that the governor of Puebla was on good terms with the murdered men, thus suspicions were in error.[117]

Nevertheless, one last glimmer of independence was still on the court. The Corona thesis—that a strike declared while a contract exists is illegal—represented a major attack against the labor movement. Courageously, on February 20, 1948, the labor chamber of the Supreme Court struck down the Corona thesis. It was understood that Justice Fernando de la Fuente, the most independent member of the Supreme Court, had been behind the move. Fernando de la Fuente then became the target of a murder attempt, after which he was less outspoken.[118] The Supreme Court, having extended itself over the events in León, backed off, and the moment of judicial independence ended.

The Right Opposition

As President Alemán shifted considerably to the right, even by the standards of his predecessor, there was profound resentment in much of the traditional base of the governing party. The Right, now primarily the Acción Nacional, the Fuerza Popular, and what remained of the Sinarquistas, continued to press its campaigns against impositions, or electoral fraud. In cases like that of Zitácuaro, Michoacán, on March 23, 1947, the AN was successful in forcing the municipal president to flee the country. At other times, students were able to force the increase of subsidies for the university. Similar episodes form a constant rather than a variable in contemporary Mexican political history.

At the beginning of the Alemán presidency there was such a long list of state and local crises that it is tempting to view the constant churning of conflict as part of the price that the government had to pay for shifting the course of the revolution. The explanation with which the PRI was most comfortable was that the Right (the AN, the Sinarquistas, and the like) was behind these events, and undoubtedly it was to some degree, but probably not to as great a degree as it liked to think. Some found the opposition to be so ineffective that they thought it must be a conspiracy, "Confidential reports are that Manuel Gómez Morín, the leader of the PAN, is an intimate adviser of President Alemán on many projects sponsored by the government."[119] This may well have been the case with the PP; however, it was less likely so with the PAN. Rather, what seems to have happened is that, from positions on both the right and the left, people were eager to take advantage of opportunities to embarrass the government. At times the internal conflicts within the official machine made it easier for outsiders to act more effectively. Finally, it must be remembered that there were still local political machines and contending factions in many regions, and a local conflict, pursued in the name of anti-imposition politics, could mask a wide variety of local/federal conflicts.

A complete mix-up occurred in the local elections in Tapachula, Chiapas, in 1946. Elections in November had seen a typical case of imposition. The machine candidate, Luis Guizar Oseguerra, had confronted Ernesto A. Córdova, candidate of the Civic Party of Tapachula. The PRI offered no candidate in the November 17 elections. When the government announced on November 20 that Guizar Oseguerra had won, it set off a series of demonstrations that lasted for the remainder of the year, culminating in a rally in which troops fired into a crowd killing nine and wounding forty-one.[120]

Unlike the similar episode in León, this one was politically messy. When the oficial mayor de gobernación arrived in Tapachula, he arrested forty-three people. Eventually, the governor of Chiapas, Gabriel Sarmiento, arrested the state attorney general, the inspector of police, and a number of policemen. On January 6, Undersecretary of Gobernación Ernesto P. Uruchurtu announced that the governor had been given a leave of absence and that two deputies had been charged with the shooting. Luis Guizar was arrested and then released.[121] The events may have simply reflected confusion in the official party. One U.S. diplomat reported: "This Embassy has learned from a confidential source in Gobernación that Señor Ernesto A. Córdova was the candidate certified by Gobernación as the official government candidate, that a brother of the Health Minister, Dr. Rafael Pascasio Gamboa, had designated another candidate and that former Governor Juan M. Esponda double crossed both Gobernación and Gamboa and put in his candidate, Luis Guizar. It was stated that this latter candidate was not wanted either by the people of the town or by the Federal Government."[122] If this statement is accurate, then the massacre becomes the by-product of official crossed wires. However, it is likely that within such a confused situation the people of the town found more room to manipulate than normally would have been possible. Clearly, the Alemán years saw rough politics.

General and Governor Edmundo Sánchez Cano, of Oaxaca, faced opposition as a number of forces came together. Merchants were up in arms over high tax increases, students were outraged at decrees adversely affecting the autonomy of the institute of arts and sciences in the state university, and a series of impositions in local elections had generated ill feelings in a number of communities. Shops closed in January 1947 until the governor rescinded a large tax increase and relented on cuts to the university budget; however, it still took federal troops to get officials into their offices. After the events at León and Tapachula, the protests in Oaxaca were played up in the local press as well as in the D.F. The minister of the interior, Héctor Pérez Martínez, went to Oaxaca, and Sánchez Cano asked for an extended leave of absence. Eduardo Vasconcelos, of the Supreme Court, was named interim governor as tension eased.[123]

The political struggles over the governorships in 1947 found a number of state governors in distress. In the first half of the year, six governors fell from office before their allotted term was over. Two were forced from office by the pressure of public opinion: Juan M. Esponda of Chiapas and General E. Sancho Cano of Oaxaca. Governor García Barragón of Jalisco was deposed by the president acting in union with the Permanent Chamber. Governor Blas Corral Martínez of Durango died of natural causes; however, his death was surrounded by scandal (see Chapter 5).

Governor Cepeda Davila of Coahuila committed suicide while on a trip to Mexico City. A strike by local taxpayers against his 400 percent increase in taxes in July 1947 may have contributed to his problems. A group of prominent citizens had also gone to Mexico City to make a countercase against Governor Cepeda Davila, claiming that he had looted 2 million pesos. The most outrageous of his initiatives was to enact a special levy for the nonexistent University of Coahuila.

The case of Governor Hugo Pedro González of Tamaulipas was ambiguous. In a bloody incident at Llera, on March 12, twelve people were killed and a larger number wounded. The government blamed the AN for inciting the crowd of farmers, who had been fired upon by government troops as they approached the Municipal Palace. Yet the picture was clouded. Reports in *El Mundo* of Tampico were undoubtedly influenced by the governor's support of the strike as a way of influencing the editorial policy of the newspaper. In addition, the fact that a proposed state tax on cotton was facing considerable local opposition made the local business community angry.

Beyond these examples in which protests against governors had succeeded were other, less successful, protests. The governor of Guanajuato held on to his office, and the new governor of Jalisco, Avila Camacho's former presidential secretary, Jesús González Gallo, made some headway against the dissidents.[124] Governor Fernando Foglio Miramontes of Chihuahua came under attack for allowing slot machines to operate in Ciudad Juárez. And opposition business interests in Sonora were especially angry at the way that governor and ex-president Abelardo Rodríguez established his own business interests as monopolies. Governor Macías Valenzuela of Sinaloa faced similar accusations. The league of industrialists in Monterrey continued the battle against the government and especially the CTM. Some two thousand petitions were filed over an alleged imposition in 1947 in Monterrey.[125]

The U.S. embassy believed that when mass demonstrations took place against imposed governors and their abuses of power, the policy of Gobernación was to correct the abuses but to keep the offenders in office, lest other groups be encouraged.[126] Such appeared to have happened in Tabasco, Nuevo León, Guerrero, Querétaro, Sinaloa, Morelos, Chihuahua, and Sonora. In Sonora, Governor Abelardo Rodríguez was forced to rescind a tax on the sale of fruits and vegetables.

Old Revolutionaries

The administration's shift to the right, corruption, and disregard for electoral propriety angered many, especially those who identified with the Cardenista traditions. Xavier Icasa shared that anger, and he had been a member of the Supreme Court in that brief moment when it had exercised a measure of independence from the executive. In discussions with a U.S. diplomat, he admitted that everyone in his circle was angry. However, everyone in the political classes simply wanted a job; and Alemán had power.[127] The pro-labor policies of the Cárdenas administration were being attacked, and the formation of the CUT seemed to signal a deep division within the revolutionary coalition. Many thought of Lázaro Cárdenas as the natural leader for those who abhorred these changes. Yet they were eternally disappointed. A few months after he left office, Cárdenas gave an interview to Betty Ross of the North American Newspaper Alliance in which he stated that he would speak no more of politics in public.[128] For the remainder of his life, he was true to his word. Cárdenas's loyalty was to the governing party even as it dismantled many of the measures that he had innovated. His withdrawal from politics was already clear at the beginning of Alemán's term.

When Alemán visited the United States in May, every newspaper in Mexico reported on his tour with headlines for the entire nine days of the journey. The press was exuberant in boasting of the success of the tour. National pride merged with a desire to gain support for future industrial development. *El Popular* was especially effusive in its praise for the president. Embarrassing issues like U.S. imperialism, the treatment of the braceros, and the rapacity of some foreign investors were ignored. Small incidents like President Truman's *abrazo* of President Alemán, the remark by Truman that he "is a great guy," and his son's inauguration into the Boy Scouts were widely reported. *Novedades* was so carried away it erroneously reported that the United States would return the flags and memorabilia that had been captured in 1847.[129]

When Lázaro Cárdenas visited the returning president and congratulated him heartily upon his triumph, it seemed to put rumors of a split between the two men to rest. President Cárdenas was, in effect, extending an additional degree of legitimacy to Alemán and his program. That the former president was then placed in charge of a huge irrigation project in his home state of Michoacán seemed to seal the deal. Those disaffected from Alemán's version of the Mexican Revolution would not find help from Cárdenas.

Alemán was not above using his influence to have a go at his old rival from time to time. At the beginning of his administration there was another outbreak of hoof-and-mouth disease. Slaughter teams again went about killing the animals of rural Mexicans. One popular version of events blamed the importation of zebu cattle from Brazil for the disease. In some press accounts, former president Cárdenas was identified as having imported the cattle. Cárdenas had been importing cattle from that country, but he was angry that his cattle were singled out. Moreover, he understood it as a political attack since both Avila Camacho and Alemán had done the same and were not mentioned.[130] Cárdenas suffered these slights in silence, and he always honored his commitment to not comment publicly upon the policies of his successors. Those who hated Alemanismo would have to find other means of expression.

Narciso Bassols and a group involved with the publication of *Combate* (including Manuel Mesa, Ricardo J. Zevada, Emigdio Adame, and Víctor Manuel Villaseñor) lambasted the government's shift to the right. They fell back on an issue around which Mexican nationalism had developed; they exposed the plan to allow foreign capital to re-enter the Mexican petroleum industry. This battle intensified when Fidel Velázquez returned as head of the CTM. Only after this change, and after *Combate* had been investigating the issue, did Lombardo Toledano and his group at *El Popular* "pretend to have discovered the issue," in the phrase of Víctor Manuel

Villaseñor.[131] Throughout the Alemán years they continued to fight the plan.

By the end of Alemán's *sexenio*, pressures were boiling over with some frequency. In 1951 dentistry students at UNAM began to frolic in the tradition of water-throwing in the countryside on San Juan's Day. Fun gave way to broader political frustration as the number of student protesters quickly grew to four thousand. The government's response eventually left one hundred fifty students injured. Although there is nothing new about student riots, the attempt to blame the episode on Communist dentists was innovative, if somewhat lame.[132]

Many workers no longer looked to their old leaders. After being on strike for four months in 1950, the coal miners at the ASARCO mine in Nueva Rosito organized another hunger march on Mexico City; at some points, up to five thousand miners participated.[133] When they finally arrived in the capital, in April 1951, their numbers were reduced to twenty-two hundred. As they camped out on an athletic field under considerable media attention, the miners confronted their leaders for failing to support their struggle. It was a dramatic moment.

There was considerable disquiet within the PRI. On the third day of the PRI's 1953 convention, General Jacinto Treviño dropped a political bombshell in the Palacio de Bellas Artes. As a general who held the highest rank in the Mexican Army and treasured his long relationship with President Calles, he raised the issue of false elections: "For forty-two years you have been talking about effective suffrage. When have we had it? When has it been respected?" He attacked the "sycophants and hypocrites of the revolution" and singled out William Jenkins, the sugar baron, banker, and movie magnate; former president Abelardo Rodríguez; and Jorge Pasquel, for maintaining a fuel distribution monopoly. Many in the audience shouted him down, but there was also a significant minority within the PRI that supported him.[134] The PRI appeared to be generating its own opposition.

The Selection of Ruíz Cortines

There was considerable speculation that President Alemán might try for a second term, possibly using the Korean War as a pretext to continue in office. Indeed, Luis Morones of the CROM had met with presidential secretary Rogelio de la Selva in August 1951 before coming out in favor of a second term for President Alemán. This was seen as the president bringing out his stalking-horse. However, in his annual address to the nation on the first day of September the president disclaimed any interest in a second term. As one diplomat put it, "Embassy discussions suggest that perhaps even the president was taken back by the enthusiastic reception given by everyone to his disavowal to run for office again and the immediate readiness of everyone around him to take him at his word."[135]

Mexico had accumulated a number of ex-presidents as the party faced the selection of 1952. General Cárdenas was probably the most influential former president, at least with those who identified with earlier currents of the Mexican Revolution. Portes Gil had been effectively removed from a position of significance when he became ambassador to India. Avila Camacho's influence diminished to the point of obscurity, and Abelardo Rodríguez's sway was limited to the northwest and to the world of business, although at times he could still assert himself in the capital. Generals Ortíz Rubio and Adolfo de la Huerta exercised only minor influence.

Several candidates were mooted for the 1952 election. As minister of the interior, Ruíz Cortines was a leading candidate; however, his health was believed to be poor, and some still accused him of having collaborated with U.S. authorities during the invasion of Veracruz in 1914. Nevertheless, his reputation for honesty stood for a great deal in the later phases of the Alemán administration. Ramón Beteta, the finance minister, was a possible candidate although the fact that he was married to a woman from the United States was widely believed to eliminate him. Furthermore, he was not immune from accusations of corruption.[136]

The ministers of communications and of agriculture, García López and Ortíz Garza, were also mentioned occasionally. By far the most frequently discussed candidate during the 1950–51 run-up to the selection was the president's nephew, the head of the DDF, Fernando Casas Alemán. But it seems that the nephew failed to show adequate respect for the uncle as the selection approached, and it was Miguel who ruined Fernando's chances at the end of 1951. Casas Alemán and his associates had jumped the gun when they made it clear which members of the Alemán administration would have to go. At the top of their list was Senator Carlos Serrano, chief of the Dirección de Seguridad; rumors abounded that Serrano threatened Casas Alemán's life should he become the *tapado*. Then Casas Alemán publicly upstaged his uncle at the dedication of the Lerma waterworks on September 4, 1951, where his supporters passed out Casas Alemán lapel buttons and even wore them on the platform in front of the president. They followed that occasion with an advertising campaign that the president viewed as impertinent.[137] Thus, Adolfo Ruíz Cortines won his party's nomination on October 14, 1951. When the president named Serrano's longtime confidant Ernesto Uruchurtu to replace Ruíz Cortines as minister of the interior for the final months of the administration, he was making a political statement.

The same pattern began to emerge in the run-up to the 1952 election as General Henríquez Guzmán initially floated his candidacy on the left wing of the PRI, complete with rumors of former president Cárdenas's support. This time, however, he did not pull out as the PRI named its candidate. His campaign served as a rallying point for the disaffected, and after the election, many of his followers were arrested. Henríquez Guzmán's dependence on building contracts from the government for the Pan American Highway and other construction projects limited his willingness to offend the official party. It is likely that his candidacies were preemptive moves to incapacitate the Cárdenas wing of the PRI. That had been the pattern in the 1946 campaign, and the effect of Henríquez Guzmán's efforts in 1952 was much the same. Again, it seems useful to separate Henríquez Guzmán from the Henriquistas. The police were following those who flocked to his banner. Whatever their leader's ultimate relationship with the president might be, it is clear that such Henriquista figures as General Marcelino García Barragán, General Celestino Gasca, General Luis Alamillo Flores, Ernesto Soto Reyes, Professor Graciano Sánchez, Ing. Cesar Martino, and Agustín Guzmán Velasco were under a police surveillance that consisted of recording their public statements and their movements.[138]

Further evidence of the pantomimelike nature of the opposition parties can be seen in the agreement between the PRI, the Federación de Partidos del Pueblo Mexicano (Henríquez Guzmán's party), and the Partido Popular to the effect that the minor parties would submit joint nominees for positions of deputies and senators. Thus the election still saw only token opposition to the PRI. The PCM and the PP agreed to support Lombardo Toledano for president in the 1952 elections; however, his candidacy had little effect. Lombardo's long years of sophistry in favor of the PRM and the PRI had undermined his credibility even among his former followers, and his enemies were determined. Official election results were that he won only 2 percent of the vote. Few seriously charged electoral fraud in this case.[139]

The diminishing influence of labor is best seen in the loss of strength and autonomy of the membership in unions. U.S. sources believed that the CTM's active membership had decreased from 1,000,000 (or 1,500,000 including friendly unions) in 1940 to between 400,000 and 600,000 members in 1946 and then to only 250,000 to 300,000 members by 1951. Moreover, they believed, based upon sources within Gobernación, that whereas Lombardo Toledano might have commanded one million votes in 1946, by 1952 the CTM was totally under the influence of the PRI. Union after union paid the price of co-optation. Between the two elections, the CGT saw its membership decrease from 25,000 members to 5,000 members. The railroad workers had held their membership at about 65,000 to 70,000 members; however, after Campa pulled out they were completely dominated by the PRI. The mining unions in the SITMMSRM saw their membership drop from 80,000 to 52,000 between the two elections as their independence also diminished. Similar losses of membership and autonomy occurred within the FSTSE, the CNC (although that organization continued nationally to claim millions of peasants as members), the COCM, the CNT, the power workers' STERM, and the electrical workers' SME. The Partido Popular's UGOCM undoubtedly exercised more autonomy; however, its membership was only a fraction of the 625,000 members it claimed. The U.S. embassy attaché believed that a more accurate figure would have been 20,000 to 50,000 members.[140] A measure of the taming of labor under Alemán can be seen in that no labor organization openly supported a candidate other than the nominee of the PRI in 1952. The unions carefully delayed their conventions until after the official nominee was revealed.

The most vigorous campaign to influence the PRI's selection procedure emerged in a press release on April 15, 1950, through a document called "In Defense of the Cárdenas Regime." At one level, the document was a response to recent hostile articles against Cardenismo in *Excélsior* by Victoriano Anguiano and in *Hoy* by José Rubén Romero. At another level, it was an attempt to focus opinion upon the degree to which the Alemán administration had diverted the course of the Mexican Revolution. Former President Cárdenas's hand was seen behind this document because two of his closest associates had signed the petition. Ignacio García Tellez was the ex-president's present private secretary and had been his minister of the interior. Silviano Barba González was the ex-president's first cousin and had been an intimate friend since their childhood. The statement safely focused upon the repudiation of

Miguel Alemán and Adolfo Ruiz Cortines during the presidential campaign. *Courtesy Hermanos Mayo, Archivo General de la Nación, Mexico City*

reelection. U.S. embassy sources learned that Cárdenas and Alemán had engaged in an unsatisfactory meeting on April 8, and the release of the document was Lázaro Cárdenas's response.[141] Undoubtedly, the episode formed part of the bargaining process leading toward the party's selection of the next candidate. The ploy blocked any talk of Alemán's reelection.

The selection of Adolfo Ruíz Cortines as the candidate of the PRI opened a new stage in Mexican politics—the era of the institutionalized candidate. Ruíz Cortines had spent virtually his entire adult life within the governing party. Formerly, candidates had held governorships, been generals, or had held some other position before reaching the highest office. Born in Veracruz in 1894, Ruíz Cortines received a minimal education. After only three years in secondary school in Jalapa, he entered the Constitutionalist forces of General Treviño and fought at the battle of Ebano. From being paymaster of the division, he moved on to working with the High Commission that reviewed military records in Mexico City. It was while he was working as a clerk in the 1930s in the DDF that his career took off when Miguel Alemán took him under his wing.

Ruíz Cortines's career then followed Alemán's. When Alemán was elected governor of Veracruz in 1936, Ruíz Cortines became his secretary general, which made him acting governor whenever

Alemán was out of the state. When don Miguel became minister of the interior, don Adolfo moved up to become his executive officer; and when Alemán ran for president, Ruíz Cortines was the campaign manager. They were also business partners in a number of deals, including the Veracruz pineapple project. However, Ruíz Cortines never held a major post in his own right.

There was an old accusation against Ruíz Cortines that he had collaborated with the U.S. occupational forces in Veracruz back in 1914, which was unlikely since he was only twenty at the time and not in any position of importance. U.S. diplomats privately looked at their records to see if the accusations had any basis but were unable to find any record relating to him. When the state legislatures of Veracruz, Aguascalientes, Guanajuato, and Guerrero announced that their investigations had found no support for the charges, it cleared the way for his selection.

As Alemán's minister of the interior, Ruíz Cortines displayed unquestioned loyalty. He became wealthy without especially developing a reputation for corruption, certainly by the standards of Alemanismo. U.S. diplomats thought that his money came from Axis nationals in the early stages of World War II; his funds clearly did not come from his family. Ruíz Cortines never outshone his mentor, and he advanced by specializing in the faithful implementation of instructions. As one diplomat of the period rather succinctly put it, "Party loyalty has been his chief concern."[142]

Imposition politics remained a characteristic of the Alemán years, even to the end. On March 16, 1952, members of the PRI clashed with supporters of the FPPM when both groups tried to hold a rally at the same time in the same place. One person died and twelve were wounded. On the evening of March 21, 1952, several thousand people in Oaxaca demonstrated against the promulgation of a new tax by Governor Manuel Mayoral Heredia. When they approached the governor's palace, they were met with shots; three were killed and twenty were wounded. In this case, charges of official corruption abounded. Businesses stayed closed in Oaxaca until April 2.

The tame nature of the union movement could be clearly seen when on July 29, 1951, General Henríquez Guzmán announced his candidacy for president. The response of the docile union movement was, of course, negative. Fidel Velázquez was especially innovative in describing the rules of democratic politics. He faulted Henríquez Guzmán, like General Almazán and Lic. Padilla before him, for making the fundamental mistake of launching his political campaign by attacking the administration he proposed to succeed.

Adolfo Ruiz Cortines is sworn in as president of Mexico. *Courtesy Hermanos Mayo, Archivo General de la Nación, Mexico City*

By the end of his term, President Alemán had come to dominate the Cárdenas wing of the party. Old revolutionaries were still unable to rally around a candidate opposed to the changes of the 1940s. Without Cárdenas's direct participation, Cardenismo remained a sentimental and increasingly nostalgic memory. The hegemonic domination of Alemán's forces may be revealed by a small incident. Of all the economists in the country, Jesús Silva Herzog was perhaps the one most closely identified with ex-president Cárdenas's program. He had headed the Silva Herzog Commission that investigated the petroleum industry, and his recommendations had been a central link in the chain of events that led to the petroleum expropriation in 1938. By November 1950 it was stunning to see Jesús Silva Herzog write to the president, denying a report in *Excélsior* asserting that he had been active in an opposition movement. He assured the president that he was dedicating himself to cultural roles and would not participate in any political activity, a response that President Alemán said *"enteréme con satisfación."*[143] A most revealing glimpse of the circles in which Alemán moved came when the government of Major Oscar Osorio in El Salvador recommended Miguel Alemán for the Nobel Peace Prize, a suggestion that the Nobel Prize Committee "noted with displeasure."[144]

First Word/Last Word

By the time the contours of Miguel Alemán's counterrevolution had become clear, many of the country's most eloquent voices had passed into the ranks of the opposition. Daniel Cosío Villegas was a prime example. As a young historian and economist he had represented his country at the Bretton Woods conference. His contributions to the intellectual life of his country—which continued for decades—were already notable. Moreover, his ability to give institutional expression to intellectual concerns was unique. It was a courageous move, therefore, in 1947, when he published the article "La Crisis de México." Cosío Villegas argued that the government gave the appearance of a "revolution exhausted." Although the program of the Mexican Revolution had never been totally unified, there had been, nevertheless, three fundamental propositions that served as a common denominator for that great movement. The first proposition was a commitment to oppose the unending retention of power by a small group of leaders, known as *continuísmo*. The second was a commitment to decrease the high level of inequity among Mexicans. Finally, the third was a commitment to end the domination of Mexico by foreigners. In Cosío Villegas's view, the Alemán government was shaky on all of these fundamental points.[145]

Notes

1. *Excélsior*, December 28, 1947.
2. Eckstein, *El ejido colectivo en México*; Stavenhagen, *Estructura agraria y desarrollo agrícola en México*.
3. *Diario Oficial*, February 12, 1947.
4. Dulles, *Yesterday in Mexico*, 76–77.
5. *Excélsior*, July 22, 1947
6. Blanca Torres, *Hacia la utopía industrial* (Mexico: El Colegio de México, 1984), 57–58.

7. For petitions complaining against squatters, or *paracaidistas*, see the file in AGN, RP/MAV, 444.1/7.

8. *Diario de Yucatán*, January 10, 1949.

9. Robert C. Wysong to secretary of state, January 20, 1949, USNA/ 59, 812.00/1-2049.

10. Report for 1946–47 from the Confederación de Camaras de Comercio to the president, AGN, RP/MAV, 433/216.

11. "Revision of Mexican Commercial Bank Reserve Requirements," May, 16, 1950, USAN/59. 812.14/5-1650.

12. Torres, *Hacia la utopía industrial*, 78–79.

13. Roberto Amorós to Nazario S. Ortiz Garza, November 1, 1949, and accompanying memorandum from Luis G. Legorreta, October 27, 1949, AGN, RP/MAV, 508.1/263.

14. C. H. Bateman to E. Bevin, February 24, 1947, PRO/371, 60940.

15. Report for 1946–47 from the Confederación de Camaras de Comercio to the president, AGN, RP/MAV, 433/216.

16. These letters can be found in AGN, RP/MAV, 002/6072.

17. The balance sheet and detailed list of board members for June 1951 may be found in AGN, RP/MAV, 530/115.76.

18. S. Walter Washington to secretary of state, August 15, 1947, USNA/ 59, 812.5043/8-1547.

19. S. Walter Washington to secretary of state, January 6, 1947, USNA/ 59, 812.00/1-647.

20. The Roundtable was a broad gathering of Lombardistas, members of the Acción Socialista Unificada, and other independent figures on the left where Valentín Campa, Narciso Bassols, Miguel Angel Velasco, and others met to discuss Mexico's postwar condition. See Carr, *Marxism and Communism in Twentieth-Century Mexico*, 156–64.

21. After that, Luis Garcia Larragaña regularly refused an audience with the president to delegations of workers on strike. AGN, RP/MAV, 432.2/10. See also AGN, RP/MAV, 432/244A.

22. *El Popular*, February 7, 1947.

23. Charles R. Burrows to secretary of state, December 23, 1949, USNA/ 59, 812.00/12-2349.

24. Middlebrook, *The Paradox of Revolution*, 109.

25. Jubilation in the conservative press followed the U.S. congressional override of President Truman's veto of the Taft-Hartley Act. See *Excélsior*, *El Universal*, *Novedades*, and *La Prensa*, June 24, 1947. Within a few days, the U.S. model was being urged on the Mexican government; *Novedades*, June 26, 1947. For the complete reforms of the labor law that the president wanted to implement, see Secretaría de Trabajo y Prevision Social, Memorandum, October 14, 1947, AGN, RP/MAV, 545.3/46.

26. Alkaline solvents are used to dissolve the waxes that build up during petroleum refining. These solvents are so strong they will also dissolve human flesh. "Isomerization" refers to the process of creating long-chain carbon molecules for high-octane fuel. People working around this process frequently suffer from damage to the eyes and lungs.

27. Telegram from F. Biora to Alemán, December 11, 1948, AGN, RP/ MAV, 432/57.

28. These estimates are reconstructed by Middlebrook, *The Paradox of Revolution*, 117–18.

29. Espinoza Toledo, "La consolidación del sindicalismo institucional en México, 1941–1952," 301–12.

30. Carlos Romero Sagaón to President Alemán, August 21, 1948, AGN, RP/MAV, 565.32/82. For an excellent study of these complex relations, see Middlebrook, *The Paradox of Revolution*, 107–55.

31. Presidential secretaries routinely denied these requests on March 15, 1952, and September 12, 1952, AGN, RP/MAV, 432/244A.

32. Petitions to the president, May 27, 1947, and his response of June 11, 1947, AGN, RP/MAV, 432/174.

33. Yllanes Ramos, Confederación Nacional de Cameras de Industrias, to Alemán, August 12, 1947, AGN, RP/MAV, 432/56.

34. The reports on these events may be found in AGN, RP/MAV, 432/223.

35. Sindicato Industrial de Trabajadores Mineros y Metalúrgicos to Alemán, June 1, 1948, AGN, RP/MAV, 4322/341; workers at the Nash factory to Alemán, April 10, 1948, AGN, RP/MAV, 432/380; Ford workers to Alemán, October 5, 1949, AGN, RP/MAV, 432/450.

36. Juan de Zengotita to secretary of state, June 4, 1947, USNA/59, 812.00/6-447.

37. Ezequiel Teyssier to Alemán, April 20, 1950, AGN, RP/MAV, 432.2/5.

38. Adrian Huerta of the CTM in Puebla to Alemán, September 15, 1949, AGN, RP/MAV, 432.3/47. For a similar story, see Joaquin Evangelista et al. to President Alemán, July 6, 1948, AGN, RP/MAV, 541.1/3.

39. STFRM to the minister of defense, Gilberto R. Limón, July 21, 1949, AGN, RP/MAV, 432.3/34; *Prensa Grafica*, November 23, 1949.

40. Cristobal Alvarado Muñoz to President Alemán, March 27, 1950; Fidel Velázquez to Alemán, April 12, 1950, AGN, RP/MAV, 433/43.

41. Thurston to secretary of state, January 5, 1950, USNA/59, 812.062/1-450.

42. Manuel Morales to Alemán, July 3, 1948, AGN, RP/MAV, 432/188.

43. Roberto Ortíz Gris, representing twenty-eight PEMEX drillers, to Alemán, June 28, 1948, AGN, RP/MAV, 432/114.

44. Juan García Gómez and Juan Gómez Martínez to Alemán, July 12, 1948, AGN, RP/MAV, 601.1/229.

45. These petitions to the president are in AGN, RP/MAV, 545.3/82.

46. *Washington Post*, March 16, 1946.

47. Memorandum of conversation between Guy Ray and Miguel Alemán, March 29, 1946, USNA/59, 812.00/3-2946.

48. Ambassador Thurston to secretary of state, December 30, 1949, USNA/59, 812.00/12-3049. Jorge Prieto Laurens and Arturo Amaya of the Frente Popular Anti-Comunista de México regularly went to the president for the cost of their anti-Communist advertisement in the press and for subsidies. Jorge Prieto Laurens and Arturo Amaya to Rogelio de la Selva, May 21, 1952, AGN, RP/MAV, 621/2286.

49. Campa, *Mi testimonio*, 204–6.

50. Charles R. Burrows to secretary of state, December 23, 1949, USNA/59, 812.00/12-2349.

51. Col. Marcelino Inurreta of the Dirección Federal de Securidad to Rogelio de la Selva, July 7, 1947, AGN, RP/MAV, 544.61/5, and additional anti-Communist denunciations that were directed to the president.

52. Report of the arrest of Manuel Terrazas, n.d., AGN, RP/MAV, 549.44/874.

53. S. Walter Washington to secretary of state, June 26, 1947, USNA/59, 812.00/6-2647.

54. James C. Powell, Jr., to Roy Richard Rubottom, August 24, 1951, USNA/59, 712.00/8-2451.

55. See circular #202 of the Centro Patronal del D.F., February 1, 1947, AGN, RP/MAV, 432/92.

56. Barry T. Benson, "Revisions of the Cinematographic Law," September 24, 1952, USNA/59, 912.44/10-3151.

57. William R. Laidlaw to secretary of state, February 17, 1950, USNA/59, 712.00/2-1750.

58. Harvey R. Wellman, "Weekly Financial Report," April 22, 1949, USNA/59, 812.516/4-2249.

59. Report of the Comisión Intersecretarial Sobre Inversión de Capital Extranjero to Rogelio de la Selva, private secretary to the president, November 18, 1949, AGN, RP/MAV, 545.22/58.

60. Embassy to Acheson, "Presidential Proposal to Erect New Steel Plant near Acapulco," June 15, 1952, USNA/59, 812.331/1-1552.

61. For the reaction within the Alemán administration to these articles, see C. Koons to A. Ruiz Galindo and comments by Ruiz Galindo, December 26, 1947, AGN, RP/MAV, 704/170.

62. See letters from R. S. Kersh, Westinghouse; Donald P. Gilles, Republic Steel Corporation; and William R. Kuhuns, editor of *Banking*, the journal of the American Bankers Association, to the president, AGN, RP/MAV, 002/6072.

63. Ibid.

64. Confidential report from Murray Shields, vice president, Bank of Manhattan, February 16, 1951, AGN, RP/MAV, 294/20676.

65. Ruiz Galindo to the president and various project proposals, April 7, 1947, and the report of the effectiveness of these measures by the Confederación de Cámaras Industriales to the president, October 7, 1949, AGN, RP/MAV, 512.23/4, and associate documents.

66. See, for example, Dr. O Gómez de Molina, general manager of Eli Lilly y Compañía de México, to President Alemán, February 3, 1948, AGN, RP/MAV, 111/3660.

67. Lauro E. Doblado and Daniel Quirín to President Alemán, April 6, 1949, and the Asociación de Exhibidores Independientes de Monterrey to President Alemán, March 25, 1949, AGN, RP, MAV, 523.354.

68. Marte Gómez to the president, June 3, 1950, and April 29, 1952, AGN, RP/MAV, 008.2(8)/1706.

69. Office of Strategic Services, "Private U.S. Investment as a Source of Friction in Selected Latin American Countries," April 30, 1953, USNA/165, Research and Analysis Report # 5985.1.

70. Ibid.

71. The record of the 15th Meeting of the Bankers Association may be found in AGN, RP, MAV, 433/487. It was also covered in *Hoy*, May 14, 1949.

72. *Diario Oficial*, November 12, 1948; Beteta to Alemán, November 11, 1949, AGN, RP/MAV, 545.23/311.

73. Carlos M. Cinta, general manager of N.D. & R., to the president, June 30, 1949, AGN, RP/MAV, 565.1/85.

74. Messersmith to W. Carrigan, December 11, 1945, Messersmith Papers.

75. Ceceña, *México en la orbita imperial.*

76. Valuation of these ranches, n.d., n.a., AGN, RP/MAV, 101/37.

77. Navarro Elizondo to Alemán, December 2, 1948, and July 26, 1948, AGN, RP/MAV, 562.11/158.

78. Roberto Chellet Osante to President Alemán, March 24, 1949, AGN, RP/MAV, 562.4/1.

79. Report from Ilo C. Funk, "Possible Assistance in Developing New Pineapple Industry in Veracruz," February 12, 1946, USNA/59, 812.5034/2-1246. See also USNA/59, Box 4474, 812.00-TA/6-2253, for the Point Four projects in Mexico during the period.

80. Embassy to secretary of state, August 23, 1950, 812.02/8-2350, and July 26, 1950, 812.02/7-2650.

81. Axel Wenner-Gren to Alemán, September 8 and October 14, 1949, AGN, RP/MAV, 512.2/67.

82. Leonard Reinsch to Rowley, January 31, 1947, Truman Library, Ross Papers, File 8.

83. *Newsweek*, December 17, 1951.

84. Guy Ray to secretary of state, February 8, 1946, USNA/59, 812.00/2-846. *Time* reported an episode relating to Alemán and an actress in its article "Man of Affairs," February 11, 1946. Beteta's response was "*no merece commentario de nuestro parte*" in *Excélsior*, February 8, 1946.

85. S. Walter Washington to secretary of state, March 19, 1948, USNA/59, 812.00/3-1948.

86. Mabry, *Mexico's Acción Nacional*, 38–49.

87. *Excélsior*, December 8, 1945.

88. *Excélsior*, December 18, 1945.

89. Soto, *Emergence of the Modern Mexican Woman*, 128–32.

90. Macías, *Against All Odds*, 140–45.

91. Report to the president from Rodolfo Sánchez Taboada on the conference "Mujeres Representativas de México," January 23, 1947, AGN, RP/MAV, 433/46.

92. Thurston to secretary of state, January 2, 1947, USNA/59, 812.00/1-247. *El Popular*, January 3, 1947, reported that right-wing parties were behind the events.

93. Report entitled "Political Situation in Mexico after Eight Months of the Government of President Alemán," August 1, 1947, USNA/59, 812.00/8-147.

94. "Annual Report for 1948" to the Foreign Office, January 6, 1949, PRO/371, 74076.

95. Espinosa de los Monteros to Rogerio de la Selva, March 5, 1948, and Alemán to Snyder, n.d., AGN, RP/MAV, 545.22/150.

96. Banco de México circulars #1071 and #1072. Merwin L. Bohan to secretary of state, June 25, 1947, USNA/59, 812.50/6-2547.

97. Report entitled "Mexico's Food Supply Situation," November 13, 1952, USNA/59, 812.03/11-1352.

98. This position not only is substantiated by modern research, but it also may even have underestimated the phenomenon.

99. Juan de Zengotita to secretary of state, October 30, 1947, USNA/59, 812.00/10-3047.

100. See the various petitions from December, 1947, AGN, RP/MAV, 436.1/5.

101. *Diario Oficial*, January 14, 1948.

102. Aguilar Camín, *Saldos de la revolución*, 126.

103. S. Walter Washington to secretary of state, January 10, 1947, USNA/59, 812.00/1-1047.

104 . Martín Luis Guzmán was president; Magistrate of the Superior Court Paul Carranza Trujillo and General Esteban Calderón were vice presidents; and Daniel Cosío Villegas, the historian, was secretary. The treasurer was the head of the silver workers' union, Antonio Pozzi, and interestingly, Jesús Reyes Heroles, later ideologue of the PRI, was head of technical affairs.

105. The information on *Tiempo*'s subsidy comes from J. Edgar Hoover to Jack D. Neal, chief of the State Department's Division of Foreign Activity Correlation, February 18, 1947, USNA/59, 812.00/1-647.

106. J. E. Hoover to Jack Neal, Department of State, February 18, 1947, USNA/59, 812.00/2-1847.

107. "Current Political Trends in Mexico," Franklin C. Gowen to secretary of state, May 24, 1951, USNA/59, 712.00/5-2451.

108. Washington to secretary of state, March 17, 1948, USNA/59, 812.00/3-1748.

109. R. Smith Simpson to the Department of State, February 24, 1950, USNA/59, 712.00/2-2450.

110. *El Popular*, December 17, 1945.

111. The U.S. embassy understood that Alemán and Ruíz Cortines gave *El Popular* 30,000 pesos per month. Franklin C. Gowen to the Department of State, June 30, 1953, USNA/59, 712.00/6-3053.

112. Messersmith to S. Braden, January 31, 1946, USNA/59, 812.00/1-3146, and February 22, 1946, USNA/59, 812.00/2-2246.

113. All of the press covered these events of June 20, 1948. For the U.S. reports, see Dwight Dickerson to secretary of state, June 24, 1948, USNA/59, 812.00/6-2448, and June 29, 1948, USNA/59, 812.00/6-2948.

114. Juan de Zengotita to secretary of state, January 5, 1947, USNA/59, 812.00/1-547.

115. C. H. Bateman to E. Bevin, August 10, 1949, PRO/371, 74079.

116. S. Walter Washington to secretary of state, August 4, 1947, USNA/59, 812.00/8-447.

117. Report entitled "Refusal of the Supreme Court to Investigate the Honey Murders," August 11, 1947, USNA/59, 812.00/8-1147.

118. S. Walter Washington to secretary of state, March 18, 1948, USNA/59, 812.00/3-1048.

119. Washington to secretary of state, January 24, 1947, USNA/59, 812.00/1-2447.

120. *El Nacional*, January 9, 1947. *El Universal* said that it happened on December 31.

121. *El Universal*, January 5, 1947.

122. "Federal Government Officials Report Tapachula Incident Settled," January 10, 1947, USNA/59, 812.00/1-1047. See also 812.00/1-47.

123. *El Nacional*, January 13, 1947; S. Walter Washington to secretary of state, January 20, 1947, USNA/59, 812.00/1-2047.

124. In a rare moment, an AN candidate in Jalisco, Emilio Madero, praised J. Jesús González Gallo for holding clean elections and for not indulging in nepotism. *El Universal*, March 24, 1947.

125. For the U.S. embassy's version of these conflicts, see S. Walter Washington to secretary of state, March 26, 1947, USNA/59, 812.00/3-2647.

126. S. Walter Washington to secretary of state, August 4, 1947, USNA/59, 812.00/8-447.

127. S. Walter Washington to secretary of state, January 6, 1947, USNA/59, 812.00/1-647.

128. *Excélsior*, February 11, 1941.

129. *Novedades*, May 5, 1947.

130. Washington to secretary of state, April 10, 1947, USNA/59, 812.00/4-1047.

131. V. M. Villaseñor, *Memorias de un hombre de izquierda: De Avila Camacho a Echeverría*, 1:15.

132. *Excélsior*, June 25, 1951.

133. Earlier strikes in the mining industry led to a general strike in 1944 and an earlier hunger caravan in 1947. See Manuel J. Santos, "La caravana del hambre," *Boletín de Cemos/8 Memoria*, 1, no. 8 (January-February 1985): 191–92.

134. All of the press covered the speech. The U.S. report on these events was "Second National Assembly of the PRI," February 13, 1953, USAN/59, 712.00/2-1353.

135. Charles R. Burrows, first secretary of embassy, to secretary of state, October 6, 1951, USNA/59, 712.00/10-650.

136. U.S. diplomats regularly puzzled over her "anti-American" positions. Although they recognized that Ramón Beteta had experienced discrimination while a student at the University of Texas, they were unable to distinguish between anti-Americanism and anti-imperialism. Charles R. Burrows to secretary of state, August 18, 1950, USNA/59, 712.00/8-1850.

137. Charles R. Burrows to secretary of state, October 6, 1951, USNA/59, 712.00/10-650. This version is based upon conversations with Francisco Buch de Parado, a friend and business confidant of President Alemán. General León Lobato, Serrano's subordinate as chief of police of the D.F., was reported to have kept Casas Alemán and Henríquez Guzmán under close observation. In addition, see the Memorandum of conversation with Francisco Vazquez de Mercado, head of the Partido Nacionalista de México, and R. Smith Simpson, September 4, 1951, USNA/59, 712.00/9-451.

138. Police reports to the president, November 23 to 28, 1952, AGN, RP/MAV, 252/350.

139. The official returns were Ruíz Cortines, 2,713,000; Henríquez Guzmán, 579,000; González Luna, 285,000; and Lombardo Toledano, 72,000.

140. Report entitled "Mexican Elections in 1946 and 1952 . . . ," February 12, 1952, USNA/59, 712.00/2-1252.

141. Charles R. Burrows to secretary of state, April 19, 1950, USNA/59, 712.00/4-1850.

142. Franklin C. Gowan to secretary of state, September 25, 1951, USNA/59, 712.00/9-2551.

143. J. Silva Herzog to Alemán and his response, November 11, 1950, AGN, RP/MAV, 001/10691.

144. Franklin C. Gowan to secretary of state, September 26, 1952, USNA/59, 712.00/9-2652.

145. Cosío Villegas, *Extremos de América*, 3–27. Cosío Villegas's instincts about the U.S. influence were sound. One propaganda report noted that many U.S.-written columns were placed in Mexico City publications each week, including three in the magazine *Atisbos*, five in *El Universal*, and the by-line "Tablero Mundial" in *El Universal*. The USIS was also able to block an essay by Lombardo Toledano in *Hoy*. "Report for September 1952," October 6, 1952, USNA/59, 712.00/10-652.

5

The Politics of Corruption

"Let the chips fall where they may."

—Miguel Alemán

Corruption, unlike pregnancy, is a matter of degree. Between the Sermon on the Mount and Dog Hill[1] there may be an enormous difference; however, between the highest and the lowest standards of personal and public honesty, every possible position is occupied, degree by degree. In these finely sliced gradations of honesty lies a problem. We know that the difference between sharp business practice and theft can be extraordinarily fine, yet the highest moral reflections on the problem are not always very helpful in that they do not deal with the degrees of corruption. One can take an absolutist position, condemning every kind of corruption, but going that far removes one from the mainstream of daily life. (Harry Truman reputedly made his contemporaries nervous when he bought his own postage stamps; when he mailed a personal letter, he took out his own stamps and placed one on his letter, using government stamps only for official business.[2]) By contrast, some toleration of corruption may flow from the titillation of a good scandal; or, an acknowledgment of the universality of corruption may merge with the desire to get in on the action.

If problems of degree make the problem of corruption difficult to grasp at the individual level, the problem is only compounded when the historian tries to relate greed to the broad patterns of development within society. The very concept of corruption asserts the propriety of the status quo. Indeed, it assumes the dominance of the laws of nation-state over regional, kinship, or familial claims. A case can be made that a degree of corruption can, at times, increase social justice. Within a closed system, it can make room for people to survive, and it may also lead to income redistribution. This is especially so when there is a general perception that society operates in ways bereft of social justice. Yet widespread corruption—especially in a period when the general public is being asked to "tighten the belt" in the name of some national cause—can throw perceptions of political legitimacy into question.

The difficulty is that in one context corruption can lead to a more just society, whereas in another context the opposite can occur. Within an extremely hierarchical system, corruption may reinforce patterns of submission and dominance. It may also represent a prior commitment to family and personal networks as opposed to claims by society and the law. Or systems of bribes may simply be a way of remunerating poorly paid functionaries. There is an inevitable stratum of corruption in every society; still, the spirit of the age also sets the norms, degrees, and parameters of toleration. In the United States, for example, there were much lower levels of corruption in the Truman/Eisenhower period than in the Nixon/Reagan era; to a considerable degree this disparity reflected the standards that were set at the top of the political and social pyramid.

In Mexico, poverty and corruption have always cohabited. For example, Laurens Perry has explored the ways that minority republicanism led to different levels of corruption within the Restored Republic.[3] State expenditures and military projects traditionally were sources of personal enrichment (Manuel Avila Camacho got his start as Venustiano Carranza's paymaster). Both favors to central members of the Sonora dynasty and labor corruption of the CROM were well-known aspects of public life before the 1930s. Poverty and underdevelopment undoubtedly exacerbated the phenomena, although some commentators looked the other way. James Wilkie, in his interview with Ramón Beteta on the industrial development push of the late 1940s, said that "the thing that many people do not understand is that in Mexico there is no robbery; there are no frauds, should we say, but people do earn a lot from government contracts. When there is a high rate of economic development there are a lot of people who earn high profits from their contracts; that is the way things are." Beteta was quick to agree with Wilkie that there was no theft, joking that when he left office "they accused me of having stolen the reserves of the Bank of Mexico."[4]

Recently, an extreme example of the rationalization of corruption emerged in Stephen D. Morris's *Corruption and Politics in Contemporary Mexico*:

Corruption is a crucial mechanism in Mexico's unique governing style. By allocating spoils, corruption helps undermine the potentials of organizations to threaten the system and thus helps alleviate class-based demands. Although widespread corruption may result in low levels of trust in the performance of government, the goals of the system or the policies of the government may not be questioned. Indeed, blaming human avarice for the system's failures provides an easy escape for the government, thereby taming a potentially politically explosive issue.[5]

It is difficult to accept this recrudescence of structural functionalism. Certainly, corruption can undercut reform movements, as the experience of the 1940s clearly demonstrates. However, a high level of cynicism or a belief that the president is indeed a crook may undermine authority. And the notion that corruption helps "bolster feelings of legitimacy among the political elite by offering material benefits to those who play the political game" goes too far.[6] In a hypothetical case where, say in the name of privatization, a high official appropriates a public asset for personal gain, there is no one else who benefits or is bought off and class friction is augmented, not alleviated. Perhaps this is a case where it is useful to remember a fundamental proposition from the physical sciences—Occam's Law.

Personally, we all have to come to our own position on these matters. But for historians, individual foibles matter less than the impact of corrupt activities on society. A consideration of Mexico's development program of the 1940s forces the observer to confront these problems since the acquisitive urge became prominent—some would say dominant—and corruption became a historical issue as it drastically changed the program of the Mexican Revolution. The evidence of corruption is substantial and emanates from many sources. Whereas the historian tries to be sensitive to the quality of the evidence, we are scarcely in a position to hold trials in which judicial force and legal rules of evidence are in effect.

The attempt to write a history of the 1940s without substantial reference to the corruption of the era seriously distorts the reality of the age. Blanca Torres, one of the few historians to work seriously on the post-1940 period, mentions corruption only four times in her book. The first reference is to corruption among members of ejidos. There is a reference to *"functionarios y empresarios beneficiados"* who took advantage of wartime regulations for personal enrichment. Corrupt practices by foreign companies are noted, and finally, there is a reference to the resentment over the corruption surrounding the hoof-and-mouth disease campaigns.[7] The overall impression from the book is that the corruption was a minor phenomenon, no different from corruption in most other times and places. Yet, this is an example in which a prudent and balanced tone, even a sense of moderation, seriously distorts history. Even if a significant percentage of the accusations that abound in the historical record were to be thrown out as hearsay, enough direct evidence would still be left to force the historian to confront the issue of the impact of corruption upon the development program of the nation.[8] Individual corruption in high places proliferated to the point that little peccadillos grew to change the direction of Mexican development.

This atmosphere of generalized corruption had not always been pervasive before 1940; certainly the period of the Cardenista reforms is not as riddled with these accusations. The period of Cardenismo was probably the least corrupt period in Mexican history. To a considerable degree, the Cardenista reforms motivated people in positions of authority in the Cárdenas administration to work for the public good and to set aside ageold practices of personal enrichment at the public's expense. Significantly, Cárdenas set the tone by releasing government employees from the old practice of giving back part of their salary to the governing party.[9]

The only accusation against Lázaro Cárdenas that I have found in the archives came from the American consul in Mexico City, George P. Shaw. He erroneously accused Cárdenas of being pro-German. Shaw reported that a network existed in Michoacán involving the president's brother, Damaso Cárdenas, the ex-chief of police of the DF, General José Manuel Nuñez, and Gabino Vázquez, the head of the Agrarian Department. The suggestion was that in spite of being antibusiness, Cárdenas was an investor in land and in the Hotel Artega, and that he was active as a lime exporter from Michoacán. None of this was illegal or unethical; it was simply kept out of sight. Shaw claimed that a system of timber export permits issued by Governor Ireta linked Cárdenas to a "levy of tribute" and that the former president benefited from higher timber prices. Even if this was so, by the standards of the 1940s, this was almost saintly behavior.[10] The commitment to major reform in the 1930s held down the level of corruption to historically low levels.

It is also important to note, as the work of Jeffrey Rubin demonstrates, that standards set by the national government did not automatically apply to state politics. Rubin rightly points out that Cárdenas by no means dominated all of the state and local political machines. Indeed, a model of domestic diplomacy may provide an appropriate vehicle for understanding the relationship between the national Cardenista project and the local authorities.[11] To take an extreme example, the (Maximino) Avila Camacho/Batista/Jenkins machine prevailed in Puebla with an extremely high level of contempt for the Cardenista project, yet the president supported that machine against the CTM's FROC.[12] Patterns of corruption were unchanged in some states and regions, even at moments of the most intense reform under Cárdenas.

After the Cárdenas administration, matters changed at the center, and many senior officials seemed to be at the heart of numerous shady deals. This was a well-known fact at the time. A popular joke of the day asked: "What are the three great evils of Mexico?" "Santa Anna's leg, Obregón's arm, and Alemán's teeth" was the reply.[13] Unlike the Echeverría jokes of the 1970s, which communicated strong middle-class opposition to the reforms of that period, Alemán was widely viewed, even at the time, as being unusually corrupt. Political humor expressed contempt for prevailing practices at the same time that it also revealed a sense of powerlessness. Even the PRI machine politician Emilio Portes Gil, in his final comment on the Alemán years, admitted, "Unfortunately many of his friends, abusing the trust he had placed in them, took advantage of politics to dedicate themselves to large business deals."[14]

Now that there is access to the rich historical record for the period, it is clear that the people who had jumped to conclusions about corrupt officials during the 1940s had spotted only the tip of the iceberg. Corruption took many forms, and at times, corrupt practices shaded off into sharp business deals. By sorting the history of corruption into a taxonomy, from minor to major, from subtle to blatant, and from the idiosyncratic to the systemic, we can understand better how corruption grew to be a major factor in the dismantling of the early Cardenista version of the Mexican Revolution.

Direct Looting

Although it is rare to find evidence of government officials simply looting the public coffers, there were cases when that occurred. In 1949 the *teserero general de la nación*, Luis Ríos Chimal, was charged with fraud. It was alleged he had falsified receipts when American Airlines paid 3 million pesos to the Mexican Treasury in taxes. Ríos Chimal cashed the checks; however, the funds did not find their way into the public accounts.[15] The fraud was clear; only the lack of political cover was remarkable.

Governor Blas Corral Martínez, of Durango, found himself in an unusual political situation in 1947. While he was undergoing medical treatment at the Mayo Clinic in Rochester, Minnesota, his death was prematurely reported. The state legislature, in a moment of euphoria, named a new governor, and a number of the top state officials of the Corral Martínez administration resigned. A constitutional and political battle ensued since the acting governor was a member of the opposition Acción Nacional party. Word then came from New York that Corral Martínez was alive after all. During the confusion, his relatives were charged with having looted the state treasury while Corral Martínez was at the Mayo Clinic. The next governor, José Ramón Valdez, released details on the empty state treasury that he inherited.[16]

In Oaxaca at the beginning of 1947, there was a popular protest against the governor, Sánchez Cano. He had offended the business community with innovative taxes, the students by cutting the university budget, and others by the politics of imposition. Popular protest grew until it took the army to protect officials from the local population. Even entering their offices was risky, so great was the public anger. The governor was eventually forced out, and afterward there were reports that he had left the state treasury "completely bereft of funds."[17]

Sometimes a sudden appearance of wealth led to only one conclusion. A British diplomat noted about Ramón Beteta: "A few years ago he was poor, now he is rich but had not sufficient sagacity to camouflage his sudden accretion of wealth. The mansion he is building for himself and his bejewelled American wife has not escaped the notice of either his chief or the public."[18] By far the most serious allegation of direct appropriation of funds from the Avila Camacho administration was reported by a British diplomat: "According to my informant the worst discovery was that ninety-three million dollars for which valid receipts were given by the late Minister of Finance cannot be accounted for." Alfonso Caso was reported to be hard at work running down these irregularities.[19] Apparently, it was a thankless task, for he soon gave up the job and returned to academic life.

When direct looting was established, it was child's play for a competent auditor to uncover the theft. Only the political will was required to prosecute. Moreover, not much of a defense could be mounted against such direct theft. The main impact of these thefts was on the immediate programs that were denied funds as a result of the misappropriation. Thus schools existed only on the books, and roads remained unmade.

The Abuse of Authority

The tendency to use one's position to augment one's personal wealth was common. A report from Lieutenant Colonel Maurice C. Holden, the assistant U.S. military attaché, explained that the National Security Police—which had been organized by President Alemán on December 1, 1946, to protect the president's life, to keep the president abreast of subversive activities, and to coordinate the other police functions within Mexico—had become extremely corrupt. The FBI trained a number of young graduates from the Mexican Military Academy for future positions in the National Security Police. Therefore, the information the FBI picked up from Mexican trainees may well have been highly reliable since internal confidences were being exchanged from one police agency to another. By 1947, Colonel Marcelino Inurreta was the commander of the National Security Police, and the second in command was Juan Ramón Gurrola. As the military attaché put it, "Both are persons of questionable character and recent information indicates their involvement in dope-smuggling activities. It appears that they are using the organization as a front for illegal operations to amass personal fortunes. Carlos I. Serrano, close adviser to the President, has unlimited power over National Security Police and is fully cognizant of its 'side-line' operations."[20]

Colonel Inurreta had, in this version, been paymaster of the Federal District Police Force during the Avila Camacho administration. While in that position he had purchased a prestigious home. During the Alemán campaign, he mortgaged the home for 85,000 pesos and, using a friend's name, applied the funds to the purchase of a restaurant. He played a dangerous game: "After the election he told Colonel Serrano, one of the President's closest advisers, how much money he had spent on the campaign, and that he had mortgaged his home in order to obtain the money, and in proof of this he exhibited the mortgage papers. Colonel Serrano informed President Alemán of this and arrangements were made to refund Inurreta the 85,000 pesos and also to give him the job as head of the National Security Police."[21]

The U.S. attaché learned of these details when the second in command, Juan Ramón Gurrola, called on U.S. Treasury officials to find out how much they knew about dope smuggling into the United States. "After the U.S. Treasury agent left, Gurrola was heard to brag that he had found a gold mine of information, implying that he would receive information which would assist him in his illicit dope operations." The case against Juan Ramón Gurrola was also strengthened when a Cadillac driven by his nephew, Francisco Gurrola, was seized by U.S. customs officials on June 25, 1946, at Laredo, Texas. The car contained sixty-four cans of opium. Francisco Gurrola was tried, convicted, and sentenced to three years in a federal penitentiary in Texas. According to this account, the third in command, Colonel Manuel Magoral, allegedly controlled marijuana sales in Mexico City. The documentary record does not make it clear whether the president and other high officials of the government knew about the smuggling activities of the department; the drug-running may have simply been conducted by a small group around Colonel Serrano. Lieutenant Colonel Holden believed that the National Security Police systematically engaged in personal violence, protection rackets, blackmail, and the penetration of banking records. These police were, in Holden's view, "nothing but a Gestapo organization under another name," and he found it alarming that in military and police circles, Colonel Serrano was thought to be the second most powerful man in the country.

Subsequent investigations by U.S. embassy personnel raised questions concerning Serrano's involvement in the smuggling. U.S. Treasury officials admitted that their evidence linking Serrano to the automobile carrying cocaine that had been seized in Laredo was circumstantial. Nevertheless, these Treasury agents learned that Angel González, brother of the attorney general, had been threatened by Serrano and had left the country in fear for his life.[22] In response to Serrano's action and to his request to the United States to return the car to him, these Treasury officials were believed to have leaked this information to the syndicated columnists Drew Pearson and Walter Winchell; this enraged Serrano, who threatened to go to the United States to sue Pearson. Ambassador Thurston concluded: "I received the impression as I watched Serrano that he undoubtedly represents all that is evil and vicious and dangerous, and that there is nothing that he would not do without a qualm. At the same time I likewise received the impression that in this particular instance he may well be entirely innocent."[23] In any case, the episode ended with a sacrificial offering. Juan Ramón Gurrola was fired, and he went into unofficial exile in Chile. Thus, the episode reverberated no higher than the second in command in the National Security Police.

Another case of political gangsterism left a trail that went even higher into the Alemán administration. The murder of opposition Senator Mauro Angulo of Tlaxcala on Avenue Insurgentes on February 17, 1948, caused a furor that focused attention on state terrorism. U.S. diplomats learned that the four main suspects were members of Alemán's inner circle: Jorge Pasquel was believed to be the main narcotics importer; Enrique Parra "arranges many affairs, both financial and amorous"; Senator Gabriel Ramos Millan was active in banking circles and known "for bringing pressure on bankers to extend credit for persons whom the president wishes to honor"; and Colonel Carlos Serrano was the owner of several houses of prostitution and directed *pistoleros*.[24]

In another example of slightly less blatant, but still fairly unimaginative, corruption, five members of the board of directors of the Banco del Pequeño Comercio wrote to the president denouncing the director of the bank, Juan de Dios Bojórquez, for corrupt practices. According to his fellow directors, Bojórquez was guilty of paying excessive rent on the bank's premises, of channeling repair work through his son, of commiting irregularities in hiring and accounting, of maintaining *aviadores* (people carried on a payroll who do no work but only "fly in" on pay day to collect their checks), and of extending high-risk credit to his friends and compadres. In short, the directors accused the manager of gravely abusing his position.[25]

There were other notorious examples of simple corruption. Governor Cepeda Davila, of Coahuila, shot himself after a popular protest against his increasing state taxes by 400 percent in July 1947. Pressure had mounted on him when it was revealed that he had placed a 2-million-peso line item on the state budget for the State University of Coahuila. Sadly, that state did not have a university in 1947.[26] And Governor Betancourt of Puebla admitted openly that his contribution to President Alemán's electoral campaign had diverted funds, which had been allocated by the state legislature, away from public projects.[27]

In 1947 there was a campaign against the former governor of Baja California, Rodolfo Sánchez Taboada, who was accused of having made a personal fortune out of his office. Sánchez Taboada had been active in calling for the expulsion from the PRI of those who joined the Partido Popular, and many who felt the pressure became willing to talk about his malfeasance.[28] The allegations did not damage his career, however, for he was soon named president of the PRI.

At times, the direct abuse of authority grew in scale and threatened major institutions; then, only the diversion of public funds staved off disaster. In 1949 the Banco Nacional de México owned 60 percent of the stock in the Banco del Pacífico in Baja California. According to the information that a British diplomat gained from the manager of the National City Bank in Mexico City, the Banco del Pacífico had "suffered a loss of about 12 million pesos . . . through the activities of a politician in Baja California." Although it was feared in banking circles that this loss would redound upon the Banco Nacional de México, "Mr. Richardson had been assured that the Government had come to the assistance of both the Banco Nacional de México and the Banco del Pacífico and that both would continue to operate in a normal way."[29] The episode reveals how the government regularly applied public funds to bail out the private sector.

In 1949 the Banco de Comercio and a number of smaller banks split off from the Mexican Bankers Association over a proposal to remove the tax-free status on 50 percent of sight deposits. In a major Mexican innovation, these funds were required to be lodged with the Banco de México to finance projects of industrialization. Thus the Banco de Comercio's move was a repudiation of government policies. It is understandable in light of these events in Baja California that the Banco Nacional de México (BANAMEX) supported the government's proposal to remove this tax advantage. The indirect tax benefits were valued less than the direct subsidy. Of course, the gift of 12 million pesos of the public's money to the bank to cover the officials' looting represented a major diversion of funds.

Another more insidious kind of abuse of authority occurred when allegations of corruption were used as a weapon against those whom the authorities wanted to punish for other reasons. Allegations of corruption against small fish could be used as a kind of barrier, protecting those in charge from new competitors. In August 1947 the minister of the interior, Héctor Pérez Martínez, was fired and replaced by the president's nephew, Fernando Casas Alemán. In one account of the dismissal, Pérez Martínez's error had been to issue gambling permits "behind Miguel Alemán's back."[30]

Something of the political style of the period emerges from the glimpse we have of a visit by Miguel Alemán to Coatzacoalcos in May 1950. It was a major event for that remote city. Alemán arrived with an entourage of fifteen hundred. The PRI had raised some 250,000 pesos from local merchants who had to pay from 500 to 1,000 pesos each or face official problems. The sweetener was a promise that the government would use the occasion to pave streets and improve the water system. The construction company run by the exceedingly well-connected Manuel Suárez, Techo Eterno Eureka, received 4.5 million pesos from state and local funds, but the work was never done.[31]

The president was deeply involved in the administration of the radio station XEX, which was running at a loss and receiving public subsidies from the Comisión Nacional de Inversiones in 1948. Alonso Sordo Noriega, the original manager of the station who still held 49 percent of the shares, wrote to the president accusing the board, Senator Bermúdez, and the station manager, Alvarez Garza, of maintaining contradictory accounts that "demonstrate an important concealment of the financial condition of the Difusora, which in my opinion, is indisputably illicit." In total, he alleged and documented—with more than one hundred pages of accounting records—a monthly loss of 35,000 pesos, or 1.6 million pesos since he had been overseeing the accounting of XEX.[32]

It was always possible to focus upon corruption to embarrass a political opponent. Such appears to have happened at the end of 1948 when Antonio Betancourt Pérez, the general director of the Commission of Vigilance of the DDF, was arrested for authorizing an increase in the price of milk in return for a 70,000-peso bribe from the Unión de Ganaderos of the state of Mexico. After his arrest, Betancourt Pérez accused Alejandro Carrillo of being behind the episode. In this case, given his contempt for Carrillo, President Alemán insisted that justice be done, wherever the chips might fall.[33]

Kickbacks

It is important to realize that even though the 1940s was a period of extreme corruption, not all officials were so inclined. Ezra Sensibar was the president of Construction Aggregates and also of the Mexican affiliate, Fomento Termoeléctrico S.A. At the very end of the Cárdenas administration, he was involved in the negotiation of a major contract, worth 60 million pesos, to rebuild the port facilities at Frontera, Manzanillo, Mazatlán, and Tampico. Saying that it was not proper to bind the new administration to such a long-term project, the Cárdenas administration deferred these negotiations in November.

When the negotiations resumed under the Avila Camacho administration they were in the hands of General Jara, the minister of the navy, and his assistant, Colonel Teodulo García. "According to Sensibar, General Jara had his hand out in a big way. Sensibar said that while his company recognized that small gratifications might be required from time to time it would have no part in paying any real graft, such for instance as the 10% or 15% required by General Maximino [Avila Camacho] in his Department." Sensibar did acknowledge that the design and building of the port works had been hindered by corrupt practices, by officials who held their positions as political rewards and who knew nothing about port construction, as well as by General Jara's decision to locate the shipbuilding yards in his home state of Veracruz in spite of its poor harbors. Ambassador Messersmith was concerned about this graft since the Export-Import Bank was funding the port construction; he worked to keep the negotiation away from the Ministry of the Navy. The Department of Finance was a far better option, since Eduardo Suárez was "honest and sincere in this matter and had shown no desire to benefit personally." U.S. officials, therefore, tried to channel the contract in that direction.[34]

During World War II the export of cattle from Mexico to the United States was prohibited due to the inflationary effect in Mexico and the diversion of resources from the war effort. Food shortages and high prices made the issue of hunger a highly sensitive one. The Department of the National Economy was therefore entrusted with the power to issue export permits. Minister Francisco Xavier Gaxiola, a close confidant of Abelardo Rodríguez, abused that position. In September 1941 he signed an agreement with Honorato González and two other promoters by which export permits were issued for the export of fifty thousand head of cattle. González would pay Gaxiola's brother-in-law two pesos per head, half of which would be returned to Gaxiola. The FBI report on the deal noted that it was rare to have such an agreement in writing, "a fact which may be taken as an instance of the openness by which Gaxiola can be bribed."[35]

The consul general of Mexico, Ricardo C. Hill, was indicted for having engaged in wartime profiteering in New York City during World War II. In 1947 a grand jury charged him with having broken price and export control regulations. He faced a maximum of thirty-six years in prison and fines of $360,000.[36] He clearly had abused his diplomatic status while representing his country in the United States.

Frequently, purchase orders were simply inflated. The Mexican ambassador to Italy was involved in negotiations with three Italian industrialists: Inocentti, Guani, and Calme. Mexico was trying to arrange the acquisition of a seamless pipe-making factory; PEMEX was desperate for pipe. Apparently, the Italian industrialists had an innovative technique for the production of such pipe. Since postwar regulations made it difficult for Italians to invest abroad, they were willing to sell the technology to Mexico. Referring to another country that had made a similar arrangement, the ambassador noted that in buying the $4-million factory, "Confidentially I knew that the people charged with the purchase by their government put in a bill for eight million dollars."[37] The ambassador did not spell out the way in which the additional $4 million were to be divided.

By 1949 the repayment of the railroad loans was delayed because of diversions of the money. U.S. officials were angry that the Mexican officials preferred to purchase railroad track rather than to pay other obligations: "As you know, the National Railway owes the American Association of Railroads about $2,000,000 [dollars] for back payments on car per diems, etc. A Mexican official told me a few weeks ago that the money to pay this debt was given by Hacienda to the Nacional but instead of being used for that purpose was sidetracked to establish letters of credit for steel purchases in the United States. The reason, of course, is the kickbacks that certain people are obtaining or hope to obtain."[38]

Wartime contracts provided a great deal of opportunity for kickbacks and false contracts. In the purchase of new railroad cars, for example, a web of conspiracy linked U.S. corporations to purchasing authorities in Mexico. According to one report, a number of businessmen operating in Mexico—A. Z. Phillips, General Enríque Estrada, and Alexander Kleyff—provided links between the Hastings group (Senator Hastings and Axel Wenner-Gren) and General Maximino Avila Camacho. After Wenner-Gren and Phillips were blacklisted for operating in the interests of the Axis, the others carried on their operations. In the first wartime purchase of 1,000 box cars, the average bids were in the range of $3,200 each. However, that price was passed over for a bid of $3,880 from the Magor Car Corporation, whose function was to sublet the manufacture of the railroad cars to the Ralston Car Corporation and arrange for the distribution of the $680 per car. Additional purchases of 500 box cars, 200 gondolas, and 70 hopper cars added another million dollars to the group's profit. Even this was small pickings for Wenner-Gren. Before his blacklisting he had been working on a project of a new bank, "to bring about the transfer of all funds of the Government Railways and Petroleos Mexicanos to said bank as a depository and thus have the money of these two agencies for use and control and thus indirectly control the railways and the oil industry."[39]

The $30-million Export-Import Bank loan for highway construction was also a target of the Hastings/Wenner-Gren/Maximino group. Since the payments were handled through the National City Bank, U.S. authorities had access to the information. In these cases as well, the main effect was to divert U.S. funds from the war effort; however, by wartime standards the amount of money was small. At other times, kickbacks appeared like normal business practice—a cost of doing business. Pan American Airways sent 25,000 pesos per month to the Department of Tourism, "which represents the payment of Pan American Airways, Inc., for the month of October, 1949."[40]

Hidden Deals

Business figures frequently established intimate relations with political patrons; money and political protection formed a symbiotic union. Perhaps the best-known example was the close association between Maximino Avila Camacho, when he was governor of Puebla under Cárdenas, and William O. Jenkins, the American entrepreneur who dominated the sugar industry in Atencingo, film distribution in Mexico City, and, eventually, the Banco de Comercio. David Ronfeldt's excellent history of the ejido at Atencingo demonstrates how the foreigner William Jenkins abused the local population with impunity. There were frequent calls for Jenkins's expulsion from Mexico. In 1939, Deputy Emilio N. Acosta sought to enlist local residents to occupy Jenkins's properties. On May 7 there was a pitched battle between peasants and workers from the region and the soldiers who were protecting Jenkins's property. James B. Stewart, the American consul in Mexico City, noted that the governor of Puebla, Maximino Avila Camacho, was "undoubtedly a secret partner of Jenkins and in his fight with Acosta lined up the CTM." This informal arrangement saw Jenkins offer Maximino business opportunities and financial rewards all the while that Maximino provided political cover for Jenkins.[41] This relationship continued throughout the 1940s.

In the territory of Baja California Norte, Governor Alberto Aldrete was President Alemán's appointee. Having contributed 3 million pesos to the president's campaign, Aldrete was in a position to form a construction company, which he named Constructora de Baja California. U.S. contractors complained to their embassy that even though the company did not own a single piece of construction equipment, the firm received some of the largest contracts in the territory. Moreover, funds supposedly going to public works projects had been diverted to the purchase of the sumptuous hotel and Casino Playa in Ensenada. Aldrete was also able to use his position as governor to underwrite his private borrowing in the United States for his brewing interests.[42]

In another case, Nacional Distribuidora y Reguladora S.A. (N.D.&R.) purchased a large shipment of coffee beans from El Salvador, through the Mexican trading company Fomento Económico Mexicano S.A. (FEMSA). Eventually it was discovered that the beans were of too low a quality for the contracted price. It seemed a simple enough problem. However, it then developed that Luis Viñas León, the treasurer of the Chamber of Deputies, intervened on behalf of the importer, Alberto J. Avramow, pointing out to the president that during the 1946 election campaign Avramow had made a 25,000-peso contribution to Fernando Casas Alemán, Aarón Sáenz, and Ramón Beteta.[43] This was the kind of link that led officials to demur when N.D.&R. was charged with corruption and blamed for the inflation of the period; the directors responded that they were only partially responsible for these problems.[44] In this instance, the veil of secrecy under which these deals had taken place worked against N.D.&R.'s ability to defend itself.

A change of government regulations could influence business practices significantly. ASARCO officials complained to the U.S. embassy about a deal being done in association with the classification of gold. Gold was pegged at $35 per ounce, as it had been for some time. But if the gold could be reclassified as industrial gold the price went up to $38 per ounce. Pushing through nearly 15,000 kilos of gold per year, the potential difference added up to a considerable amount, and company officials were upset that the difference in the price did not go to the producer but became "personal profits to influential persons."[45]

In the town of Tecate, Baja California, a series of false financial representations threatened the viability of the entire community, as corruption endangered the region's further development. Governor and entrepreneur Alberto V. Aldrete wrote to the president in 1950, begging for his intervention against Nacional Financiera and the Banco de México's accusations that Aldrete's firms had acted fraudulently. He pointed out that he had founded eight businesses and that these charges, which were against his son, Alberto, were threatening the prosperity, if not the existence, of the entire town of Tecate. He begged that he be allowed to continue running at least the technical side of his brewing businesses.[46]

According to an auditors' report, the Banco de México had to cover a million-dollar loan from the Bank of California to Aceites Vegetales S.A. and the Tecate Brewery, which had been fraudulently funneled through the Pacific Vegetable Oil Corporation. Luis Legorreta of the Banco Nacional de México eventually became involved in the restructuring after the Aldrete interests were impounded. It was a fairly typical case of fraud by the legal standards of the day, and the banks' capital was secured. The impact was so acute in Tecate, however, that the town went into decline as a result of the fraud.[47]

Sometimes corruption merged with inefficiency. The Monte de Piedad is widely known as the government's pawnshop. Descended from colonial welfare institutions, it loaned small amounts of money to the very poor at high interest rates. In fact, by 1949 it was virtually insolvent. Although it carried a book value of 41.2 million pesos, it had made nine loans of roughly 32 million pesos that were nonperforming. In addition, 82,700 poor and lower-middle-class families had had their savings deposited in the bank. The accounting was in such bad shape that it was impossible to determine exactly what had happened. The auditor cautioned extreme secrecy because if the situation became more generally known it could precipitate a panic and failure.The worst part of the situation, in the auditor's view, was that the union knew about the desperate situation. The solution, therefore, was to dissolve the union.[48]

Payments for Services Rendered

In some cases, money simply changed hands to buy political favors. Strong popular resistance against the monopoly position of the Henequeneros de Yucatán was generated by the Frente de Defensa de la Industria Henequenera in 1949. The issue centered upon the demand of the ejidatarios of the town of Hoctún for higher pay and also their requirement that officials follow the law relating to social security rights. The movement gained force when the *Diario de Yucatán* reported their case sympathetically, much to the consternation of local officials, as well as of the functionaries of the (PRI-dominated) Socialist Party of the Southeast.[49] Kidnapping the local leaders was intended to thwart mass demonstrations, and troops even blocked the access to Mérida to keep local farmers from demonstrating. At one crucial point, Mario Souza, chief of the Agrarian Department, went to Mérida to oversee the settlement. In the report of the U.S. consul in Mérida, "It is the opinion of certain well informed persons in Mérida that Souza will probably return to Mexico City richer by several thousand pesos, and that he will do nothing to interfere with local officials."[50]

Students in Mexico have long demonstrated against what they call the *prensa vendida*, or the press that has sold its integrity to the political authorities. There is archival evidence for this phenomenon. In July 1947, for example, the Cía. Editorial Mexicana of Monterrey wrote to the president reminding him that it had been the first editorial group in the state to adhere to the principles of Alemanismo. The group then asked him for subsidies for the newspapers it produced.[51] Although there is no record of the government's response to that request, a student newspaper, *Ases Universitario* (University aces), did ask for and receive a subsidy of $750 per fortnight, a not inconsiderable sum for students in the 1940s.[52]

The reasons why the press did the government's bidding are clear. Many leading figures of the day held stock in the conservative newspapers. In the case of *Novedades*, for example, shareholders in 1946 included Jorge Pasquel, "who is at least partially a front for [President] Alemán," and, reportedly, Aarón Sáenz and Abelardo Rodríguez. Prisciliano Elizondo of the Monterrey Group was also a shareholder in *Novedades*; old enmities had been superseded.[53] Similar arrangements existed with other newspapers and magazines.

One of the more interesting cases of a hidden deal relates to the repeated semicandidacies of General Miguel Henríquez Guzmán. In 1946, Henríquez Guzmán gave the appearance of intending to run for the presidency against the official candidate, but he withdrew before making much of a run for the office. At the time most observers simply assumed that the cost was so high and the chances were so poor that he had to face political reality. Nevertheless, his semicandidacy served a purpose. It gave the elections the appearance of a democratic contest. It also consumed vital months leading up to the elections and crowded the field for other prospective candidates. It is, therefore, extremely interesting to find in the correspondence of George Messersmith a bitter complaint about the contracts for the gas pipeline from Poza Rica to Salamanca. The Henríquez Guzmán brothers won the pipeline contract for their construction company over U.S. engineering bids. The contract was awarded on a cost-plus basis, estimated to be worth 100,000 pesos or more. Messersmith maintained that a U.S. contractor could have done the job for 40,000 pesos, including the materials.[54]

In fact, the case of the Henríquez Guzmán brothers was even more politically sensitive. The investment banker, Carlos Trouyet, drew a distinction between the governments of Avila Camacho and Alemán: "During the time of General Maximino Avila Camacho the Henríquez Guzmán brothers had a working understanding with General Maximino and got most of the road building and construction contracts." The Henríquez Guzmán brothers, Ing. Evaristo Araiza, Carlos Trouyet, and others formed the company Constructora Industrial S.A. This firm did work of a good quality, and its understandings were honored even after Maximino's death. Ramón Beteta had been pressuring General Henríquez Guzmán, through his brothers Jorge and Luis, not to declare for the presidency in 1946. Trouyet confided that Alemán was worried since he feared that the army would support the general, given Alemán's civilian background.[55] This would account for the government's generosity in the Poza Rica-Salamanca pipeline.

Inside Information

The conjunction of business and government interests created enormous opportunities. Never was this more so than during the administration of President Alemán. In the strictest confidence, Messersmith reported to Robert L. Gardner, the vice president of the World Bank, that "there are a group of about five around the President whose actions are notorious and are causing unfavorable comment."[56]

Diplomats were frequently diplomatic—that is, reticent to discuss what they knew, even years after the fact. Merwin L. Bohan, who was embassy counselor for economic affairs in Mexico City from 1945 to 1960, when talking about Alemán and Beteta, said, "I'm not going to discuss his [Beteta's] morality etc. because I don't think that's quite proper."[57] Nevertheless, Bohan did recount a story about Beteta that revealed something of the tone of the era. Beteta issued a decree in 1948 prohibiting U.S. businessmen from bringing their cars into Mexico. After Bohan had pressured Beteta repeatedly to rescind the decree, Beteta finally told him, "No, I'm not going to fix it up." Bohan responded, "Mr. Minister, but why?" at which point Beteta replied, "Look, I asked you for a dozen things and you didn't get replies on any of these things for me out of Washington." Bohan said, "But Mr. Minister, you were only up there a month ago and you just got a hundred million dollars out of the U.S. government." He answered, "Sure, *we* got it. You didn't help us. You didn't get it for us."[58]

U.S. diplomats were approached during the Alemán campaign in 1946 by Manuel Nieto, the Ford distributor in Veracruz and the head of a delegation of pineapple growers in Veracruz. Nieto wanted the USDA to provide chemical analysis of the growers' land, as well as technical information on the preparation, fertilization, planting, and processing of pineapples. The spokesman for the group offered to pay 50 percent of the USDA's costs; the planter-politicians Governor Adolfo Ruíz Cortines and PRI candidate Miguel Alemán would pay the other half. The consortium planned to plant some 890 hectares of land in pineapples, and, in confidential discussions, candidate Alemán indicated that after the election the government would spend 120 million pesos improving roads to service the plantations. Additional government funds would also be committed to improving local ports, and irrigation would be provided through the Papaloapan River projects. Alemán's pineapple group was trying to break the monopoly of the Pineapple Growers Association in Loma Bonita and the Isla region of Veracruz.[59] Eventually, a Point Four program under President Truman was organized to aid the pineapple industry in Veracruz. In the end, these politicians did not have to pay since the funds to support these various initiatives became categorized as U.S. aid to underdeveloped countries. This is an excellent example of the interaction between the private vested interests of officials—especially their ability to instigate public projects under the rubric of development—and the dominant belief in development.

Favorable treatment of the pineapple industry was explained when the government of President Alemán issued a decree exempting pineapples from export duties; by contrast, the duty on bananas was 3.25 pesos per stem. It certainly made economic sense to abolish export taxes; however, the president's involvement in the

Veracruz industry suggests that factors other than economic theory were in play.[60]

Former director of the Banco de México Antonio Espinosa de los Monteros found his experience in the United States useful in 1946. The north of Mexico was energy poor before the great discoveries of natural gas. The United States had regularly denied export of this resource during the war years. Espinosa de los Monteros positioned himself to take advantage of this situation. With associates in the governing circle, he bought a controlling interest in the Compañía Mexicana de Gas. They next approached the Federal Power Commission as wartime regulations were lifted and obtained the first allocation of gas to Mexico. To block domestic competition, permits were given only to Gas Industrial de Monterrey S.A. Espinosa de los Monteros wrote to the president's private secretary, "It will be necessary to delay for ten long years the exploration for gas in Northern Mexico [to aid the] interests of our company."[61]

When a major economic development takes place, theoretical economists are inclined to look for market forces rather than for individual hidden hands, in the tradition of Adam Smith, founder of their discipline. The community's reaction was frequently more straightforward and to the point, as in its response to the devaluation of June 1948. There was a public outcry against insider trading practices. The outrage that was focused on government officials was so great that President Alemán believed it necessary, in defense of the directors of the Banco de México, to promise to publish lists of those banks and individuals involved in large exchange transactions on the eve of the devaluation.[62] There certainly had been an economic basis to this development; the country's large wartime reserves had been eroded rapidly by inflation, investments, and opulent expenditures after World War II. Finance Minister Beteta appears to have bet, erroneously, that the U.S. Treasury and the IMF would bail out the peso in 1948. His use of statistics was unimpressive in his speech to the Mexican Bankers' Association on the eve of the devaluation.

Beteta gained some short-term comfort in that the public was reassured of the strength of the peso, even though many in financial circles knew that the peso was in trouble. When the devaluation came on July 22, 1948, accusations of insider trading proliferated, and the government circle was widely believed to have profited from the devaluation. The head of the DDF, Fernando Casas Alemán (the president's nephew), was booed off a soccer field when he tried to officiate at the opening of a match. The government felt political heat and published a list of individuals who had traded (some nineteen million dollars) with luck on the eve of the devaluation; however, as one diplomat put it, "Attention riveted on what was not disclosed."[63]

The weekly magazine *Presente* accused the Sáenz family of having made $1.5 million by purchasing dollars on the eve of the devaluation. The issue was sensitive because Josué, the son of Aarón Sáenz, was the director of credit in the Ministry of Finance. It was alleged that Aarón Sáenz Cournet, a cousin of Josué, had done the insider trading based on information from Josué and using capital from the elder Aarón. All of the Aarón Sáenz family wrote the president in private, vigorously denying any involvement, and the matter was turned over to the attorney general to investigate.[64] The allegations died.

The technical experts in the IMF and the U.S. Department of the Treasury concluded that the July 22 devaluation fundamentally reflected "a current account deficit and not speculation until the last weeks before" the decision to abandon the rate of 4.85 pesos to the U.S. dollar, a rate that fell to 7 to 1 in early August. Mexico counted upon drawing rights to $22.5 million in the IMF and another $13 million in the U.S. Treasury stabilization agreement—a figure subsequently increased to $25 million—to see the nation through. In return, the recommendations of the IMF and the Treasury were being "rigorously followed."[65]

Carlos Serrano, the head of the secret police, again approached the U.S. embassy after the columnist Drew Pearson wrote about his alleged involvement with running narcotics into the United States. Apparently thinking that it would help his cause, Serrano made a number of accusations against other members of the administration. He asserted that both the minister of the economy, Ruiz Galindo, and the minister of war, General Limón, were making a lot of money out of their offices. He even asserted that Limón had pocketed $10,000 of the $50,000 the president had recently given the army's polo team for an international tour.[66]

The president was frequently accused of setting up his friends and close political associates with monopoly positions. In the second National Assembly of the PRI, in 1953, General Jacinto Treviño accused Alemán's close political aide Jorge Pasquel of running an officially sanctioned monopoly distributing fuel.[67] Similarly, Alemán's friend Antonio Díaz Lombardo was allowed to have the "notorious bus monopoly."[68]

Development in Acapulco

William O'Dwyer was a former mayor of New York City who would be shown to have close links to the mobster Frank Costello during the televised 1951 Kefauver anticrime hearings in the U.S. Senate. President Truman had sent O'Dwyer to Mexico as ambassador to take the heat off investigations of the New York City Tammany Hall machine. O'Dwyer quickly found an environment to his liking in the deals surrounding the development of Acapulco. He referred to his "very good friend" Ing. Melchor Perusquía in the following way: "Mr. Perusquía is a very dear friend of President Alemán and his official capacity is Collector of the Port of Acapulco and is also the head of the Board of Improvement. In short he could be referred to as the 'Emperor of Acapulco.' "[69]

Since the town of Acapulco was surrounded by ejido lands, land deals and the alienation of public beaches in the fabulous resort generated continuous scandals. One common pattern was for politically powerful people to initiate legal proceedings taking the land of local villages (ejidos) for their own property. Visitors to the famous Caleta Beach in Acapulco frequently comment upon a striking old mansion that is on a tiny island a few meters from the popular beach. (The actual construction was carried out by General Jorge Enríquez, who had the contract to build the road to Zihuatenejo.) There is archival evidence that Maximino Avila Camacho and, after his death, his widow, Margarita Richardi de Avila Camacho, were involved in a most blatant act of corruption by transferring the island to their personal title. In that case it was the national patrimony, rather than ejido land, that was the origin of their freely acquired property.[70]

The ejido of Icacos lost its land to a golf course, a housing subdivision, and a company formed by the ubiquitous Manuel Suárez of Techo Eterno Eureka who also managed to gain most of the southern shore of the Bay of Acapulco. In the understanding of the U.S. vice consul, "No cash will be paid, but the city will be entitled to an amount of work on civic improvements such as a new market, improved street sewage, and so on." Suárez was suppose to do work equal to the value of the land, and he also received many contracts to do work in the port. Most of the work was done with sewage pipe and construction materials made by Suárez's company, and recurrent delays were an accepted form of raising the price of the projects.[71]

At one point, even that phantasmal organization, the Confederación Nacional de Campesinos (CNC), wrote to the president complaining about the process by which the presidential decree of January 9, 1947, had dispossessed the ejidos "El Jardin" and "Garita de Juárez" of their lands. The land was turned over by decree to the Junta Federal de Mejoras Materiales. Melchor Perusquía argued that even though the peasants "did nothing" with the land, that the Junta had offered them each a lot, a typical house, and 7,000 pesos, the people still resisted their dispossession. This was understandable when one realizes that the ejido "El Jardin" alone had lost 20,480,000 square meters of frontage on the road to Pie de la Cuesta.[72]

Another deal in Acapulco was with the U.S. oilman J. Paul Getty. Apparently, the negotiations between Miguel Alemán and Getty had been going on since 1941. At stake were 500 hectares belonging to the Ejido del Marquez, at Puerto Marquez in Acapulco. Getty's agents indicated that they would proceed with the contract with the Junta Federal de Mejoras Materiales de Acapulco "for the acquisition, development and improvement of land belonging to the Ejido del Marquez provided a satisfactory decree and satisfactory title could be obtained. Mr. Getty is extremely interested in this project and would extremely appreciate its favorable consideration."[73] The president's response to Getty was "get in touch with Señor Melchor Perusquía, President of the Committee of Material Improvements of Acapulco, who has instructions on how to manage and resolve this kind of problem."[74]

The use of the state to channel resources into programs of industrialization coincided with the private interests of important functionaries. Thus, the minister of the economy, Antonio Ruiz Galindo, was the recipient of a state subsidy to support his industrial efforts. Indeed, he wrote to President Alemán asking him "to please extend for two years more" (1953 and 1954) the subsidy of 1,250,000 pesos that had first been given to him on September 23, 1947, and was then subsequently extended each year after 1948, while he was a minister. From the internal evidence in his letter to the president, it is likely that he was not paying interest on the "subsidy."[75] Whether he ever intended to repay the money, the minister used the national treasury as a commercial bank—without the inconvenience of repayments.

Thus far we have seen that there was a wide range of corrupt practices in the 1940s. Some of these practices were fairly unimaginative, such as the payment of bribes, direct looting, and the gift of money to favorites. Wartime projects also provided considerable opportunity for a range of corrupt activities, from direct kickbacks to the giving of construction contracts to friends; the ability to direct public resources to powerful figures generated real political strength. More sinister still was the systematic use of corruption to break the independence of the union movement.

Discrediting Labor

The role of corruption in paying for political obedience was critical in relation to the labor movement. In an environment in the late 1940s that was rapidly becoming less favorable to the labor movement material rewards were important in convincing union leaders to resist rank-and-file pressure for independence. It is commonly observed that there are three kinds of unions in Mexico: company unions (*sindicatos blancos*), or yellow dog unions as they were called in the U.S. labor movement; government-controlled unions (*sindicatos charros*); and independent unions. Corruption applied in conjunction with repression played a persuasive role in convincing union leaders to shift from an independent stance. Moreover, corruption and endemic violence in the struggles between different unions in the 1940s had the important impact of discrediting the union movement among the general population.

In March 1948 the leadership of the Confederación Unica de Trabajadores (CUT) accused the secretary general of the CTM, Fernando Amilpa, of "trying to alienate for himself lands that were given to all of the workers who belonged to that labor organization." The lands in question had been given to the union in 1939 by President Cárdenas, and opposition unionists thought that they should not pass into the hands of Amilpa.[76] Many labor supporters recognized that serious damage was inflicted on their cause as these charges and countercharges resounded.

Allegations of official union gangsterism and corruption proliferated. Union leader Palomino Roja wrote to the president about the case of José Martínez Torres, a baker, who refused to give money for the campaign of *charro* union leader Jesús Yurén. In retaliation, the baker was kidnapped, thrown into the penitentiary, and charged with murder, although eventually released.[77] Without trying to play judge and jury in these cases, several points are noteworthy. These examples of official union violence are common. Officials had to be helping the *charro* unionists as they were quickly released and their opponents put in jail. And finally, it is bizarre that the petitioners still appealed to the president in the faith that he would do the right thing.[78]

Hidden deals abounded in the union movement. Businessmen frequently boasted of keeping union leaders on the payroll; they thought that bribes were a bargain in order to have the union leaders keep their workers in line. Direct allegations of these practices were made to diplomats by the management of the Compañía de las Fábricas de Papel de San Rafael y Anexas S.A., where managers claimed to carry twelve union officials on the company accounts, and the Fabrica de Papel Coyoacán, and also by the bottlers of Coca-Cola, Orange Crush, and Mission Orange. In each of these cases, union officials from the Sindicato de Trabajadores en General de la Industria de Aguas Gaseosas y Similares were alleged to have regularly accepted bribes to keep their unions in line with management objectives.[79]

Charro union leaders were frequently accused of corruption.[80] Petitions to the president singled out Fidel Velázquez, Fernando Amilpa, Jesús Yurén, Alfonso Sánchez Madariaga, and other CTM officials as corrupt.[81] The president regularly denied an audience to the petitioner and merely sent the complaint along for a legal opinion, at which point the matter died. However, widespread knowledge of corruption in the union movement created deep divisions between honest and dishonest unionists; at the same time, it sent out the signal that dishonesty was tolerated.[82] In addition to their "divide and rule" benefit to the government, these charges of corruption also discredited the labor movement in the broader community.

At times, national political strategies depended on corruption in the union movement. At the height of the battle over petroleum nationalization in 1938, the companies saw the potential of corruption for dividing the unions and hurting the government. They found their man in Juan Zamora, the local petroleum union chief in El Ebano, San Luis Potosí, and encouraged him to divert pay from the union members and to steal equipment from PEMEX. They provided markets for the stolen equipment and also subsidized opposition union factions. The theft of equipment forced union leaders into either silence or opposition, and factions proliferated in the petroleum workers' union. The diversion of pay into Zamora's pockets also had the desired effect of pitting worker against worker. Eventually, the case became notorious, and the government arrested Zamora and his associates; they were charged with collusion with the foreign petroleum companies.[83] Since the

companies were courting rebellion, these machinations went beyond normal labor politics. By supporting rebellion, the companies exposed themselves to retaliation from the central government.
After all, contesting state sovereignty was not normal business practice, even in the petroleum industry.

Another political use of corruption was especially notable in
the period. Banking had always been the Achilles' heel of the land
reform movement. Several land reform and cooperative banks had
been set up over the years to deal with a twofold problem. It has
frequently been noted that the land reform program had been struc-
tured around the prohibition against the ejidos' using their land to
guarantee borrowing. This has usually been viewed as a safety
measure against foreclosure. In fact, the unwillingness of commercial banks to lend to *campesinos* also reflected considerable urban
and class bias. The solution was to establish rural banks and cooperative banks to lend to these alternative forms of development.
These public-sector banks became among the most notoriously corrupt in Mexico, and they seriously undercut and discredited the
ejido and cooperative movements. It is interesting to examine the
composition of the boards of directors of these public-interest banks.
In the case of the Banco Nacional Fomento Cooperativo, Ramón
Beteta led a contingent of seven government officials. Another four
directors were from banking and industry. Moreover, many of the
most important private bankers in the country sat on the boards of
these banks, and it is fair to say that endemic corruption in these
banks reflected official tolerance.

Perhaps the most tantalizing suggestion of the political use of
corruption emerges from a series of FBI reports. A New Jersey businessman, Henry Grunewald, wrote to J. Edgar Hoover about a business deal linking Mexican petroleum to the Barbar Asphalt
Corporation, one of the largest firms in the United States at the
time, and later the Pantux Corporation, which was formed exclusively for the deal. Some 150,000 to 200,000 barrels of PEMEX oil
were shipped to New Jersey each month at the bargain price of
85 cents per barrel f.o.b. Tampico. Pantux Corporation was organized by several businessmen—Joseph Slutzker, Harry Tepper, and
Joseph Silverman—with Luis Felipe Contreras owning a major block
of the stock in association with the Lombardo Toledano brothers.

It is unlikely that this was a licit business deal—selling petroleum well below market prices—and major finder fees were also
involved. Even if the Lombardo Toledano brothers' law firm had
done work for the Pantux Corporation, it is difficult to understand

why they would have had a percentage involvement in the deal. Grunewald wrote to the FBI because at one stage there were also plans to sell Mexican oil to the USSR, and he wanted to check the legality of that idea. Another FBI report, made when Vicente Lombardo Toledano was in the United States, stated that Lombardo had indeed visited the offices of the Barbar Asphalt Corporation in Newark, thus linking him personally with the company.[84]

This information explains two mysteries of Mexican politics. First, observers wondered about Lombardo Toledano's personal finances for even though he had a wealthy father Lombardo's spending habits were lavish—especially on his political activities. Second, such an arrangement would also explain his slavish fidelity to the presidents with whom he so frequently disagreed and his unwillingness to make an issue of corruption.[85] These interpretations are reinforced by the U.S. diplomats' belief that Ruíz Cortines continued Alemán's practice of giving Lombardo Toledano 30,000 pesos per month to keep *El Popular* going.[86]

The leverage that government officials had over the business community was great. A wide variety of rules and regulations could be invoked to punish an uncooperative firm. Elections offered a moment at which pressure could be applied to the business community. Businesses were expected to contribute to the campaign of the *tapado*. The closer one was to the center of power, the higher the amount expected. A close confidant of Ezequiel Padilla, Albarrán, confided to a U.S. diplomat that Aarón Sáenz raised somewhere between 600,000 and 700,000 pesos in campaign contributions for the Alemán campaign in 1945. Sugar was a regulated commodity, and Sáenz expected the government to set felicitous prices for his sugar and also to enforce exclusive contracts that kept producers under the control of his sugar refineries.[87] Competitive trade practices represented a major threat to those who dominated sugar production, and therefore, munificent campaign contributions seemed entirely realistic.

Political power was frequently used to maintain a monopoly position. There was the sad story of a shopkeeper who sold his business for 20,000 pesos, with which he bought a refrigerator truck. Purchasing fish in Veracruz, he headed for Mexico City only to learn how the system worked. After being stopped at Jalapa, Puebla, and the border of the Federal District for the usual *mordidas*, or bribes, he was eventually told, after paying, that he would not be allowed to bring fish into the Federal District "without the consent of the local fish monopoly." Similar setups prohibited restaurant owners from purchasing beef except from the Chihuahua slaughterhouse. The corn market was centralized and controlled in Toluca. Owners' associations even kept outsiders from entering the bus business in Mexico City.[88] In every instance the recipient of official favors was expected to come to the aid of the party as elections approached. Similar arrangements clearly acted against the public good by preventing competition in these and many other fields.

Changing the Rules

As blatant as theft and influence peddling might be, an argument can be made that the sale of political influence may even be more damaging. Corruption could be devastating for those who attempted to innovate. Mexican Silk Mill Incorporated S.A. provides a case in point. The firm went into bankruptcy in 1939. Under the Cardenista legislation, it was then possible for the workers to purchase the mill and try to run it themselves. In 1944, after years of litigation before the Junta Federal de Conciliación y Arbitraje, the workers actually gained legal recognition as the only privileged creditors of the bankrupt company. Manuel Campanella was named as the firm's receiver. While in that position he was supposed to oversee the financial reorganization of the enterprise as a cooperative. The workers paid 1,885,000 pesos and became the owners of the reconstituted firm by 1947. When the workers demanded to see the accounts, Campanella refused their request and it quickly became apparent that he had a great deal to hide. Campanella was eventually convicted of a 10-million-peso theft in 1948. His crime decapitalized the operation and prevented the new owners from taking control of the firm that they had purchased. An important industry went down. The workers lost their investment and became even more outraged when the administration issued Campanella a writ of protection in 1949 despite his conviction for fraud.[89] Power brokers were willing to go to extreme lengths to ensure that the cooperative model of development failed.

The 1934 Organic Law of Monopoly was originally intended to foster infant industries. In practice it came to mean the virtual invalidation of the antimonopoly prohibitions of Article 28 of the 1917 constitution. Anderson, Clayton and Company S.A. managed a breakthrough in overcoming the antimonopoly laws in 1952. The ministers of agriculture and of the national economy had sought to prohibit the powerful firm from engaging in additional cotton ginning in Torreón on the grounds of monopoly practices. One might not immediately think of the world's largest agribusiness as a candidate for protection under the Organic Law of Monopoly; however, the courts thought differently. In March 1952 a district judge in Torreón upheld the company and granted A. C. & Co. an injunction (*amparo*) on the grounds that antimonopoly efforts by the government represented "anachronistic fruit of a classical liberal ideology which belongs to the past."[90] Economic theory could be used quite selectively.

An Extreme Case

The most public case of corruption was undoubtedly that of Maximino Avila Camacho, the president's brother. A great embarrassment to the administration, he was crude, violent, dishonest, and a nouveau riche. Maximino's survival in the cabinet was due entirely to his relationship with the president. He had an inflated ego and an exaggerated sense of his own importance. He boasted of a visit to Washington to the U.S. consul in Ciudad Juárez: "He described the reception in Washington D.C. and the ovation he received as something which he had never before seen in his life; the crowds were so thick, translating his own words, that one could hardly stick a needle between the people who were standing so close to each other."[91]

Maximino is the sort of figure whom historians of scandal love. Yet there was far more to him than his bizarre psychology. He was more hostile to the Cardenista tradition than anyone else in the PRM, and his personal greed was boundless. His position in his brother's administration was that of minister of transportation and communications. Thus, he headed the agency of the government that issued contracts for telecommunications, road building, and many other kinds of public works: he became known as "Mr. 15 percent." As one British diplomat explained, "It appears that General Maximino has succeeded in making enemies largely due to the cancellation of road building concessions which were granted by his predecessor [in the Avila Camacho government] to influential politicians and generals, which Maximino has felt it necessary to cancel on the pretext of awarding such contracts to his own friends, prominent amongst whom was Wenner-Gren." [92]

Axel Wenner-Gren was General Maximino's close friend, and Maximino's business dealings with the blacklisted entrepreneur were quite an embarrassment to the Allies and to the Avila Camacho administration. It was widely believed that Wenner-Gren was

paying kickbacks to General Maximino, and when the entrepreneur was placed on the Allies' blacklist it gave an opening to
the enemies of Maximino as well as to the opponents of graft in
general.

Typical of the style of the man was Maximino's birthday celebration, in August 1942. He gave himself a party to end all parties. The celebration at the end of Maximino's term as governor of
the state of Puebla represented the end of an era as well as his
birthday. He had the state legislature declare him to be the *"hijo
predilecto del estado,"* and his name was inscribed in gold on the
wall of the legislative chamber, an honor formerly paid only to
Alvaro Obregón and Emiliano Zapata. One British diplomat in attendance declared, "These celebrations partook of the nature of a
Roman orgy." Governor Gonzalo Bautista threw Maximino a birthday dinner for twelve hundred people, who ate from gold-embossed
plates. An estimated five thousand people visited Puebla at the
height of the birthday celebrations. At one moment during the festivities, Maximino appeared in the city's bullring in a pure white
traje de luz, the traditional bullfighting costume, accompanied by
his Spanish girlfriend, the bullfighter Conchita Cintrón, who was
similarly attired. The British intelligence report on the celebrations

Charros (probably Maximino Avila Camacho and his Spanish girlfriend, bullfighter
Conchita Cintrón) in front of bullring. *Courtesy Hermanos Mayo, Archivo General de
la Nación, Mexico City*

concluded with the comment, "In the evening he gave a ball on a truly regal scale."[93]

He was described by his archenemy Lombardo Toledano, in a speech to the CTM leadership at the Universidad Obrero upon his return from a visit to the United States. According to Lombardo Toledano, "General Maximino, as he is generally known, is a rare type, worthy of study by psychologists. . . . He boasts of twenty houses in the Chapultepec Hills, twenty automobiles, and half a million pesos worth of fine, pure blooded, Arabian horses; he affirms in a loud voice that he has two hundred silk suits with two hundred pairs of shoes."[94]

Sometimes Maximino's efforts to obtain a payoff accidentally became public knowledge. In Sonora in 1942, Governor Macías expelled all employees of the Department of Communications and Public Works from the state in retaliation for the difficulties that Maximino was placing in the way of the completion of a highway. The contract had been issued by General de la Garza to a rival construction firm, headed by General Yocupicio, prior to Maximino's tenure in office. The problem was that Maximino was not receiving his share of the contract.[95] Consequently, a major road project was halted over the right to collect graft.

Maximino had been a deadly enemy of the CTM when he was the governor of Puebla in the Cárdenas period. His technique for blocking the CTM was to build up lesser unions to offset the main labor organization, an approach that generated labor conflict in Puebla for decades. Even at his birthday party, when the CTM tried to organize a protest against the squandering of public funds to assuage the governor's ego, Maximino responded by having the local transport workers' union organize a counterdemonstration on his behalf.

Maximino Avila Camacho was a business partner and political protector of William Jenkins, the former American consul in Puebla who had become extremely wealthy from his interests in sugar, land, films, and banking. (Jenkins had gone to Mexico after being expelled from Vanderbilt University. He had violated university rules by marrying Mary Street while he was still an undergraduate.) Maximino handled the political cover for Jenkins in the face of bitter opposition from workers and ejidatarios, and Jenkins cut Maximino in on the economic action in Puebla. Mexicans frequently found it very difficult to understand how such a caricature of the rapacious foreign exploiter as William Jenkins could survive the nationalistic reforms of the Mexican Revolution. Maximino Avila

Camacho was the answer. His corruption was boundless. The governorship provided small pickings by the standards he achieved as minister of communications and transportation under his brother a few years later.

Maximino also associated with U.S. criminals. The mayor of San Antonio, Texas, wrote to FDR to point out that "all the racketeers in the United States are now passing through San Antonio in and out of Mexico."[96] Even at the height of the austerity crisis following the crop failures of 1942–43, Maximino used these contacts for personal gain. One U.S. diplomat accused Maximino of manipulating commodity prices, especially the price of rice from the Nueva Italia and Lombardia haciendas. Maximino was also accused of being at the pinnacle of a system of *mordidas*, or semiofficial bribes, and even with having instituted a system of scalping tickets for popular attractions throughout the country. Many businessmen were appalled by his activities.[97]

Vicente Lombardo Toledano, Alejandro Carrillo, and the delegate Daniel Rodríguez of Michoacán also accused Maximino of hoarding commodities. Even Fernando Amilpa, then the president of the Senate, openly discussed the problem of official corruption, always arguing, of course, that the president was doing his best to crack down on offenders. Avarice was not the only impulse that motivated the president's brother. One diplomat of the period reported that Maximino had arranged the deportation of two Spaniards as a response, "not to any political question, but to the competition with Maximino over the dancer, Conchita Martínez."[98]

General Maximino did make friends. He frequently entertained Fulgencio Batista of Cuba. Another friend, John A. Hastings, was a former New York senator who had been linked to the Jimmy Walker scandal in New York City. During the period, he headed up the "Hastings Group" in business. His close links to the Swedish (pro-Nazi) businessman Axel Wenner-Gren created a maze of business dealings involving Maximino Avila Camacho. One British diplomat confided, in an internal report to the Foreign Office, that Maximino was a friend of Sir Harry (a mining magnate) and Lady Oaks and that he was embarrassed that the duke of Windsor had allegedly called Maximino "one of the great men of our age."[99] State Department economic intelligence believed that the Hastings Group, including Maximino, had amassed $100 million.[100]

Before the United States entered World War II, the U.S. government worked hard to impress Maximino. During Maximino's 1941 trip to Washington, Vice President Wallace, Secretary Hull, and others showed him the sights of the capital and entertained him at the Metropolitan Club, a routine for friendly guests. A military escort of "five or six armored cars" was provided for his sightseeing. More interesting still, U.S. officials assigned Major Lawrence Higgins, chief of the Foreign Liaison Section of the army, to serve as translator. Higgins was also the son-in-law of Maximino's business partner, William O. Jenkins of Puebla.[101] This attempt to court Maximino did not work. Even after Mexico joined the Allies, Maximino maintained his business partnership with Axel Wenner-Gren. High officials of the two countries worried that "Maximino's well known strong armed tactics," as Eduardo Villaseñor put it, would be the "logical entry point for Fascist penetration in Mexico." This concern was not entirely speculative since it was known that Maximino kept a large picture of Mussolini in his bedroom in his house in Puebla.[102]

At one time Maximino harbored illusions about following his brother into the presidency. This, however, was not going to happen; his increasingly public corruption offended even many of the hard-line right wingers in business and politics. Eventually, opposition within the PRM forced him to call a press conference with his favorite newspapers to deny his candidacy. He began the interview by stating, with typical modesty, "You know there is no lack of people who see me as a possible presidential candidate." The interview of May 20, 1943, served as a sort of self-indictment. Maximino, after denying his interest in higher office, claimed that he was not antilabor or anti-Cárdenas; it was only that he had a good sense of humor and kidded around a lot. Maximino denied that his personal fortune was as large as it was often made out to be, saying that he had only about three million pesos. He also denied having any interest in the Mexico City slaughterhouse; therefore, he was innocent of manipulating wartime meat prices. Neither did he own, as was widely rumored, a new skyscraper on the Paseo de la Reforma (the building in which the headquarters of the National Railways was located) or the "1-2-3" chain stores. He admitted that he owned a home in Acapulco but denied that it was worth a million pesos. He offered to sell the residence to anyone for 50,000 pesos, a price that was widely ridiculed but reportedly precipitated many purchase offers.[103]

Harold D. Finley, the first secretary of the American embassy, estimated that Maximino's fortune was increasing at close to three million pesos per week. He also granted credence to a series of rumors that were circulating widely about Maximino's activities. For example, the general was said to have been involved in increasing the price of corn for tortillas and of benefiting from the higher prices. He applied to the Ministry of the National Economy for permission to export rice to the United States, where it was in short supply. While processing his application, the Department of the National Economy discovered that he was sitting on forty thousand tons of rice, which would have brought nearly one million dollars on the U.S. market.

In 1941 an earthquake struck Mexico City. The owner of one skyscraper on the Paseo de la Reforma invested heavily in repairing the building. Finley reported that Maximino approached the owner of the building, offering him a very low price, a figure less than the cost of the repairs, for the newly repaired edifice. When the owner refused, Maximino contrived to withhold the building's safety inspection permits. Thus, Maximino's offer became one that the owner could no longer refuse. Similarly, Maximino was said to have obtained a mansion on the Avenida de los Insurgentes—a property that occupied a square city block—by threatening to increase enormously the annual rates the owner would have to pay on the property. Finley marveled at the tolerance others showed for the man's activities.[104]

The magazine *Hoy* published a long interview with Maximino, conducted by the journalist and historian José C. Valadés. Using his influence as a financial supporter of *Hoy*, he was trying to appear respectable by having Valadés conduct the interview.[105] In acute financial trouble, *Hoy* had been vulnerable to Maximino's influence and money. In 1940 the magazine had backed General Almazán, and its circulation had dropped from thirty thousand readers per week to between eight thousand and ten thousand. Valadés had to weather a storm of derision in the wake of the interview. Popular jokes asserted that Maximino was even buying the recently erupting volcano at Paricutín, since he could not resist anything that was going up. He made another offer in the article to sell a property called "El Batan," which he had acquired from former President Ortíz Rubio for 75,000 pesos. The second secretary of the U.S. embassy placed a figure of 500,000 pesos as a more accurate price and reported that Maximino's phones again rang hot as he received thirty offers at that price within twenty-four hours after the article appeared.[106]

After being named minister of transportation and communications, Maximino became active in combating not only the Left but also Foreign Minister Padilla, whose diplomatic triumph at the Rio

Conference had made him an early front-runner in the maneuvers over the 1946 nomination. According to Guy W. Ray, the chief political officer of the U.S. embassy, Maximino, acting as a front for his brother, had been using articles in the magazines *Hoy* and *Así* to attack Padilla. In Ray's view, the articles were in *Así* because "*Así* is generally supposed in newspaper circles to be subsidized by the President principally for the purpose of making public attacks on persons who have become prominent or who are out of line with his policies."[107]

Hoy was more closely linked with Minister Maximino Avila Camacho whereas *Así* was thought to be instructed by President Manuel Avila Camacho. Maximino also used his position as minister of transportation and communications to subsidize and to extend the privilege of free mail delivery to the friendly magazine *Tiempo*. He also was reported to have plans to start four newspapers: in Mexico City, Puebla, Ciudad Juárez, and Veracruz.[108] Friends and foes alike of the administration tended to view Maximino as an embarrassment to the president. This information suggests that the president was actually using his brother as a "stalking-horse" to test popular reaction to his policies before he implemented questionable tactics and maneuvers. Other suggestions also point toward this conclusion.

There is evidence that Maximino may have been acting for his family in some of his most dishonest activities. After his death, the revelations about Maximino's personal corruption stunned even the most jaded observers. A family feud erupted as prospective heirs battled over the massive fortune that Maximino had accumulated during his political career, first in Puebla as a silent partner of William Jenkins and later as a minister in his brother's government. The feud over the estate became public on December 2, 1946, when the motion picture actor, Jorge Vélez, was gunned down in the streets on the eve of his wedding to Margarita Richardi, Maximino's widow. In spite of Jorge's wounds, and in spite of a second attempt on his life in the hospital, the wedding was celebrated, in the hospital, a few days later. No one was charged with the crime, and a further attempt on the lives of the pair took place on January 25 as they were attempting to seek safety outside of the country. Machine guns were fired from a speeding car near the Mexico City airport; although the newlyweds were not killed, the bullets hit Margarita's sister-in-law, Teresa Bonfigli de Richardi.

This spectacle of Maximino's heirs treating Mexico City to a running shoot-out near the airport in an attempt to prevent Jorge

Vélez and Margarita Richardi from taking Maximino's fortune out of the country created a furor. The press made it page one news. The public, suffering from wartime inflation and a rapidly declining standard of living, demanded action, and at first it appeared that a trial associated with the "dance of the millions" was in the offing. Figures as high as 400 million pesos were reported to be involved, an enormous sum in 1946. Clearly, the Avila Camacho family was becoming a focus for the frustrations of the era.

The government was outraged to see the most questionable practices of the revolutionary family aired in public. The federal district attorney, General and Lic. Carlos Franco Sodi, initially told the press that justice would proceed, "fall who may." The following day President Alemán demanded the full application of the law, using the same phrase; Luis Manuel Avila Binder, Maximino's son by his first wife, Armando Armenta Barradas, described as "a notorious gunman," and Emilio Romero, Jorge Vélez's chauffeur, were arrested for the crime. In addition, a warrant was issued for the arrest of another brother of Maximino, Gabriel Avila Camacho, described as the "intellectual author" of the attack.

The public was doubly shocked when Jorge and Margarita left the country on January 31 in order not to testify. Word spread that the pair had left with the approval of the authorities to avoid a public trial. This version of events was reinforced when, on February 3, Gabriel Avila Camacho was released due to lack of evidence. Major newspapers including *Excélsior*, *Novedades*, and *La Prensa* had reported the events as evidence of a profoundly corrupt system, so the government decided to suppress the charge of murder against relatives of the former president. By the end of January word was around in press circles that the president had told journalists to lay off the issue: after January 30 the press suspended its critical editorials.[109] Political allies stopped trying to defend Maximino. The best that the friends of the administration could do was to say nothing.

Maximino's represented the most blatant private accumulation of wealth; yet the president's brother also calls to mind the grotesque caricatures that colonial systems generated. Franz Fanon, in *The Wretched of the Earth*, added a psychological explanation to similar phenomena elsewhere by arguing that this kind of crude imitation of wealth and ostentatious display of ill-gotten gains was common in neocolonial contexts. But the story of Maximino is more than an example of individual excess. His activities covered every category of corruption. He looted public funds directly, and the percentage he demanded of public contracts was notable because it was higher than the traditional payments required. He used his office, both in Puebla and in the Ministry of Transportation and Communications, to enrich himself and his friends and to hurt his enemies. His use of corruption to divide the labor movement was highly developed; the complex and violent nature of the movement in Puebla echoed his manipulations long after he departed the scene. Even his country's involvement in World War II failed to slow down his acquisitive efforts.

The question of responsibility for this staggering record of corruption cries out for an answer. The historical judgment of the *porfiriato*, for example, seems to be that although Porfirio Díaz was personally honest, he traded tolerance of corruption for political support. Of the Avila Camacho years there can be no such observation—the corruption went right to the top. Although President Avila Camacho enjoyed a relatively clean reputation while he was in office, once he was out of power, different stories quickly emerged. A U.S. diplomat reported, "The comments concerning the Ex-President are illuminating. Now that he is out of the Presidency, people seem to be able to express their real opinions and the number that I have gathered is anything but complimentary. My friends no longer talk of him as the 'Sir Galahad' of purity and honesty. In fact they say that he has cleaned up immense wealth, and since I have been talking to his bankers, they ought to know." [110]

In this account, the U.S. diplomats had learned that President Avila Camacho had been the silent partner of a number of major figures in his administration:

> They say that it is an undoubted fact that he was a silent partner of his brother Maximino, who was described as the best collector in Mexican history. It is also said that he is the silent partner of Manuel Suárez, who operates under the name Techo Eterno Eurika. Suárez has huge "cost-plus" public works contracts spread over the Republic, including port works, municipal involvements, real estate developments, schools, and public buildings in Veracruz and elsewhere and appears to be cleaning up a fortune on the contracts.

In the archival collection of the AGN in Mexico City are bank statements belonging to President Avila Camacho. He had one dollars account with the First National City Bank, and a small and a large account with the Banco de México. Detailed statements have survived for several months in 1942 and 1943. In August 1942, the month with the best records, there were deposits into his account of 500,000 pesos on August 6 and an even 1 million pesos on

August 13. What these sums were for is not indicated, and it is difficult to think of a licit reason why such large and even sums would have been deposited, especially when one recalls that the exchange rate was three pesos to one dollar. Even if the 1-million-peso deposit represented a legitimate transaction, it shows how well the president had done since entering politics.[111]

President Alemán's reputation for corruption was legendary, however, even while he was in office. Indeed, a casual reading of the press of the period amazes the reader. Whatever part of the country the president was visiting, he regularly retired to one of his haciendas on weekends. Even before becoming president he had accumulated considerable property in Veracruz. "It seems that he was the owner of 'Mocambo,' an extremely valuable property consisting of a large part of the waterfront land extending from Veracruz south to Boca del Río, including the resort Hotel Mocambo."[112]

Alemán's business interests were numerous. Frequently, these interests were hidden from the public view by partnership agreements with his associates, or *prestanombres*. Manuel Suárez, the Spanish industrialist, benefited enormously from his business deals with Presidents Avila Camacho and Alemán as well as with General Maximino Avila Camacho. When the Export-Import Bank financed the Hilton Hotel in Mexico City, the project was owned by Suárez and Alemán and then leased back to the Hilton Hotel Corporation to administer. This partnership also enjoyed "immense public works projects," including road and street construction, sewers and water systems, port works, and land deals. Often the partners only showed negotiable government notes to banks in order to raise the capital to proceed, putting up no capital of their own. For the Centrál Sanalona, the partners financed this sugar mill and property "almost 100 per cent by Government funds and by an Eximbank credit through Nacional Financiera." The National Investment Bank was also influenced by Suárez's close relationship with President Alemán. In 1953 the U.S. embassy learned that Suárez had an 80-million-peso debt with Nacional Financiera "which he is unable to service or liquidate." By 1950 Suárez's relationship with Alemán had cooled and Nacional Financiera was forced into a loss by renegotiating his loans.[113]

Companies that wanted advantages from the government commonly gave the president lucrative properties to facilitate the desired agreements. The La Paz Development Company found that its program "has progressed quite rapidly since the 'word' has circulated that the President endorsed the plan" after "the President, who incidentally has just been given a large seaside estate at La Paz . . . ," had reason to support the project. General Olachea ran the project in association with American investors, led by George F. Nicol, who "have so far succeeded pretty well in getting what they want."[114] Support of the local military leaders was also guaranteed by means of these arrangements.

Many individuals in Mexico who were privy to even a glimpse of the spirit of the age were horrified. Fernando de la Fuente was a courageous member of the Supreme Court, who was deeply upset about the growing level of corruption. He was one of the judges who had stood against the government at the time of the massacre at León in early 1946. "From a source within his family it has been learned that a short time ago he let it be known that he was considering exposing to the public some of the fraud in which President Alemán himself was alleged to be involved." In March 1948 shots were fired in an attempt on his life, after which he kept his silence.[115]

U.S. Corruption: The U.S. Army Air Corps Scandal

The highly unusual role of the United States in facilitating Mexican trade, investment, and development programs during World War II inevitably placed American diplomats in much closer contact with corruption than was the norm during peacetime. In their daily dealings with high officials and with U.S. businessmen operating in Mexico, diplomats inadvertently compiled a detailed record of corruption, one that is quite unique. However, in several instances, U.S. officials dealing with Mexico also crossed the line.

There was a scandal involving the Export-Import Lumber Company of Buffalo, New York, the U.S. firm charged with delivering Mexican mahogany for the construction of PT boats to the Defense Supplies Corporation, a subsidiary of the BEW. The initial contract for $2.5 million board feet of mahogany was to be produced for Export-Import Lumber by the Tehuantepec Lumber Company, a subsidiary of Resource Corporation International of Chicago. Unfortunately, the officers of Resource Corporation International were under indictment at this time, and the owners of Export-Import, a father and son, had no experience in the business. According to the General Accounting Office's audit, an initial advance of $500,000 and a further payment of $1.7 million for a mahogany plantation were lost. The plantation was seized by the Allied Property Custodian, but not before the $1.7 million payment had been distributed to Axis investors. The poor records of the firms made an audit impossible, although auditors did determine that the real value of the plantation was $60,000. The matter was complicated because a senior forestry official of the BEW was also an ex-official of Resource Corporation International.[116] Eventually, U.S. investigators concluded that the "senior forestry specialist of the BEW . . . was under indictment for fraud."[117] Given the enormity and speed of wartime purchasing, it is surprising that such cases were relatively infrequent.

Blatant examples of corruption were not limited to civilian contractors. There was a scandal when it was discovered that U.S. Army Air Corps officials were diverting airplane engine parts to private sales. The Lend-Lease Program for the Mexican air force was both incompetently and corruptly administered on the U.S. side during the war. The situation was such a mess that by 1943 the Army Air Corps sent Major Herman W. Brann to Mexico to investigate complaints emanating from the military attaché to the embassy in Mexico City. Major Brann's final report was one that, in George Messersmith's phrase, "does us no credit."[118]

The Lend-Lease Program for the Mexican air force was initiated in April 1942. By 1943 approximately one railroad car per week was arriving with aviation parts, mainly at the air force base in Puebla. There was no record of what exactly was being sent, or by whom, and the Mexican air force authorities had no influence upon what material was shipped. Apparently, as the Mexican authorities opened the crates it was not even clear what much of the material was for. By the end of 1943, only 10 percent of the material thus arriving had been opened, identified, and recorded; some twenty-eight hundred cases were still unpacked. In addition, the U.S. records at Duncan Field, San Antonio, were also very poor.[119] The program was out of control. By the end of 1943, 174 aircraft had been delivered, even though there were only 165 pilots in the entire Mexican air force.

Apart from the administrative incompetence there were several other problems. The material was addressed to the chief of the presidential general staff, General Jesús Salvador Sánchez y Sánchez. General Gustavo Salinas was the commanding general of the Mexican air force, and General Salinas worked closely with Major Brann in his investigation. Their work was highly sensitive. The lack of records on both sides signaled to a number of Mexican functionaries that U.S. officials were skimming off profits, and the Mexicans took pains not to embarrass the U.S. officials. The investigation proceeded slowly. Moreover, General Sánchez and his wife were the co-owners of a munitions and war materials sales company, and there were suggestions that they had discovered a new source of supply.

A spot audit of only a small percentage of the material in the warehouse also revealed that Mexico had been overcharged by $150,000 for what it had received. Major Brann could only observe that the total would be very much higher. Depressingly familiar pricing practices abounded, like charging $45 for a 3/8" X 1/8" plug that could be purchased at any automobile supply store for 10 cents, or overpricing a simple adaptor by $116, or charging a 1/2" washer as a $19.20 housing magneto.

It was never established, according to the U.S. records that have survived, who was profiting from the false pricing. It was noted, however, that once the strange material arrived in Mexico some U.S. personnel started selling obviously useful items, such as tires. Furthermore, the president's colorful brother, General Maximino Avila Camacho, took over some C-60 Lockheed airplanes, refitted them, and personally leased them to the Compañía Mexicana de Aviación, which was then a subsidiary of Pan American Airways.

The Army Air Corps scandal combined incompetence with malfeasance on the U.S. side; only after the fact did some Mexican officials take advantage of material that was going to waste. Even as their comrades were dying in combat—and this was happening at the very same time as the costly Doolittle mission to bomb Tokyo, in April 1942—some Air Corps officials were cashing in on their opportunities. The sacrifice of fellow fliers weighed heavily upon Major Brann's mind as he investigated this corruption; the episode also put U.S. officials on the defensive.

The U.S. Navy and Mexican Light and Power

U.S. officials were certainly not above questionable deals. After George Messersmith left the State Department, following his monumental battle with Spruille Braden over policy towards Juan Domingo Perón in Argentina, he returned to Mexico as president of the largest foreign firm in the country, Mexican Light and Power Company (MEXLIGHT). In that position he tapped his considerable range of contacts within the U.S. government to the advantage of his new employer. Writing in 1949 to Paul J. Reveley of the Division of Mexican Affairs in the State Department, he thanked Reveley for helping in the negotiations with the U.S. Navy over the rental of a mobile electrical generating station that was mounted on a railroad train more than a tenth of a mile long. Two of these gigantic trains had been built for the U.S. Navy as insurance against power failures should an enemy attack destroy a major generating facility in the United States. The unit consisted of six cars, a 225-ton boiler car mounted on eight axles, and a 275-ton steam turbogenerator mounted on twelve axles. Three additional freight cars carried peripheral gear for this mobile power station. It was, in the judgment of one expert, "one of the engineering marvels which came out of the war."[120] Reveley helped Messersmith reduce the price of the rental from $600 to $400 per day: "As soon as I heard from him [Messersmith's agent] that the price was $400 I knew that you and Ruth [Reveley's wife] had been helpful in the matter, for without your intervention I am sure that they [the U.S. Navy] would have stuck at $600. I can not tell you how deeply we appreciate getting the train for $400 a day because it means a tremendous lot to the company."[121]

Someone in the State Department calculated that the former ambassador had saved his new employer $73,000 per year by tapping his former State Department colleagues for favors. The deal undoubtedly helped Mexico overcome a serious drought, which was limiting its power-generating capacity in the Bajío in 1949. Messersmith also thought that this arrangement generally facilitated his dealings with Martínez Báez and Sánchez Cuen within the Alemán administration in favorably resolving tariff issues, adjusting contractual provisions, and solving labor problems. The ability to use the U.S. Navy's generator allowed the Mexican administration to avoid power shortages, and this strengthened Messersmith's hand in bargaining with the government on other matters.

Ambassador Messersmith's intervention in the MEXLIGHT case neatly allows the analyst to focus on the limits between good business and corruption. U.S. diplomats frequently posed, with some degree of veracity, as protectors of the Mexican people against the rapacious appetites of the more acquisitive domestic functionaries. Messersmith was attacked after the war by the Left for exercising undue influence on the government, an accusation that was correct. Thus, at a mass meeting in the *zócalo* on December 21, 1945, a number of speakers had called for his dismissal. Again on January 12, 1946, the ambassador was attacked by the left-labor alliance for his close collaboration with the Sinarquistas, a charge that was hyperbolic.[122] At the same time, an editorial in the *Laredo Times* attacked Messersmith for quite different reasons. Messersmith was informed by Lanz Duret, editor and owner of *El Universal*, that the head of the Artes Gráficas union, one of Lombardo Toledano's associates, had "told Lanz Duret that he was willing to pay any amount for its [*Laredo Times* article] publication."[123] As Messersmith defended himself against those he now called the Communists—a term he would not have applied so crudely during the war—he wove his personal defense around the issue of corruption. "There are a lot of people in the Mexican Government who are as crooked as a ram's horn, and who don't particularly like me because I have stood in their way in making improper personal gains at the expense of the Mexican masses."[124]

The U.S. ambassador was able, with a degree of truthfulness, to represent his action as a defense of the Mexican people by opposing corruption. Yet this defense of the victims of corruption also enabled him to set aside the issue of the impact of the return of U.S. investment and to base his self-justification on the wartime cooperation between the two countries. The Left's attack on Messersmith, on the spurious grounds of collaboration with the Sinarquistas, gave quite an opening to the conservative press, and they leapt into the breach.[125] Messersmith would have been more vulnerable on the MEXLIGHT case and in terms of an infamous case of influence peddling involving one of the best connected international law firms in the United States, Sullivan and Cromwell.

Sullivan and Cromwell: Miller and Sabalo

Another kind of corruption surrounded Edward G. Miller, President Truman's assistant secretary of state for Latin America from 1949 to 1952. Before coming to Washington, he had been a partner in what was probably the most powerful law firm in the foreign policy arena, Sullivan and Cromwell. John Foster Dulles was the best-known partner at the time. Before joining the Truman administration, Miller had represented a client with oil interests in Mexico, Sabalo Transportation Company. Sabalo was, as one historian recently said, "a store front" for El Aguila Oil Company. It was also informally linked to and protected by Rafael Sánchez Tapia, a close adviser to Lázaro Cárdenas and former President Ortiz Rubio.[126]

Sabalo Transportation Company was one of those firms that had been nationalized by President Cárdenas in 1938 and that had owned rich petroleum rights in Poza Rica, Veracruz. At the time, there was an outstanding issue associated with a petroleum loan for Mexico. Soon after Edward Miller was appointed, the State Department made representations to Mexico demanding that foreign oil companies be allowed to reenter the industry. The demand reveals an intriguing conjunction among Miller's long association with Sabalo, Sullivan and Cromwell's representations to the State Department and the Congress, the State Department's pressure on the Alemán administration to find a way to allow private capital back into the Mexican oil industry, and Mexico's eventual capitulation to this pressure. Miller's conflict of interest in the case—as a diplomat pursuing a settlement for the same party that he had formerly had as a client—attracted critical attention in the press.

Dean Acheson relied upon technicalities in his defense of the Miller-Sabalo relationship. First, he emphasized that the State Department's representations to Mexico occurred one month before Miller took up his post in 1949. Second, Acheson stressed that Miller had severed his formal association with Sullivan and Cromwell when he became the assistant secretary of state for Latin America. Finally, upon his appointment, Miller had announced that he would have nothing to do with the Sabalo case.[127] To accept Acheson's sophistry it would be necessary to ignore the reality that Miller continued to press his colleagues in the State Department to support the interests of his former client. A memorandum to President Truman made this clear:[128] "During the past week Mr. Allen Dulles visited Mexico and is reported to have told Minister Bermúdez that if the Mexican government would see fit to do something about the Sabalo Transport Company, a Mexican company with American stockholders, he would use his influence with Assistant Secretary of State Miller, with Senator John Foster Dulles, and with a very close friend of his, Secretary of State Dean Acheson." In Mexico, even at the time, it seemed obvious that the State Department was doing Sullivan and Cromwell's bidding.

MEXLIGHT

This explication of corruption suggests that the closer to the top of society, the more political the use of corruption. No one would suggest that George Messersmith, John W. Snyder (Truman's secretary of the treasury), or Eduardo Villaseñor were involved with ordinary crimes. But the record of the Mexican Light and Power Company, in the Truman Library, provides an interesting example of the gradations of corruption. In 1943, Eduardo Villaseñor drew the wrath of President Avila Camacho and Ambassador Messersmith by suggesting that Mexico might do better economically by maintaining a businesslike attitude and bargaining for the best price for raw materials rather than by tying them unconditionally to the Allied war effort. Not only was Villaseñor brought to heel, but he quickly recanted. After President Truman sacked both Messersmith and Braden over the treatment of Perón in Argentina, Messersmith returned to Mexico as the head of Mexican Light and Power Company, which was, in 1953, legally a Canadian corporation with headquarters in Toronto but in reality dominated by its major shareholders, Sir Reginald Leeper and Sir Bernhard Binder in London and Brussels, respectively.[129]

Records of the Board of Directors of MEXLIGHT have survived in the Truman Library and in the Messersmith papers at the University of Delaware; the most interesting part of that story is that Messersmith approached a number of important former Mexican officials and entrepreneurs to invite them to become members of the MEXLIGHT board: Eduardo Suárez, Luis G. Legorreta, Guillermo Barroso (president of CONCAMIN), and Arthur Ross. More importantly perhaps, Messersmith also organized a sort of junior board, called MEXLIGHT's Mexican Advisory Committee, which included Carlos Prieto of the Fundidora, Juan Ortíz Monastario of the Banco Comercial Mexicano, and Carlos Mendieta of the Banco de Comercio.[130] By mixing former government officials with figures in the private sector, he was clearly holding out the prospect of rewards for suitable public officials. Even Villaseñor joined the junior board, together with Salvador Ugarte of the Banco de Comercio and Gaston Azcárraga of the Monterrey Group in 1957.[131] The prospect of future rewards for favorable policy pronouncements changed official attitudes considerably.

The direct rewards of board membership were not insignificant. For attending a few meetings, John Snyder received lavish expenses—$565 for a trip from Toledo, Ohio, to the D.F. in 1953, and $7,000 every six months for fees and unspecified services.[132] In addition to their fees, members could apply information indirectly. Most useful to the company, other government officials could dream of becoming members of the board if they pursued policies comforting to MEXLIGHT, and this pattern prevailed even after the company was nationalized some years later. The possibility of rewards for these officials enabled Messersmith to report to board members, "We are going through a difficult labor negotiation and the President and Carrillo Flores showed great understanding and gave us real help."[133]

In the last analysis, corruption that shifts the rules of the game may be the most important because it can set structures in place that are enduring. It is sobering to reflect upon Steve Bechtel's dictum, "It is more effective to do a man a favor than to ask him for one."[134] Bechtel should know; as the head of the largest engineering corporation in the United States he was highly dependent upon favorable government rulings and contracts for his business. George Messersmith made much the same point when he reflected upon the effectiveness of favoring selected reporters with information rather than with direct bribes to influence the media.[135]

The diversion of foreign investment funds from the industrial development program to private use showed just how critical the issue of corruption had become. One British diplomat blamed the devaluation of 1948 on the diversion of funds into private purses: "It is equally well known how this balance [of foreign reserves] has for the most part been frittered away on motor cars, washing machines, radios, expensive foodstuffs, etc., only a lesser part having been spent on essential capital goods required either for replacements or the development of local industries."[136]

Conclusion

The historian of Mexico in the 1940s has to decide how to deal with this rich and complex record of corruption. It is beyond reason to ignore the cumulative record of corruption during the era. Since the same names and accusations come from many separate sources within the archives of the United States, Britain, and Mexico, the triangulation effect—when the same information is corroborated from different sources—gives me confidence that even if some individual accusations are exaggerated, the overall pattern cannot be dismissed. Certainly, it is necessary to resist a sense of propriety that asserts that historians cannot deal with the public record of corruption. After all, high officials perpetrated the fraud and theft; we can surely mention it!

In addition to the triangulation effect, there is a second kind of evidence that convinces me that the record of corruption is essentially true. Once Alemán left office and went on a tour of Europe, many of his close associates joined a chorus criticizing the corruption of the era. General Jacinto Treviño drove the point home when he denounced corruption at the 1953 convention of the PRI. *Excélsior* discussed a plan by Ruíz Cortines to expropriate ill-gotten land from Alemán and his friends, including Ramón Beteta, Carlos

Serrano, Nazario Ortíz Garza, and Carlos Oriani. *Excélsior* also explained how Alemán and his associates had systematically obtained the land under the guise of land reform, having used their inside information to absorb land with no apparent owner.[137]

On August 28, 1953, the leader of the Federación de Partidos del Pueblo Mexicano, which was the Henriquista party, submitted a legal brief to Attorney General Carlos Franco Sodi accusing Alemán and thirty-two other high officials of his administration with corruption. Among these Alemanistas were Ernesto Uruchurtu, Flores Muñoz, Angel Carvajal, and Antonio Carrillo Flores; also mentioned were Gilberto Limón (Defense), Nazario Ortíz Garza (Agriculture), Ramón Beteta (Treasury), Agustín García López (Communications), Manuel Gual Vidal (Education), Antonio Martínez Baez (Economy), Rafael Pascasio Gamboa (Health), Antonio Carrillo Flores (NAFISA), and Carlos I. Serrano, among others. The brief was delivered just before the annual presidential address and the expected return of Alemán to Mexico, and its political timing was well planned. In part, it was in retaliation for the police harassment that the Henriquistas had been receiving. With a few exceptions, the press, due to its close connections with the government, ignored the allegations, which died quietly once they were inside the legal establishment.[138]

Supreme Court Justice Corona openly characterized the Alemán administration as a "moral cesspool." And Ruíz Cortines actually expropriated the 650,000-hectare Hacienda Palomas in Chihuahua and threatened to do the same to the 500,000-hectare Green *latifundia* in Sonora. Even Ernesto Uruchurtu, a figure not previously tainted by reform, joined the anticorruption campaign by cracking down on the heart of the problem—cinemas that overcharged.[139] The old economic nationalist José R. Colin also said that there were many "merchants, industrialists, bankers, and contractors who profited under the protection of the past government."[140] From Cuba, the historian Herminio Portel Vila published "Mexico: 1953," which included an open letter from General León Ossorio y Agüero accusing Alemán of corruption because of what the general had learned while serving in the army.[141]

Perhaps the most crucial consequence of corruption in the 1940s in Mexico was that it undermined reform. Rewards were offered to individuals as incentives for jettisoning the idealistic elements of the Cardenista project. Nowhere was this more obvious than in the sector of banking established to underpin agrarian reform. Misuse of funds and embezzlement flourished there in ways the same bankers, who sat on the boards of directors of the public agrarian banks, would never permit in their own private institutions. Or again, in the labor movement, a new class of labor activists, the *charros*, became skilled in the techniques of raising and then dashing the hopes of workers who were involved in labor disputes. At crucial moments, bribes undercut union solidarity with great effectiveness. As a result, central reforms in the areas of agrarian and labor policy were systematically weakened.

Corruption and inefficiency began to undercut the alternative vision represented by the tradition of economic nationalism. In early 1949, in response to the president's order to prepare a new Ley para la Vigilancia de Organismos Descentralizados y Empresas de Participación Estatal, the Ministry of Finance initiated a study of the reasons for the failures and poor performances of public enterprises. The study, by Rafael Mancera, covered PEMEX, Ferrocarriles Nacionales, Nacional Distribuidora y Regularidora, the Comisión Federal de Electricidad, Institución Mexicano de Seguro Social (IMSS), Comisiones de Caminos, various retirement funds, and eight trading companies. After commenting on the enormous share of the national economy that these state enterprises represented, the Mancera report arrived at a remarkably clear conclusion. Overall, the performance of these enterprises was "disastrous." It was easy to account for this:

> Of course, the case of each institution is different and it is not possible to go into each case in detail in this brief memorandum, but it is virtually certain that a large part of each disaster may be attributed to *a fact that is common to each and every one of these Institutions.*
>
> This common cause is the following: the absurd composition of the Boards of Directors of these Institutions.
>
> In effect, as one reviews the various boards one by one, we always find the same circumstances:
>
> I—The majority or the totality of its members *are individuals who are ignorant of the activities of the institution;* this means they do not properly exercise the role of a director or that, when they do so, they make bad or illicit policy; as a result the business of the institution is not managed expertly.
>
> II—The naming of directors is not a process of selecting experts, *rather it is the protection of high officials, which fundamentally serves their political influence and their nepotism.*
>
> III—The directors are selected absurdly, with individuals who are dysfunctional, frequently at odds, thus sowing the seed of future failures.

IV—Among the directors there is always one person, be it the general manager or another, who takes on the direction of the institution, *using the rest of the directors as a way of legitimizing his acts or at least of avoiding responsibilities.*

V—There is always one person outside of the institution who is really in control, using the institution for personal ends rather than for the purpose for which the institution was founded.[142]

This incisive internal analysis from the subsecretary of finance— the Mancera thesis—concluded by arguing for openness and accountability as the obvious remedies for the disastrous performances of these enterprises. Sadly, the lack of adequate public attention to the performance of public enterprises reverberated down through the years. It was a major factor in the bankruptcy of the state in 1982 and in the return to neoliberalism the decade after that.[143] Above all, the pitiful performance of public enterprises eroded belief in an alternative vision of the nation's development.

When a political group that has been committed to reform, at least partially in the interest of the public good, drops the pretense and/or the reality of promoting progressive reform (changes to the system that favor those people who are at the bottom of the socio-economic pyramid), then corruption grows. Decision makers develop a cynical view of the state as a "milch cow" to be linked to an individual mode of development, that is to say, they develop a "get yours" view of government. Hypocrisy increases, since it is very difficult to organize a political rally on the theme of "I got mine." And if it is possible to drape individual booty with theories of development, that is sublime.

One Latin Americanist remarked, during the Nixon era, that Latin America is far more democratic than the United States because there everyone can offer a bribe, whereas in the United States one has to be a General Electric to exercise this prerogative. There may be a grain of truth in that observation. Indeed, the difference between politicos taking bribes and executives organizing "golden parachutes" for themselves at shareholders' expense is slight. Better still, if one is fighting an unjust system, a degree of popular justice, even revenge, can result from a well-conceived piece of larceny. Few of us feel too bad when abusive tax strippers or monopolists suffer a loss. The well-planned sting is the stuff that feeds our Walter Mitty complexes.

Yet when corruption becomes so endemic that it diverts a considerable portion of a country's development funds into private pockets, things have gone too far. Even this partial, surviving record of the corruption of the 1940s makes one reflect on alternatives. When the government shifted funds in the budget away from the social program of the revolution, it meant that a clear choice had been made to have more mansions in the Pedregal or Lomas and less infrastructure, welfare, health care, and education. And when stolen funds found their way into foreign bank accounts, even the multiplier effect of the spending was exported away from Mexico. As similar cases emerged around the country over the years, the aggregate impact of corruption added another fundamental explanation—to those offered by dependency perspectives—to the nation's problems of underdevelopment. Clearly, corruption was at the core of the country's problem of poor income distribution.

This extraordinary public record of corruption begs the question of how the corruption could have happened. The Mexican system of extreme political centralism was at the heart of the problem. Absolute power is vested in the hands of the president for six years. The president is unrestrained by law, by the audit of public funds, or by the kind of political reality that flows from an independent legislature and judiciary. The lack of presidential accountability is aided immeasurably by an extremely high level of secrecy. Finally, there is the phenomenon that Carlos Fuentes has described in *The Death of Artemio Cruz* as *la chingada*. This tradition—of abusing the weak without a trace of conscience—is also central to the process.

The solution to this problem is really quite simple. Secrecy must disappear, especially from the expenditures of the state, and a new level of accountability must be complemented by a political reform that ensures that the governing machine does not count the votes. Also a broader process of consultation must complement alternative centers of decision making. Above all, an alternative political culture must replace the status quo.[144] Watching Juan Ortega Arenas, the head of a supposedly independent union—the Unidad Obrera Independiente (UOI)—interact with workers at the Volkswagen plant in Puebla in the 1970s, complete with his retinue of followers and limousines, made me realize that even if by some miracle he had come to replace Fidel Velázquez as the head of the CTM little else would have changed.

What was unique about the Mexican experience of corruption is that this massive transfer of resources to the few existed within a context of fervent nationalism and a widely supported push for industrial modernization. The mechanism of mass political organization of the state provided cover for those who abused their positions. The entire process was accompanied by the increasingly empty rhetoric of the Mexican Revolution.

Notes

1. Dog Hill is the large compound in which President José López Portillo built a group of five mansions for his family members at the height of the economic crisis of 1982. The name came from his campaign pledge to fight like a dog against corruption. The opulent symbol of debt-financed corruption was within clear sight of a major highway entering Mexico City. For a time at the end of his term, López Portillo was forced to follow his funds outside of the country, so bitter was the popular reaction to the corruption of his term of office.

2. Truman was the last American president to emerge from office at roughly the same submillionaire level at which he entered politics, a pattern that was not dominant among the Mexican leaders in this period. After leaving the presidency, Truman returned to his old house in Independence, Missouri, to live out his days.

3. Perry, *Juárez and Díaz: Machine Politics in Mexico*, 12–17.

4. Wilkie and Wilkie, *México Vista en el Siglo XX: Entrevistas de Historia Oral*, 66–67.

5. Morris, *Corruption and Politics in Contemporary Mexico*, 41.

6. Ibid., 66.

7. Blanca Torres, *Hacia la utopía industrial*, 66, 98, 212, 263.

8. As John Gledhill put it in his study of the *ejido* Emiliano Zapata in Michoacán, "A concern with the scandalous becomes an analytical necessity if one wishes to explain the realities of Mexican social and political life," John Gledhill, *Casi Nada*, 12.

9. Miller, *Culture and State in Mexico in the Sexennium of Manuel Avila Camacho*, 36.

10. Report "Political Situation in Mexico," from the American consul in Mexico City, George P. Shaw, to secretary of state, June 28, 1941, USNA/ 59, 812.00/31715.

11. For an analysis of the alternative historiographical currents dealing with Cardenismo, see Knight, "*Cardenismo*: Juggernaut or Jalopy?" 73–108.

12. Rubin, "Decentering the Regime: Culture and Regional Politics in Mexico," unpublished manuscript, 1994, 13–21.

13. In the first two instances, the loss of leaders' limbs in battle was linked to the price the community paid for their leadership. The reference to teeth was a play on the slang usage of the term "bite" to describe a bribe.

14. Portes Gil, *Autobiografía de la revolución mexicana*, 749.

15. AGN, RP/MAV, 444.1/294, and *Excélsior*, March 28, 1949.

16. S. Walter Washington to secretary of state, August 4, 1947, USNA/ 59, 812.00/8-447.

17. *Ultimas Noticias*, January 23, 1947.

18. Bateman to Bevin, January 11, 1947, PRO/371, 60940.

19. C. H. Bateman to Bevin, August 18, 1947, PRO/371, 60943.

20. Lt. Col. Maurice C. Holden to secretary of state, July 16, 1947, USNA/59, 812.105/9-447.

21. Ibid.

22. F. X. Di Lucia to Raymond G. Geist, April 23, 1948, USNA/59, 812.20/5-2648.

23. Ambassador Thurston to Paul J. Reveley, Division of Mexican Affairs, May 26, 1948, and F. D. Sharp to W. Washington, April 16, 1948, USNA/59, 812.20/5-2648.

24. S. Walter Washington to secretary of state, "Political Gangsterism in Government . . . ," March 3, 1948, USNA/59, 812.00/3-348. See also 812.00/2-1848 for additional accusations against Pasquel and Parra.

25. Letter from five company directors to President Alemán, February 6, 1951, AGN, RP/MAV, 433/152-A. The president was not moved by the accusations against Bojórquez.

26. S. Walter Washington to secretary of state, August 4, 1947, USNA/ 59, 812.00/8-447.

27. Ibid.

28. *Excélsior* and *La Prensa*, March 17, 1947.

29. W. W. McVittin, commercial counselor of the British embassy, to the Foreign Office, February 10, 1949, PRO/FO, 371/74086.

30. Thurston to secetary of state, August 28, 1947, USNA/59, 812.00/ 8-2847.

31. Louis F. Blanchard, American consul in Coatzacoalcos, to secretary of state, June 30, 1950, USNA/59, 712.00/6-3050.

32. Alonso Sordo Noriega to President Alemán, December 6, 1948, AGN, RP/MAV, 512.32/7 and 512.32/8.

33. Washington to secretary of state, December 18, 1948, USNA/59, 812.00/12-1847.

34. Herbert S. Bursley to Philip Bonsal, December 26, 1942, USNA/ 59, 812.642/16.

35. J. Edgar Hoover to A. Berle, December 16, 1941, USNA/59, 812.00/ 31845.

36. Merwin L. Bohan to secretary of state, March 5, 1947, USNA/59, 812.50/3-547.

37. Ambassador Francisco del Rio y Cañedo to President Alemán, May 3, 1949, AGN, RP/MAV, 705.1/209.

38. Paul J. Revely to Horace H. Braun, January 18, 1949, USNA/59, 812.51/1-1849.

39. This was a report received in Washington from a contact in Saint Louis, possibly C. D. Hicks, and forwarded to the chargé d'affaires in Mexico City, February 24, 1942, USNA/59, 812.51/2581. See also the report "Mexican Projects of Senator Hastings," February 6, 1942, USNA/59, 812.51/2573.

40. Pan American Airways to Juan de Dios Bojórquez, president of the National Commission of Tourism, October 24, 1949, AGN, RP/MAV, 545.22/187.

41. James B. Stewart to secretary of state, May 29, 1939, USNA/59, 812.00/30744.

42. S. Walter Washington to secretary of state, August 4, 1947, USNA/ 59, 812.00/8-447.

43. Letter from Luis Viñela León to the president's secretary, Rogerio de la Selva, June 13, 1949, AGN, RP/MAV, 606.1/2.

44. Federico Alcala, president of the Unión de Concesionarios de Tiendas Populares de la República Mexicana de la N.D. & R., to the president, April 1, 1947, AGN, RP/MAV, 606.1/2.

45. Report entitled "Manipulation of Mexican Gold Exports and the Effect on Mining and Smelting," by Horace H. Braun, June 30, 1948, USNA/59, 812.516/6-3048.

46. Alberto V. Aldrete to President Alemán, February 10, 1950, AGN, RP/MAV, 522/27.

47. Ibid.

48. Auditor's report to the president, July 25, 1949, AGN, RP/MAV, 545.3/56-A.

49. *Diario de Yucatán*, January 10, 1949.

50. Robert C. Wysong to secretary of state, January 20, 1949, USNA/59, 812.00/1-2049.

51. Cía. Editorial Mexicana to President Alemán, July 15, 1947, AGN, RP/MAV, 704/165.

52. *Ases Universitarios* to President Alemán, n.d., AGN, RP/MAV, 704/365.

53. David Thomasson to Guy Ray, July 31, 1946, USNA/59, 812.911/7-3146.

54. Messersmith to Clayton, January 18, 1946, GSM Papers.

55. Memorandum of conversation between Braun and Trouyet, February 13, 1946, USNA/59, 812.00/2-1346.

56. Robert L. Gardner diary, July 27, 1948, Robert L. Gardner Papers, Truman Library.

57. Interview with Merwin L. Bohan, #224, February 1977, 37, Truman Library.

58. Ibid., 39–40.

59. Ilo C. Funk, American consul in Veracruz, to secretary of state, February 12, 1946, USNA/59, 812.5034/2-1246.

60. *Diario Oficial*, July 26, 1947.

61. Antonio Espinosa de los Monteros to J. Jesús González Gallo, July 2, 1946, AGN, RPMAC, 577/180.

62. *Presente*, August 11, 1948.

63. T. G. Rapp to Ernest Bevin, August 12, 1948, PRO/FO, 371/68000.

64. *Presente*, July 29, 1948. For the denials from the Aarón Sáenz family, see AGN, RP/MAV, 565.32/1-3.

65. Frank A. Southland to John W. Snyder, June 10 and August 8, 1948; Beteta to Snyder, August 12, 1948, Truman Library, John W. Snyder Papers.

66. S. Walter Washington to secretary of state, March 19, 1948, USNA/59, 812.00/3-1948.

67. "Second National Assembly of the PRI," February 13, 1953, USNA/59, 712.00/2-1353. Pasquel's political position also allowed him to dominate professional baseball during the era. See La France, "Labor, the State, and Professional Baseball in Mexico in the 1980s," 112–14 .

68. "Report for June 1953," USNA/59, 712.00/7-753.

69. Edward Miller to Ambassador William O'Dwyer, December 12, 1950, Truman Library, Edward G. Miller, Jr., Papers, Box 3.

70. These legal documents may be found in AGN, RP/MAV, 545.22/43; John L. Toppings, vice consul in Acapulco, to secretary of state,

August 31, 1942, USNA/59, 812.00 Guerrero/47; and Toppings to secretary of state, September 30, 1942, USNA/59, 812.00 Guerrero/48.

71. Toppings to secretary of state: December 5, 1942, USNA/59, 812.00 Guerrero/49; March 18, 1943, USNA/59, 812.00 Guerrero/52; and the Report for April, USNA/59, 812.00 Guerrero/53.

72. General Gabriel Leva (CNC) to President Alemán, April 12, 1947, and Melchor Perusquía to the secretario de bienes nacionales, March 22, 1947, AGN, RP/MAV, 618 (727.1) /13196.

73. David S. Hecht [Getty's agent] to Alemán, August 1, 1949, AGN, RP/MAV, 705.1/226.

74. Ibid. See also the president's instructions, September 12, 1949, and the ensuing telegram from Alemán's secretary, Roberto Amorós, to Getty's lawyer, Guillermo R. Tamayo, of September 13, 1949, AGN, RP/MAV, 705.1/226.

75. Petition from Ruiz Galindo to the president, AGN, RP/MAV, 545.22/146-7.

76. Telegram from the CUT to the president, March 19, 1948, AGN, RP/MAV, 564.4/145.

77. Palomino Rojas, Secretario general del Sindicato Unico de Panaderos y Similares, to the president, June 26, 1945, AGN, RP/MAC, 542.1/1060.

78. This was a widespread phenomenon. See Prieto Laurens and Melchor Ortega of the Partido Democrático Mexicano to the president, May 13, 1946, AGN, RP/MAC, 544.1/33-4. They complained to Avila Camacho about the "imposition" of Alemán.

79. S. Walter Washington to secretary of state, November 25, 1947. See associated reports by Juan de Zengotita and Irving Glen Tragen, USNA/59, 812.5043/11-2547.

80. See, for example, Tomás Palomino Rojas, secretary general of the purged CTM, to President Alemán, October 26, 1947, AGN, RP/MAV, 433/26.

81. Tomás Palomino Rojas to the president, October 4, 1945, AGN, RP/MAC, 542.1/1060. Complaints about corruption in the railroads are in AGN, RP/MAC, 542.22/6.

82. Letter from the national executive of the CUT to Alemán, March 19, 1948, ANG, RP/MAV, 564.4/145-9.

83. For a further discussion of this episode, see Ruth Adler, "Experiments in Worker Participation in the Administration of Industry in Mexico during the Presidency of Lázaro Cárdenas." For this episode Adler cites the archive of Section 20 of the STPRM, Poza Rica, Veracruz, File no. 013-3, and Circular #31 of the Consejo General de Vigilancia, September 9, 1938.

84. Henry Grunewald to J. Edgar Hoover, October 14, 1941, and PEMEX to Joseph Stutzker, September 26, 1941, USNA/59, 812.00/31825. Hoover to Berle, November 25, 1941, 812.00/31834. (Hoover and/or his agents did not understand the relationship between events in Mexico and New Jersey.)

85. These material factors also reinforced Lombardo's absolute commitment to the domination of the state over the labor movement, in both an ideological and a bureaucratic sense. Some authors have dismissed material motivation in favor of desire for political power to explain Lombardo's slavish attitude toward the governing party. See Chassen de

López, *Lombardo Toledano y el movimiento obrero mexicano (1917–1940)*, 274–75.

86. Franklin C. Gowan to secretary of state, June 30, 1953, USNA/59, 712.00/6-3053.

87. John W. Carrigan to secretary of state, August 10, 1945, USNA/59, 812.00/8-1045.

88. Report on "Restrictive Business Practices in Mexico," May 13, 1952, USNA/59, 812.054/5-1352.

89. José Echandi Pomez et al. to President Alemán, April 4, 1949, AGN, RP/MAV, 432/244.

90. Barry T. Benson, commercial attaché, to secretary of state, June 10, 1952, USNA/59, 812.054/6-1052.

91. William P. Blocker to secretary of state, May 9, 1941, USNA/59, 812.00/31673.

92. Secret report from Bateman to the Ministry of Information, February 24, 1942, PRO/FO, 30571.

93. Intercepted report from the Asiatic Petroleum Corporation of New York to G. Leigh-Jones, St. Helen's Court, London, September 8, 1942, PRO/FO, 371/30571.

94. J. Edgar Hoover to A. Berle, "Vicente Lombardo Toledano," June 6, 1942, USNA/59, 812.5043/61.

95. Ibid.

96. Maury Maverick to President Roosevelt, February 5, 1941, USNA/59, 812.00/31629 1/2.

97. A report entitled "Third Congress of the CTM" from W. K. Ailshie to secretary of state, April 2, 1943, USNA/59, 812.504/2196.

98. Report from Guy W. Ray to secretary of state entitled "Confidential Report Furnished the Embassy on Political Activities in Mexico, Especially as Regards Vicente Lombardo Toledano and Former President Lázaro Cárdenas," January 10, 1944, USNA/59, 812.504/2255.

99. Secret report by Ian Davidson to the Foreign Office, March 3, 1941, PRO/FO, 371/26067.

100. Bursley to Welles, February 20, 1940, USNA/59, 812.00/31741.

101. Bursley to Welles, February 26, 1941; 812.00/31746, Bursley to Welles, March 21, 1941; and 812.00/31748, S. Woodward (War Department) to secretary of state, April 14, 1941, USNA/59, 812.00/31744.

102. Memorandum of conversation between Edward G. Trueblood, second secretary of embassy, Eduardo Villaseñor of the Banco de México, and Professor Arthur P. Whitaker, January 23, 1942, USNA/59, 812.00/31871.

103. *Excélsior* and *La Prensa*, May 20, 1943.

104. Report from Harold D. Finley to secretary of state, entitled "General Maximino Avila Camacho Says That He Is Not a Candidate for the Presidency of Mexico," May 20, 1943, USNA/59, 812.00/32154.

105. *Hoy*, May 22, 1943, and in translation in the *Mexico City Post*, May 22, 1943.

106. Guy W. Ray to secretary of state, "Interview by local writer with General Maximino Ávila Camacho, Brother of the President of Mexico and the Minister of Communications, in Which the General Asserts he has No Presidential Ambitions and Attempts to Justify His Possession of a Large Fortune," May 25, 1943, USNA /59, 812.00/32156.

107. Ibid.

108. Guy W. Ray to secretary of state, March 24, 1943, "Political Situation in Mexico," USNA/59, 812.00/32132.

109. Report from Dwight Dickerson to secretary of state, "Spectre of Maximino Avila Camacho Rises to Plague the Alemán Government," February 6, 1947, USNA/59, 812.00/2-647.

110. Ambassador Thurston to secretary of state, December 12, 1946, and Horace H. Braun's memorandum of December 4, 1946, USNA/59, 812.00/12-1246.

111. The monthly bank statements had no account number, only the president's name; they are found in AGN, RP/MAC, 565.1/78. The 500,000-peso deposits were recurring, although they were not made on the same day each month.

112. Ambassador Thurston to secretary of state, December 12, 1946, and Horace H. Braun's memorandum of December 4, 1946, USNA/59, 812.00/12-1246.

113. Report on "Suárez-Hilton Hotel Project and Information Concerning Manuel Suárez y Suárez," July 26, 1950. Suárez's properties included Techo Eterno Eureka, S.A., Inmuebles Urbanos, S.C., Compañía Azucarera de Navolato, S.A., and the Centrál Sanalona, S.A., USNA/59, 812.02/7-2650

114. "Plan to Develop the Southern Territory of Baja California as Tourist Resort," February 17, 1950, USNA/59, 812.021/2-1750. See also 812.021/4-2750 for the detailed advantages the company received from the Mexican government, including an 80 percent reduction in taxes, plus generous concessions.

115. Washington to secretary of state, March 18, 1948, USNA/59, 812.00/3-1048.

116. The report by Lindsay C. Warren, comptroller general of the United States, was quoted by Jones, *Fifty Billion Dollars*, 364–66.

117. As cited in Fossedal, *Our Finest Hour*, 96.

118. The information relating to the U.S. Air Corps scandal can be found in a letter from Ambassador Messersmith to Philip W. Bonsal, December 30, 1943, USNA/59, 812.24/12-3043, and the report from Major Herman W. Brann, "Lend Lease Aviation to Mexican Air Force," December 11, 1943, USNA/59, 812.24/12-3043.

119. Mistakes abounded: aluminum too soft for aircraft use was sent; air searchlights were wasted; parts did not correspond to engines and aircraft; tires and instruments were useless. A seven-year supply of oil rings arrived from Kelly Field, Texas, without the accompanying pistons. In short, material that was not needed arrived while critical items were absent.

120. Merwin L. Bohan to secretary of state, January 26, 1947, USNA/59, 812.50/1-2947. In 1947, the plant went to Mexican Light and Power, and it was later used by the Cía. Eléctrica Guanajuatense, a subsidiary of Electric Bond and Share Co.

121. George M. Messersmith, president of Mexican Light and Power, to Paul J. Reveley, Division of Mexican Affairs, November 3, 1949, USNA/59, 812.34/11-349.

122. *El Popular*, January 9, 1946.

123. Messersmith to Carrigan, January 12, 1946, USNA/59, 812.00B/1-1246.

124. At this point Messersmith began to see a Communist conspiracy linking Moscow, through the Agencia Noticiera Latinoamericana, with *El Popular, La Voz de México*, and *Nosotros*. Messersmith to Carrigan, February 7, 1946, USNA/59, 812.00B/2-746.

125. See *Excélsior*, January 11, 1946, for a response in which Messersmith's efforts were identified with the government and the progress of the nation.the Scripps Howard chain was able to place an article in *Ultimas Noticias* on January 10 under the title "Lombardo Considered as a Saboteur of Friendship." The terms of the debate on foreign investment were being narrowed.

126. Schuller, "Cardenismo Revisited," 249–51.

127. Memorandum from Dean Acheson to John Kee, chairman, House Committee on Foreign Relations, September 16, 1949, Truman Library, Edward G. Miller, Jr., Papers, Box 3.

128. The settlement was also linked to steel exports to Mexico. State Department memorandum on "Mexican Oil Loan," n.a., August 17, 1949, and Oscar L. Chapman to Truman, August 3, 1951, Truman Library, HST Official File, 146.

129. John Snyder—who also became president of Willys Overland Motors—joined the board of MEXLIGHT in 1953 after the change of administrations in the United States.

130. Minutes of the Board of Directors, November 4, 1954, GSM Papers.

131. Minutes of the Board of Directors, June 24, 1957, GSM Papers.

132. John Snyder to G. L. Stewart, secretary of MEXLIGHT, September 14, 1953, and Stewart to Snyder, December 31, 1953, Truman Library, Snyder Papers.

133. Snyder to Messersmith, April 8, 1954, Truman Library, Snyder Papers.

134. McCartney, *Friends in High Places, the Bechtel Story*, 156.

135. Messersmith to Acheson, January 11, 1946, GSM Papers.

136. T. G. Rapp to Ernest Bevin, August 12, 1948, PRO/FO, 371/68000.

137. *Excélsior*, June 26, 1953.

138. Franklin C. Gowan to the Department of State, September 2, 1953, USNA/59, 712.00/9-253.

139. "Report for July," August 6, 1953, USNA/59, 712.00/8-653.

140. *Excélsior*, July 17, 1953.

141. *Bohemia*, September 20, 1953.

142. Rafael Mancera to President Alemán, September 23, 1949, AGN, RP/MAV, 545.3/156 (emphasis in original). This initiative provoked a fury of opposition from those administering public enterprises.

143. Judith Adler Hellman's interviews with managers of recently privatized enterprises make it abundantly clear that there was absolutely no consultation by the Salinas de Gotari government as it set off to privatize over a thousand state enterprises during that administration, 1988–1994. Judith Adler Hellman, "Mexican Popular Movements, Clientelism, and the Process of Democratization," *Latin American Perspectives* 81 (Spring 1994): 124–42.

144. Manuel Buendía commented on the tendency to glorify corruption within the political elite and for convicted officials to be quickly reemployed in other positions of trust when their incarceration ended. *Excélsior*, January 24, 1983.

6

The Battle for the Mexican Media

There are two fundamentally different kinds of politics. First, there is the struggle to attain and use the power of the state. At the core of state power is force. The triumph of the nation-state over claims of family, friends, kin, and region—what the Mexicans call the *patria chica*—is one of the great historical stories of the past two centuries. Nothing is more central to the exercise of state power than the monopolization of legitimate force in the hands of the government. This level of politics is a world where a small number of hard realists struggle to build a coalition of forces strong enough to stay in power. The higher the degree of political legitimacy, the less likely raw force is on open display. Antonio Gramsci increased our understanding of this process immeasurably when he introduced the concept of political/cultural hegemony in the 1920s. The many civic institutions that augment and complement the power of the state have become the subjects of entire fields of study. The tendency of so many people to identify with and define themselves in terms of the nation attests to the triumph of state power.

There is another kind of political power. Politics is also a struggle over the way to look at public issues. In this arena the "numbers men" are not always the best exponents of a point of view. Thus, interest groups, journalists, social scientists, historians, and a wide range of commentators force their way into the rarefied world of political practitioners. In this universe of alternative perspectives, people put forth their own views of the proper role of the state or of what items deserve to be promoted to the top of the political agenda. There are even rare moments when a great moral issue—such as war, slavery, or revolution—can dominate an era. Then, the most skilled political mechanics may find it impossible to hide from the great issue or an idea when its time has come. This is the battle for the "hearts and minds," as it was called during the time of the Vietnam War.

In this century, mass communications media have replaced earlier forms of patron-client relationships to mediate political debate and provide the arena for the battle over alternative political views. Increasingly, the channels of mass communication arbitrate alternative perspectives, if frequently at an infuriatingly simplistic level. The printed word, increasingly augmented by the spoken word on radio and by visual images on television, compete for people's loyalties and affiliation. We increasingly appreciate the importance of the psychology of confabulation—the mixing of ideas, images, stories, lessons, and experiences—as we constantly modify our understanding of the world. In this process the importance of the mass media grows.

A new perspective on the media's role has emerged in Jesús Martín-Barbero's *De los medios a los mediaciones*.[1] The process involves not just the molding of popular belief by the media but also its mediation between the public's attitudes and those who control the media. Thus, pressures from the marketplace and the state intermingle in the individual's mind with elements of national culture, popular memory, and personal life experience. Contradictory images and different ways of reporting coexist with selective memories; therefore, modern media studies have moved away from a simple model in which powerful media interests impose their will and/or their message on the powerless to an analysis of mediation and feedback effects.

For Mexico in the 1940s, as we have seen in Chapter 1, great themes of the age—the quest for industrial modernization and the move from rural to urban areas—were much in evidence, even from this distance. Films or songs in the ranchero tradition in Mexico were clearly part of the process of negotiating the shift from rural to urban life.[2] Yet the form of discourse initiated at the political summit could still be central. For example, in recent years Indian activists have made the distinction between what they now call *indianismo*, or "Indianism"—the culture of the Indian community—and what was called in the 1940s *indigenismo*—the Cardenista effort to incorporate the Indian into the mestizo nation on the government's terms. The president gave this effort an official start in 1940, as Cárdenas inaugurated the First Inter-American Indigenist Congress, held in Pátzcuaro. His speech shocked many as he called the Indians a "factor for progress"; however, it was a form of progress on the president's terms, clearly resting on a desire to Mexicanize the Indians, not to indigenize the Mexicans. In a different way this is the same point that Marjorie Becker highlights in *Setting the Virgin on Fire* when she discusses the state in its religious struggles,[3] or that Néstor García Canclini makes as he discusses the process of integrating peasant traditions, including folklore and *artesanías*, into the national character. The process also incorporated elements of a considerable shift from religious to secular cultural symbols.[4]

Recently, Roger Bartra has approached the problem from a different angle. He offers a delightful critique of some excessive, if well-known, treatments of national characteristics by focusing upon the images of peasants and the rural past, a kind of "paradise subverted" in relation to the evolution of national identity. It is a healthy corrective. Bartra's analysis focuses upon the dangers of these national myths. Allegedly national characteristics are tackled in an engaging way, and mythical space is analysed in terms not so much of multiple and obscure origins as of its use and function in contemporary Mexico. From this perspective, Bartra uses the metamorphosis of the axolotl into the salamander as a metaphor for the Mexican's relationship between a primitive past and the contemporary postrevolutionary crisis in Mexico, or, as he put it, "the birth of a modern myth based on the complex mediation and legitimization process in a society in which the revolutionary forces that constituted it have declined."[5]

Bartra proposes, in effect, a complex model in which the ruling classes appropriate popular culture through nationalist stereotypes that only partially relate to the proletarian culture from which they are taken. However, as selected elements of popular culture are appropriated and crafted by the mass media, some of these elements feedback to influence the behavior and identity of the lower classes in their daily life. Empathy and fantasy are at the heart of this process. Yet before the owners of the new media can manipulate the popular culture, the rulers of Mexico have to own and control the rapidly changing channels of mass communication.

At midcentury, contemporary concerns about media reductionism were not as prevalent as they are today. The written text was sovereign—challenged only by the arrival of the spoken word on the nearly vacant airways and, of course, by oral traditions. Newspapers circulated locally and in small print runs. Readers were urban and readership extremely restricted since literacy was still limited. Nevertheless, the media represented the cutting edge of modernity. Not only distant news, as world war approached, but also the inside word on national affairs and on matters of interest from sports to fashion gained a new prominence. Above all, a new lifestyle was promulgated by innovations in the media of communications.

Just as one kind of power flows from the command of state policies, another kind of power is generated by the capital required to control a media empire. Normally, these two sources of power operate in tandem and create an irresistible force. If they diverge, the potential for unrest and even chaos is great; however, the space for positive change and participation in the political process by those who command neither fortunes nor political structures may also increase. What is clear is that there were certain moments in the mid-twentieth century when the channels of mass communications were being allocated for the foreseeable future. This chapter is primarily interested in that process.

Britain and the Mexican Media

In Mexico the battle to control the media involved Britain, the United States, private media companies, and a number of important Mexican entrepreneurs. The initial control became indelible since the victors' heirs still control most of the channels of mass communications. Although a few new players have either created new channels or taken over existing media empires, the impact of the first victories still resonates. What is fascinating is that Mexicans managed to retain a significant degree of control of their media in the face of the overwhelming influence from the North. A three-cornered battle for the Mexican media ensued between British, U.S., and Mexican media magnates.

The approach of World War II brought rivalries to Mexico. Germany especially had a considerable presence in Mexico in the 1930s. In electricity, hardware, pharmaceuticals, industrial chemistry, and international banking, German executives led their industries. There was a brief flirtation between the Cárdenas government and German interests in the lead-up to the expropriation of the petroleum industry. And figures on the far right were predisposed to favor Germany as a way of combating the USSR without embracing Britain. José Vasconcelos, for example, associated with the German propaganda agent Arthur Dietrich, who had offices on Calle

Viena #17 in Mexico City on the eve of World War II.[6] He also accepted German funds to support the magazine *Timón*.

Alarmed by the superior financial backing enjoyed by German representatives in Mexico, and by some early propaganda success that Germany had had on radio and in print, two Allied representatives joined forces in 1939 to form the Inter-Allied Propaganda Committee. Robert H. K. Marett, formerly with El Aguila Petroleum Company but then representing the British Ministry of Information, and the anthropologist Jacques Soustelle, representing France, were the main figures behind Anglo-French cooperation in Mexico. José Luis Ortíz Garza notes that Soustelle's father was a close friend of Marett and that this facilitated the coordination of the British and French efforts.[7]

In the most recent authoritative study of the topic, Nicholas John Cull notes that the Inter-Allied Propaganda Committee and "yet another British office had sprung up at Rockefeller Center. Known as the British Overseas Press Service, it collected British bulletins and American clippings to supply British publicists in Latin America, Asia, Europe and the colonies."[8] In reality, the accomplishments of these two closely linked groups went considerably further than the mere collation of clippings.

Agents of the Inter-Allied Propaganda Committee were active in Mexico on the eve of the Second World War.[9] Documents in the British archives provide the most detailed account of their propaganda effort. The extent and depth of that effort is surprising. Modern states seem to pursue their war aims on the propaganda front as well as on the battlefield; however, in this case the techniques the Inter-Allied Propaganda Committee developed provided the means to penetrate and manipulate the Mexican media to such an extent that a pattern was established that the United States would soon emulate. This experience formed a bridge between wartime propaganda and subsequent cultural imperialism.[10]

British propaganda developed unevenly in the twentieth century. A major propaganda effort had been waged during the First World War within the United States aimed at convincing that country to enter the war. Lord Beaverbrook, the minister of information, and Viscount Northcliffe, the director of enemy propaganda, had supervised that effort; both men were press magnates in their own right.[11] Although the impact of their effort is still a matter of debate, it is clear that isolationist sentiment in the United States during the interwar period blamed the British propaganda effort for pulling the country into the war. Such studies as Harold Lasswell's *Propaganda Techniques in the World War* and J. D. Squire's *British Propaganda at Home and in the United States from 1914–1917* reinforced the impression generated by the Nye Committee that in this instance the United States had been drawn into the war by nefarious foreign forces.

American sensitivities combined with financial pressure emanating from the British Treasury to reduce the British propaganda effort in the Western Hemisphere in the interwar years. The news department of the Foreign Office maintained only a fraction of the propaganda effort that the United Kingdom had supported during the First World War. Reuters, for instance, lost a lucrative wartime contract with the British government and was able to negotiate only a piece-rate payment for the material that the government wanted included on the Reuters wire service.[12]

The Foreign Office generally followed the policy that restraint and indirect influence were more effective than obvious manipulation. Between the wars the Foreign Office pioneered regular press briefings and began to issue information to favored journalists, but within Latin America the office maintained only a limited effort. The Foreign Office administered an Official News Service and disseminated news through the Cables and Wireless Branch. The office also published a *Weekly London Letter* and generally promoted British culture, an effort that culminated in the creation of the British Council in 1934. These efforts were slight in comparison with the periodical *América Latina*, published during World War I, and the Latin American *Supplement* of *The Times*, which was published for a few years following the war.[13]

As the policy of appeasement became more controversial during the period of Fascist expansion, some opponents of the strategy became involved in an attempt to revive the propaganda effort to further their view. Rex Leeper, head of the news department of the Foreign Office, had been working in that direction since the Germans reintroduced conscription in March 1935. Anthony Eden called him the "early prophet of the Nazi menace."[14] Hence, it was the Foreign Office, rather than the British Broadcasting Corporation (BBC), that revitalized the British propaganda effort.

Events in Europe insured the success of a pro-British propaganda offensive. A shift in popular opinion in the United States followed Hitler's occupation of Prague. Christopher Warren reported back to Leeper that the British could abandon their policy of restraint since "the fact remains that today the United States has arrived at a pitch of unneutral thought which even a short time ago we should hardly have dared to hope for."[15] This change of attitude in the United States seems to have also freed British diplomats to pursue their cause in Mexico.

The Allied propaganda effort eventually thrived since war seems to be the easiest issue around which to mobilize massive human and material effort. Sacrifice in the name of the nation can change priorities in many ways. Popular aspirations may be thwarted by wartime manipulations, and elites may reach goals that are denied them in more normal times. Even though Mexico was only peripherally involved in the military aspects of World War II, the Mexican fidelity to the Allied cause changed the country irrevocably. Mexico's unqualified support for the United States during the war and the importance of its economic contribution to the Allied side might suggest that the war was popular in Mexico. The reality was not that simple. Official support for the war was initially paper thin and should not be equated with popular enthusiasm for the Allied cause.

British propagandists understood that the Mexican people were overwhelmingly indifferent to the war in its early stages and that the position of the Avila Camacho government related more to internal political considerations than to the war itself. For the vast majority of the Mexican population, the war was a distant event about which they knew very little. I. D. Davidson represented the expropriated British petroleum interests in Mexico in the period in which relations between Britain and Mexico were suspended. He was a major source of information on Mexico for the British Foreign Office. He argued that in 1940 the public opinion that mattered in Mexico was held by perhaps 2 percent of the population, one-half of whom lived in the Federal District. He reported to Whitehall that fully half of the Mexican people did not know that a war was going on.[16] As late as 1942, British diplomats were writing back to London, "little popular zeal was shewn for the cause [the declaration of war] Mexico has espoused."[17] In September, a diplomat still bemoaned "the average Mexican's apathy toward the war and his dislike of the United States." Enthusiasm for the war was restricted to a "small circle" in the capital.[18]

The problem for the British was that domestic political positions in Mexico had predisposed various groups against the Allied cause before the war began. Davidson proposed a way to categorize politically active Mexicans. To his surprise, old-wealth Mexicans remained essentially *porfirista* (supportive of the old dictatorship of Porfirio Díaz). They favored the Axis, "and more than anything they feel that Germany stood for the antithesis of communism." Next were the "middle class professionals," and they were divided. Most of them, Davidson thought, supported Germany; however, they were not as anti-British as the upper class. They were motivated by the fear of the "colossus of the North." This group was nationalistic and did not consider Germany a threat to Mexico. In another category were the politicos of the governing party, who followed "the official policy of the government [which] is to be pro-Ally, but not for a moment do I [Davidson] believe this represents the true feelings of those in power."[19] It was true that the Cardenista wing of the party saw both the United Kingdom and the Axis powers as the arch enemies of the people. Thus the governing party was only superficially committed to the Allied cause.[20] Its propaganda effort faced considerable obstacles as the Inter-Allied Propaganda Committee set out to influence public opinion in Mexico for the Allied cause.

British diplomats and businessmen seemed to understand that while their effort was aimed at influencing public opinion in favor of the Allied cause in the present period, it was also directed at maintaining long-term influence within the American sphere of influence. "After all [wrote Davidson] the idea of publicity in Mexico at the present time is presumably not to obtain any immediate advantage, even if such were possible, but to lay a basis for British commercial influence and British trade."[21]

The likelihood that the United States would emerge far stronger after the war, at least in the Western Hemisphere, was accepted,

> The immediate objective of the U.S. government is to develop Mexico's enormous resources as a set-off to the loss of overseas sources of supply. . . . The establishment of a vast economic entity under the effective control of the United States, exercised through the agency of the new and revised techniques of dollar diplomacy does not necessarily involve a return to isolation, since it would also have the effect of enormously strengthening the position of the United States.[22]

Britain embarked upon its propaganda campaign with the twin goals of keeping a presence in Mexico and stimulating Mexican enthusiasm for the war in order to keep raw materials flowing for Allied production.

Between the German invasion of Poland and the fall of France, the Inter-Allied Propaganda Committee was primarily a British project, and after France fell to the Nazis, British control was absolute, although committee members went to some lengths to include French representatives in their activities. Perhaps the French involvement made the campaigns appear more broadly based, and it is likely that the French participation made the committee's activities more appealing to many members of the Mexican intelligentsia who were traditionally Francophile.

Initially, the temptation to launch its own publication seemed attractive. The committee started a magazine, *Noticias Gráficas*, only to discover that the editor, according to a British member of the committee, was a French lady of "advanced leftist opinions." It was difficult to control the magazine's content, and the exercise cost the committee 35,000 pesos before it decided that the experiment had been awkward and ineffective.[23] Davidson also agreed that the committee was wise to abandon the direct approach to propaganda.[24]

It was a century-old tradition in Mexico to subsidize newspapers to influence editorial policy. In 1940 the committee had paid subsidies to *El Popular*, the newspaper of the CTM. However, those payments had not resulted in the degree of influence for which the committee had hoped. One British committee member said, "I still think that it was a mistake to pay blackmail. However, if a majority of the French representatives on the Committee vote for a renewal of the subsidy, I will not object."[25] The German experience with propaganda confirmed the Allied view that neither acquiring one's own newspaper nor paying outright bribes was the most effective approach toward propaganda. In the opinion of the committee, the German experience had been a virtual model of what not to do. The Germans subsidized the magazine *Timón*. "If our experience is any guide [wrote one diplomat] we can only rejoice at this development as we know just how much it costs to start a news magazine."[26] In spite of the Germans' success in attracting the well-known Mexican politician and writer José Vasconcelos to their cause, the committee was unperturbed. They understood that Vasconcelos's pro-Axis position was grounded in the conservative tradition of *hispanidad*, that is, in an anti-U.S. stance and a fear that traditional Spanish values were being eroded under the influence of the English-speaking world.

Sometimes a direct financial contribution would be based upon the calculation that political favor could be gained in high places. When Emilio Portes Gíl started the weekly newspaper *Candíl*, the committee agreed to contribute 500 pesos per month to the project. The British members on the committee believed that Portes Gíl was close to the Mexican president and that this would augment their influence.[27]

The organization of the paper industry in Mexico created an indirect opening for British influence. The Mexican government controlled a semiofficial agency called Productora é Importadora de Papel S.A. de C.V. (PIPSA), the function of which was to ration and distribute newsprint to newspapers throughout the country. Mexico was not self-sufficient in paper, and the major foreign suppliers were located in Canada. Bonham-Carter urged the Foreign Office to make maximum use of this situation, but warned that pressure should be subtle because obvious and heavy-handed tactics could precipitate a backlash.[28] Another propaganda agent, Thomas Ifor-Rees, suggested that the officials of PIPSA should be forced to deal directly with the Canadian government's trade commissioner. Since supply blockages could be blamed on the war, Ifor-Rees urged his government to "take action which would put an effective check to German propaganda in the local press and ensure that fairer publicity be given to the Allied war news and anti-Nazi material."[29] Even in its twilight, the Empire still had its uses.

Direct pressure could be generated in other ways. The example of the important Mexico City newspaper *Novedades* is instructive. As appeasement gave way to war, *Novedades* was strongly pro-Axis. But two factors seem to have persuaded the owners to change their newspaper's stance, and by 1940 even British propaganda agents judged *Novedades* to be "100 percent pro-Ally."[30] The first factor was the owners' consternation over the German-Soviet pact of 1939. The second one was that alliance dashed any conservative hopes that the appeasement policy might turn the Germans against the Russians rather than against France and Britain. Events in Europe were reinforced by a campaign on the part of the committee to convince the British and French companies in Mexico to shift their advertising funds away from the less friendly newspaper *Excélsior* to *Novedades*. As the owners of *Novedades* became distressed by the Axis powers' pact with the Soviet Union, a bonanza of advertising revenue reinforced their resolution to shift sides.[31]

The Inter-Allied Propaganda Committee also began to prepare its own material. It brought out five thousand copies of Herman Rauschning's book *Hitler Told Me*. Based upon the author's extensive interviews with Hitler, the book contained, according to Bonham-Carter, "conveniently nasty remarks about Mexico." The committee complemented the book with a pamphlet and a poster to broaden its impact.[32] Hitler's speeches provided a rich source of material to use against the Axis powers. A series of Hitler's pamphlets appeared, and in each case a British writer produced an introduction for the Spanish version. The committee published *Germany's National Religion*, with a foreword by G. K. Chesterton; *The Racial Concept of the World*, foreword by Sir Charles Grant Robertson; *Germany's Foreign Policy*, foreword by the Duchess of Atholl, MP; *The Nazi Party and the State*, foreword by Sir John Murray; and *The Redistribution of the World: Adolph Hitler's Reichstag Speech*, with a foreword by Viscount Cranbourne.[33]

The most detailed surviving report on Allied propaganda activities relates the committee's activities for April 1940. In that month, the committee produced four new pamphlets: *Report of Cardinal Hlond to the Pope on the Situations of the Catholic Church in Poland* (50,000 copies printed at a cost of 1,535 pesos), *German Atrocities in Poland* (10,000 at 335 pesos), *This Is What Hitler Thinks* (20,000 at 1,600 pesos), and *Naval Strength and the Losses of the Belligerents* (50,000 at 1,652 pesos). In addition, the committee distributed 61,284 copies of eight reprinted publications, including 39,980 copies of the *Treatment of German Nationals in Germany* and 7,480 copies of *This Is What Hitler Thinks*.[34]

The committee also developed a distribution network, including a mailing list, to place its material in the hands of opinion makers in Mexico. It sent propaganda to 5,500 doctors and dentists, 1,400 lawyers, 1,300 teachers, 800 government functionaries, 930 engineers, 4,600 businessmen, 2,300 mayors, and 6,000 religious leaders. It even donated material to barbershops.[35]

The war gave the propaganda committee an opportunity to be useful to the Mexican media. Rapidly developing political and military events created a need in the Mexican press for photographs and maps relating to the war. The committee sprang into action to make the editors' work easier. In addition, it opened new channels of communication with the press.[36] In April 1940 the British members of the committee were able to submit 280 photographs to the Mexico City press of which 119 were published. The French propagandists offered the metropolitan press another 150 photographs of which 31 were published in that month alone.[37] Out of this day-to-day contact grew the most important propaganda breakthrough of the war.

News services had developed during the second industrial revolution (1870–1910) in response to the need for more rapid communications. Their historical evolution was initially related to the need for a rapid flow of information for financial purposes. In

Europe, Reuters emerged as the main British news service and was challenged by the Havas News Service of France. Reuters was loosely tied to the British government whereas Havas was closely linked to the French government. As late as 1900, the American Associated Press operated entirely within the United States. In the age of the robber barons, Reuters and Havas arranged a division of the world. In 1876, Reuters agreed that Havas should have Latin America in return for Reuters enjoying a monopoly over coverage of Australia and the Far East.[38] The key to that monopoly position was the control of the transatlantic cables.

On the eve of the Second World War, Havas News Service was still the most important wire service in Latin America although the U.S. agencies were increasing in importance. Moreover, Havas News Service was the key to the activities of the Inter-Allied Propaganda Committee. Mexican newspapers obtained material from Havas via the Anta Agency in Mexico. But the costs were too high to cover distribution of the Havas material in Mexico. The propaganda committee subsidized the Anta Agency with 4,000 pesos per month (then equivalent to £222). This was an exceptional opportunity for the committee. The Mexicans were unaware of the Allied financial intervention so the subsidy was not an affront to nationalistic sentiments. As one propagandist reported, "At the beginning of the war it was found necessary for the Allied Committee to subsidize Anta in order that this pro-Ally news service should receive the widest distribution possible." Indirect manipulation of a news service had the advantage of being out of the public eye and an efficient way to influence news published through the entire media. Control was a vital part of the arrangement. As the report explained, "This financial dependence of Anta upon the Allied Committee is, of course, a most important factor in the present situation; for whatever sort of news Havas may issue, Anta is in a position to ensure that only that part of it which is either neutral or friendly to the Allied cause reaches the Mexican press."[39]

Agents of the Allied committee worked with the Anta Agency on a daily basis from the committee's headquarters on Hamburgo #42 in Mexico City. They closely monitored the agency to insure that unfriendly material would not slip through. Material on the Anta wire came from several sources. Havas News Service in New York was the most important source, followed by Havas News Service in London and the Reuters News Service. The British Official Wireless Service was less useful to the committee. The committee expressed pleasure with this arrangement: "The Anta News Service as published in Mexico is carefully studied each day in this office, and I can state with certainty that since the collapse of France little or no unfavorable news has been published under the Anta signature." The committee did worry about how long the Havas representative in Mexico, Monsieur Gés, would "stand for this tampering with their service by Anta," and Gés hid behind the position that he had not received instructions from his superiors. "My impression is that he is waiting to see which way the cat will jump and that he is chiefly concerned with keeping his job."[40]

Domination of the news services was the most important achieve-ment of the Inter-Allied Propaganda Committee during the war. This meant a new level of sophistication for the printed word; readers would not even know that the committee was influencing their "freedom" of thought. Journalists too might not be aware of this intervention and certainly would not know the extent of the committee's influence. It was no longer necessary for the committee to produce all of its own material since a single intrusion at the news service level would be reflected in articles throughout the country.

The April 1940 record allows us to examine the activities of the committee in some detail, with reference to both the magnitude of its propaganda effort and the content of the material it produced.[41] The committee claimed a record of rapidly increasing successes between December 1939 and April 1940. Each month the committee was able to place more articles in the metropolitan press. The respective number of articles from December to April were 38, 69, 104, 228, and 251. In addition, the committee was channeling material through "our Mexican [cinematic] news service *Servicio Mundial*." That subsidiary sold its stories to an average of thirty-two provincial newspapers. The average number of the committee's articles published in the provincial newspapers between January and April were, respectively, 193, 308, 416, and 480. Thus in April 1940 the propaganda committee placed a total of 731 articles in scores of newspapers throughout Mexico.

Only a few regional newspapers were sympathetic to the German position: *La Opinión* of Puebla, *El Regional de Culiacán, Ecos de la Costa* of Culiacán, *El Heraldo Michoacano* of Morelia, and *El Diario del Sureste* of Mérida. In the capital, the major newspaper *Excélsior* and especially its afternoon supplement *Ultimas Noticias* were a major concern. Committee members had a series of meetings with

editorial staff members and tried to direct advertising away from
Excélsior toward the more friendly *Novedades*. This had some effect,
but not as much as the Allies hoped. The other newspaper in the
capital that was pro-Axis was *La Prensa*. The committee was convinced that *La Prensa* was accepting funds from the German embassy. Apart from in these few newspapers, Allied propaganda
material was being used throughout the Mexican press. Of the 251
articles placed in April 1940 in nineteen Mexican newspapers,
Novedades led with 94, *Journal Français de Mexique* had 44, and—by
this time—*Ultimas Noticias* had 19. The committee's success in planting material in *Novedades* was overwhelming, but diplomats were
equally pleased with having changed the trajectory of *Ultimas
Noticias* and *Excélsior*.

A number of themes are evident in the articles that the committee placed in the press. Reasonably enough, the most numerous
articles reflected interest in the events of the war. Of course, any
propaganda effort would portray one's own war effort as strong
and successful and stress the mendacity and venality of the other
side—a more tenable position in World War II than most. The
themes that were unique to this period emphasized the fate of neutral countries in the wake of the German army, the impossibility of
the continuance of the German-Soviet pact, and the suffering of
the Catholic populations of conquered countries. All of these themes
were calculated to strike a receptive chord in Mexico. The religious
issue was more tricky than most. Wanting to offend neither the
Catholic Church nor the strong tradition of anticlericalism, the committee limited itself to describing the tragic fate of Catholic populations who were brutalized by the Nazi war machine. As one
propaganda agent put it, "Robbed of its political content Catholic
propaganda should be of the utmost importance here in influencing the more conservative sector of popular opinion which is often
inclined to be pro-German."[42]

The propaganda committee also showed great interest in
Mexico's radio stations, which were in private hands. The oldest
radio station in the country was XEB. It was owned by El Buen
Tono Tobacco Company. The next oldest station, XEW, the "Voice
of Latin America from Mexico," as it called itself, was owned by
Emilio Azcárraga Vidaurreta and had been founded in 1930.[43] Both
XEW and its sister station XEQ took their news releases from American Associated Press and from the Havas-Anta Service. Even though
the committee suspected Azcárraga of harboring pro-Axis sympa-

thies, the committee's achievement in controlling the news at the Havas-Anta Service neutralized that position.[44] And Azcárraga's relationship with President Avila Camacho soon brought those radio stations around. The committee suspected that radio stations XEL, XEAI, XEBZ, and XESM accepted German money, although the British consul general confessed that listeners who complained about these stations in the early years of the war were not always able to distinguish between "what was German propaganda and what is simply bad news."[45]

Despite some difficulties, the committee was able to place 116 transmissions on Mexico City radio stations by April 1940. Regularly scheduled radio reports from the Anta Agency were carried by stations XEB, XEW, XERC, XEFO, and XEBZ. XEQ also transmitted Anta material but at irregular intervals. The committee was also experimenting with retransmitting their material from Havas-Anta via XEQ into the interior, first through a local station in Veracruz. This was seen as a test case for retransmission throughout the country.[46]

It is difficult to capture the nature of the Allied propaganda that was broadcast over the Mexican radio stations because of the ephemeral nature of radio. The titles of the radio programs suggest that the emphasis was somewhat different from the material issued to the Mexican press. On the radio, the most frequent theme was that the Allies were fighting for Western culture against the onslaught of Nazi barbarism—a not indefensible position. The radio broadcasts also seem to have differed from the press propaganda in emphasizing individual testimony against the Nazis. H. G. Wells and Professors Le Criox and Leyva were presented regularly on radio. Suffering by individuals was also stressed. The series "Diary of a Young Polish Girl" was aired, as was "Christianity and the French Youth." This personal approach was probably intended to reduce the great issues of war and politics to a more human and immediate scale. Twenty-five of the recorded 116 programs were based upon this format.[47]

Cinema in Mexico is a mass passion. The government has traditionally intervened with regulations and subsidies to keep tickets cheap. Theaters are enormous and attendance is regular among a high percentage of the Mexican population. In short, cinema is a natural target for the propagandist and was so during the 1940s. Yet the film industry proved to be difficult to penetrate for the Inter-Allied Propaganda Committee. The committee had started a news short called *Servicio Mundial*, but the newsreels it produced were obviously propaganda. It had also prepared, edited, and translated one Polish and three French documentary films.[48]

The committee experienced great difficulty in getting its material released in Mexican cinemas. One French film distributor suggested that this was due to "the competition of American film companies who are jealous of the Mexican market."[49] This comment is both fascinating and revealing since the distribution of films in Mexico in this period was a monopoly controlled by William Jenkins. His control of the large sugar refinery at Atencingo, the motion picture distribution business in Mexico City, and, eventually, the Banco de Comercio was matched by his involvement with the local Avila Camacho political machine in Puebla.

It is extraordinary that the Allied committee was unable to place its propaganda in the cinemas controlled by the Jenkins group. It is tempting to write this off to Jenkins's extreme right-wing political ideology; however, another explanation may be equally relevant. As we have seen, Jenkins's longtime silent partner in Puebla was the infamous Maximino Avila Camacho. The president's brother was plugged into an international pro-Fascist network and was initially so favorable to the Axis cause that he was reported to have a picture of Benito Mussolini hanging over his bed in his mansion in Puebla. Since Maximino provided political protection for Jenkins—in return for business opportunities—against the constant demands that Jenkins be expelled for violating Article 30 (expulsion being the constitutional penalty for a foreigner who meddles in Mexican politics) and since Maximino's pro-Axis attitudes were still clear at this time, this relationship may have been the origin of the committee's problem.[50]

The committee tried to get around the Jenkins-Maximino film blockade by using United Artists to release a British film entitled *The Lion Has Wings* about an RAF raid on the Kiel Canal, but, when the trailer was previewed at the Balmori Cinema in Mexico City the crowd's response was so hostile that management withdrew the film.[51] Other propaganda films were eventually screened at the Alameda theater, but only infrequently. The committee appears not to have been able to place its propaganda in the motion picture houses in Mexico City, except through the relatively ineffective news shorts.[52]

In the period in which wartime attitudes and alliances were being formed, the Inter-Allied Propaganda Committee was extraordinarily successful in placing its propaganda in the Mexican press

and on the airwaves. It certainly must be given some credit for turning Mexican public opinion around during the early stages of the
Second World War. The sheer volume of its effort is striking. The
British agents devised subtle and indirect techniques of media
manipulation. The Allied propagandists seem to have had a fairly
good understanding of Mexico, and this level of realistic understanding aided their cause. Their skill in charting a course through
the sensitive religious issue is evidence of this. And the fact that it
was British—and even more, French—propaganda agents who first
carried the burden of the anti-Fascist effort rather than American
agents helped to dissociate the Allied cause from the traditional
antigringo attitudes of the vast majority of the population.

It is fortunate that the record of the activities of the Inter-
Allied Propaganda Committee has survived for April 1940, for matters quickly changed. With the fall of France in June 1940 the Havas
News Service sided with the Vichy government. Thereafter, from
the point of view of the Allies in Latin America, Havas's material
was unacceptable. No longer could the office in Mexico City simply modify material from the Havas wire.[53] Instead, Reuters, the
Associated Press (AP), and the United Press International (UPI)
became the reliable sources for pro-Allied news during the remainder of World War II.

As already discussed, the British propaganda effort in Mexico
was effective in devising techniques for the manipulation of the
media in the early phases of World War II. Unprecedented quantities of foreign news were inserted into the Mexican communications network without the Mexicans being aware of the intervention.
There is little doubt that this intervention molded attitudes toward
the Allied cause. In the long run, this effort turned out to be pre-
liminary to the massive effort of the United States to replace European influence. It was quite remarkable that even as the United
States was handling its interests after relations had been severed
between London and Mexico City, Britain was still able to mount
this indirect effort to influence Mexican public opinion.[54] British
success in this did not go unnoticed in Washington, and the U.S.
government resolved to make up for lost ground.

The United States and the Mexican Media

On the eve of U.S. entry into World War II, the American news agencies Associated Press and United Press International were gaining

Articles Placed by the Inter-Allied Propaganda Committee, March 17–22, 1941

Papers	AP	UP	ANTA	T/oceanic	Exclusive	International	Total
El Nacional		826	649		20		1,495
El Popular			883	233	127		1,243
Novedades			2,301		85	211	2,597
El Universal		836	603	176	7		1,622
El Universal Grafico		464	204	162	70		900
Excélsior	2,768			115	213		3,114*
Ultimas Noticias				143	320		889*
La Prensa			474	305			779

*Error in the total data figure reflects the quality of statistical estimates in the 1940s.

on Anta. Figures on the origins of news stories for the week of March 17–22, 1941, are found in the table (facing page).[55] Provincial newspapers relied even more heavily than did the main Mexico City papers on the U.S. news services.

Wartime Propaganda and Advertising

As war began, important segments of the Mexican press held a hostile attitude toward the United States and the government's desire to cooperate with the Allies. *Excélsior* was so hostile toward the Allies as the war began in Europe that its management would not even cooperate with the timing of government announcements, and the editor's decision to print a provocative interview with the president-elect's brother, in which some pro-Fascist sympathies were revealed, was seen as an act unfriendly to the administration and the war effort.[56] The U.S. government's blacklist covered 180 firms and individuals in Mexico, including radio stations XEG in Monterrey and XEBZ in Mexico City and the newspapers *La Prensa* and *Hoy* in the capital and *El Norte* in Monterrey.

Criticism was aimed at the United States as late as the November 7, 1942, issue of *Hoy*, and *El Occidental* in Guadalajara ran a sustained campaign aimed at countering Foreign Minister Padilla's willingness to allow Mexicans living in the United States to be subjected to military conscription. Padilla responded by placing a pro-Allied article in *El Universal* and in the *New York Times* on November 8. The U.S. embassy was counting on the influence Manuel Suárez had as a shareholder in *Hoy* to change that paper's policy, especially since Suárez was so close to the president.[57] Nevertheless, for some time, a group around Maximino Avila Camacho—including Alemán and Gaxiola—as well as Acción Nacional leaders Efraín González Luna in Guadalajara and Manuel Gómez Morín blocked the effort to bring all sectors of the press into the war effort. This group briefly attempted to join with *El Popular* and to influence the editorial policy of *Tiempo* by sharing material with Lombardo Toledano and the CTM; however, this alliance was doomed, so long a time had its members been antagonists.[58]

The problem of *carestía*, wartime shortages and high prices, was blamed on cooperation with the United States in the war effort. A few editors drew the obvious conclusion that wartime cooperation was causing considerable suffering; Alvarez de Castillo, for example, the publisher of *El Informador*, pointed out that rumors were rife in Guadalajara that gasoline shortages were directly attributable to the war effort.[59] Most of the mainstream press and the Left combined their forces to deny this obvious linkage. This denial became more difficult in April 1943, however, when Eduardo Villaseñor, the president of the Banco de México, made his important speech criticizing the strategy of wartime cooperation with the United States on the grounds that Mexico was gaining very little from the arrangement. Ambassador Messersmith was extremely perturbed that he did not have the influence to prevent *Novedades* from running an editorial supporting Villaseñor.[60]

As they planned their own press campaign, U.S. diplomats understood that it was vital to target the "big four" newspapers in Mexico City—*El Universal, Excélsior, Novedades,* and *La Prensa.* Of these opinion makers, *El Universal* was the country's leading newspaper and was close to the governing party[61]; *El Nacional* was essentially a government organ, only slightly less official than *Diario Oficial;* and *Excélsior* was extremely conservative and, at some points, close to being a voice of the Grupo Monterrey and COPARMEX. Its evening tabloid, *Ultimas Noticias,* was open in its sympathy for the Axis cause in the early war years.[62] Each of the big four had circulation in the range of 70,000 to 80,000 daily newspapers, with 90,000 to 100,000 sold on Sunday.

The Inter-Allied Propaganda Committee in Mexico City quickly organized a campaign aimed at convincing sympathetic corporate advertisers to withdraw their business from unfriendly newspapers. U.S. diplomats joined this Franco-British effort, and the Rockefeller committee produced its own blacklist, which included Excélsior. The paper's management was alarmed. The committee had been pressuring Rodrigo de Llano, president of the board of the Excélsior group, for some time. This preemptive move by the OIAA was a grave threat. Excélsior responded by having Kent Cooper of Associated Press argue that the Rockefeller committee was in error. By April 1941, Josephus Daniels was able to report that *Excélsior* and *Ultimas Noticias* were pro-American and pro-British, noting that *Excélsior* had never been pro-German. At a board meeting of *Excélsior* attended by Allied diplomats, Miguel Ordorica, the pro-German editor of *Ultimas Noticias,* was given an indefinite leave of absence.[63] By May, *Excélsior* had shifted to the use of the Associated Press as its news service. Overall, the AP furnished 37.2 percent of wire service material by May, whereas United Press International provided 12.1 percent and Anta 26 percent. In that month, only *El Mundo* of Tampico, *El Porvenir* of Monterrey, and *Diario de Yucatán* and *La Opinion* of Torreón still displayed a significant number of unfriendly headlines: 18, 9, 4, and 7, respectively.[64] By September the committee was turning its attention to the small newspapers, *La Reacción, Hombre Libre, Omega, El Sinarquista, México Nuevo, La Semana, Diario Español, Nuevo Día,* and other very minor publications.[65]

The pressure from the Inter-Allied Propaganda Committee had an effect. Juan Malpica Silva, his son Javier, and his nephew Enríque all approached U.S. consulate officials in Veracruz after learning that the Inter-Allied Committee had placed *El Dictamen* on the blacklist for corporate advertising. Producing voluminous copy for the consulate officials, Malpica Silva blamed the newspaper's reputation for being pro-Axis on advertisements placed by Acción Nacional party leaders. He acknowledged that one editor was completely pro-German; however, "He stated that he was very anxious to rid himself of the editor, and that he had some hope in that the man had made himself so disagreeable to the staff that the syndicate was trying to have him ousted." By April 15 the paper was able to report that the offending editor, Luis Fregoso Rojas, had been removed, and it also indicated that it would make more use of Allied press services.[66] The newspaper was then removed from the blacklist for the goal had been to mold press behavior, not to punish, except in the last instance.

Another pressure point for the Allied press officers was available because newsprint was imported from the United States and Canada. Building upon the earlier British effort, U.S. diplomats approached the PIPSA board, which was headed by Alfonso Teja Zabre. At the beginning of the war, he indicated to these officials that he would be willing "to undertake to import newsprint and paper only for publications friendly to the United States and the United Nations." However, the president thought that *Omega* and *Hombre Libre,* the most recalcitrant magazines, were so small as to not merit using this mechanism. Both magazines appeared three times a week, were edited by Daniel R. de la Vega, and had a combined circulation of less than ten thousand. They were anti-Avila Camacho, "more anti-British than anti-American," anti-Jewish, and anti-Communist. The second secretary of the U.S. embassy, Guy Ray, thought that an indirect approach would be far more effective than openly denying newsprint or imported machinery to pro-Axis newspapers.

At the end of December 1941 all of the editors of provincial newspapers were invited to the U.S. embassy in Mexico City. " After lengthy talks these editors all agreed that the United States and Canada could not reasonably be expected to furnish newsprint to papers which persistently attacked the United States and the Allies."[67] As just noted, Ray thought the indirect approach was effective, and, since no threats were made, there was no resentment. To a considerable degree, this was because the war also created considerable opportunity for the press officers to be useful to the Mexican media. Having a source at hand, where editors could check the details of military developments and obtain maps and photographs and other reliable information related to the military campaigns, gave press officers a reason to deal with editors on a daily basis. And not having access to that information could place a newspaper at an obvious disadvantage.

A number of approaches were mooted. Raleigh Gibson pursued a plan to produce a humorous pulp magazine for wartime propaganda. "It would consist principally of war propaganda cartoons drawn by local artists with an occasional humorous dig at American tourists and their foibles to remove it from the straight propaganda category. (British propaganda in Mexico makes pretty dull reading because it is so obviously propaganda.)" The railway union, STFRM, agreed to take fifteen thousand copies of the magazine and with that base the committee could print five thousand copies for the small subsidy of $125 or ten thousand copies with an embassy subsidy each month, which would no longer be required if sales reached thirty thousand to forty thousand copies.[68] This project offered the possibility of tapping a new segment of the population. In the main, however, direct subsidies were losing favor.

The tradition of offering local magazines and newspapers subsidies for special editions on July 4 each year was also dropped. The resulting issue was so obviously propaganda that diplomats tried to compel editors to appeal to U.S. companies for those traditional subsidies, as the editors of *El Universal*, *El Nacional*, *El Popular*, and *Hoy* discovered in 1942. However, U.S. corporate managers were cool to this suggestion since wartime restrictions in the United States were already reducing their exports and sales to Mexico, making their advertising in that country pointless. Since the embassy press unit was following a strategy of using advertising as an enticement to woo newspapers away from their Axis sympathies, this decline represented a serious development. Ray, therefore, turned to Nelson Rockefeller for help from Rockefeller's new organization, the Office of Inter-American Affairs.[69]

Nelson Rockefeller and the Office of Inter-American Affairs

The U.S. propaganda effort superseded the European influence. Nelson Rockefeller, the Coordinator of the Office of Inter-American Affairs (OIAA) between 1940 and 1945, organized a massive effort aimed at replacing the former preponderance of influence by the Europeans. In August 1942, he obtained a ruling from the U.S. Treasury Department granting tax deductions for expenditures that U.S. firms made to advertise in Latin America. That ruling was subsequently extended to cover more than 40 percent of the radio and newspaper revenues generated in activities in Latin America. Additional pressure was applied to newspapers in Latin America through the control of newsprint. As summed up by Edward Jay Epstein, "With a staff of some 1200 in the United States, including mobilized journalists, advertising experts and public opinion analysis, and some $140 million in government funds (expended over five years) the Rockefeller Office mounted a propaganda effort virtually unprecedented in the annals of American history."[70]

The OIAA supported cultural exchanges, grants, teacher exchanges, a media program, and a wide range of cultural activities. Coordinating committees, formed primarily of expatriate businessmen, were established in each country in the hemisphere. These were linked to the Office of Strategic Services (OSS) under the direction of Colonel William "Wild Bill" Donovan.[71] Shortwave broadcasts grew into a massive public relations effort, followed by media support programs. Even the film industry was brought into the war effort. Initially, this meant implied newsreels reporting the military events; however, that effort was expanded to include Hollywood feature films. The most innovative activity of the committee was convincing the Disney studios to enlist in the war effort. Thereafter, Donald Duck learned about Lake Titicaca, and the little-known "Gaucho Goofey" joined in to make pro-war cartoons for the Latin American audience. Full-length cartoons, including "Saludos Amigos" in Spanish and "José Carioca" for Brazil, were extremely popular.[72] In 1943, President Avila Camacho awarded Aztec Eagles, the highest award that the government can give to a foreigner, to the OIAA, Walt Disney, and Louis B. Mayer of MGM Studios for their wartime efforts.

Under Sydney Ross the OIAA also organized twenty-eight trucks with portable generators, projectors, and sound equipment to tour the country endlessly, showing propaganda films in even the smallest towns. Paramount, Columbia, and MGM all produced special newsreels for these sound trucks. By December 1943 an estimated ninety thousand Mexicans were viewing these popular projections each month. Ross even noted that sales of products by advertisers such as Colgate Palmolive increased in an area after the sound trucks had worked the region. (By the end of the war, Colgate Palmolive had developed 48,000 outlets for their products in Mexico.)[73] For many rural people in remote regions, these were the first motion pictures they had ever seen. Noting this, Grant Advertising bought the Compañía General Anunciadora S.A. for 1 million pesos and became the first U.S. advertising company in Mexico. Soon advertisements from Ford, Coca-Cola, Jantzen, and many other U.S. firms appeared regularly in the Mexican media.[74] These advertising initiatives seemed to represent the cutting edge of modernity.

At an important moment in the history of Mexico, internal forces opposed to the Cardenista tendencies of the Mexican Revolution were interacting with the Allied propaganda effort to bring the idea of a community of interests between Mexico and the major industrial powers of the West to the fore. The war provided the great events around which such cooperation could build in ways that would have been far more difficult in peacetime. The historical conjuncture of the internal political situation with the war created an opening in which foreign manipulation of the communications media developed. This phenomenon did not end with the termination of hostilities.

As World War II drew to its close, Warren Lee Pierson, the president of the Export-Import Bank, shifted to the private sector and became president of the American Cable and Radio Corporation and of All American Cables and Radio. Given the centrality of Export-Import Bank financing for the radio industry, this move was not without its significance for Mexico. Messersmith wrote to Pierson urging him to maintain a consulting relationship with the bank and to keep the Mexican need for future capital in mind.[75] Pierson continued to play an important role by overseeing links between the U.S. and Mexican media companies.

By the time of the selection of Miguel Alemán, U.S. press officers had characterized the political affiliations of the major newspapers in Mexico City. Although *Excélsior* was quite conservative, it "will never attack the decisions or the tendencies of the Government in Presidential elections." *El Universal* and *El Universal Gráfico* were also unwilling to attack the government, but they exercised only minor political influence. *La Prensa* was quite sensational and influenced only extreme Catholics. *Novedades* was equally to the right, but was more judicious and therefore more influential. *El Popular* was understood to speak only for Lombardo Toledano, and it no longer exercised much influenced over the working class, and *El Popular* was openly identified with the PCM. *Omega* and *Hombre Libre* were quite critical of the government, but they had slight influence. No magazines were thought to be politically influential.[76]

From time to time there was an attempt by those critical of the United States to found a magazine like *Indice*, started by Narciso Bassols and Alonso Aguilar in July 1951. The journal generated great attention and concern in the U.S. embassy; however, it had folded by 1952.[77] After that, U.S. diplomats viewed seven newspapers and twelve periodicals as "pro-Communist."[78] Moreover, the refusal of the United States to loan money to PEMEX after the war—not to mention exclusion from the Marshall Plan—created considerable resentment across the Mexican political spectrum. René Capistrán Garza, for example vilified Mrs. Roosevelt after the U.S. rejection of a petroleum loan for PEMEX: The two were linked, as José Pagés Llergo, the director of *Hoy*, explained to Phil Raine, a diplomat, in 1949.[79] Still, this problem would not fundamentally shift the relationship between the two countries.

Mexico and the Korean War

President Alemán had already made it abundantly clear to U.S. officials that Mexico's support for the U.S. position would be even greater in the Cold War than it had been in World War II. On the eve of his departure to Washington to head the Mexican Desk at the State Department, Guy Ray met with the president and Beteta. Alemán used the opportunity to make some fundamental points. Alemán assured Ray of Mexico's support in the event "of a war or even a struggle of ideologies" against the USSR. When Ray pressed him for what Alemán meant, "he said that the comparison he had

in mind was, first, that Mexico would declare war immediately
against Russia in the case of hostilities between the United States
and Russia, and second, that this time Mexico would be better prepared to render effective military aid."[80]

Continued Mexican support for U.S. foreign policy was not at
issue. The question was what the public would be told and what
agreements would be made in private. On January 30, 1950, the
UPI correspondent in Mexico City, Vincent Wilber, published similar articles in three Mexico City newspapers: *El Nacional, El Universal* and *Excélsior* under variations of the title "What Latin America
Might Be Expected to Contribute to the Defense of the Continent in
the Event of War." Wilber had based his articles on an internal study
prepared by the U.S. embassy. The version in *El Popular* was, not
surprisingly, the least friendly to the United States. The study reported that the United States expected Latin America to provide
raw materials, military bases, and troops if another war started.
U.S. diplomats, who were upset that the report had been leaked,
were amazed that so little attention was paid to the allegations beyond the editorials in *El Popular*.[81] U.S. influence still remained great
among Mexican editors.

In 1952, Lanz Duret, the editor of *El Universal*, approached the
press officer of the U.S. embassy. He was "very disturbed" over an
article in *The New Yorker*, which had identified *El Universal* as one
of the newspapers around the world unfavorable to the United
States. As a gesture, Armando Chavez Camacho, then editor of *El
Universal Gráfico*, was promoted to director of *El Universal*. His "extremely cooperative attitude with the Embassy in using material"
played a role in his advancement. The newspaper was unionized,
and some journalists were "only lukewarm" toward U.S. interests.
When a critical advertisement was published in *El Universal*, embassy officials quickly approached Duret, who explained that because of the journalists' union nothing could be done about the ad.
Apparently, another journalist, Valencia Solís, was bitter about the
treatment he had received in the United States "because of his dark
skin," and an editor had been "treated badly by customs or immigration officials at the border." Nevertheless, the embassy was not
unduly concerned, "The Embassy believes that Lanz Duret will do
everything possible to maintain cordial relations with the United
States. Vigilance is necessary to keep the unionized staff in line and
this can only be done by contacts with leading staff members and
with Lanz Duret himself."[82]

The Allied Radio Network

At the beginning of the war, William Paley, president of CBS, and John Royal, vice president of NBC, toured Latin America making contact with the most important broadcasting companies in the region for the OIAA. It was recognized that "a large proportion of the population of the American democracies cannot read and many are located so far from ways of communication that they seldom read newspapers." Therefore, it was proposed to establish a network of radio stations to cover all of Mexico and then to extend the network to the entire Western Hemisphere. "In this way all of the people would be given entertainment and news service with which the information would be included that would raise their morale and interest in democratic government."

A monumental decision was then made by the wartime propaganda experts "to coordinate these two powerful means of instruction, the newspapers and the radio, [and] place the operation of the radio broadcasting network in the hands of the Compañía de Inversiones y Transportes, S.A." The initial idea was that each newspaper would still exist as a separate identity but that the new radio effort would be merged with the older stations in a national network: "A nation wide service of this type would provide a very much better advertising medium than the present arrangement. In addition to the advertising of products made in Mexico, which should alone make the operations profitable, the Mexican network reaching the entire country should receive a large amount of advertising business from the United States' firms making products for sale in Latin American countries. This should greatly increase United States business in Mexico."[83] The Allied desire for a national network for wartime propaganda merged neatly with the government's propaganda program, "La Hora Nacional," which was reorganized and renamed "La Hora del Ejército" for the duration of the war. Each Sunday night, on every radio station in Mexico, the program became the centerpiece for news about the war. Programs such as Félix Palavicini's "Interpretación Mexicana de al Guerra" or XEW's "Tribuna de la Libertad" and "La Verdad es . . . ," narrated by Manuel Bernal, also rallied support for the war effort.

The budget for the radio project was initially limited to $175,000. It provided for broadcasting special notices three times a day over a network of forty-seven stations. "Content of all programs is subject to the absolute control and supervision of Guy W. Ray, second secretary of the embassy, with whom all scripts must be cleared. Any deviation from an approved script is ground for cancellation with a termination of liability for all amounts then due or to fall due." Ray, who became something of a proconsul for the media, sent warnings through PIPSA to penalize newspapers and electronic outlets that accepted advertising from the German pharmaceutical houses such as Bayer, including their extremely successful brands Aspirina and Cafiaspirina. Unfortunately, these brands had become generic terms; however, the committee worked to replace them with the more politically acceptable Mejoral. Ray was successful in inserting a clause in the contract between each newspaper and PIPSA to the effect that it would cut off the import of newsprint from Canada if a newspaper was blacklisted by the U.S. embassy. As word spread within the industry, the threat alone made it unnecessary to go any further.[84]

This propaganda effort was not the only factor behind the reversal of the popular attitude toward the war, from opposition to support. German attacks on Mexican shipping in 1942 were certainly central to this reversal; still, it is difficult to avoid the conclusion that wartime propaganda efforts supplemented government policy and played an important role in the shift in popular opinion from indifference and hostility to the war effort to enthusiastic support for it. There was also a commercial component to this shift.

Business in the United States pushed for links with the new Mexican media network to provide "a large market for radios made in the United States." Turning to the industry more directly, the media diplomats estimated that the replacement value of the entire radio system in Mexico was $5 million; therefore, they proposed to make individual contracts with Mexican media owners and provide $1 million (a figure that was soon doubled) in new equipment that would enable the existing owners to move old equipment to remote stations to complete a national radio network.[85] The larger stations would benefit by receiving more technically advanced equipment.

Emilio Azcárraga's XEW and XEQ were the central stations linked to both NBC and CBS in the United States and to a further eighteen stations throughout Mexico. This position for Azcárraga's network was remarkable given the frequency of U.S. intelligence reports acknowledging his earlier pro-Axis proclivities. XEW's manager, Othón Vélez, had been especially noted for his pro-Axis views. By July 1942 the U.S. embassy concluded that Azcárraga had no links with the Nazis. Testimony by the U.S. radio executives was crucial in Azcárraga's rehabilitation. Apparently, his links with the U.S. radio networks and the prominence of his stations in Mexico overcame doubts expressed by the intelligence and diplomatic communities as the United States and Mexico entered the war.[86]

Azcárraga's transmitters for XEW were so powerful that an agreement between the two countries was reached on March 29, 1941, on the frequency of radio broadcasting stations in order to provide maximum power to the Allied network. Mexican frequencies were modified so as not to clash with U.S. stations as far away as Denver and Salt Lake City. Thus it was clear government policy to fix the Azcárraga radio network at the heart of Mexican broadcasting even as it ensured that the U.S. model of commercial radio would grow in Mexico and that cross-media ownership would prevail. This was the key that allowed newspapers owners so quickly to gain radio stations and owners of existing radio stations to forge networks. U.S. technical support cemented the new arrangement.

Technical Assistance

In 1941 the Banco Nacional Financiero of Mexico applied to the Export-Import Bank for $2 million for printing equipment for newspapers in Mexico City. The loan, in the name of the Compañía de Inversiones y Transportes S.A. (CITSA), was for ten years at 4 percent. The company put up $500,000. The plan was for the four largest newspapers to coordinate their efforts by establishing a single printing plant that would have color printing capacity. The plant would be based upon the same technology recently installed by Southland Paper Mills at Lufkin, Texas, and the equipment would be purchased in the United States.

The United States was keen to use Mexico to send pro-Allied material to South America, where it believed that the Axis influence was strong. There was even a proposal to print a magazine called *Chamaco* for children. The newspapers that would benefit comprised 98 percent of the circulation in Mexico City—they were *La Prensa, Excélsior, Novedades,* and *El Universal.* For the four leading newspapers, the new level of technology would in effect provide a barrier to other newspapers that might want to compete with the established newspapers. The Banco Nacional Financiero had the support and underwriting of Nacional Financiera.[87]

Hollywood and Mexico

The export of movies from the United States provided important extra income for Hollywood. Will H. Hays, the president of the Motion Picture Producers and Distributors of America, pressured the State Department to understand the situation. He asserted that the industry represented an invested capital of $2 billion and that it employed 250,000 Americans and produced 80 percent of the world's screen entertainment with a weekly audience of 95,000,000 at home and 150,000,000 abroad. Moreover, Hays emphasized that the industry expended $225 million each year and generated $500 million in tax revenue.

It was imperative, therefore, for the government to understand that "foreign markets provide the margin of revenue on which the qualitative superiority—hence the world supremacy—of the American motion picture depends."[88] The industry earned one-third of its production cost from foreign distribution—roughly ninety million dollars a year. This was a vital margin; however, it was earned in foreign currencies. "*Dollar exchange* [Hays's emphasis], therefore, is the indispensable link between quantity and quality, the *sine qua non* of the industry's success." Countries such as Britain and Spain, which tried to put mechanisms in place to regulate the exodus of payments, were the bête noire of the industry. Here was an industry, like cotton, that generated tremendous pressure for open door, antieconomic nationalism policies.

There was a struggle over the control of the motion picture industry in Mexico that had protectionist implications. Film companies in Mexico were fairly weak, even as a new generation of stars emerged in the 1940s. Over the decade, the Mexican industry grew to consist of four studios: Churubusco, Azteca, Clasa, and Tepeyac. In 1949 those studios produced 107 films. They purchased 80 percent of their raw film from Eastman Kodak Company. In that same year production ran ahead of demand, and the studios had a backlog of some seventy films.[89] Still, for most of the decade the film studios were relatively weaker than the actors or the unions.

By the 1940s the actors had formed their own union, the Sindicato de Trabajadores de la Producción Cinematográfica (STPC), to challenge the STIC. The dispute between the rival unions was extremely bitter; however, Mario Moreno's popularity and his personal relationship with the president carried the day. The new union openly defied Fidel Velázquez and the CTM, who were clearly upstaged by Mario Moreno, Jorge Negrete, and María Félix. Both presidents of the 1940s openly supported the STPC against the STIC.[90]

On August 11, 1945, the STIC decided to try again, this time focusing on the U.S. film distributors. A strike was declared after the negotiations fell through at the end of July. The STIC, headed by Salvador Carrillo, an associate of Lombardo Toledano, timed the strike to coincide with the change of government. Francis Alstock, head of the motion pictures division of the OIAA, was involved in the negotiations. Mexican distributors viewed the STIC demand for broader coverage in the industry as intolerable and refused to view it as a dispute that affected only the U.S. interests.[91] The U.S. officials were convinced that Mexicans in the industry were so well paid, even by U.S. standards, that the strike was really a Lombardista attempt to keep U.S. motion pictures out of Mexico and replace them with Soviet films.[92] Jorge Piño Sandoval, writing in *Excélsior*, supported that view.[93] When the STIC presented the Soviet film entitled *The Collective Farms of the USSR* at the Alameda theater on August 16 it seemed to support Piño Sandoval's case. Since the major leaders of the CTM and the STIC, including Fidel Velázquez and Alejandro Carrillo, had been in attendance, that seemed possible. Moreover, union leaders boasted that they had an additional forty Soviet films ready to project if theater owners went ahead with their threat to close the theaters.

Negotiations were bitter, as management wanted to take away the confectionery concession that Salvador Carrillo enjoyed in the nation's cinemas. Eventually, the president turned the dispute over to Trujillo Gurría, the minister of labor, with instructions to settle matters. He also told Fidel Velázquez that this was not to be treated as a case of U.S. imperialism since the U.S. industry was aiding the Mexican filmmakers.[94] An agreement was reached on September 7, 1945 (without Salvador Carrillo), in which management gained additional control over the workers (the use of time clocks was at issue) in exchange for a 32 percent wage increase. Management was delighted with the settlement since the STIC was reduced to covering only the workers in distribution and exhibition. U.S. diplomats understood that the president's support for the STPC had doomed the STIC attempt to cover all workers in the industry and to keep U.S. films out of Mexico.[95]

Relations continued to deteriorate between the STIC and the STPC until the latter union, in an extraordinary general assembly, decided to withdraw from the CTM, so bitter were the feelings.

Jorge Negrete spoke openly at that assembly on the way that the CTM had attacked the STPC for expressing horror about the massacre in León in January. Mario Moreno also spoke, in a subdued but bitter tone, about the attitude of the CTM leadership toward the actors' union, and Gabriel Figueroa supported their views in the name of the technical and manual workers in the film industry.[96] By this time President Alemán was also supporting the STPC whereas months earlier, during the electoral campaign, when he still felt he needed CTM votes, he had not been willing to do so.

After the war, the exceptional period of daily U.S. participation in the Mexican media waned. However, the United States Information Service (USIS) was still active in Mexico. In 1953 the USIS managed to place excerpts from *One Who Survived*, by Alexander Barmine, in thirty-four provincial newspapers in installments. Clearly, propagating the Cold War was a high priority, one that was especially welcomed by the major daily newspapers and by the Periodistas Unidos de América group of newspapers. As the USIS boasted, "Zinc engravings were supplied [to] each newspaper and the entire matter was handled without attribution to the Embassy." The USIS was were also trying to place material on the bracero issue to convince Mexicans that rumors of ill-treatment were exaggerated.[97]

Mexican Media Interests

Several entrepreneurs had come to dominate the Mexican media industry since a "French group," under Constantino de Tárnava, had started the first radio stations in Monterrey and Mexico City after 1921 to advertise the products of its cigarette company, El Buen Tono.[98] None of the early media pioneers was more important than the Azcárraga Vidaurreta brothers, Raúl and Emilio. Born in Tampico and educated in Texas, Raúl had started a radio sales business and a motor garage before opening the first station, CYB (later XEB), in Monterrey. Emilio opened radio stations XEW and XEQ in association with Charles W. Horn, a former executive of the RCA and NBC radio organizations. Emilio's marriage into the Milmo family, one of the founders of the Monterrey Group, undoubtedly enabled him to tap the capital to race ahead. Emilio Azcárraga was, even at the beginning of his media career, reported to be extremely wealthy. Initially, Emilio Azcárraga was understood to be sympathetic to the Axis cause, and he favored Almazán in 1940. However, that quickly changed, as the close link between politics and the media was reinforced by Emilio's personal relationship with the president in the Avila Camacho years.

Emilio Azcárraga developed techniques to avoid being totally dominated by the U.S. media giant. He soon started his second station, XEQ, with backing from CBS to compete with his own—RCA-backed—XEW chain, founded in 1930. Then, station XET, "El Pregonero del Norte," attained legal standing in 1935. It started as a private corporation with an initial capital of 65,000 pesos, and Azcárraga shared the foundation stock with businessmen José F. Muguerza, Guillermo Guajardo, Francisco Zertuche, Adolfo Rodríguez, Fernando Muguerza, Raúl Cueva, Rodolfo Junco de la Vega, and Joel Rocha. By the late 1930s, the French Buen Tono group had given up on the business and sold off its stations, thus strengthening the Azcárragas' hand.[99]

By 1950, Azcarrága's capital base was about 500,000 pesos, which made XET the most sophisticated station in Monterrey, with more than double the capital of its nearest rival, XEFB. In the intervening years, Cevercería Cuauhetémoc had bought a sizable block of shares from some of the founding shareholders. The station was closely linked through ownership arrangements with the local newspapers *El Norte* and *El Sol*.[100]

Alonso Sordo Noriega was another media magnate. A member of the governing party, he became a player in the media as Avila Camacho's radio director during the 1940 campaign. After the election he became the director of radio station XEX, and the U.S. embassy assigned a radio expert, Bill Ray, to help the group with technical problems; the relationship provided advanced equipment to the group for years. By 1947 his network had grown to eighty-four radio stations.[101] Nevertheless, his path was not as easy as this overview might suggest.

An interesting record of the relationship between the government and Radio de México S.A. (station XEX, "La Voz de México") has survived. Frustrated by Antonio Bermúdez in his attempt in the early years of the station's life to get a subsidy from PEMEX, Alonso Sordo Noriega approached President Alemán directly. His account of the history of the station was that when he founded the station, it had been with the collaboration of the CFE and PEMEX. At the time the CFE and PEMEX had agreed that Sordo Noriega should have 40 percent of the stock in the station and 15 percent of the profits. However, the Secretaría de Bienes Nacionales granted him only 8 percent and then froze him out of the management of the station—prohibiting him even from selling space on the air to advertisers. According to Sordo Noriega, this was to make him look bad to the president. Sordo Noriega's approach seems to have worked, for the president intervened to give him ninety days to show an improvement in the station's business, an arrangement that Bermúdez then rescinded.

By May 1948 the accumulated losses of the station since its founding were over 1.6 million pesos and, at the time of the president's intervention, the deficit was growing at the rate of 210,000 pesos per month. The specific accounts were a matter of controversy between Bermúdez and Sordo Noriega; what is clear is that their battle was over the control of the station. Both men understood that the government would cover the losses through advertising from PEMEX, the Lotería Nacional, and direct subsidies. Clearly, vital management decisions were made in the presidential office, and the programs were vetted by the administration. These agreements helped the station rebound in the second half of 1948, as its deficit fell to $20,000 per month by the end of the year.[102] Nevertheless, the station landed back in the government's hands, and the matter was settled permanently only at the beginning of 1951 when the government sold radio station XEX to Romulo O'Farrill.[103]

In addition to supporting the most popular radio stations directly, the government wanted to make radio widely available to the population. Therefore, it also attempted to create a domestic manufacturing industry to build radios. By 1949 ten radio manufacturing plants operated in the country with an annual output of 116,000 receiving sets. The wartime propaganda effort thus merged in a number of ways with the political agenda of the governing party after the end of hostilities to support the rapid growth of the radio industry.

Television

By the time of President Alemán the PRI-Azcárraga relationship had provided a foundation television license (XEW-TV) that was the origin of the country's most important television giant, Televisa. The ownership was shared among the Azcárraga, Alemán, and O'Farrill families as well as other members of the Monterrey Group.[104] The importance of the new medium can be seen by the fact that by 1951 Televicentro already represented a $3-million investment. Alemán's son, Miguel, Jr., maintained a lifelong association with Televicentro, reflecting the initial agreements. The other initial license went to Romulo O'Farrill, who had a long-standing relationship with the president involving motor vehicle distributorships and media interests. His new television station, which was actually the first on the air, complemented his radio station and *Novedades*.[105]

At first, television came slowly to Mexico. As late as the end of 1950, one industry survey concluded that only 1,854 television sets had been sold in the entire republic. Although televisions were playing in store windows throughout the capital, there was considerable buyer resistance since only one station, the O'Farrills' XHTV, was on the air, from 5:00 P.M. to 10:00 P.M. Rómulo O'Farrill, Jr., was the president of XHTV, Televisión de México S.A., and he enthusiastically reported to U.S. diplomats that his firm had already invested 400,000 pesos in the station. In its rush to be the first station on the air, XHTV operated out of extremely limited quarters in the National Lottery Building. But plans were under way for a new building to house XHTV, radio XEX, and *Novedades*, all O'Farrill properties. By January 1952 there were thirty television stations already operating or at the stage of testing in Mexico.[106]

In contrast to the possibility of manufacturing radios domestically, manufacturing televisions was more difficult. Television sets could not be built for the tiny Mexican market, and U.S. equipment entered the market freely. The import tariff of January 18, 1951, placed only a 0.6 percent tariff on receivers and parts, a 1 percent tariff on sets in cabinets, and a 2 percent tariff on sets that were combined with radios or phonographs.[107]

Others quickly tried to catch up with the O'Farrills' lead. Work progresed on the antenna for XHGC, Televisión Nacional, owned by Ing. González Camarena. Camarena took pride in having designed and built much of the equipment himself. Because XHGC was housed next to station XEQ, cooperation was already emerging. Camarena's investment before going on the air was 560,000 pesos. The president authorized a plan to install the station's transmitters on national parkland on the slopes of Ixtaccihuátl in order to transmit from Puebla to Cuernavaca.

Emilio Azcárraga, the owner of radio station XEW, approached his new media outlet, XHWT, on a grand scale. On Avenida Chapultepec #26 in Mexico City he built a giant complex of twenty-three studios for both radio and television, eventually known as Televicentro. Projected to cost 30 million pesos, the complex included administrative offices, technical studios, two theaters that would each seat over one thousand spectators, and even a studio designed and decorated for puppet shows and other children's material. His plan was to charge people from 3 to 5 pesos to watch a program being recorded. Cameras were designed into the recording studios so that they could be moved through the aisles. Three television stations were to run from the building: one for sports, another for films, and a third for live shows. The technical equipment came from General Electric in the United States.[108]

By the end of 1950 a new law of *radiodifusión* had been added to the general law of communications to cover television. Permits began to be issued to cover the republic.[109] Emilio Azcárraga's position was already so dominant that, in 1950, when a license was issued for a new television station in Matamoros, the owners, Pedro de Lille, Manuel de Leal, W. B. Miller, and Noel Alrich Solano, publicly announced—apparently before reaching an agreement—that they hoped Azcárraga would take over the station.[110]

Control of the Media

At the beginning of the decade, *Novedades* was owned and managed by Ignacio F. Herrerías, who founded the paper in the 1930s on the profits that he had made from comic strips. Until the beginning of the European war in 1939, he accepted a regular subsidy from the German embassy. After the war began, Herrerías turned to the British for subsidies. He also enjoyed substantial loans from the Mexican government that helped his paper to grow to roughly the same size as the three other major newspapers. The editor of *Novedades* was René Capistran Garza, a well-known conservative writer and a close friend of the archbishop. His salary was generally characterized by those in the industry as "enormous." Although he flirted with the Falangists before the war, clearly sympathizing with Franco in Spain, he moved toward the Allies after the war broke out. *Novedades* published an English-language page, which was paid for by the Allied Information Office, that is, the British. The paper's debt was high compared to that of *Excélsior* or *El Universal*.[111] This made possible the takeover of the paper by a family that had exceptionally close relations with the presidents of the 1940s.

U.S. diplomats tried to keep tabs on the changing ownership patterns in the Mexican media. At the end of July 1946, David Thompson wrote to Guy Ray, who was then in charge of the Mexico desk in the Department of State. He confirmed earlier reports that President Alemán had direct interests in *Novedades*. The four chief investors in the paper were Jorge Pasquel, Prisciliano Elizondo, Antonio Díaz Lombardo, and José Clemente. Pasquel was a baseball impresario "who is at least in part a front for Alemán." He also had been in an altercation in Nuevo Laredo with a customs agent whom he killed. "Ex-president Portes Gil is said to have got Pasquel out of this scrape for a hefty consideration." Elizondo was a banker, contractor, and capitalist from Monterrey. He also had a reputation as a maker of governors. Díaz Lombardo had made his fortune in bus lines, banks, and hotels, whereas Clemente was in firearms, jewelry, and money lending. Thompson was not able to confirm the presence of Aarón Sáenz or Abelardo Rodríguez on the board of *Novedades*.[112]

By the late 1940s, Rómulo O'Farrill, Sr., and his son, Rómulo, Jr., owned a major slice of the country's media interests, including part of *Novedades*, *The News*, radio station XEX, and Channel 4-XHTV, as well as automobile and truck distributorships (Automotriz O'Farrill, the assembly plant for and distributorship of Packard and Mack trucks), and other interests. They had been extremely close to President Avila Camacho (Rómulo, Sr., married his niece, Hilda Avila Camacho, in 1942) and President Alemán, and they maintained a cordial relationship with Ruíz Cortines. Although they had initially attempted to fight the near monopoly of Emilio Azcárraga in Mexico City (radio station XEW, television station Channel 2-XEW-TV, and radio station XEQ), the O'Farrill family found that major advertisers such as Colgate Palmolive and Proctor and Gamble were not willing to break from the Azcárraga stations in a significant way and channel enough advertising to XEX. According to Rómulo O'Farrill, Jr., his father did not have either the time or the inclination to devote to the business, so the family came to an agreement with Azcárraga in which the two magnates' interests in XEX and XEQ were merged, with the O'Farrills holding 50 percent, Azcárraga 25 percent and station managers Emilio Balli and Sancristobal the remainder. The arrangement did not cover XHTV, Channel 4, which was the first station operating in Latin America.[113]

Newspapers

El Universal was the oldest newspaper in Mexico, having been founded in November 1916. By the end of the 1940s, *El Universal* was edited and published by Miguel Lanz Duret, who, however, was frequently considered to be less gifted than either his father or

Felix Palavicini, who had controlled the newspaper at the time of World War I. Miguel's younger brother Fernando was also becoming active in the administration of the paper. The stock in the newspaper was controlled by the Duret and Figueroa families, which were interrelated by marriage. The editor of the paper in the war years was José Gómez Ugarte, and the paper relied on the UPI news service.[114]

Founded in March 1917, *Excélsior* was later taken over by people close to the Grupo Monterrey; however, in the late 1940s it became a cooperative run by Rodrigo de Llano. U.S. diplomats believed that "there is probably more *esprit de corps* among the employees and journalists of *Excélsior* than any other paper in Mexico City." The paper relied on the Associated Press for its news and frequently took articles from the North American Newspaper Alliance and featured articles by G. F. Eliot and Walter Lippmann.[115]

La Prensa was a daily tabloid run by Luis Novarro, with Fernando Mora the editor. It was pro-Allies after the war began, although it had accepted a subsidy from Germany before the war. Since its tabloid style tended to focus upon murders, violence, and other individual crimes, it was of less importance to the Allies. After the United States entered the war, however, *La Prensa* used a great deal of material prepared by Nelson Rockefeller's OIAA.[116] Novarro suffered a debilitating illness in the war years, after which his paper was run by a "triumvirate," one member of which was Manuel Espejel, an employee of the Press Section of the Presidency.

El Popular was the organ of the CTM and as such was dominated by Vicente Lombardo Toledano and Alejandro Carrillo. The paper had been hostile to the Allies until the German invasion of the USSR, after which *El Popular* became an ardent supporter of the Grand Alliance. Of interest, even as the government asserted greater control over the CTM, Lombardo Toledano and Carrillo maintained their control of *El Popular* throughout the decade, even supporting the Partido Popular. By the end of the war, *El Popular* was down to a circulation of twenty thousand to twenty-five thousand, so inept had been its long-running apologia for Lombardo Toledano; circulation crashed to only about twelve thousand by the end of the decade.[117]

El Nacional was the official government newspaper, and it was run by Raúl Noriega. The paper was extremely dull and had all the vices of an official propaganda outlet; therefore, it had the smallest circulation, around four thousand. *El Nacional* was not the same as *Diario Oficial*, which was the government's official gazette.[118] Finally, *La Voz de México* was the newspaper of the PCM. Its editor was Carlos Sanchez Cárdenas. The government's domination of the "big four" newspapers was so complete that it could ignore these small voices of dissent.

The hand of the government could be seen in or behind the ownership arrangements in three major newspapers in Mexico City; however, with *Novedades, Excélsior,* and *El Universal,* not to mention PIPSA, that relationship was hidden. By contrast, everyone knew that *El Nacional* was a semigovernment organ, and this gave the impression that the "big three" were more independent of the government than was the case.[119] Even the powerful regional media baron, José García Valseca, had gotten his start as Maximino Avila Camacho's chauffeur before he founded a publishing empire based on the comic book *Pepín*.[120]

Magazines

Hoy was the largest news magazine at the beginning of the decade. José Pagés Llergo was its editor. The magazine, however, had supported General Almazán in the 1940 election, and, as a result, its circulation fell from thirty thousand to about ten thousand by 1942. Hernández Llergo was reputed to be highly skilled in obtaining subsidies for his magazines. The stock of the magazine was owned by Manuel Suárez, the well-known Spanish businessman. Not only did Suárez make his peace with the Avila Camacho brothers after the election, but they also became his silent partners in the venture. Maximino Avila Camacho was understood to control a share of the magazine by the time he joined the cabinet. *Hoy*'s best feature were the cartoons on its covers by Antonio Arias Bernal; they commanded a great deal of attention and were prominently displayed around the country as each new issue emerged.

Todo was a magazine similar in appearance to *Hoy*. Run by Luis Ledesma, *Todo* had a circulation of about twenty thousand and was less reliant on subsidies than other publications. *Estampa* was a small magazine run by Spanish refugees from Fascism. It struggled in Mexico, with a circulation of about two thousand and was understood to be kept afloat by contributions from Spanish refugees. *Así* was also a very small, if somewhat scurrilous, magazine. *Continente* patterned itself on *Fortune* magazine in the United States, but it had a circulation of scarcely one thousand. *La Nación* was the magazine of the Acción Nacional party, and *El Sinarquista* represented that movement. U.S. diplomats worried a great deal about their inability to influence these magazines. After Mexico entered the war, however, these magazines trimmed their pro-Axis positions considerably.[121]

Selecciones de Reader's Digest quickly grew to be the largest circulating foreign magazine in Latin America. In 1940 the OIAA had been influential in getting the first Spanish-language edition of *Selecciones* published. The techniques of selected marketing and linking subscriptions to possible gifts were already used by the magazine. Above all, the formula used by the magazine communicated the Allied point of view without obviously appearing to be propaganda. A Spanish version of *Life* soon followed. These magazines were frequently monitored by people like the journalist Salvador Novo for the OIAA media specialists to evaluate their impact on the Mexican people.[122]

The newest major news magazine was *Tiempo*. Martín Luis Guzmán was the owner and director of *Tiempo*. A supporter of the Adolfo de la Huerta rebellion in 1924, Guzmán kept a low political profile until the time of Avila Camacho. He was particularly upset over the pro-Catholic attitudes and policies of the president, which Guzmán viewed as violating the constitution of 1917. Reportedly close to Lombardo Toledano, he charted a different course. At the time of the October 1945 celebrations of the coronation of the Virgin of Guadalupe, Guzmán received material support from Raúl Noriega, director of *El Nacional*. At that time he also had a successful interview with candidate Miguel Alemán, in which Alemán reportedly gained approval and promises of financial support for a new liberal party that would do battle over religious issues. Alemán's support then led to the founding of the Partido Nacional Liberal Mexicano (PNLM) on March 17, 1946. With Guzmán as president and Raúl Carranza, a magistrate of the Superior Court, and General Esteban Calderón as vice presidents, the party attracted some distinguished figures including Daniel Cosío Villegas as secretary, Antonio Pozzi of CONCAMIN, Jesús Reyes Heroles, then a law professor at UNAM, and a foundation membership of 400. The party claimed its membership grew to 3,200 in the Federal District alone by the end of the year; however, it faded quickly after that.[123]

The Influence of the Government

The relationship between the government and the media was extraordinarily close, although not without its moments of conflict.

Perhaps the most important link between the two emerged around the issues of newsprint. During the Cárdenas presidency, the importation of newsprint had been handled by a government agency known as Productores y Importadores de Papel S.A. (PIPSA). The agency imported newsprint to Mexico duty free, whereas anyone trying to import newsprint outside of the official monopoly had to pay a duty of $14 per ton. By the 1940s, PIPSA had so abused its powers that the owners of the largest newspapers in Mexico City were looking for a way around this situation. To make matters worse, on the eve of his inauguration, President Avila Camacho and his fabled brother Maximino were reported to have decided to start a new newspaper in Mexico City that would be nominally independent but in fact would be under their control. Thus in the wake of the 1940 election, Mexico's press barons faced two immediate threats.

The directors of *El Universal*, *Novedades*, *Excélsior*, and *La Prensa* all approached the president. A deal was negotiated in which the government would turn PIPSA over to these press magnates as a cooperative to run in their interests, and the Avila Camacho brothers would abandon their plan to start a new newspaper. In return, "the four newspapers in question would pledge their support to the Avila Camacho administration for its duration and, in particular, would abstain from any criticism of President Avila Camacho personally. This arrangement was put into effect, and both sides lived up to it scrupulously." The same arrangement was carried over to the Alemán administration. Guy Ray, the U.S. embassy's media officer, reported that the media executives claimed that since this deal was voluntary, the arrangement had not limited their freedom of expression. They frequently remarked that "it is neither patriotic nor in good taste to criticize the President of the country personally."[124] Therefore, it became a fundamental ground rule of Mexican politics that when a coordinated press campaign appeared, it had presidential approval, or at the very least, such a campaign could be called off by the political authorities. The presidents of the 1940s monitored the media through the Presidential Press Bureau and the Information Section of Gobernación. U.S. diplomats understood that substantial payments to media executives regularly accompanied significant requests.[125] Nevertheless, these Mexican mechanisms of media control were hidden and relatively innocuous by comparison with those in some other countries in Latin America, where the arrest and incarceration of independent journalists was far more common.

In 1944, Avila Camacho bowed to conservative pressure and created a commission to censor comic books. The Comisión Calificadora de Publicaciones y Revistas Ilustradas was scarcely an inquisitorial body. Lacking powers of enforcement, it tried over several decades to guard the nation's morality from the comics. As Anne Rubenstein put it, "On a small scale, the members of the Commission fought out a three-way conflict among strict social traditionalism, modernizing revolutionary nationalism, and transnational capitalist culture which was being played out through this period in many facets of Mexican life."[126] However, media interests defended themselves.

By 1950 the radio interests in Mexico were able to organize their own associations. In Monterrey, a close friend of Emilio Azcárraga's, Enríque Serna Martínez, was elected head of the Association of Owners of Radio Stations.[127] The idea was to create a united front in dealing with the government. But if the government was diligent in monitoring the political content of radio transmissions, it was doubly keen to control the new visual medium. From the earliest days of television, the practice was for the station to clear its programs with the government. Early didactic programs like "Practical Advice for Housewives," talks about museum collections, and shorts from Spain were soon replaced by a great deal of material from the United States. For example, in 1951 the U.S. embassy cleared twenty-nine additional titles for screening on Mexican television for the month of September alone.[128]

Techniques of Protectionism

As World War II ended, U.S. diplomats made a concerted effort to shelter U.S. filmmakers from protectionist measures in Mexico. Seeing the industry—in addition to being a major export — as a way of propagating U.S. values and products, diplomats developed a series of techniques with which to combat protectionism. The Motion Picture Producers and Distributors of America (MMPDA) under Will Hays specialized in monitoring protection efforts by the USSR, Spain, Britain, and Mexico.

In a move that went beyond efforts to counter Mexican protectionism by means of constant demands for free trade in media products, U.S. officials found a way to limit competition from the South. The Achilles' heel of Mexico's film industry was access to raw film stock, which was then only produced in the United States. Although the Mexican industry could produce films, it depended upon U.S.

supplies to make multiple copies of films for export. OCIAA film expert Frank Fouce, as early as 1944, spotted this as a critical pressure point since many completed films were in storage awaiting release due to a lack of film stock for copies. By 1947 the Mexican government was protesting that the low U.S. quota of raw film stock was indirectly limiting Mexican film exports. Moreover, as Seth Fein points out, Mexican protectionism was impossible since the United States provided a larger market for Mexican films than did other Spanish-speaking markets. Mexican domestic profits were roughly the same as the sale of tickets in the United States and far exceeded revenue earned elsewhere in the Spanish-speaking world. In addition, cooperation between U.S. and Mexican studios also undercut any protectionist tendencies in the film industry.[129]

There were, nevertheless, a few minor attempts to protect the Mexican media from U.S. influence, especially along the border. English-language stations operated under significant restrictions. For example, station XEG operated from Monterrey. Initially founded by William Richard Cammack, the station was registered under the name of Angel Lozano Elizondo. The station had a special permit from the government to allow it to broadcast in English. It attracted a large number of preachers in Texas who found its rates for the time cheap and made their money back easily from the faithful. U.S. advertisers also liked the cheap rates they were able to organize through an office in Fort Worth. (Rates were higher in the winter when atmospheric conditions were more propitious.)[130]

The most important protectionist measure was the prohibition against dubbing foreign-language films into Spanish. This was a calculated attempt to make the domestic cinema more attractive to Mexicans. However, these attempts were of minor consequence, and it was immediately recognized when television came to Mexico that the prohibition against dubbing could not apply to the new media.

A more serious effort was made to protect the fledgling electronics industry. On July 11, 1947, the government prohibited the importation of assembled radio sets. Within two years there were ten domestic producers, employing 450 workers, manufacturing all of the name brands from the United States: RCA, GE, Philco, Motorola, and Zenith, among others. Tax exemptions were granted in return for an agreement by the manufacturers to produce tubes and components in Mexico, which was not implemented. An estimated 1.2 million sets were in operation by the beginning of 1950.[131] In the end, the electronics industry never overcame problems of quality and small production runs. In short, protectionist measures were far less important than the rise of the Mexican media magnates.

Conclusion

The battle for control of the Mexican media took place in various stages. The propaganda battle between the Great Powers on the eve of World War II inevitably came to Mexico as the Inter-Allied Propaganda Committee launched its innovative program. The British and French triumphed initially by devising techniques to penetrate the Mexican print media by subsidizing and monitoring the international news services.

To a considerable degree, the Franco-British Inter-Allied Propaganda Committee caught the U.S. propaganda agents napping. Their response was a renewed effort by press officers in the U.S. embassy and the creation of Nelson Rockefeller's OIAA, to the considerable annoyance of the State Department diplomats. By the time they designed their own media effort for the war, they had learned that indirect methods were far more effective than direct propaganda. They learned this lesson by watching the forlorn German experience in directly subsidizing *Timón*. Not only was this German effort crude, obvious, and heavyhanded, it was also a financial black hole.

Mexico's great strategic decision to offer complete support to the Allies in World War II, in the hope that it would lead to the country's industrialization, doomed the pro-Axis press. Close wartime cooperation, control over the source of newsprint, and the campaign aimed at reducing advertising income for pro-Axis newspapers quickly brought all but a very few editors into the Allied camp for the duration of the war. The reluctance of the U.S. propaganda officers to use their heaviest weapons, as in the case of PIPSA, was well rewarded since little bitterness accompanied the about-face by a considerable segment of the print media.

The opportunity to be useful by producing great volumes of background material, maps, photographs, and accounts of military campaigns earned U.S. media officers considerable influence. In addition, by providing new state-of-the-art equipment for cooperative media outlets, wartime projects increased the technological sophistication and dominance of the strongest newspapers and radio stations. Thus the pinnacle players in the media game emerged from the war with strong positions and large bank balances, just as television appeared on the horizon.

Ironically, the very strength and independence of the Mexican media magnates, and their ability to resist domination by the giant conglomerates from the North, depended upon favors they gained during the period of wartime cooperation. As the war ended, the financial strength and technological sophistication of their operations also placed them in a strong position to ward off future competitors. Finally, their close relationship with the governing party cemented their place at the heart of the Mexican system of mass communications. For its part, the government learned that its indirect relationship with the "big four"—*El Universal, Excélsior, Novedades,* and *La Prensa*—served it better than the crude, boring, and obvious efforts of *El Nacional* or of "La Hora Nacional." This lesson was even more effective as it was applied to the electronic communications media. The arrival of television simply meant the forward retention of the media bosses' dominance in an even more powerful new communications medium.

Notes

1. Martín-Barbero, *De los medios a los mediaciones,* 95.
2. Ibid., 95–97 and 143–49.
3. Becker, *Setting the Virgin on Fire,* 156–62.
4. García Canclini, *Las culturas populares en el capitalismo* (Havana: Casa de los Américos, 1981), 172; Rowe and Schelling, *Memory and Modernity,* 64–74.
5. Bartra, *The Cage of Melancholy,* 80.
6. Schuller, "Cardenismo Revisited: The International Dimensions of the Post-Reform Cárdenas Era, 1937–1940."
7. Ortíz Garza, *México en guerra,* 25–26.
8. Cull, *Selling War,* 130.
9. An earlier version of the history of the British propaganda effort in Mexico was published as Niblo, "British Propaganda in Mexico during the Second World War," 114–26.
10. In recent years an enormous debate has challenged the use of this term. Undoubtedly, critics of the concept of cultural imperialism, such as John Tomlinson and John Sinclair, have a point in that new media empires have emerged in Brazil and Mexico, and the two-way flow of cultural influences has made the matter more complex. However, at midcentury the influence was overwhelmingly one way. These critics go too far if they muddle the central reality of influence flowing from the Great Powers toward countries such as Mexico. This is not to say the impact of media on the population is automatically what owners desired.
11. Taylor, *Beaverbrook,* 192.
12. Taylor, *The Projection of Britain,* 43.

13. Ibid., 55–61.

14. Ibid., 182.

15. Ibid., 76.

16. I. D. Davidson to F. Goodbar, January 4, 1940, London, Public Record Office, Foreign Office, File 371, #24217 (hereafter, PRO/371, #24217).

17. Annual Report, March 31, 1942, PRO/371, #24217.

18. Foreign Office Internal Report, September 15, 1942, PRO/371, #24217.

19. I. D. Davidson to F. Goodbar, January 4, 1940, PRO/371, #24217.

20. It is clear that Davidson underestimated the degree to which President Lázaro Cárdenas had acted to commit Mexico to the Allied cause, even before the Japanese attack on Pearl Harbor. See President Cárdenas's revealing letter to Elena Vázquez Gómez, SRE, 39-10-10, June 21, 1940.

21. I. D. Davidson to F. Goodbar, January 4, 1940, PRO/371, #24217.

22. C. H. Bateman to the Foreign Office, November, 17, 1941, PRO/371, #30590.

23. Bonham-Carter to K. G. Grubb, March 12, 1940, PRO/371, #24218.

24. Davidson to Goodbar, March 5, 1940, PRO/371, #24217.

25. Bonham-Carter to K. G. Grubb, March 12, 1940, PRO/371, #24218. The comment neatly glossed over the distinction between an ethical objection to subsidies and a recognition that the result was not as effective as those paying might have expected.

26. Ibid. The concern Allied diplomats gave to these ephemeral publications seems far beyond their influence, judging by the extremely small print runs.

27. Bonham-Carter to Grubb, April 19, 1940, PRO/371, #24218.

28. Bonham-Carter to Grubb, May 7, 1940, PRO/371, #24218.

29. T. Ifor-Rees to Grubb, April 26, 1940, PRO/371, #24218.

30. Bonham-Carter to Grubb, March 12, 1940, PRO/371, #24218.

31. "Report on Allied Propaganda in Mexico," April 1940, PRO/371, #24218.

32. Bonham-Carter to Grubb, March 12, 1940, PRO/371, #24218.

33. Legation Report, June 3, 1940, PRO/371, #24218.

34. "Report on Allied Propaganda in Mexico," April 1940, PRO/371, #24218.

35. Bonham-Carter to Grubb, March 19, 1940, PRO/371, #24218.

36. Report of the consul general to C. R. Bock, July 22, 1940, PRO/371, #24218.

37. "Report on Allied Propaganda in Mexico," April 1940, PRO/371, #24218.

38. Tunstall, *The Media Are American*, 30

39. Report from the consul general to the Ministry of Information, July 22, 1940, PRO/371, #24218.

40. Ibid., July 22, 1940.

41. The detailed information in this section comes from "Report on Allied Propaganda in Mexico," written by R. H. K. Mavett and filed with the Foreign Office, April 1940, PRO/371, #24218.

42. C. R. Bock to the Ministry of Information, July 29, 1940, PRO/371, #24218.

43. Monsiváis, "Notas sobre la cultura popular en México," 98–112.

44. Consul general to the Ministry of Education, June 4, 1940, PRO/ 371, #24218.

45. Ibid.

46. "Report on Allied Propaganda in Mexico," April 1940, PRO/371, #24218.

47. Ibid.

48. Bonham-Carter to Grubb, March 12, 1940, PRO/371, #24218.

49. "Report on Allied Propaganda in Mexico," April 1940, PRO/371, #24218.

50. For the Jenkins kidnapping, see Katz, *The Secret War in Mexico,* and Zorilla, *Historia de los relaciones entre México y los Estados Unidos,* 343–44; for Jenkins's activities at Atencingo, see Ronfeldt, *Atencingo,* 3–38. In the end, under threat from the Mexican Congress, he lodged his enormous fortune in the Mary Street Jenkins Foundation (the largest private foundation in Latin America), with the requirement that the lion's share of the funds be spent in Puebla.

51. This reception contrasted dramatically with the film's enthusiastic reception in the United States, where it was released with commentary by the well-known foreign correspondent Lowell Thomas. Despite what its maker, Alexander Korda, admitted was "propaganda in the crudest sense of the word" and what Cull called "a tawdry script," it was a box office hit. Cull, *Selling War,* 48–49.

52. "Report on Allied Propaganda in Mexico," April 1940, PRO/371, #24218.

53. Tunstall, *The Media Are American,* 139.

54. For the history of the British petroleum settlement, see Meyer, *Su Majestad Británica contra la revolución mexicana, 1900–1950,* 472–525.

55. Josephus Daniels to secretary of state, April 7, 1941, USNA/59, 812.911/306.

56. Guy W. Ray to secretary of state, August 31, 1942, USNA/59, 812.00/32035.

57. Messersmith to secretary of state, November 5, 1942, USNA/59, 812.00/32072-1/2.

58. Ray to secretary of state, March 24, 1943, USNA/59, 812.00/32132.

59. Ray to secretary of state, June 9, 1944, USNA/59, 812.00/32399.

60. Messersmith to Duggan, June 15, 1943, USNA/59, 812.516/668; *Novedades,* June 11 and 12, 1943.

61. Ray to secretary of state, December 29, 1944, USNA/59, 812.00/ 12-2944.

62. Even in the latter stages of the war embassy propaganda officers thought *Excélsior* mischievously misquoted the president to favor the Axis powers. George Messersmith to Nelson Rockefeller, March 15, 1945, USNA/59, 812.00/3-1545.

63. Josephus Daniels to secretary of state, April 10, 1941, USNA/59, 812.911/307, and enclosure from Kent Cooper to Duggan, April 16, 1941, USNA/59, 812.911/311. An investigation established that the blacklisting of *Excélsior* had been based on anachronistic information. H. Notter to Duggan, May 2, 1941, USNA/59, 812.911/311.

64. Daniels to secretary of state, June 23, 1941, USNA/59, 812.911/315.

65. J. F. McGurk to secretary of state, September 30, 1941, USNA/59, 812.911/331.

66. Josephus Daniels to secretary of state, April 18, 1941, USNA/59, 812.911/310.

67. Ray to secretary of state, December 11, 1942, USNA/59, 812.911/487.

68. Dudley T. Easby to John Dreir, March 18, 1942, USNA/59, 812.91/364.

69. Messersmith to secretary of state, June 3, 1942, USNA/59, 812.911/400 and associated memorandum.

70. Edward J. Epstein, "Power is Essential . . . ," London, *Sunday Times*, December 14, 1975, as cited in Tunstall, *The Media Are American*, 140.

71. Erb, "Nelson Rockefeller and United States-Latin American Relations, 1940–1945," 98–105.

72. Ibid., 122–24. In 1975, A. Dorfman and A. Mattelart wrote an interpretation of the way they saw dominant cultural values propagated through the Disney comics, *How to Read Donald Duck*. This brought forth a torrent of cultural commentary. For an interesting review of the variety of readings of the Disney comics, see Tomlinson, *Cultural Imperialism*, 41–45.

73. Ortíz Garza, *México en guerra*, 53–56.

74. Ibid., 61.

75. Messersmith to Pierson, January 31, 1945, USAN/59, 812.51/1-2645.

76. Messersmith to secretary of state, March 24, 1945, USNA/59. 812.00/3-2445. Embassy officials thought *Omega* and *Hombre Libre* were "calculated to appeal to the riff-raff of the country." Dudley T. Easby to John Dreir, March 18, 1942, USNA/59, 812.91/364. This sanguine assessment demonstrates that press diplomats focused only on the use of state power and not on the broader climate of political opinion.

77. Bassols was a well-known and highly articulate voice on the independent left. Aguilar was a concern due to his background in studying banking at Columbia University and his work as head of financial studies in Nacional Financiera. R. S. Folsom to the Department of State, July 24, 1951, USNA/59, 912.63/7-2451. Bassols, *Obras*, 933–43.

78. Franklin C. Gowan to the Department of State, August 23, 1953, USNA/59, 912.63/8-2853.

79. P. Raine to secretary of state, August 19, 1949, USNA/59, 812.51/8-2349.

80. Memorandum of conversation between Guy Ray and Miguel Alemán, March 29, 1946, USNA/59, 812.00/3-2946.

81. Charles R. Burrows to the Department of State, February 3, 1950, USNA/59, 912.61/2-350.

82. Forney A. Rankin to the State Department, September 23, 1952, USNA/59, 912.61/9-2352.

83. Banco Nacional Financiero to Export-Import Bank, August 14, 1941, USNA/59, 812.51/2520. At the time there were 28 radio stations in Mexico City, 13 in Tijuana, 9 in Monterrey, 8 in Guadalajara, 7 in Nuevo Laredo, and 5 in Ciudad Juárez, Merida, and Chihuahua.

84. Wallace K. Harrison to Dudley T. Easby, March 14, 1942, USNA/59, 812.911/346.

85. Moving the old equipment enabled existing owners to establish new stations in Sierra Mojada, Veracruz, Acapulco, Guadalajara, Oaxaca, Tuxtla Gutierrez, Durango, Campeche, Mérida, and San Luis Potosí.

86. Ortíz Garza, *México en guerra*, 129–36.

87. Banco Nacional Financiero to the Export-Import Bank, August 19, 1941, USNA/59, 812.51/2519.

88. Will H. Hays to Francis Colt de Wolf, chief, Telecommunications Division, Department of State, October 13, 1944, USNA/59, 800.515/10-1344.

89. Abbey Schoen to the Department of State, October 5, 1950, USNA/59, 812.00/10-550.

90. Huer, *La industria cinematográfica Mexicana*, 121–28; Mora, *Mexican Cinema*, 69–70.

91. Ray to secretary of state, August 13, 1945, USNA/59, 812.504/8-1345.

92. Ray to secretary of state, August 21, 1945, USNA/59, 812.504/8-2145.

93. *Excélsior*, August 13, 1945.

94. Ray to secretary of state, August 31, 1945, USNA/59, 812.5045/8-3145.

95. W. K. Ailshie to secretary of state, October 10, 1945, USNA/59, 812.504/10-1045.

96. *Excélsior*, February 12, 1946, and W. K. Ailshie to secretary of state, February 13, 1946, USNA/59, 812.5045/2-1346.

97. Franklin C. Gowan to the Department of State, March 9, 1953, USNA/559, 712.00/3-953.

98. Mejía Prieto, *Historia de la radio y la TV en México*, 14–15; Fernández Christlieb, "La industria de radio y televisión," 240–41; Sinclair, "Mass Media and Dependency," 120–21.

99. Fernández Christlieb, "La industria de radio y televisión," 244–45; Sinclair, "Mass Media and Dependency," 122.

100. Stanley G. Slavens to the Department of State, March 17, 1950, USNA/59, 912.40/3-1750.

101. Leonard Reinsch to Rowley, January 31, 1947, Truman Library, Ross Papers, File 8.

102. Alonso Sordo Noriega to Alemán, December 6, 1948, and accompanying documents, AGN, RP/MAV, 512.32/8.

103. Report on XEX, February 3, 1951, AGN, RP/MAV, 512.32/8.

104. Sinclair, "Mass Media and Dependency," 122 and 127. He notes that by the late 1970s Televisa had become a conglomerate controlling 45 companies.

105. *Newsweek*, December 17, 1951.

106. Secretaría de Comunicaciones y Obras Públicas, report on television stations, January 26, 1952, AGN, RP/MAV, 466/262.73.

107. Raymond J. Barrett to the Department of State, January 25, 1951, USNA/59, 912.44/1-2551.

108. Ibid.

109. Jorge Rivera and Robles Maldonaldo in Tijuana; Cía. Mexicana de Televisión in Matamoros; Carlos Matiscal Gómez in Monterrey; Azcárraga's XEW, O'Farrill's XHTV and XEQ, and Guillermo González Camarena in Mexico City.

110. Peter J. Raineri to the Department of State, November 3, 1950, USNA/59, 812.00/11-350.

111. Ray to secretary of state, December 11, 1942, USNA/59, 812.911/487.

112. David Thompson to Guy Ray, July 31, 1946, USNA/59, 812.911/7-3146.

113. Eugene Delgado-Arias to the Department of State, March 13, 1953, USNA/59, 912.40/3-1353. The information was based upon a conversation with Rómulo O'Farrill, Jr.

114. Ray to secretary of state, December 11, 1942, USNA/59, 812.911/487.

115. Ibid.

116. Ibid.

117. Ibid. Lombardo Toledano also tried to start a rival news service, Agencia Noticiera Latinoamericana (ANLA).

118. Ray to secretary of state, December 11, 1942, USNA/59, 812.911/487.

119. Ray to the Department of State, April 20, 1950, USNA/59, 912.60/4-2050.

120. Rubenstein, "Bad Language, Naked Ladies, and Other Threats to the Nation," 114.

121. Ray to secretary of state, December 11, 1942, USNA/59, 812.911/487.

122. Ortíz Garza, *México en guerra*, 99–100.

123. J. E. Hoover to Jack Neal, Department of State, February 18, 1947, USNA/59, 812.00/2-1847.

124. Messersmith to secretary of state, December 11, 1942, and to secretary of state, June 3, 1942, USNA/59, 812.911/487; Guy W. Ray to the Department of State, April 20, 1950, USNA/59, 912.60/4-2050.

125. Ray to the Department of State, April 20, 1950, USNA/59, 912.60/4-2050.

126. Rubenstein, "Bad Language, Naked Ladies, and Other Threats to the Nation," 136.

127. Stanley G. Slavens to the Department of State, March 17, 1950, USNA/59, 912.40/3-1750.

128. Raymond J. Barrett to the Department of State, January 25, 1951, USNA/59, 912.44/1-2551. See the supplement from Webb, acting for J. A. Graffis, to the Department of State, September 7, 1951, USNA/59, 912.44/9-751.

129. Fein, "Hollywood, U.S. Relations, and the Devolution of the 'Golden Age' of Mexican Cinema," 106–20.

130. G. Slavens to the Department of State, March 17, 1950, USNA/59, 912.40/3-1750.

131. Abbey Schoen to the Department of State, October 5, 1950, USNA/59, 812.00/10-550.

Conclusion

A lthough life in an era can never be adequately captured in a single study, the overview of Mexico in the 1940s in Chapter 1 argues that numerous aspects of life were dominated by a new vision of industrial and urban modernity. Led by the state, this view of things modern was not just a theoretical construct. Rustic life and values were rapidly being superseded by a new vision of a modern, urban, industrial nation. Although this transformation was not limited to the 1940s, Mexico changed enormously from the mid-1930s to the mid-1950s as the country reordered its priorities to commit massive resources to a program of rapid industrialization. The push for industrial modernization merged neatly with revolutionary nationalism and with opportunities offered by participation in the Grand Alliance during World War II.

The Mexican political system was profoundly linked to the project of industrial modernization, even though it meant the repudiation of many aspects of the revolutionary past. There was both hope for and promise of a prosperous future. Ethical passion was driven by the desire to escape from the poverty of a rural past that must not be romanticized, and national pride asserted the country's right to join the world's major industrial powers in a new age. At its best moments, the vision of modernity offered material emancipation from poverty, disease, and want. Moreover, paid work and the never-ending products of industry gave concrete meaning to a modern lifestyle, and most individuals longed to be part of that future.

The rural exodus accelerated as cities grew, and in field after field of human endeavor new worlds were conquered. Abelardo Rodríguez and the forty new industries he started represent one kind of possibility, if, at times, in a somewhat embarrassing way. In fields closer to our own, a figure such as Daniel Cosío Villegas personifies cultural modernism as he founded learned institutions, academic departments, and professional journals, pursued a journalistic career, wrote histories, and negotiated treaties, eventually becoming a kind of political/moral institution of one, negotiating with and challenging presidents with an alternative vision of freedom.

The cultural manifestations of modernity frequently linked many of the country's most creative individuals in near worship of the economically active state. Even the most radical of Mexico's creative masters, from Rivera to Siqueiros, were united in opposition to their political masters as they sought state support for their art and resisted the shift in the Mexican Revolution to a more conservative stance. Perhaps no sphere more clearly reveals the ambiguities involved in depending so strongly on the state than does the cultural. People involved in literature and theater were especially unwilling to engage the massive social changes that were buffeting the country. Film was perhaps the most compromised of all the arts as mechanisms of social control were perfected to dominate that influential creative medium; however, people still flocked to the cinemas. Some areas such as education, art, archaeology, and anthropology did especially well, since their efforts so neatly lined up with nationalism. Aspects of popular music and sports were most clearly linked to a rejection of the project of industrial modernization. It is no coincidence that state-dominated unionists became known as *charros*.

The most destructive impact of this new vision of industrial modernity was on the peasant and artisan economies. Many of Mexico's most enduring problems flow from the diversion of resources away from these areas—a matter of hostile state policy. Furthermore, the unbelievable growth of Mexico City stands as a monument to the push of the peasants leaving the countryside combined with the highly political effort to industrialize. Although it was not immediately apparent, the catastrophic effect of industrialization on future employment became a national tragedy.

Three presidents, from Cárdenas to Alemán, contributed to the general accommodation with the United States that shifted the radical nationalism of pre-1938 Cardenismo to a more orthodox pattern of unlimited private capital accumulation. Although some aspects of this could be seen in the final two years of the Cárdenas administration, it was President Avila Camacho who locked into place the swing away from economic radicalism. His ability to shift the political agenda so dramatically in a more conservative direction without precipitating rebellion was, in a broad sense, linked to Mexico's involvement in the war effort. His international strategy was to exchange support for the Allied cause for help with industrialization.

More immediately, the political intricacies of the era allowed Avila Camacho to adopt a "moderate" stance between the parties of the Right and the Left even as the president moved away from the radical aspects of the revolution. Similarly, within the governing PRM, he occupied the middle ground between the caudillos of the Right and the Lombardistas and Cardenistas of the Left. The Left's absolute commitment to the cause of the USSR made them tolerate an assault on the living standards of the vast majority of the population in the name of international antifascism. The sphinxlike silence of Lázaro Cárdenas after 1940 made opposition to the new approach extremely difficult.

Official corruption also had a deeply debilitating effect on the idealism of the revolution even as the government introduced a regime of virtually unlimited private accumulation backed by the state. Domestic politics placed commitment to industrial modernization at the top of the political agenda during the 1940s. The economically active state aided foreign and domestic investors by granting direct and indirect subsidies, tolerating corruption, and molding the rules of the game to favor the politically and economically strong. Taxes became optional for the well connected. And foreign investors, who flocked back to Mexico after the war, quickly learned that a highly placed politician was invaluable as a silent partner.

The strategy of development was based upon a massive transfer of resources from the poor to the rich and from the country to the city. Land and labor reform were stifled in order to place the developers' interests at the top of the national agenda. The suppression of economic nationalists, independent unionists, and the Left was a matter of high (and frequently violent) priority. Finally, corruption increased massively to offer rewards to those who were well connected or flexible enough to adapt to the new approach. Within revolutionary institutions, corruption played an especially divisive role as those on the take split and demoralized those who were committed to earlier versions of revolutionary change.

By the 1940s the lingering role of the revolution was to contribute a torrent of anachronistic rhetoric as cover for this new approach to development. President Cárdenas surrounded himself with highly orthodox economic advisers, even at his most radical moments, and their influence initiated a process by which the great reformer of the 1930s moved away from radical nationalism after 1938. His eventual refusal to condemn the excesses of the Alemán administration was also deeply debilitating to opponents of the new approach.

The system of presidential autocracy continued to deepen throughout the decade. The lack of popular input in the selection of each new president was matched by an arrogant use of presidential power, as each incumbent acted without check or accountability for his six-year period in office. Even the shocking abuse of force by the authorities in León in January 1946—which led the governing party to change its name—was without legal remedy.

There was a moment when several Supreme Court justices, most notably Justices Roque Estrada, Carlos Angeles, and Fernando de la Fuente, tried to apply a judicial remedy to what must be acknowledged to have been state terrorism. However, a few shots by a *pistolero* brought that assertion of judicial independence to an end. Presidents would remain above the law. Miguel Alemán represented an extreme version of presidential arrogance as he amassed a vast fortune, cloistered himself behind his expanded presidential guard, and focused upon his relationship with international capital. The astonishing growth of Acapulco, with which Alemán was so closely associated, is best understood as the building of a pleasure dome where international business deals were cemented. Tourism followed capital.

The development of executive centralism took place within the context of two great historical phenomena: revolutionary nationalism and the deeply held belief in the importance of industrial modernization. Wartime cooperation with the United States promised to speed the process of industrialization. Nationalism and modernism—which were then unproblematic concepts—provided the political cover that allowed the governments of Mexico after 1938 to increase the power of an extremely narrow circle of political decision makers and link them with an equally small number of private investors.[1] This formula produced one of the most unequal patterns of distribution of income and wealth in the world, by some measures outstripping even Brazil and India.

Political debate was egregiously inadequate as these changes occurred. Opposition parties on the right, especially the PAN, were sensitive to the concerns of small business and segments of the middle class; they usually focused on opposing the electoral imposition that the governing party was so adept at fostering. In essence, they limited their concerns to violations of political liberalism at election time. However, as they faulted the governing party for its electoral machinations, they also rejected the social goals and reforms of the revolution that had promised so much to workers and peasants. Their political liberalism was, therefore, inevitably tainted with the oppression of the prerevolutionary past.

Political discourse generally ignored the intimate links between big business and the governing party, and those links were generally kept out of public view. A chasm divided the interests of international and domestic capital; however, the former group won the ideological battle. Foreign corporations, with only a few exceptions, quickly learned that quiet arrangements with the most important politicians generated invaluable political cover for their operations in Mexico.

On the left, the CTM, the Lombardista alternative, and the PCM all made their peace with the government's swing to the right, initially in the name of the war effort and the battle against fascism. Yet too frequently they also replicated the authoritarian centralism of the dominant political culture. Debates over the public versus the private sector, or the meaning of each president's variation on the theme—as an "ismo" was added to the presidential surname— were vacuous. There was a convergence between the broad Left and many in government who frequently equated progress with the goal of nationalization of the means of production. This simple formula was a significant factor that eventually led the country into the debt trap by the 1970s.

The state was committed to a pattern of expanding the public sector while surreptitiously, but powerfully, aiding the process of private accumulation. This meant that the state supported the development push with capital and public guarantees for private borrowing, even as it provided the markets for industry. During the most rapid period of Western postwar expansion the government was able to make the pattern of debt-financed expansion work; however, as the world economy confronted the limits of this approach by the early 1970s, the Mexican model began to unravel, politically at the time of the Olympics in 1968 and then for all the world to see by the economic collapse of 1982.

Clearly, there is an urgent need to understand better the limits and thresholds after which point debt quits working as an expansion mechanism and becomes a burden, and eventually an anchor around the neck of future generations. A call for a return to neoliberalism—state-of-the-art economic theory, 1890s style, for the 1990s—led to a bargain basement sell-off of the public sector,

which had been built over three generations. New crises of speculation were not long in coming, as the "Christmas crisis" that began at the end of 1994 demonstrated.

Mexico provides an extreme example of how the official vision
of progress, as encompassed in the national income accounting system, is leading the world toward devastation. No place better demonstrates the cost of focusing only on the short-term sale than does
Mexico City. The price of disregarding the fate of the majority of
the population as well as of the environmental damage created in
the process of production is apparent for all to see in that once great
city, as birds fall from the sky if they are so imprudent as to try to
fly on a bad pollution day. Clear air was not valued until it was
lost.

Creating a political system to enforce the model of development that ravished the peasant and artisan sectors led directly to
the growth of urban slums and precluded the countryside from
providing a healthy base for society. (Here the extreme contrast with
the solid rural base of the more durable postwar economic
"miracles" in Japan and Western Europe needs to be highlighted.)
It also pitted the political system against the interests of the vast
majority of the Mexican people, to the point that understating population growth is all that is left as a "solution" to problems of underdevelopment. Little wonder that in the end there is profound
disillusionment.

As industry became ever more sophisticated, it became clear
that a theory of exploitation based upon surplus value had to yield
to a recognition that the system treats ever larger segments of the
community as expendable. Under the worst possible scenario,
Mexico's final comparative advantage under NAFTA may simply
be as a repository for the effluence of its "trading partners."

Battered by tidal waves of change in the second half of the twentieth century, Mexicans in large numbers dropped away from the
great modernization project—in which they had found no home—
and tuned into the *telenovelas* that are aired in perpetuity on the
stations owned by the victors in the media wars of the 1940s. For
this is as close as most Mexicans will ever get to Alemán's great
promise of an industrial utopia, a promise that provided a fundamental mechanism of legitimization for the state after the Mexican
Revolution.

The debt crisis, the collapse of the Left, the revival of neoliberalism, the concomitant destruction of the economically active state,
and the fire sale of the public sector are more than any single gen-

eration should have had to confront—not to mention the political crisis of 1968 and the financial crashes of 1976, 1982, 1987, and 1994–96. As those problems were compounded by extraordinarily high rates of unemployment, by inequality, and, now, by extreme environmental decay, a crisis of understanding—some would say an exhaustion of alternatives—emerged. Finally, as cocaine (the world's most precious commodity, by free-market criteria) put down roots as it traveled north across the national territory, the paradigm shifted from politics to crime, even within the core of the party of the highly institutionalized revolution.

At the heart of the contemporary crisis was the collapse of the tradition of economic nationalism now compounded by the never-ending current account deficit, that is to say, depression recycled to the debt crisis through the mechanisms of the economically active state. After the state mortgaged the people's future and the decision makers took public assets and/or played capitalist with a guarantee from the public finance system, people's belief that human intervention could make things better was profoundly weakened.

Direct solutions of human problems, not the pointless construction of ineffective bureaucracies, are urgently required. Above all, the political debate and concrete policies must address the rules of the game rather than pretend to extend pathetic handouts that somehow never get to those for whom they are intended.

For those who think that the shift to neoliberalism in the 1980s and 1990s represented a change in kind, rather than in degree, from the model of development adopted in the 1940s, it is useful to recall Cosío Villegas's lamentation at the time of the Chapultepec Conference of 1945: "No one understands the degree to which Latin America is tied to the engine of those United States which are resolved to intervene in a most dangerous game of universal power."[2] The implementation of NAFTA in 1994 was the final implementation of proposals that Will Clayton first made at the Havana Conference in 1947, which were only partially realized at the time.

This research confirms the scarcely original point that human action formed the world in which we live, although not in the way the decision makers imagined. By addressing the way the rules of the game affect outcomes, political discourse can rise out of the swamp of irrelevance that it has occupied for far too long. This means a return to a holistic analysis combining concrete political policies with real economic interests (as contrasted to playing mathematical games with doubtful numbers).[3]

Understanding the concrete social effects of central structures—laws, regulations, taxes, accounting rules, and technology—is required in order to address *los grandes problemas nacionales*.[4] If concrete analyses are located within a set of values committed to a reduction in poverty, inequality, and environmental destruction, then there may still be an alternative to the nihilism, social disintegration, and despair that surround us today. If the next attempt to improve life for most Mexicans is to succeed better than the last, reformers will have to see the target clearly before they can hit the mark.

Notes

1. The widespread and extremely hostile reaction to Frank Tannenbaum's suggestion, in 1950, in *Mexico: The Struggle for Peace and Bread* (New York: Alfred A. Knopf, 1950) that the country did not have enough resources to industrialize was another demonstration of the depth and breadth of the commitment to the project of industrial modernization.

2. Daniel Cosío Villegas, *Extremos de América*, 185–218.

3. Perhaps the most inadequate aspect of modern academic division of labor is the unwillingness of students of politics and economics to engage in each other's disciplines. Only by juxtaposing the use of political and economic power within specific contexts, and then evaluating policies, structures, and laws in terms of concrete social outcomes, can academic discourse become truly relevant. Notions of finding overriding theories that are useful at all times and places will have to be abandoned in favor of understanding the ways key decision makers have created the world in which we must live. Relevant research will—by necessity—have to cut across the boundaries of the traditional departments in academia.

4. In 1909, Andrés Molina Enríquez wrote *Los grandes problemas nacionales*, a book that was profoundly critical of the dictatorship of Porfirio Díaz and the high concentration of land ownership as represented by the *hacienda* system. It is commonly viewed as having been highly influential on the eve of the Mexican Revolution.

Bibliography

Archives and Manuscript Collections

Archivo General de la Nación, Mexico City
    Ramo de Presidentes
        Lázaro Cárdenas, 1934–1940
        Manuel Avila Camacho, 1940–1946
        Miguel Alemán Valdez, 1946–1952
        Adolfo Ruíz Cortines, 1952–1958
Biblioteca de Relaciones Exteriores, Mexico City
Biblioteca Miguel Lerdo de Tejada, Mexico City
Hemeroteca Nacional, Mexico City
Library of Congress, Washington, DC
    Josephus Daniels Papers
Public Records Office, London
    Records of the Foreign Office FO 371
Franklin D. Roosevelt Library, Hyde Park, New York
    Adolf A. Berle Papers
    Henry Morgenthau, Jr., Papers
    Franklin D. Roosevelt Papers
        President's Personal File
        President's Secretary's File
        Press Conferences
Harry S. Truman Library, Independence, Missouri
    Merwin L. Bohan Papers
    Will L. Clayton Papers
    Robert L. Gardner Papers
    Roman L. Horne Papers
    Edward G. Miller, Jr., Papers
    John W. Snyder Papers
    Harry S. Truman Papers
        President's Personal File
        President's Secretary's File
        Press Conferences
United States National Archives, Washington, DC
    General Records of the Department of State, Record Group 59
    General Records of the Department of the Treasury, Record Group 56

Photographic Records of the Office of War Information, Record Group 208
Records of the Office of Inter-American Affairs, Record Group 229
University of Delaware, Newark, Delaware
George S. Messersmith Papers

Primary Sources

Acheson, Dean. *Present at the Creation: My Years in the State Department*. New York: W. W. Norton, 1969.

Alamillo Flores, Luis. *Memorias: Luchas ignorados al lado de los grandes jefes de la revolución mexicana*. México: Editorial Extemporaneos, 1976.

Almazán, Juan Andreu. *Memorias de General Juan Andreu Almazán: Informes y documentos sobre la campaña política de 1940*. México: Editorial Quintana-Impresor, 1941.

Bassols, Narciso. *Obras*. México: Fondo de Cultura Económica, 1964.

Campa, Valentín. *50 años de oposición en México*. México: UNAM, 1979.

Cárdenas, Lázaro. *Ideario político*. México: Editorial Era, 1972.

Davies, Howell, ed. *The South American Handbook*. London: Trade and Travel Publications, 1940–50.

Gaxiola, Francisco Javier. *Memorias*. México: Editorial Porrúa, S.A., 1975.

Hull, Cordell. *The Memoirs of Cordell Hull*. 2 vols. New York: Macmillan, 1948.

Jones, Jesse H. *Fifty Billion Dollars: My Thirteen Years with the RFC*. New York: Macmillan, 1951.

Laborde, Hernán. "Cárdenas, reformador agrario." *Problemas Agrícolas é Industriales de México* 4 (January-March 1952): 57–86.

Pani, Alberto J. *Apuntes autobiograficos*. 2 vols. México: Libreria de Manuel Porrúa, 1950.

Portes Gil, Emilio. *Autobiografía de la revolución mexicana: Un tratado de interpretación historica*. México: Instituto Mexicano de Cultura, 1964.

Suárez, Eduardo. *Comentarios y recuerdos (1926–1946)*. México: Editorial Porrúa, 1977.

Villaseñor, Eduardo. *Memorias-testimonio*. México: Fondo de Cultura Económica, 1974.

Villaseñor, Victor Manuel. *Memorias de un hombre de la izquierda: De Avila Camacho a Echeverría*. 2 vols. México: Editorial Grijalbo, 1976.

Wallace, Henry A. *The Price of Vision: The Diary of Henry A. Wallace, 1942–1946*. Edited by John Morton Blum. Boston: Houghton Mifflin Company, 1973.

Other Documents

Armour Research Foundation. *Proceedings of the Mexican-American Conference on Industrial Research, September 30–October 6, 1945.* Chicago: Armour Research Foundation, 1945.

Banco de México. *Transacciones internacionales de México.* México: Banco de México, 1946.

Cámara Nacional de Industria de Transformación, *Actividades durante el año de 1945.* México: Cámara Nacional de Industria de Transformación, 1945.

Central Intelligence Agency. *Situation Report: Mexico.* January 24, 1951.

Colín, José R. *Materias primas y capital extranjero.* México: Cámara Nacional de Industria de Transformación, 1945.

———. *Requisitos fundamentales para la industrialización de México.* México: Cámara Nacional de Industria de Transformación, 1945.

Lavín, José Domingo. *La industria química nacional.* México: Cámara Nacional de Industria de Transformación, 1945.

———. *Materias primas y capital extranjero.* México: Cámara Nacional de Industria de Transformación, 1943.

———. *De la necesidad de formar la industria química mexicana.* México: Cámara Nacional de Industria de Transformación, 1943.

———. *Plan inmediato de industrialización en México.* México: Cámara Nacional de Industria de Transformación, 1945.

National Foreign Trade Council. *Proceedings of the National Foreign Trade Council.* New York: National Foreign Trade Council, various dates.

Quijano, José Manuel, ed. *La banca: Pasado y presente.* México: CIDE, 1983.

Secretaría de Gobernación. *Seis años de actividad nacional.* México: Secretaría de Gobernación, 1946.

Senate Committee on Banking and Currency. *Study of the Export-Import Bank and World Bank.* 83d Cong., 2d sess. Washington, DC: Government Printing Office, 1954.

Sindicato Nacional de Telefonistas, and other unions. *La justicia social en México.* México: n.p., 1945.

Special Committee on Post-War Economic Policy and Planning. *Economic Problems of the Transition Period.* 78th Cong., 2d Sess., and 79th Cong., 1st sess. Washington, DC: Government Printing Office, 1945.

United Nations. *Second World Food Survey.* Rome: Food and Agricultural Organization, 1952.

U.S. Board of Economic Warfare. "Confidential Report on the Mexican Economy." In Stetson Conn and Byron Fairchild, *The Framework of Hemispheric Defense: The United States Army in World War II.* Washington, DC: Government Printing Office, 1960.

Books

Acuña, Rodolfo. *Occupied America: A History of Chicanos.* New York: Harper and Row, 1988.

Aguilar Camín, Héctor. *Saldos de la revolución: Cultura y politica de México, 1910–1980.* México: Editorial Nuevo Imagen, 1982.

Aguilar Camín, Héctor, and Meyer, Lorenzo. *In the Shadow of the Mexican Revolution: Contemporary Mexican History, 1910–1989.* Austin: University of Texas Press, 1993.

Alcázar, Marco Antonio. *Las agrupaciones patronales en México.* México: El Colegio de México, 1970.

Alvarado, Arturo, ed. *Electoral Patterns and Perspectives in Mexico.* La Jolla: Center for U.S.-Mexican Studies, 1987.

Arias, Patricia, ed. *Guadalajara: La gran ciudad de la pequeña industria.* Zamora: El Colegio de Michoacán, 1985.

Ariza, Luis. *Historia del movimiento obrero mexicano.* México: Ediciones del autor, 1965.

Arizpe, Lourdes. *Migración, etnicismo y cambio económico: Un estudio sobre migrantes campesinos a la ciudad de México.* México: El Colegio de México, 1978.

———. *La mujer en el desarrollo de México y de América Latina.* México: UNAM, 1989.

Aurrecoechea, Juan Manuel, and Bartra, Armando. *Puros Cuentos: La historieta en México, 1874–1934.* México: Grijalbo, 1988.

Ayala Blanco, Jorge. *La condición del cine mexicana, 1973–1985.* México: Editorial Posada, 1986.

Ballesteros, José Ramón. *Origen y evolución del charro mexicano.* México: Librería de Manuel Porrúa, 1972.

Bartra, Armando. *Los herederos de Zapata: Movimientos campesinos postrevolucionarios en México.* México: Editorial Era, 1985.

Bartra, Roger, et al. *La izquierda en los cuarenta.* México: Centro de Estudios del Movimiento Obrero y Socialista, 1985.

———. *The Cage of Melancholy: Identity and Metamorphosis in the Mexican Character.* Translated by Christopher J. Hall. New Brunswick: Rutgers University Press, 1992.

Basurto, Jorge. *La clase obrera en la historia de México: Del avilacamachismo al alemanismo, 1940–1952.* México: Siglo Veintiuno, 1984.

Becker, Marjorie. *Setting the Virgin on Fire: Lázaro Cárdenas, Michoacán Campesinos, and the Redemption of the Mexican Revolution.* Berkeley: University of California Press, 1995.

Beezley, William H. *Judas at the Jockey Club and Other Episodes of Porfirian Mexico.* Lincoln: University of Nebraska Press, 1987.

———, et al., eds. *Rituals of Rule, Rituals of Resistance: Public Celebrations and Popular Culture in Mexico.* Wilmington: Scholarly Resources, 1994.

Benjamin, Thomas. *Rich Land, Poor People: Politics and Society in Modern Chiapas.* Albuquerque: University of New Mexico Press, 1989.

Bennett, Douglas C., and Sharpe, Kenneth. *Transnational Corporations vs. the State: The Political Economy of the Mexican Auto Industry.* Princeton: Princeton University Press, 1985.

Bethell, Leslie, and Roxborough, Ian, eds. *Latin America between the Second World War and the Cold War.* Cambridge: Cambridge University Press, 1992.

Bonet, Eduardo, et al. *Bulls and Bullfighting: History, Techniques, Spectacle.* Translated by Rafael Millan. New York: Crown Publishers, 1970.

Bortz, Jeffrey. *El Salario en México.* México: Ediciones "El Caballito," 1988.

Brannon, Jeffrey, and Blankoff, Eric N. *Agrarian Reform and Public Enterprise in Mexico: The Political Economy of Yucatán's Henequen Industry.* Tuscaloosa: University of Alabama Press, 1987.

Brody, Robert, and Rossman, Charles, eds. *Carlos Fuentes: A Critical View.* Austin: University of Texas Press, 1982.

Camp, Roderic Ai. *Mexican Political Biographies, 1935–1975.* Tucson: University of Arizona Press, 1976.

———. *Polling for Democrary: Public Opinion and Political Liberalization in Mexico.* Wilmington: Scholarly Resources, 1996.

Carr, Barry. *Marxism and Communism in Twentieth-Century Mexico.* Lincoln: University of Nebraska Press, 1992.

———. *El movimiento obrero y la política en México, 1910–1920.* México: Editorial Era, 1981.

Ceceña, José Luis. *México en la orbita imperial.* México: "El Caballito," 1970.

Chassen de López, Francie R. *Lombardo Toledano y el movimiento obrero mexicano (1917–1940).* México: Extemporaneos, 1977.

Cockcroft, James. *Mexico: Class Formation, Capital Accumulation, and the State.* New York: Monthly Review Press, 1983.

Collier, George, and Quaratiello, Elizabeth L. *Basta! Land and the Zapatista Revolution in Chiapas.* San Francisco: Food First Books, 1994.

Contreras, Ariel José. *México 1940: Industrialización y crisis política: Estado y sociedad civil en las elecciones presidenciales.* México: Siglo Veintiuno Editores, 1977.

Córdova, Arnaldo. *La formación del poder político en México.* México: Ediciones Era, 1972.

———. *La ideología de la revolución mexicana: Formación del nuevo régimen.* México: Ediciones Era, 1973.

Cosío Villegas, Daniel. *Extremos de América.* México: Fondo de Cultura Económica, 1949.

————. *Historia moderna de México: El porfiriato, la vida política interior, parte segunda.* México: Editorial Hermes, 1972.

Cross, Henry E., and Sandos, Jorge A. *Across the Border: Rural Developments in Mexico and Recent Migration to the United States.* Berkeley: Institute of Government Studies, University of California, 1981.

Cull, Nicholas John. *Selling War: The British Propaganda Campaign against American "Neutrality" in World War II.* Oxford: Oxford University Press, 1995.

de la Rosa, Martín, and Reilly, Charles A. *Religión y política en México.* México: Siglo Veintiuno, 1985.

Delpar, Helen. *The Enormous Vogue of Things Mexican: Cultural Relations between the United States and Mexico, 1920–1935.* Tuscaloosa: University of Alabama Press, 1992.

de Mora, Juan Miguel. *Panorama del teatro en México.* México: Editorial Latino América, 1970.

de Orellana, Margarita. *La mirada circular: El cine norteamericano de la revolución mexicana, 1911–1917.* México: Cuadernos de Joaquín Mortiz, 1991.

Domínguez, Jorge I., ed. *Race and Ethnicity in Latin America.* New York: Garland Publishing, 1994.

Dorfman, A., and Mattelart, A. *How to Read Donald Duck: Imperialist Ideology in the Disney Comics.* New York: International, 1975.

Dulles, John W. F. *Yesterday in Mexico: A Chronicle of the Revolution, 1919–1936.* Austin: University of Texas Press, 1967.

Durand Ponte, Victor M. *Las derrotas obreras, 1946–52.* México: UNAM, 1984.

Durán Ochoa, Julio. *México: 50 años de revolución: La vida social.* México: Fondo de Cultura Económico, 1961.

Eckstein, Solomon. *El ejido colectivo en México.* México: Fondo de Cultura Económica, 1966.

————. *El marco macro-económico del problema agrario en México.* México: Centro de Investigaciones Agrarias, 1968.

Fernández Christlieb, Fatima. *Los medios de defusión masiva en México.* México: Juan Pablos Editor, 1982.

Fossedal, Gregory A. *Our Finest Hour: Will Clayton, the Marshall Plan, and the Triumph of Democracy.* Stanford: Hoover Institution Press, 1993.

Foweraker, Joe. *Popular Mobilization in Mexico: The Teachers' Movement, 1977–87.* Cambridge: Cambridge University Press, 1993.

————, and Craig, Ann L. *Popular Movements and Political Change in Mexico.* Boulder: Westview Press, 1990.

Franco, Jean. *The Modern Culture of Latin America: Society and the Artist.* Harmondsworth: Penguin Books, 1970.

————. *Plotting Women: Gender and Representation in Mexico.* New York: Columbia University Press, 1989.

Friedrich, Paul. *The Princes of Naranja: An Essay in Anthropological Method*. Princeton: Princeton University Press, 1986.

García, Gustavo. *El cine mundo mexicano*. México: Martin Casillas Editorial, 1982.

García Canclini, Néstor, et al. *La ciudad de los viajeros, travesías e imaginarios urbanos: México, 1940–2000*. México: Universidad Autónoma Metropolitana, Iztapalapa, 1996.

Garrido, Luis Javier. *El partido de la revolución institucionalizada: La formación del nuevo estado en México (1928–1945)*. México: Siglo Veintiuno Editores, 1982.

Gledhill, John. *Casi Nada: A Study of Agrarian Reform in the Homeland of Cardenismo*. Albany: State University of New York, 1991.

Gómez Maganda, Alejandro. *Acapulco en mi vida y en el tiempo*. México: Libro Mex. Editores, 1960.

González, Luis. *Pueblo en vilo: Microhistoria de San José de Gracia*. México: El Colegio de México, 1968.

González Navarro, Moisés. *Raza y tierra: La guerra de castas y el henequén*. México: El Colegio de México, 1970.

Graham, Richard, ed. *The Idea of Race in Latin America, 1870–1940*. Austin: University of Texas Press, 1990.

Green, David. *The Containment of Latin America: A History of the Myths and Realities of the Good Neighbor Policy*. Chicago: Quadrangle Books, 1971.

Greenberg, James B. *Blood Ties: Life and Violence in Rural Mexico*. Tucson: University of Arizona Press, 1989.

Haber, Stephen H. *Industry and Underdevelopment: The Industrialization of Mexico, 1890–1940*. Stanford: Stanford University Press, 1989.

Halberstam, David. *The Fifties*. New York: Ballantine Books, 1994.

Hamilton, Nora. *The Limits of State Autonomy: Post-Revolutionary Mexico*. Princeton: Princeton University Press, 1982.

Hefley, James C. *Aarón Sáenz: Mexico's Revolutionary Capitalist*. Waco: World Books, 1970.

Hernández Chavez, Alicia. *La mecánica Cardenista*. México: El Colegio de México, 1979.

Hernández Rodríguez, Rogelio. *La formación del político mexicano: El caso de Carlos A. Madrazo*. México: El Colegio de México, 1991.

Hewitt de Alcántara, Cynthia. *La modernización de la agricultura mexicana: 1940–1970*. México: Siglo Veintiuno, 1978.

———. *Modernizing Mexican Agriculture: Socioeconomic Implications of Technological Change, 1940–1970*. Geneva: United Nations Research Institute for Social Development, 1976.

———. *The Social and Economic Implications of Large-Scale Introduction of New Varieties of Food Grains, Country Report: Mexico*. Geneva: United Nations Research Institute for Social Development, November 1974.

Holland, William. *Medicina Maya en los altos de Chiapas: El estudio del cambio sociocultural*. Translated by Daniel Cazés. México: Instituto Nacional Indigenista, 1989.

Huer, Federico. *La industrial cinematográfica mexicana*. México: Impreso del autor, 1964.

Jacobs, Ian. *Ranchero Revolt: The Mexican Revolution in Guerrero*. Austin: University of Texas Press, 1982.

Joseph, Gilbert M. *Rediscovering the Past of Mexico's Periphery*. Tuscaloosa: University of Alabama Press, 1986.

————, and Nugent, Daniel. *Everyday Forms of State Formation: Revolution and the Negotiation of Rule in Modern Mexico*. Durham: Duke University Press, 1994.

Karetnikova, Inga, with Steinmetz, Leon. *Mexico According to Eisenstein*. Albuquerque: University of New Mexico Press, 1991.

Katz, Friedrich. *The Secret War in Mexico: Europe, the United States, and the Mexican Revolution*. Chicago: University of Chicago Press, 1981.

Kaufman, Burton I. *Trade and Aid: Eisenhower's Foreign Economic Policy*. Baltimore: Johns Hopkins University Press, 1982.

Keen, Benjamin. *The Aztec Image in Western Thought*. New Brunswick: Rutgers University Press, 1971.

Knight, Alan. *The Mexican Revolution: Counter-revolution and Reconstruction*. Vol. 2. Lincoln: University of Nebraska Press, 1986.

Krauze, Enrique. *Daniel Cosío Villegas: Una biografía intelectual*. México: Joaquín Mortiz, 1980.

————. *La Presidencia imperial: Ascensoi y caída del sistema político mexicano (1940–1996)*. México: Tusquets Editores México, 1997.

La Botz, Dan. *The Crisis of Mexican Labor*. New York: Praeger, 1988.

Ladd, Doris M. *The Mexican Nobility at Independence, 1780–1826*. Austin: University of Texas Press, 1976.

Langford, Walter M. *The Mexican Novel Comes of Age*. Notre Dame: University of Notre Dame Press, 1971.

León, Samuel, and Marván, Ignacio. *La clase obrera en la historia de México*. Vol. 10, *En el Cardenismo (1934–1940)*. México: Siglo Veintiuno Editores, 1985.

Lewis, Oscar. *Life in a Mexican Village: Tepoztlán Restudied*. Urbana: University of Illinois Press, 1963.

Loaeza, Soledad. *Clases media y política en México*. México: El Colegio de México, 1988.

Logan, Kathleen. *Haciendo Pueblo: The Development of a Guadalajaran Suburb*. Tuscaloosa: University of Alabama Press, 1984.

Lorey, David E. *The University System and Economic Development in Mexico since 1910*. Stanford: Stanford University Press, 1993.

Loyo Brambila, Aurora. *El movimiento magisterial de 1958 en México*. México: Ediciones Era, 1979.

Loyola, Rafael, ed. *Entre la guerra y la estabilidad política: El México de los 40*. México: Grijalbo, 1986.

Loyola Díaz, Rafael. *El ocaso del radicalismo revolucionario, ferro-carrileros y petroleros: 1938–1947.* México: Instituto de Investigaciones Sociales, UNAM, 1991.

Mabry, Donald J. *Mexico's Acción Nacional: A Catholic Alternative to Revolution.* Syracuse: Syracuse University Press, 1973.

Macías, Anna. *Against All Odds: The Feminist Movement in Mexico to 1940.* Westport: Greenwood Press, 1982.

MacLachlan, Colin M., and Beezley, William H. *El Gran Pueblo: A History of Greater Mexico.* Englewood Cliffs: Prentice Hall, 1994.

Magaña, Esquivel. *Medio siglo de teatro mexicano, 1900–1961.* México: Instituto Nacional de Bellas Artes, 1964.

Martín-Barbero, Jesús. *De los medios a los mediaciones: Comunicación, cultura, y hegemonía,* México: Ediciones G. Gilli, 1987.

Martínez Assad, Carlos. *La sucessión presidencial en México: Coyuntura electoral y cambio político.* México: Editorial Nueva Imagen, 1981.

Mass, Bonnie. *Population Target: The Political Economy of Population Control in Latin America.* Toronto: Women's Press, 1979.

Mattelart, Armand. *Multinacionales y sistemas de comunicación: Los aparatos ideólogicos del imperialismo.* México: Siglo Veintiuno, 1977.

McCartney, Laton. *Friends in High Places, the Bechtel Story: The Most Secret Corporation and How It Engineered the World.* New York: Simon and Schuster, 1988.

Medin, Tzvi. *El sexeño alemanista: Ideología y praxis política de Miguel Alemán.* México: Ediciones Era, 1990.

Medina, Luis. *Historia de la revolución mexicana, periodo 1940–1952: Civilismo y modernización del autoritarismo.* México: El Colegio de México, 1979.

Medina, Luis, and Torres, Blanca. *Historia de la revolución mexicana, periodo 1940–1952: Del cardenismo al avilacamachismo.* México: El Colegio de México, 1978.

Mejía Prieto, Jorge. *Historia de la radio y la TV en México.* México: Editores Asociados, 1972.

Meyer, Lorenzo. *México y Estados Unidos en el conflicto petrolero (1917–1942).* México: El Colegio de México, 1972.

———. *Su Majestad Británica contra la revolución mexicana, 1900–1950: El fin de un imperio informal.* México: El Colegio de México, 1991.

Michaels, Albert A. *The Mexican Election of 1940.* Buffalo: Council of International Studies, 1971.

Middlebrook, Kevin J. *The Paradox of Revolution: Labor, the State, and Authoritarianism in Mexico.* Baltimore: Johns Hopkins University Press, 1995.

Molina Enríquez, Andrés. *Los grandes problemas nacionales.* México: Imprenta de A. Carranza e Hijos, 1909.

Monsiváis, Carlos. *Amor perdido.* México: Ediciones Era, 1977.

Mora, Carl J. *Mexican Cinema: Reflections of a Society, 1896–1980.* Berkeley: University of California Press, 1982.

Morris, Stephen D. *Corruption and Politics in Contemporary Mexico*. Tuscaloosa: University of Alabama Press, 1991.

Mosk, Sanford A. *Industrial Revolution in Mexico*. Berkeley: University of California Press, 1954.

Múgica Martínez, Jesús. *La confederación revolucionaria Michoacana del Trabajo*. México: Eddisa, 1982.

Murray, William J. *Football: A History of the World Game*. Hants, England: Scholarly Press, 1994.

Navarette, Ifigenia M. de. *La distribución del ingreso y el desarrollo económico de México*. México: Instituto de Investigaciones Económicas, UNAM, 1960.

Negrete, María Eugenia. *Crecimiento y distribución de la población de la Ciudad de México*. México: El Colegio de México, 1968.

Negrete, Marta Elena. *Relaciones entre la Iglesia y el Estado en México, 1929–1940*. México: El Colegio de México, 1988.

Niblo, Stephen R. *War, Diplomacy, and Development: The United States and Mexico, 1938–1954*. Wilmington: Scholarly Resources, 1995.

Novo, Salvador. *Nueva grandeza mexicana: Ensayo sobre la ciudad de México*. México: Populibros, 1965.

―――. *La vida en México en el periodo de Miguel Alemán*. México: Empresas Editoriales, 1967.

Nuncio, Abraham. *El Grupo Monterrey*. México: Editorial Nueva Imagen, 1982.

Oles, James. *South of the Border: Mexico in the American Imagination*. Washington and London: Smithsonian Institution Press, 1993.

Ortíz Garza, José Luis. *México en guerra: La historia secreta de los negocios entre empresarios mexicanos de comunicación, los Nazis y E.U.A.* México: Editorial Planeta, 1989.

Pacheco, José Emilio. *Las batallas en el desierto*. México: Ediciones Era, 1981.

Pansters, Wil. *Politics and Power in Puebla: The Political History of a Mexican State, 1937–1987*. Amsterdam: Centre for Latin American Research and Documentation, 1990.

―――, and Ouweneel, Arij. *Region, State, and Capitalism in Mexico: Nineteenth and Twentieth Centuries*. Amsterdam: Centre for Latin American Research and Documentation, 1989.

Perry, Laurens B. *Juárez and Díaz: Machine Politics in Mexico*. De Kalb: Northern Illinois University Press, 1978.

Quijano, José Manuel, ed. *La banca: Pasado y presente*. México: CIDE, 1983.

Rabe, Stephen G. *Eisenhower and Latin America: The Foreign Policy of Anticommunism*. Chapel Hill: University of North Carolina Press, 1988.

Ramírez Rancaño, Mario. *El sistema de haciendas en Tlaxcala*. México: Consejo Nacional para la Cultura y las Atres, 1990.

Ramos, Samuel. *El perfíl de hombre y cultura en México*. México: Espasa-Calpe, 1972.

Rangel Contla, José Calixto. *La pequeña burguesía en la sociedad mexicana, 1895–1960.* México: Universidad Nacional Autónoma de México, 1972.

Redfield, Robert. *Tepotzlán—A Mexican Village.* Chicago: University of Chicago Press, 1930.

Reisler, Mark. *By the Sweat of Their Brow: Mexican Immigration to the United States, 1900–1940.* Westport: Greenwood Press, 1976.

Reygadas, Luis. *Proceso de trabajo y acción obrera: Historia sindical de los mineros de nueva rosita, 1929–1979.* México: INAH, 1988.

Reynolds, Clark W. *The Mexican Economy: Twentieth-Century Structure and Growth.* New Haven: Yale University Press, 1970.

Rincón Gallardo, Carlos, and de Terreros, Romero. *El libro del charro mexicano.* México: Editorial Porrúa, 1977.

Rodríguez, Antonio. *A History of Mexican Mural Painting.* Translated by Marina Corby. New York: G. P. Putnam's Sons, 1969.

Rodríguez O., Jaime E., ed. *The Revolutionary Process in Mexico: Essays on Political and Social Change, 1880–1940.* Los Angeles: UCLA Latin American Center Publications, and Irvine: Mexico/Chicano Program, 1990.

Ronfeldt, David. *Atencingo: The Politics of Agrarian Struggle in a Mexican Ejido.* Stanford: Stanford University Press, 1973.

———. *The Modern Mexican Military: A Reassessment.* La Jolla: Center for U.S.-Mexican Studies, 1984.

Rowe, William, and Schelling, Vivian. *Memory and Modernity: Popular Culture in Latin America.* London: Verso, 1991.

Sanderson, Stephen. *Agrarian Populism and the Mexican State.* Berkeley: University of California Press, 1981.

———. *The Transformation of Mexican Agriculture: International Structures and the Politics of Rural Development.* Princeton: Princeton University Press, 1986.

Sanderson, Susan R. Walsh. *Land Reform in Mexico, 1910–1980.* Orlando: Academic Press, 1984.

Saragoza, Alexander M. *The Monterrey Elite and the Mexican State, 1880–1940.* Austin: University of Texas Press, 1988.

Schryer, Frans J. *Ethnicity and Class Conflict in Rural Mexico.* Princeton: Princeton University Press, 1990.

Soto, Shirlene. *Emergence of the Modern Mexican Woman: Her Participation in Revolution and Struggle for Modernity, 1910–1940.* Denver: Arden Press, 1990.

Stavenhagen, Rodolfo, ed. *Estructura agraria y desarrollo agrícola en México.* México: Fondo de Cultura Económica, 1974.

Stepan, Nancy Leys. *The Hour of Eugenics: Race, Gender and Nation in Latin America.* Ithaca: Cornell University Press, 1991.

———. *The Idea of Race in Science: Great Britain, 1800–1960.* London: Macmillan, 1982.

Story, Dale. *Industry, the State, and Public Policy in Mexico.* Austin: University of Texas Press, 1986.

Taracena, Alfonso. *La vida en México bajo Avila Camacho*. 2 vols. México: Editorial Jus, 1977.

Taylor, A. J. P. *Beaverbrook*. Middlesex, England: Penguin Books, 1972.

Taylor, P. M. *The Projection of Britain: British Overseas Publicity and Propaganda, 1919–1939*. Cambridge: Cambridge University Press, 1981.

Tomlinson, John. *Cultural Imperialism: A Critical Introduction*. Baltimore: Johns Hopkins University Press, 1991.

Torres Bodet, Jaime, et al. *México: 50 años de revolución: La cultura*. México: Fondo de Cultura Económica, 1962.

Torres Ramírez, Blanca. *Historia de la revolución mexicana, periodo 1940–1952: Hacia la utopía industrial*. México: El Colegio de México, 1984.

———. *Historia de la revolución mexicana, periodo 1940–1952: México en la Segunda Guerra Mundial*. México: El Colegio de México, 1977.

Tunstall, Jeremy. *The Media Are American: Anglo-American Media in the World*. London: Constable, 1977.

Tutino, John. *From Insurrection to Revolution in Mexico: Social Bases of Agrarian Violence, 1750–1940*. Princeton: Princeton University Press, 1986.

Unger, Roni. *Poesía en Voz Alta in the Theater of Mexico*. Columbia: University of Missouri Press, 1981.

Vaughan, Mary Kay. *Cultural Politics in Revolution: Teachers, Peasants, and Schools in Mexico, 1930–1940*. Tucson: University of Arizona Press, 1997.

Warman, Arturo . . . *y venimos a contradecir: Los campesinos de Morelos y el estado nacional*. México: Ediciones de la Casa Chata, 1978.

Wasserstrom, Robert. *Class and Society in Central Chiapas*. Berkeley: University of California Press, 1983.

Wilkie, James W. *The Mexican Revolution: Federal Expenditure and Social Change since 1910*. Berkeley: University of California Press, 1970.

———, and Wilkie, Edna Monzón de. *México visto en el siglo XX: Entrevistas de historia oral*. México: Instituto de Investigaciones Económicas, 1969.

Wilkie, Richard W. *Latin American Population and Urbanization Analysis: Maps and Statistics, 1950–1982*. Los Angeles: UCLA Latin American Center, 1984.

Wolfe, Bertram D. *The Fabulous Life of Diego Rivera*. New York: Stein and Day, 1969.

Wright, Harry K. *Foreign Enterprise in Mexico: Laws and Politics*. Chapel Hill: University of North Carolina Press, 1971.

Yañez Reyes, Sergio L. *Genesis de la burocracia sindical cetemista*. México: El Caballito, 1984.

Zogbaum, Heidi. *B. Traven: A Vision of Mexico*. Wilmington: Scholarly Resources, 1992.

Zorilla, Luis G. *Historia de las relaciones entre México y los Estados Unidos de América.* 2 vols. México: Editorial Porrúa, 1963.

Articles, Chapters, and Dissertations

Adler, Ruth. "Experiments in Worker Participation in the Administration of Industry in Mexico during the Presidency of Lázaro Cárdenas." Ph.D. diss., La Trobe University, 1991.

Baquiero Fóster, Gerónimo. "La música." In *México: 50 años de revolución: La cultura,* edited by Jaime Torres Bodet et al. México, 1962.

Bartra, Armando. "The Seduction of the Innocents: The First Tumultuous Moments of Mass Literacy in Postrevolutionary Mexico." In *Everyday Forms of State Formation: Revolution and the Negotiation of Rule in Modern Mexico,* edited by Gilbert M. Joseph and Daniel Nugent. Durham, 1994.

Berger, Mark T. "Under North American Eyes: Liberal Historiography and the Containment of Central America, 1898–1990." Ph.D. diss., University of New South Wales, 1992.

Binford, Leigh. "Peasants and Petty Capitalists in Southern Oaxaca Sugar Cane Processing, 1930–1980." *Journal of Latin American Studies* 23, no. 2 (May 1991): 33–55.

Bortz, Jeffrey. "Wages and Economic Crisis in Mexico." In *The Mexican Left: The Popular Movements and the Politics of Austerity,* edited by Barry Carr and Anzaldúa Montoya. La Jolla, 1986.

Brody, David. "The New Deal and World War II." In *The New Deal: The National Level,* edited by John Braeman et al. Columbus, 1975.

Cabral, Regis. "The Interaction of Science and Diplomacy: The United States, Latin America, and Nuclear Energy, 1945–1955." Ph. D. diss., University of Chicago, 1986.

———. "The Mexican Reactions to the Hiroshima and Nagasaki Tragedies of 1945." *Quipu* 4, no. 1 (January–April 1987): 81–118.

Cano, Celerino. "Análisis de la acción educativa." In *México: 50 años de revolución: La cultura,* edited by Jaime Torres Bodet et al. México, 1962.

Carr, Barry. "Crisis in Mexican Communism: The Extraordinary Congress of the Mexican Communist Party." *Science and Society* 50, no. 4 (Winter 1986): 391–414, and 51, no. 1 (Spring 1987): 43–67.

———. "Mexican Communism, 1968–1981: Eurocommunism in the Americas?" *Journal of Latin American Studies,* no. 17 (1985): 271–319.

Centeno, Miguel Angel, and Maxfield, Sylvia. "The Marriage of Finance and Order in the Mexican Political Elite." *Journal of Latin American Studies* 24, no. 1 (October 1991): 57–85.

Clash, Thomas Wood. "United States-Mexican Relations, 1940–1946: A Study of U.S. Interests and Politics." Ph.D. diss., State University of New York at Buffalo, 1972.

Cole, Richard Ray. "The Mass Media of Mexico: Ownership and Control." Ph.D. diss., University of Minnesota, 1972.

Collier, George A. "Peasant Politics and the Mexican State: Indigenous Compliance in Highland Chiapas." In *Race and Ethnicity in Latin America*, edited by Jorge I. Domínguez. New York, 1994.

Cosío Villegas, Daniel. "La crisis de México." As reproduced in *American Extremes*. Austin, 1964.

Cotter, Joseph. "The Origins of the Green Revolution in Mexico." In *Latin America in the 1940s: War and Postwar Transitions*, edited by David Rock. Berkeley, 1994.

Davis, David E. "Failed Democratic Reform in Contemporary Mexico: From Social Movements to the State and Back Again." *Journal of Latin American Studies* 26, no. 2 (May 1994): 375–408.

Díaz-Guerrero, Rogelio. "Contemporary Psychology in Mexico." *American Review of Psychology* 35 (1980): 83–112.

Durán Ochoa, Julio. "La explosión demográfica." In *México: 50 años de revolución: La vida social*, edited by Julio Durán Ochoa. México, 1961.

Elizondo, Carlos. "In Search of Revenue: Tax Reform in Mexico under the Administrations of Echeverría and Salinas." *Journal of Latin American Studies* 26, no. 1 (February 1994): 159–90.

Elizondo, Juan Manuel. "El periodo 1942–1946." *Memorias de CEMOS* 1, no. 8 (January–February 1985): 189–90.

Erb, Claude Curtis. "Nelson Rockefeller and United States-Latin American Relations, 1940–1945." Ph.D. diss., Clark University, 1982.

Espinoza Toledo, Ricardo. "La consolidación del sindicalismo institucional en México, 1941–1952." *CEMOS Memorias* 2, no. 11 (May–June 1988): 301–12.

Fein, Seth. "Hollywood and United States-Mexican Relations in the Golden Age of Mexican Cinema." Ph.D. diss., University of Texas, 1996.

———. "Hollywood, U.S. Relations and the Devolution of the 'Golden Age' of Mexican Cinema." *Film-Historia* 4, no. 2 (1994): 103–35.

Fernández Christlieb, Fatima. "La industria de radio y televisión." In *El estado y la televisión*, edited by Gustavo Esteva. México, 1976.

Fitzgerald, E. V. K. "The State and Capital Accumulation in Mexico." *Journal of Latin American Studies* 19, no. 2 (November 1978): 263–82.

Gates, Marilyn. "Codifying Marginality: The Evolution of Mexican Agrarian Policy and Its Impact on the Peasantry." *Journal of Latin American Studies*, no. 20 (1987): 277–311.

Giménez Cacho, Luis Emilio. "La constitución del sindicato industrial de trabajadores mineros." *Memorias de CEMOS* 1, no. 8 (January–February 1985): 187–88.

González Cosío, Arturo. "Clases y estratos sociales." In *México: 50 años de revolución: La vida social*, edited by Julio Durán Ochoa et al. México, 1961.

Kandt, Vera B. "Fiesta en Cuetzalan." *Artes de México* 19, no. 155 (1972): 49–74.

Knight, Alan. "*Cardenismo*: Juggernaut or Jalopy?" *Journal of Latin American Studies* 26, no. 1 (February 1994): 73–108.

———. "Popular Culture and the Revolutionary State in Mexico, 1910–1940." *Hispanic American Historical Review* 74, no. 3 (August 1994): 393–444.

———. "Racism, Revolution, and *Indigenismo*." In *The Idea of Race in Latin America, 1870–1940*, edited by Richard Graham, Austin, 1990.

La France, David. "Labor, the State, and Professional Baseball in Mexico in the 1980s." *Journal of Sport History* 22, no. 2 (Summer 1995): 111–34.

Lieuwen, Edwin. "Depoliticization of the Mexican Revolutionary Army, 1915–1940." In *The Modern Mexican Military: A Reassessment*, edited by David Ronfeldt. La Jolla, 1984.

Martínez, José Luis. "La literatura." In *México: 50 años de revolución, La cultura*, edited by Jaime Torres Bodet et al. México, 1962.

Martínez Assad, Carlos. "El cine como lo vi y como me lo contaron." In *Entre la guerra y la estabilidad política: El México de los 40*, edited by Rafael Loyola. México, 1986.

Meyer, Lorenzo. "La resistencia al capital privado extranjero: El caso del petroleo, 1938–1950." In *Las empresas transnacionales en México*, edited by Bernado Sepulveda et al. México, 1974.

Middlebrook, Kevin J. "The Sounds of Silence: Organised Labour's Response to Economic Crisis in Mexico." *Journal of Latin American Studies* 21, no. 2 (1987): 195–220.

Miller, Michael Nelson. "Culture and State in Mexico in the Sexennium of Manuel Avila Camacho." Ph.D. diss., Texas A&M University, 1992.

Mizrahi, Yemile. "Rebels without a Cause? The Politics of Entrepreneurs in Chihuahua." *Journal of Latin American Studies* 26, no. 1 (February 1994): 137–58.

Monsiváis, Carlos. "Notas sobre la cultura popular en México." *Latin American Perspectives* 5 (Winter 1978): 98–112.

———. "Sociedad y cultura." In *Entre la guerra y la estabilidad política: El México de los 40*, edited by Rafael Loyola. México, 1986.

Muñoz Ledo, Porfirio. "La educación superior." In *México: 50 años de revolución: La cultura*, edited by Jaime Torres Bodet et al. México, 1962.

Niblo, Stephen R. "British Propaganda in Mexico during the Second World War: The Development of Cultural Imperialism." *Latin American Perspectives* 10, no. 4 (Fall 1983): 114–26.

———. "Decoding Mexican Politics: The Resignation of Francisco Javier Gaxiola." *Anales* 2, no. 1 (1993): 23–39.

———. "The Experience of an Economically Active State: Mexico, from Economic Radicalism to Neo-liberalism." In *The State in Transition*, edited by Joe Camilleri et al. London, 1995.

———. "Mexico: Development without the People." *Journal of the West* 27, no. 4 (October 1988): 50–63.

Nodín Valdés, Dennis. "Mexican Revolutionary Nationalism and Repatriation during the Great Depression." *Mexican Studies/ Estudios Mexicanos* 4, no. 1 (Winter 1988): 1–24.

Olmedo, Luna. "Algunos aspectos de la balanza de pagos." *El Trimestre Económico* 9, no. 3 (July–September 1942): 14–52.

Peláez, Gerardo. "Un año decisivo." *Boletín de CEMOS* 1, no. 8 (January–February 1985): 177–78.

Rubenstein, Anne. "Mexico 'sin vicios': Conservatives, Comic Books, Censorship, and the Mexican State, 1934–1976." Ph.D. diss., Rutgers University, 1994.

Rubin, Jeffrey W. "COCEI in Juchitán: Grassroots Radicalism and Regional History." *Journal of Latin American Studies* 26, no. 1 (February 1994): 109–36.

Ruiz, Vicki L. " 'Star Struck': Acculturation, Adolescence, and the Mexican-American Woman." In *Between Two Worlds: Mexican Immigrants in the United States*, edited by David G. Gutiérrez. Berkeley, 1996.

Rus, Jan. "The 'Comunidad Revolucionaria Instituciónal': The Subversion of Native Government in Highland Chiapas, 1936–1968." In *Everyday Forms of State Formation: Revolution and the Negotiation of Rule in Modern Mexico*, edited by Gilbert M. Joseph and Daniel Nugent. Durham, 1994.

Schryer, Frans J. "Peasants and the Law: A History of Land Tenure and Conflict in the Huasteca." *Journal of Latin American Studies*, no. 18 (1985): 283–311.

Schuller, Friedrich Engelbert. "Cardenismo Revisited: The International Dimensions of the Post-Reform Cárdenas Era, 1937–1940." Ph.D. diss., University of Chicago, 1990.

Sinclair, John Graham. "Mass Media and Dependency: The Case of Television Advertising in Mexico." Ph.D. diss., La Trobe University, 1982.

———. "Neither West nor Third World: The Mexican Television Industry within the NWICO Debate." *Media, Culture and Society*, no. 12 (1990): 343–60.

Torres Bodet, Jaime. "Perspectivas de la educación." In *México: 50 años de revolución: La cultura*, edited by Jaime Torres Bodet et al. México, 1962.

Valdes, Miguel Alemán. *Miguel Alemán contesta*. Austin: Institute of Latin American Studies, University of Texas, 1975.

Vaughan, Mary Kay. "The Construction of the Patriotic Festival." In *Rituals of Rule, Rituals of Resistance: Public Celebrations and Popular Culture in Mexico,* edited by William H. Beezley et al. Wilmington, 1994.

Watanabe, Chizuko. "The Japanese Immigrant Community in Mexico: Its History and Present." Master's thesis, California State University at Los Angeles, 1983.

Newspapers and Periodicals

Atisbos (Mexico City), 1952
Bohemia (Havana), 1953
Diario de Yucatán (Merida), 1949
Diario Oficial (Mexico City), 1947–1948
Excélsior (Mexico City), 1940–1953
Fortune (New York City), 1947–1950
Hoy (Mexico City), 1939–1952
Jornadas Industriales (Mexico City), 1954
Journal of Commerce (New York City), 1947–1954
Latin American Weekly Report, August 3, 1995, WR-95-29
Mañana (Mexico City), 1944
El Mercado de Valores (Mexico City), 1952
Mexican-American Review (Mexico City), 1941
Mexico City Post (Mexico City), 1943
El Nacional (Mexico City), 1941–1947
Newsweek (New York City), 1951
New York Times (New York City), 1946
El Norte (Monterrey), 1944
Novedades (Mexico City), 1943–1947
El Popular (Mexico City), 1940–1953
El Porvenir (Monterrey), 1944
La Prensa (Mexico City), 1940–1947
Prensa Grafica (Mexico City), 1949
Presente (Mexico City), 1948
La República (Mexico City), 1942
Saturday Evening Post (New York City), 1944
Sunday Times (London), 1975
Tiempo (Mexico City), 1947
Time (New York City), 1946
Ultimas Noticias (Mexico City), 1946–1947
El Universal (Mexico City), 1939–1952
La Voz de México (Mexico City), 1940
Voz Patronal (Mexico City), 1946
Washington Post (Washington, DC), 1946

Index

Acapulco, 29; corruption in, 274–76
Acción Civica, 84
Acheson, Dean, 296
Acosta, Emilio N., 266
Adame, Emigdio, 236
Advertising, 329–33
Agrarian reform, 7, 103–6, 134–37, 184; Alemán and, 184; Avila Camacho and, 75
Agraristas, 7, 152–53
Agriculture: effect on society, 12–16, 18–19; land reform and, 187–88; religion and, 17; science and, 31; statistical errors of, 3; suppression of peasants and, 4
Aguilar, Alonso, 335
Aguilar, Cándido, 160; land reform and, 184–85
Aguilar, Magdaleno, 105
Aguilar Camín, Héctor, 95, 223
Aguilar y Maya, José: Gaxiola affair and, 129
Ahí Está el Detalle (film), 48
Ailshie, William K., 107
Aldrete, Alberto, 267–68
Alemán, Fernando Casas, 168, 199, 262; corruption and, 267; 1952 election and, 238; inside information and, 272–73
Alemán, Miguel, 2, 29, 33, 78, 90–91, 279, 350, 362, 366; Acapulco and, 274–76; anti-Communism and, 200–205; appointments of, 177–78, 179; Article 27 and, 183–88; background of, 160–63; Banco Nacional and, 210–11; business and, 207–12; Catholicism and, 138–39, 224–26; cinema strike and, 47; concluding comments on, 244; corruption and, 257, 261, 263, 269, 290–91, 299; CTM split and, 195–200; dissenter groups and, 226–27; economic nationalists and, 205–7; education and, 37; eliminates free medicine, 23; foreign capital and, 174–75; industrialization and, 25, 170–77; initial orientation of, 166–75; inner circle of, 168; inside information and, 270–73; judicial autonomy and, 230–32; labor and, 108, 190–91, 198–99; land reform and, 183–88; legislative programs of, 183–244; León violence and, 155–57; María Félix and, 49–50; Maximino shootout and, 288; military and, 169; mistresses and, 215–16; 1946 election and, 149, 159–63; *Novedades* and, 346; Partido Popular and, 227–30; personal business of, 212–15; petroleum strike and, 191–95; political reform and, 216–19; postwar economy and, 219–22; presidential selection of, 163–66; pro-business view of, 189–90; public works projects and, 171–72; right opposition and, 232–35; Ruíz Cortines selection and, 237–44; STPC and, 342; Twenty-Three Point Program of, 212; underconsumption theory and, 33–34; U.S. and, 173–74,

Alemán, Miguel (*continued*) 176–77, 235–36, 335–36; visited by Truman, 175–76; vs. old revolutionaries, 235–37
Alemán, Miguel, Jr., 215
Alemán Doctrine, 223–24
Allá en el Rancho Grande (film), 45
Allied Radio Network, 337–39
Almazán, Juan Andreu, 79; Avila Camacho candidacy and, 81; Monterrey Group and, 83; 1940 election and, 87–88; PAN and, 109; women's vote and, 217–18
Alstock, Francis, 341
Altamirano, Manlio Fabio, 161
Amar, Lenora, 215
América Latina, 316
American Bankers Association, 190
Amescua, Ernesto J., 187
Amilpa, Fernando, 227, 276, 277, 284
Anaconda Copper Company, 189
Anáhuac Construction Company, 83
Andrade, José Luis H., 192
Angeles, Carlos, 155, 364
Anguiano, Raúl, 40
Anguiano, Victoriano, 229; attacks Cárdenas, 240
Angulo, Mauro, 227, 261
Anta Agency, 322–23
Anthropology, 41–42; "battle of the bones," 42
Anticlericalism, 18, 224–25; Avila Camacho and, 94–95; education and, 222; Monterrey Group and, 83; victory over, 139
Anti-Communism, 96–97, 106, 109–10, 113, 192–94, 200–205, 237; newspapers and, 335; Rodríguez and, 112
AOCM (Alianza de Obreros y Campesinos de México), 195
Araiza, Evaristo, 134, 197; Avila Camacho and, 92–93; corruption and, 270
Archaeology, 41–42
Arenas, Juan Ortega, 302
Arendáriz, Antonio, 190

Arizpe, Lourdes, 8, 13
Around the World in Eighty Days (film), 49
Arreguín, Enrique, 95
Arriola, María, 218
Art and artists, 38–41
Artisans, 21–23
ASARCO (American Smelting and Refining Company), 172, 237, 267; labor disputes and, 122
Asi, 349; Maximino Avila Camacho and, 287
Atzcapotzalco petroleum refinery, 194
Authors' Rights Law, 222
Automobiles and auto manufacturers, 10–11, 25, 26. *See also* Industrialization
Aviation: growth of, 12
Avila Binder, Luis Manuel, 288
Avila Camacho, Ana Soledad de, 76, 114
Avila Camacho, Emiliano, 77; FBI and, 88
Avila Camacho, Gabriel, 77, 288
Avila Camacho, Hilda, 347
Avila Camacho, Manuel, 2, 238, 254, 362–63; Alemán and, 162; Axis nationals and, 117–18; background of, 76; cabinet and, 89–90, 97–98; candidacy of, 79–81; Catholicism and, 94–95, 102, 106, 138–39; changes Supreme Court, 93; cinema strike and, 47; comic books and, 352; corruption and, 289–90; decline of, 166; dissenter groups and, 226–27; dramatic policy changes of, 75; education and, 95–96; as family man, 77; first actions as president, 89–92; fondness of war, 115; foreign investment and, 92, 100; Gaxiola affair and, 124–31; growth of state sector and, 132; helps CROM, 101–2; hotel project and, 214; *Hoy* and, 349; industrialization and, 137–38; kickbacks and, 264; labor and, 98–99, 106–8, 122; land reform and, 8, 103–6,

134–38; legacy of, 140–41; León violence and, 153–60; Monterrey Group and, 83, 85, 151, 158–59; newspapers and, 351; 1940 election and, 87–88; 1940s politics and, 108–14; 1946 election and, 149–50, 165; O'Farrill and, 347; politics of, 100–101, 110, 112–14; power of, 78–79, 121; PRM and, 86–87; radio and, 324; shifts to right, 92–103; "*soy creyente,*" 94, 114, 138; strategies of Avilacamachistas and, 91; use of contracts, 123, 265; windfall of, 115–20; women's vote and, 218; workers' housing and, 135

Avila Camacho, Margarita Richardi de: corruption and, 274

Avila Camacho, Maximino, 7, 230; attacked by CTM, 100; corruption of, 6, 274, 281–91, 293; death of, 164; embarrassing behavior of, 139–40; Gaxiola affair and, 126–27; hidden deals and, 266–67; labor and, 103; William Jenkins and, 326

Avila Camacho, Rafael, 77

Avilez, Bernardo, 104

Avramow, Alberto J., 267

Ayala Blanco, Jorge, 44

¡*Ay, Jalisco no te rajes!* (film), 45

Azcárraga Vidaurreta, Emilio, 46, 82, 214–15, 324–25, 338, 339, 342–43; television and, 344–46

Azcárraga Vidaurreta, Raúl, 342

Aztecs, 38, 40

Azuela, Mariano, 56

Baillerés, Raúl, 168, 212

Ballesteros, Jorge Ramón, 62

Ballet Folklórico, 55

Balli, Emilio, 347

BANAMEX (Banco Nacional de México), 133–34, 138, 190, 210; corruption and, 262; *ejidos* and, 188

Banco Agricola, 104

Banco Cinematográfico, 52

Banco de Comercio, 262

Banco del Pacífico, 262

Banco del Pequeño Comercio, 19, 261

Banco de México, 177; inside information and, 272; luxury credits and, 220–21; U.S. loans and, 174

Banco Ejidal, 104

Banco Internacional, 211

Bank of America, 190

Barbar Asphalt Corporation, 278, 279

Barmine, Alexander, 342

Barradas, Armando Armenta, 288

Barragán, Manuel L., 82, 151

Barragán, Marcelino García, 23, 234

Barrios, Roberto, 185

Barros, José, 190

Barroso, Guillermo, 297

Bartra, Armando, 58

Bartra, Roger, 57, 313

Baseball, 65

Basketball, 61, 65

Bassols, Narciso, 126, 229, 236, 335

Bateman, Alan, 24

BBC (British Broadcasting Corporation), 316

Beales, Carlton, 66

Beaverbrook, Lord, 315

Bechtel, Steve, 298

Becker, Marjorie, 313

Beezley, William, 63

Beltrán, Alberto, 40

Beltrán, Dr. Gonzalo Aguirre, 7

Bemis, Samuel F., 24

Benítez, Fernando, 42

Berger, Mark, 24

Berle, Adolf A., Jr., 24

Bermúdez, Antonio J., 178, 263, 343–44

Bernal, Antonio Arias, 349

Betancourt, Carlos I., 231

Betancourt Pérez, Antonio: corruption and, 263

Beteta, Ramón, 138, 168, 171, 177–78, 217; Alemán's personal business and, 212; anticlericalism and, 225; Banco Nacional and, 210–11; corruption and, 254, 258, 267–78, 298–99; hotel project and, 214; inside information and, 270–72; investments and, 210; León

Beteta, Ramón (*continued*)
    violence and, 157; moderation
    of, 91–92; 1952 election and,
    238; rent control and, 211–12
BEW (Board of Economic Wel-
    fare), 291–92
Binder, Sir Bernhard, 297
Birth control, 32
Blake-Taylor, H., 112–13
Bloque de Obreros y Campesinos,
    102
Blos, Marsden, 190
Blumenthal, A. C., 166, 212
Bobadilla, Luis, 81, 106–7
Bohan, Merwin L., 174, 206, 270,
    271
Bojórquez, Juan de Dios, 261
Bonampak, 42
Bonfigli de Richardi, Teresa, 287
Bonilla, Roberto, 154, 156
Borlaugh, Norman, 31
Bortz, Jeffrey, 4
Boxing, 64
Braceros, 28–31
Braden, Spruille, 154–55, 175
Brann, Herman W., 292, 293
Braun, Horace H., 174
Bretton Woods Conference (1944),
    164, 244
Britain: Inter-Allied Propaganda
    Committee and, 315; Mexican
    indifference and, 317–18;
    Mexican media and, 314–27;
    news services and, 321–22;
    Novedades and, 346; paper
    industry and, 320; propaganda
    and, 316, 321
British Overseas Press Service,
    315
Brothels, 15
Buch de Parada, Francisco, 174–
    75; Alemán's personal busi-
    ness and, 212
Bueno, Torres, 140
Buenrostro, Efraín, 90, 128
Bullfighting, 63–64
Buñuel, Luis, 51
Business, 365; Alemán and, 207–
    12, 217; postwar downturn,
    219–22. *See also* Industrializa-
    tion; Media
Bus service, 11

Cabareteras, 50–51
Cabotage, 207
Cabral, Regis, 33
Cabrera, Luis, 77
Caciques, 6, 8
Calabacitas Tiernas (film), 48–49
Calaveras, 40
Calderón, Celia, 38
Calderón, Esteban, 225
Calles, Plutarco Elías, 82, 90, 111–
    12; Monterrey Group and, 83;
    supports Almazán, 88; World
    War II and, 117
Calles, Rodolfo Elías, 84
Camacho Bello, Eufrosina, 76
Camarena, González, 345
Camisas doradas, 100
Cammack, William Richard, 353
Campa, Valentín, 108, 195;
    Communism and, 110, 202–3
Campanella, Manuel, 280
Campesinos, 1, 5, 10, 12–16
Campobello, Nelly: women's
    issues and, 218
Candil, 112
Cano Martínez, Pablo, 153; León
    violence and, 156
"Cantinflas," Mario Moreno, 47–
    49
Capital, 133–38, 207
Caravelo, Marcelo, 78
Cárdenas, Damaso, 256
Cárdenas, Lázaro, 2, 8, 17, 163,
    238, 362–64; Alemán and, 162,
    177; cinema and, 46; corrup-
    tion and, 256; defense of, 240–
    41; destruction of caudillos
    and, 89; education and, 37,
    222; expulsion of Calles and,
    111–12; FBI and, 88; "14-Point
    Speech," 84; Gaxiola affair
    and, 125–26, 130; Germans
    and, 314; Indians and, 42, 312–
    13; industrialization and, 135;
    Japanese and, 119; kickbacks
    and, 263–64; land reform and,
    103; Manuel Avila Camacho
    and, 77–78, 81, 86, 90, 166;
    Maximino Avila Camacho and,
    79; Monterrey Group and, 83;
    1940 election and, 87; 1946
    election and, 149; old revolu-

tionaries of, 235–37; politically left position of, 110–11; strategies of Avilacamachistas and, 91; swings to right, 79, 84–85; taxes and, 132–33; Vidriera factory and, 84; war shortages and, 131; women's vote and, 217; World War II and, 116

Carestía, 34, 133

Carmena, Rosa, 51

Carmona, Manuel, 154

Carr, Barry, 99

Carranza, Delfino, 154

Carranza, Raúl, 225

Carranza, Venustiano, 26, 77, 254

Carrillo, Alejandro, 124, 189, 202, 224, 341; anticlericalism and, 225; corruption and, 263; encourages wartime cooperation, 122; Gaxiola affair and, 126; Maximino Avila Camacho and, 284; opposes Avila Camacho, 95

Carrillo, Salvador, 341

Carrillo Flores, Antonio, 34–35, 37, 138, 299

Carvajal, Angel, 299

Casa de España en México, 36–37

Cash economy, 19–21

Caso, Alfonso, 168

Caso, "Scarface," 8

Caso family, 8

Castellanos, Julio, 38

Caste War, 12

Catalán, Rafael, 89

Catholicism: Alemán and, 224–26; anti-Communism of, 106; attacks comic books, 59; Avila Camacho and, 76–77, 94–95, 102, 138–39; blamed by Lombardo Toledano, 228; education and, 222; Monterrey Group and, 83; muralists and, 39; 1946 election and, 150; political rallies and, 16; propaganda and, 324; silence on corruption, 226

Catholic Right, 139

Cattle, 236; export of, 264; zebu, 236

Caudillos (landowners), 2, 6; conflicts of, 8; land reform and, 105

CCNC (Confederación de Camaras Nacionales de Comercio), 170, 187, 221

Cedillo, Saturnino, 2; opposed by Cárdenas, 89; rebellion of, 78, 87

Celebrations, 16–20

Cement: industry, 133; replacing adobe in construction, 13–14

Cementos Atoyac, 133

Censorship, 222; of films, 53; "gag law," 222

Census: artisans and, 21, 22; errors of, 1–3, 4; labor force and, 20; literacy and, 37–38, 58–59

Centro Patronal del Districto Federal, 206

Cerdán, Giorgio: antilabor position of, 100; fights with CTM, 91

Cervantes, Elizabeth Curtiss, 124

CGT (Confederación General de Trabajadores), 99; National Labor Unity Pact and, 121

Chamula Indians, 7

Chapa, Ester, 205; women's issues and, 218

Chargoy, Gabriel Alarcón, 52

Charrerías, 61–62, 63, 64

Charros, 45, 61, 63; corruption and, 300; petroleum strike and, 192

Chase, Stuart, 66

Chávez, Carlos, 58, 168

Chávez, Julio César (boxer), 64

Cházaro, Eduardo Hernández, 161

Chemical Bank and Trust Company, 190

Chesterton, G. K., 321

Chiapas violence, 7, 233

Chilangos, 35

Child labor, 123–24

Childs, Marquis W., 77

Cholula, 23

"Christmas crisis," 366

Churchill, Winston, 200

CIA (Central Intelligence Agency), 178

Cinema, 42–53, 325–26; *cabaretera* and, 51; cowboy films and, 44–45; growth of, 46; *indigenista*, 45; María Félix and, 50; popularity of, 42; propaganda and, 43; racism and, 49; social control and, 52–53; strike and, 47–48; U.S. influence on, 43
Clark, Lew B., 174
Clayton, Will, 175
Clemente, José: *Novedades* and, 347
Clendinnen, Inga, 40
Clothing: industrialization and, 24–25; rural, 16
Club Smyrna, 54–55
Cluck, Hugh, 205
CNC (Confederación Nacional de Campesinos), 7, 98, 275; Avila Camacho candidacy and, 80, 81; declined membership of, 240; land reform and, 105, 186
CNIT (Cámara Nacional de Industrias de Transformación), 34, 206, 222
CNOP (Confederación Nacional de Organizaciones Populares), 98
CNT (Confederación Nacional de Trabajadores): declined membership of, 240; union fragmentation and, 195
Coal, 10
Cocaine, 260, 367
COCM (Confederación de Obreros y Campesinos de México), 99; declined membership of, 240; union fragmentation and, 195
Cold War, 200–205. *See also* Anti-Communism
Cole, R. R., 189–90
Colectivos: land reform and, 105
Colin, José R., 206, 299
Collier, George, 104
Colonias, 27
Combate, 236
Comedians, 48, 58
Comedia ranchera, 44–45
Comic books, 58–60, 352
Comisión Intersecretarial Sobre Inversión de Capital Extranjero, 207

Communism, 96–97, 106, 109–10, 112–13, 192–94, 200–205, 237, 335. *See also* Anti-Communism
Compadrazgo, 120
Compañia Oriental de Cemento Portland S.A., 133
CONCAMIN (Confederación de Cámaras Industriales), 225
Consejo Obrero Nacional, 191
Constitution (1917), 222, 225; Article 27, 183–88, 229
Contreras, Ariel José, 79
Contreras, Luis Felipe, 278
Contreras, Magdalena, 117
Conway, George, 170
COOC (Coalición de Organizaciones Oberas y Campesinas): union fragmentation and, 195
Cooper, Kent, 330
COPARMEX (Confederación Patronal de la República Mexicana), 109, 330; Monterrey Group and, 83; PRM and, 82–83
Córdova, Ernesto A., 233
Corn, 13–14, 32
Corón, Jesús Chiñas, 192
"Corona thesis," 194, 231–32
Corporativism, 109
Corral Martínez, Blas, 234, 258
Corridos, 40–41
Corruption. *See* Politics
Cortéz, José Lino, 134
Cosío Villegas, Daniel, 37, 61, 225, 244, 361, 367; Gaxiola affair and, 127
Costello, Frank, 274
Courtship, 15
Covarrubias, Miguel, 38
CPN (Confederación Proletaria Nacional), 190; National Labor Unity Pact and, 121; union fragmentation and, 193, 195
Cranbourne, Viscount, 321
Cricket, 65
Cristiada, 16, 18
CROM (Confederación Regional Obrera Mexicana), 99, 101, 164, 190, 198, 237; anti-Communism and, 202; Avila Camacho and, 102; corruption and, 254; National Labor

Unity Pact and, 121; union fragmentation and, 195
Cruz, Emilio, 230
CTAL (Confederación de Trabajadores de América Latina), 101, 194; Avila Camacho and, 102; petroleum strike and, 193
CTM (Confederación de Trabajadores Mexicanos), 8, 47, 164–65, 190, 194, 227, 230, 236, 276–77, 365; Alemán and, 139; Avila Camacho candidacy and, 80–81; congress of 1941, 98; declined membership of, 240; Fidel Velázquez and, 99; fights with Cerdán, 91; Gaxiola affair and, 125–26; government funds and, 103; labor meeting of 1941 and, 101–2; León violence and, 157–58; Maximino Avila Camacho and, 79, 97, 100, 283; Monterrey Group and, 83, 84; National Labor Unity Pact and, 121; 1946 election and, 165; petroleum strike and, 191, 193; Six Year Plan and, 80; split in, 195–200; STPC and, 340–42; union fragmentation and, 195; war shortages and, 131
Cuen, Sánchez, 294
Cuetzalan, 17–18
Cueva, Raúl, 343
Cull, Nicholas John, 315
Currency, 19–20
CUT (Confederación Unica de Trabajadores), 190, 235, 276; union fragmentation and, 195; violence and, 198

Dances and dance ceremonies, 17, 18
Daniels, Josephus, 78, 81, 330
Davidson, I. D., 317–19
Davila, Cepeda, 234, 261
Day, Dorothy, 66
Decina tragica, 28
De la Fuente, Fernando, 231, 232, 364
De la Selva, Rogelio, 204, 237

De la Vega, Rodolfo Junco, 343
Del Castillo, F. Gregorio, 53
Del Río, Dolores, 45–46, 49, 51–52; encourages wartime cooperation, 122
Democracy, 150; Avila Camacho and, 76
Denegri, Carlos, 67
Departamento de Asuntos Indígenas, 42
Diario de Puebla, 79
Diario de Yucatán, 186, 269, 331
Díaz, Porfirio, 41, 150, 289; Gaxiola affair and, 127. *See also* Porfirian theory; *Porfiriato*
Diáz de León, Jesús, 192
Díaz Lombardo, Antonio: inside information and, 273; *Novedades* and, 347
Dietrich, Arthur, 314–15
Diplomats: inside information and, 270–71
Disney, Walt, 333–34
Doña Barbara (film), 49
Donovan, William, 333
Dope smuggling, 260
Dorados, 109
Dulles, John Foster, 162, 295
Durán, Pedro, 192

Easter parades, 17
Echevarría, Canto, 5
Echeverría, Luis, 150
Economic nationalists, 205–7
Education, 7, 35–36, 38, 222–24; Avila Camacho and, 95; improvement of, 37
Eisenstein, Sergei, 43–44
Ejidos, 4–5, 7, 12, 138, 183–84; Acapulco and, 274; agricultural finance and, 187–88; Avila Camacho and, 94, 104; conflicts of, 8; corruption and, 269; land reform and, 185–86
El Colegio de México, 35
Election of 1940, 87; FBI and, 87–88
Election of 1946, 149–58; Alemán and, 159–79; corruption and, 150; frontrunners, 149–50; results, 166
Electricity, 8–9, 137–38

El gendarme desconocido (film), 48
"El Gitano," 152
Elguero, Pepe, 124
Elitism, 150–51
Elizondo, Angel Lozano, 353
Elizondo, Juan Manuel: labor disputes and, 122; land reform and, 185
Elizondo, Prisciliano: corruption and, 269; *Novedades* and, 347
El Mundo, 331; land reform and, 105; Llera violence and, 234; murder of editor, 219
El Nacional, 33, 226, 336, 355; description of, 348–49; land reform and, 135; León violence and, 154, 155; propaganda and, 332
El Norte: propaganda and, 329
El Popular, 319, 335, 336; Alemán's visit to U.S. and, 236; attacks Abelardo Rodríguez, 100; budget reduced, 224; Communism and, 204; corruption of, 279; CTM and, 348; Gaxiola affair and, 125, 126; labor disputes and, 107; León violence and, 154, 155; Partido Popular and, 229; PCM plot and, 97; petroleum strike and, 192; propaganda and, 329, 332; war shortages and, 131
El Porvenir, 331
El Universal, 33, 58, 59, 335, 336, 355; Avila Camacho and, 351; founding of, 347–48; Gaxiola affair and, 125; León violence and, 155; Monterrey imposition and, 159; 1946 election and, 149; PCM plot and, 97; propaganda and, 329, 330, 332
El Universal Gráfico, 335
Employment: cash economy and, 19; *empleomania*, 190–91; housing and, 23; industry workers and, 23–24; paid work and, 20–21; rural wages, 4–5; statistical errors of, 3, 4; workers' conditions, 21
Encina, Dionicio, 97, 141
Enganche, 44
Enríquez, Jorge, 274

Entertainment: rural, 15–16
En Tiempos de Don Porfirio (film), 46
Entrepreneurs, 177–79
Espaldas mojadas (film), 43
Espinosa de los Monteros, Antonio, 179; inside information and, 272
Esponda, Juan M., 234
Estampa, 349
Esto, 61
Estrada, Enríque, 265
Estrada, Roque, 155, 364
Eucharistic Congress (1948), 225
Eugenics movement, 41
Excélsior, 96, 243, 320, 324, 330, 335–36, 355; Avila Camacho and, 351; Cárdenas and, 117, 240; corruption and, 298–99; founding of, 348; Gaxiola affair and, 125; Honey murders and, 231; León violence and, 154–55; Maximino shootout and, 288; Monterrey Group and, 83, 159; PCM plot and, 97; propaganda and, 329
Export-Import Bank, 174–75, 207, 334; corruption and, 266, 290; hotel project and, 214; kickbacks and, 264; newspapers and, 339
Export-Import Lumber Company, 291–92
Extraordinary Congress (1940): Communism and, 110

Fabela, Isidro, 202
Faenas charras, 61–62
Falange (Spain), 109
Fanon, Franz, 288
Fascism, 88
FBI (Federal Bureau of Investigation), 278, 279; Alemán and, 161; Avila Camacho cabinet and, 90; Axis citizens and, 119; Communism and, 110; Gaxiola corruption and, 264; National Security Police and, 259; 1940 election and, 87–88
FCDM (Frente Constitucional Democrático Mexicano), 110
Fein, Seth, 353

Félix, María, 47, 49–50, 54, 216, 341
FEMSA (Fomento Económico Mexicano S.A.), 267
Fencing, 65
Fernández, Emilio "El Indio," 45, 50, 53
Festivals, 16–20
Figueroa, Esperanza Oteo: women's issues and, 218
Figueroa, Gabriel, 342
Films. *See* Cinema
Finley, Harold D., 126, 285–86; Gaxiola affair and, 126–27, 129
Fishing, 23
Flemming, Lamar, 24
Flores Villar, Miguel, 135–37
Flor Silvestre (film), 45, 49
"Flowery Wars," 17
Fogarty, Federico Sánchez, 202
Folk medicine, 19–20. *See also* Health care
Fondo de Cultura Económica, 35, 37
Food. *See* Agriculture
Football, 64–65
Fortín de las Flores, 28
Fortune, 207–8
Fosdick, Raymond B., 31
Fouce, Frank, 353
Foucher, Brito, 140
Foy, Amos B., 190
FPPM (Federación de Partidos del Pueblo Mexicano), 299; clashes with PRI, 242
Franco, Francisco, 35, 200
Frente de Defensa de la Industria Henequenera, 186, 268
Friede, Juan, 40
Friedrich, Paul, 8
FROC (Frente Regional de Obreros y Campesinos), 8, 79
FSTSE (Federación de Sindicatos de Trabajadores al Servicio del Estado): declined membership of, 240
Fuentes, Carlos, 302
Fuentes, Fernando de, 49
Fuerza Popular, 232
FUPDM (Frente Unico Pro Derechos de la Mujer), 217

Galindo, Alejandro, 43
Gamboa, Rafael Pascasio, 233; corruption and, 299
Gamio, Dr. Manuel, 33–34, 42
Gangsters, 261, 276
Gaos, José, 37
García, Teodulo: kickbacks and, 264
García Canclini, Néstor, 313
García Gallegos, Guillermo, 96–97
García López, Agustín, 178; corruption and, 299; 1952 election and, 238
García Tellez, Ignacio, 90; CROM and, 102; labor disputes and, 122; National Labor Unity Pact and, 121
García Valseca, José, 61, 349
Gardner, Robert L., 270
Garrido, Luis Javier, 85
Garrido, Tomás, 2; opposed by Cárdenas, 89
Garza, Alfonso Díaz, 211
Garza, Alvarez, 263
Garza, Isaac, 82
Garza, Luis, 82
Garza, René Capistrán, 335, 346
Garza, Virgilio, Jr.: arrested, 84
Gavaldón, Roberto, 44
Gaxiola, Francisco Xavier, 124–31; kickbacks and, 264
Gente de orden, 7
Germans, 117–19, 314–15, 317–20, 322–25, 331, 338, 348, 354. *See also* Nazis
Germany's Foreign Policy, 321
Germany's National Religion, 321
Getty, J. Paul, 275
Gibson, Charles, 39
Gibson, Raleigh, 119, 332
Gilles, Donald, 189
Gold, 267
Gómez, Marte R., 209; Avila Camacho cabinet and, 90
Gómez, Rojo, 165
Gómez Morín, Manuel, 139, 332
Gómez Z., Luis, 194–95
González, Angel, 260
González, Francisco Rojas, 56
González, Honorato: kickbacks and, 264
González, Hugo Pedro, 234

González, Luis, 5, 11
González, Pablo, 78
González Beytia, José, 186
González Escobar rebellion, 82
González Gallo, Jesús, 92–93, 234; Gaxiola afffair and, 128–29; Japanese and, 119–20
González Salinas, Felix, 151
Good Neighbor Policy, 101, 176
Gramsci, Antonio, 311
Grand Coulee Dam, 9
Gruening, Ernest, 66
Grunewald, Henry, 278, 279
Guajardo, Guillermo, 343
Guerrero, Anacleto, 78, 84; land reform and, 105
Guerrero, Enríque, 62
Guerrero, Nicéforo, 154
Guerrero, Xavier, 38
Guerrilla action, 117
Guízar, Tito, 44–45
Guízar Oseguerra, Luis, 233
Gurría, Trujillo, 341
Gurrola, Francisco, 260
Gurrola, Juan Ramón, 259, 260
Guthrie, Woody, 9
Gutiérrez Gurria, Alfonso: PCM plot and, 97
Guzmán, Martín Luis, 225, 350

Haberman, Robert, 66; helps CROM, 101
Hacendados, 7, 63
Halberstam, David, 32
Hamilton, Nora, 84–85
Hastings, John, 284; Alemán's personal business and, 212
Hastings Group, 265; Maximino Avila Camacho and, 284
Havas News Service, 322, 327
Hay Muertos que No Hacen Ruido (film), 48–49
Hays, Will H., 340, 352
Health care: folk medicine and, 19–20; industrial workers and, 23; rural, 16; science and, 31, 32
Hearst, William Randolph, 43, 139
Henequen, 5; government monopoly, 186–87, 268–69
Henequeneros de Yucatán, 186–87, 268–69

Henríquez Guzmán, Miguel, 165, 239, 242; corruption and, 269–70; 1946 election and, 149
Heredia, Manuel Mayoral, 242
Hernández, Lindoro, 160
Heroles, Jesús Reyes, 225
Herrerías, Ignacio F., 346
Hess, Jerome S., 176
Hewitt de Alcántara, Cynthia, 31; land reform and, 105
Higgins, Lawrence: Maximino Avila Camacho and, 285
Hill, Ricardo C., 264–65
Hillman, Stanley, 175
Hitler, Adolf, 320–21
Holden, Maurice C., 259–60
Hollywood, 334, 340–42; Alemán and, 160
Hombres pajaros, 18
Honey murders, 230–32
Hoof-and-mouth disease, 31, 236, 256
Hoover, J. Edgar, 278
Horn, Charles W., 215, 342
Horses, 19, 60–61
Hospitals. *See* Health care
Housing, 135; increase of, 23; peasants', 13
Hoy, 27, 335, 349; attacks Cárdenas, 240; Gaxiola affair and, 124–31; Maximino Avila Camacho and, 286–87; propaganda and, 329, 332
Huerta, Adolfo de la, 238
Hughes, Morris, 97
Hull, Cordell, 284
Hurtado, Elías, 102

Ibañez, Eulalio, 192
IBEC (International Basic Economy Corporation), 32
Icasa, Xavier, 190, 235
Ifor-Rees, Thomas, 320
IMF (International Monetary Fund): inside information and, 272–73
Immigration, 41
IMSS (Instituto Mexicano de Seguro Social), 221
Inafectabilidad, 103
Inclán, José, 117

Indians: archaeology and, 42; Chamula, 7; cinema and, 45; in literature, 56; national identity and, 312–13; as scapegoats, 41

Industrialization, 2, 361–62, 364, 366; Alemán and, 170–77, 189–90, 235–36; Avila Camacho and, 137–38; democracy and, 150; excluded from Marshall Plan, 220; growth of state sector and, 132; international business and, 207; science and, 31–35; Six Year Plan and, 80; of television, 214–15; U.S. and, 206, 291–98; World War II and, 115

Industry: artisans and, 22; Avila Camacho and, 89, 92–93; business elite and, 4; cash economy and, 19–21; employment and, 3, 23–24; Monterrey Group and, 82; prosperity of, 23; statistical errors of, 3; suppression of peasants and, 5

Infante, Pedro, 45

Instituto Indigenista Interamericano, 33–34, 42

Instituto Nacional de Antropología e Historia, 42

Instituto Nacional de Bellas Artes, 55

Instituto Nacional Indigenista, 7

Inter-Allied Propaganda Committee, 315, 320–23, 326–28, 330–31, 354

Inter-American Indigenist Congress, 312

International business: Alemán and, 207–12

Inurreta, Marcelino, 204, 259

Irrigation, 171–72

Islas Bravo, Antonio, 158–59, 231

Italians, 118–19

Jai alai, 65

Janitzio (film), 45

Japanese, 118–20

Jara, Heriberto, 90; kickbacks and, 264

Jaramillo, Barreto, 117

Jaramillo, Rubén, 117

Jefe politico, 6

Jenkins, William, 52, 98, 103, 230, 237, 285, 326; corruption and, 266–67; Maximino Avila Camacho and, 283–84; monopoly of, 209

Jockey Club, 61–62

Johnson, Lyndon B., 9, 210

Jones, Gus T., 119

Juárez, Benito, 40

Junta de Administración y Vigilencia de la Propiedad Extranjera, 117–18

Juventudes Nacionalistas, 109

Kahlo, Frida, 38, 76

Kawage Ramia, Alfredo: Gaxiola affair and, 124, 125, 128

Keen, Benjamin, 40

Kefauver, Estes, 274

Kennan, George: León violence and, 155

Kersh, R. S., 189

Kleyff, Alexander, 265

Knight, Alan, 24

Koons, Charles, 207

Korean War, 335–36

Kuhns, William, 190

Kuznits, Simon, 221

Labastida, Rodolfo, 198

Labor unions, 102–3; actors and, 340–41; anti-Communism and, 203–4; Avila Camacho and, 80–81; battles of, 109; CTM split and, 195–200; curbing of, 190–91; declined membership of, 240; discrediting of, 276–80; disputes and, 122–23; education and, 222–25; falling standards of living and, 221; Gaxiola affair and, 130; General Bobadilla and, 106–7; housing and, 135; National Labor Unity Pact and, 121; 1952 election and, 240; Partido Popular and, 227–30; petroleum strike and, 191–95; reform and, 363; violence and, 198, 230–32, 242; war efforts and, 122; working conditions and, 123–24, 194. *See also specific unions*

Lacaud, Julio, 133
La Nación: Gaxiola affair and, 125
Land owners, 12; conflicts of, 8;
    corruption of, 8
Land reform, 7, 103–6, 134–37,
    184; Alemán and, 184; Avila
    Camacho and, 75; *terrenos
    baldíos*, 41
Langford, Walter M., 56–57
Lanz Duret, Miguel, 295, 336,
    347–48
La Opinión, 331
La Prensa, 324, 330, 335, 355; Avila
    Camacho and, 351; founding
    of, 348; Gaxiola affair and, 125;
    León violence and, 154, 156;
    Maximino shootout and, 288;
    Monterrey imposition and,
    159; PCM plot and, 97;
    propaganda and, 329
Lara, Agustín, 54–55
Laredo Times, 294–95
Lasswell, Harold, 316
Latifundia, 104
Lauren, Prieto, 110
Lavín, José Domingo, 202, 206
La Voz de México, 343, 349; anti-
    Communism and, 204; Avila
    Camacho candidacy and, 81;
    Gaxiola affair and, 125
Lázaro, Angel, 33
Leal, Fernando, 38
Leal, Manuel de, 346
Lebaud, Captain, 77
Ledesma, Luis, 349
Ledón, Luis Castillo, 55–56
Leeper, Sir Reginald, 297
Leeper, Rex, 316
Legorreta, Agustín: Alemán's
    personal business and, 212
Legorreta, Luis, 52, 133–43, 188,
    190; Alemán's personal
    business and, 212; Avila
    Camacho and, 75; Banco
    Nacional and, 210–11; corrup-
    tion and, 268; MEXLIGHT
    and, 297
Lend-Lease Program, 292
León, Luis Viñas, 267
León violence, 153–58, 166, 342,
    364; blamed on PAN, 228
Lewis, Oscar, 5–6, 14

Liberation theology, 39
Lille, Pedro de, 346
Limón, Gilberto, 299; inside
    information and, 273
Literacy, 35
Literature and writers, 55–60
Livestock industry, 19
Llano, Rodrigo de, 330
Llergo, Hernández, 349
Llergo, José Pagés, 335, 349
Loaiza, Rodolfo T., 151
Lombardo Toledano, Vicente, 36,
    76, 93, 98, 164, 194, 197, 224,
    226, 228–30, 236, 278–79, 341;
    Alemán and, 189, 196; anti-
    Communism and, 110–13, 201–
    2; attempts labor union, 83–84;
    Avila Camacho and, 79–81, 86;
    Cárdenas and, 90; decline of,
    166; Gaxiola affair and, 126;
    labor and, 101–2, 108; León
    violence and, 157; Maximino
    Avila Camacho and, 283–84;
    1952 election and, 239;
    petroleum strike and, 192; U.S.
    view of, 165; Vidriera factory
    and, 83–84; war and, 122, 130
López, Roberto, 37
López y Fuentes, Gregorio, 56
Luce, Claire Boothe, 187
Lucha libre, 64

Macías, Anna, 218
Macías, José Natividad, 124
Madariaga, Alfonso Sánchez, 277
Magazines, 27–28, 349–50
Maglione, Luigi: anti-
    Communism of, 106
Magnum, Hall, 136
Magoral, Manuel, 260
Maldonaldo, Consuelo, 218
Malpica Silva, Juan, 331
Mancera, Rafael, 300, 301
Manolete, 64
Marett, Robert H. K., 315
María Candelaria (film), 45
Marijuana, 260
Marker, Russell, 32
Marshall, George, 176, 220
Marshall Plan, 335
Martín-Barbero, Jesús, 312
Martínez, Enríque Serna, 352

Martínez, Héctor Pérez, 231, 234, 262
Martínez, Luis María, 225; anti-Communism of, 106
Martínez, Ricardo, 38
Martínez Assad, Carlos, 52
Martínez Báez, Antonio, 294
Marxism, 35
Mass communications. *See* Media
May Day, 105–6
Mayer, George, 136
Mayer, Louis B., 139, 334
Media, 355, 362, 366; advertising and, 329–33; Allied Radio Network and, 337–39; British propaganda and, 314–27; control of, 346–47; government and, 350–52; Hollywood and, 340–42; innovations of, 313–14; Korean War and, 335–36; magazines and, 349–50; Mexican interests and, 342–44; newspapers and, 347–49; politics and, 311–12; protectionism and, 352–54; Rockefeller and, 333–35; television and, 344–46; U.S. and, 327–29
Memorias de un Mexicano (film), 26
Méndez, Leopoldo, 40
Mendieta, Carlos: MEXLIGHT and, 297
Menéndez, Miguel Angel, 56
Mesa, Manuel, 236
Messersmith, George, 78, 130, 178–79, 201, 330, 334; Alemán and, 163, 212; on Army Air Corps scandal, 292; Avila Camacho and, 115, 166; corruption and, 293–98; kickbacks and, 264; land reform and, 136–37; León violence and, 154–55; MEXLIGHT and, 170–71; 1946 election and, 149; Padilla and, 91
Mestizos, 8, 312
Metals Reserve Corporation, 24
Mexican Revolution, 35, 66, 226; Alemán Doctrine and, 223; Avila Camacho and, 75, 77; Cárdenas and, 81, 111; corruption and, 151, 255; land reform and, 7; perceived threat to, 109
Mexican Roundtable, 227
Mexican Silk Mill Incorporated S.A., 280
Mexico: changes from supporting U.S., 317; corruption and, 253–303; culture and, 35–38; devaluation of peso, 272–73; devastation of, 366; foreign business and, 189–90, 207–13, 334; foreign debt and, 117–18; growth of state sector and, 132; industrialization of, 2, 31–35, 80, 115, 132, 137–38, 150, 170–77, 189–90, 206–7, 214–15, 220, 235–36, 291–98, 361–62, 364, 366; influence on others, 66–67; labor strikes and, 191–95; political corruption of, 253–303; politics of 1940s, 108–15; postwar debt of, 220; poverty of, 189; reaction to atomic bomb, 33; Restored Republic, 254; U.S. road bonds purchase (1941) and, 11; World War II and, 114–15, 130, 141, 272, 291–93. *See also by topic*
Mexico: 50 años de revolución, 35–36
Mexico City, 362; Avila Camacho and, 76; culture and, 35–38; Davila suicide and, 234; description (1940), 28; deterioration of wages in, 4; devastation of, 366; Eucharistic Congress and, 225; housing and, 26–27; hunger march and, 237; Japanese and, 120; land reform and, 105; León violence and, 156; Maximino shootout and, 287–88; modernization of, 29; 1940 election and, 87; population growth of, 1; union battles in, 109; workers' conditions (1943), 21; Zapata's conquest and, 18
MEXLIGHT (Mexican Light and Power Company), 9, 170–71, 293–95; Messersmith corruption and, 293–95, 296–98
Michel, Primo Villa, 152

Michoacán, 5, 8; as rallying point, 16
Middlebrook, Kevin, 103, 193
Millan, Gabriel Ramos, 261
Miller, Edward G., 295–96
Miller, W. B., 346
Milmo, Patricio, 81–82
Milpas, 12
Minifundias, 12
Mining, 23; hunger march and, 237; politics and, 209–10; statistical errors of, 3
Ministry of Finance study, 300–301
Ministry of Labor, 101
Miramontes, Fernando Foglio, 90, 234–35
Mitla: archaeology and, 41
Mixcoac, 29
Modernization: health care and, 16; highways and, 11–12; production and, 24–28; resistance to, 18. *See also* Industrialization
Monastario, Juan Ortíz: MEXLIGHT and, 297
Monsanto Chemical Company, 190
Monsiváis, Carlos, 15, 43, 60
Monte Albán: archaeology and, 41
Monte de Piedad, 268
Monterrey Group, 150, 330; arrests of, 84; Avila Camacho and, 81–86; COPARMEX and, 82; corruption and, 151, 269; CTM and, 84; labor strikes and, 197; media and, 342; television and, 344
Montes, Amparo, 55
Montes de Oca, Luis, 81, 211; Avila Camacho and, 75
Morado, J. Chávez, 40
Morales, Manuel, 199
Moreno, Juan Gallardo, 190
Moreno, Manuel: violence and, 198
Moreno, Mario, 47, 340, 341, 342
Morlet, Luis Cataño, 225
Morones, Luis, 190, 237; labor meeting and, 101–2
Morris, Stephen D., 254–55
Morrow, Dwight, 66

Movies. *See* Cinema
Múgica, Francisco, 79
Muguerza, Fernando, 343
Muguerza, José F., 82, 343
Muñoz, Cristobal Alvarado, 198
Muñoz, Flores, 299
Muñoz, Rafael, 56
Muñoz, Vidal Díaz: encourages wartime cooperation, 122
Muralist movement, 38–39; Catholicism and, 39; history and, 40
Murguía, Francisco, 160
Murray, Sir John, 321
Murray, William, 65
Museo Nacional de Historia, 38
Music and composers, 57–58
Mussolini, Benito, 200

NAFISA (Nacional Financiera S.A.), 138, 172, 209; hotel project and, 214; investments and, 210, 339
Nájera, Francisco Castillo, 90, 136; anti-Communism and, 202
Naranja, 8
Nationalism, 37; economic nationalists, 205–7
National Labor Unity Pact, 121
National Security Police, 259–61
National University. *See* UNAM
Natural gas, 10
Natural resources, 24, 33, 209–10
Navarrete, Ifigenia M. de, 4
Navarro Elizondo, José: Alemán's personal business and, 213
Nazis, 140, 291–92, 316, 320–21, 325, 331, 338–39, 342, 354; Alemán and, 162–63; blamed in labor dispute, 107. *See also* Germans
N.D.&R. (Nacional Distribuidora y Reguladora S.A.), 124, 128–29, 187, 267
Negrete, Jorge, 44–45, 47, 341
Nelson, Donald, 174–75
Neoliberalism, 365–67
Neri, Elardo, 230
Neruda, Pablo, 122
Nervo, Luis Padilla, 202
Newspapers, 27, 313–14, 330–33, 347–49, 351; radio and, 337–39

News services, 316, 321–22
New York Times, 168
Nieto, Manuel, 213; inside information and, 271
Ni Sangre ni Arena (film), 48
Nobel Peace Prize: recommendation of Alemán for, 244
Noriega, Raúl, 225, 348
Northcliffe, Viscount, 315
Noticias Gráficas, 319
Novedades, 112, 320, 324, 330, 335, 346–47, 355; Alemán's visit to U.S. and, 236; Avila Camacho and, 351; corruption and, 269; León violence and, 154–55; Maximino shootout and, 288; Monterrey imposition and, 159; on U.S. motion pictures, 139
Novo, Salvador, 60
Novoa, Carlos, 177
Nuestra Señora de los Remedios, 17
Nuñez, José Manuel, 256
Nye Committee, 316

Oaxaca: violence and, 242
Obregón, Alvaro, 77, 82
Obregón, Carlos A., 152; León violence and, 155
Ocampo family, 8
O'Dwyer, William, 274
O'Farrill, F. Jimenez, 179
O'Farrill, Rómulo: *Novedades* and, 347; television and, 215, 344–45
Official News Service, 316
O'Higgins, Pablo, 38, 40
OIAA (Office of Inter-American Affairs), 341, 348, 353–54; Rockefeller and, 333–35
Ojeda, Nabor, 137
Olaguíbel, Juan Fernando, 76
Oldenburger, William, 176
Oligopoly, 133
Olivares, José Trueba, 152
Olivera Barrón, Emilio: León violence and, 153–54, 156
Olivo, Angel: encourages wartime cooperation, 122
Opium, 260
Ordorica, Miguel, 330

Organic Law of Monopoly (1934), 280–81
Oriani, Carlos: corruption and, 299
Orive de Alba, Adolfo, 174, 177
Oro, Juan Bustillo, 46
Orozco, José Clemente, 38–40
Orozco, Soledad, 76
Ortíz, José F., 134
Ortíz de Montellano, Bernardo, 56
Ortíz Garza, José Luis, 315
Ortíz Garza, Nazario S., 128, 177; corruption and, 299; 1952 election and, 238
Ortíz Rubio, Pascual, 82, 89, 238; Japanese and, 119
Osorio, Oscar, 244
Osornio, Fidencio, 2; opposed by Cárdenas, 89

Pacheco, Castro, 40
Pacheco, José Emilio, 25, 27
Padilla, Arturo, 82
Padilla, Ezequiel, 78, 81, 164; Catholicism and, 95; Lombardo Toledano and, 165; Maximino Avila Camacho and, 79, 286–87; 1946 election and, 149, 150, 166, 168; opposes Alemán, 165–66; political strategies of, 91; U.S. position of, 163
Pagliai, Bruno, 65, 166, 212, 214
Palavicini, Felix, 134
Paley, William, 337
Palmer, Thomas W., 176
Pamphlets, 321
PAN (Partido de Acción Nacional), 85, 95, 150, 219, 232, 331, 364; business and, 216–17; labor reform and, 194; land reform and, 184; León violence and, 155; Martínez death and, 258; Monterrey imposition and, 158; view of, 109
Pan American Airways, 293
Pan American Confederation of Labor, 102
Pan-American Highway, 11, 239
Pan Americanism, 24; anti-Communism and, 203
Pan American Union, 102, 176

Pansters, Wil, 8
Pantux Corporation, 278
Paracaidistas, 186
Paraza, Guadencio, 205
Parra, Germán, 179
Parra, Enrique, 212, 216, 261
Parra Vda. de Alanis, Carmen:
    women's issues and, 218
Partido Antireeleccionista Acción,
    109
Partido Nacionalista, 117
Partido Popular, 197, 239, 261,
    348; formation of, 227–30; land
    reform and, 185, 186
Pasquel, Jorge, 212, 237, 269, 273;
    murder of, 261; *Novedades* and,
    347
Passion plays, 17
Patria chica, 37, 311
Pauley, Ed, 175–76
Paz, Octavio, 57
PCM (Partido Comunista
    Mexicano), 109–10, 365; anti-
    Communism and, 202–4; Avila
    Camacho and, 96, 97; decline
    of, 141; encourages wartime
    cooperation, 122; Gaxiola
    affair and, 125; 1952 election
    and, 239
Pearson, Drew, 216, 260, 273
Peasants: agriculture and, 12–14;
    animal disease and, 236; Avila
    Camacho and, 89; celebrations
    and, 16–20; conflicts of, 8;
    entertainment and, 15–16;
    falling standards of living and,
    221; guerrillas and, 117; health
    care and, 16; Honey murders
    and, 227–30; industrialization
    and, 24–25, 362; land reform
    and, 103–6, 184–88; in litera-
    ture, 56–57; Monte de Piedad
    and, 268; national identity
    and, 313; PSD and, 110; sexual
    attitudes of, 14–15; statistics
    of, 2–3; suppression of, 4–6,
    18–19; suspicions of, 7; war
    shortages and, 130–31; William
    Jenkins and, 209
PEMEX (Pétroleos Mexicanos), 9,
    23, 25, 128, 173, 175, 178, 183,
    188, 191, 199, 201, 220, 277–78,

335, 343–44; Avila Camacho
    cabinet and, 90; corruption
    and, 265; foreign investors
    and, 207; petroleum strike
    and, 191–95
Peña, Carlos González, 61
Pequeña propiedad, 104
Pérez, Silviero, 64
Pérez Martínez, Héctor, 231, 234,
    262
Perry, Laurens, 40, 150–51, 254
Perusquía, Melchor, 274–75
Pesquería, Ignacio F., 229
Petroleum: beginning use of, 9–
    10; expropriated by Cárdenas,
    79; increased consumption of,
    11; strike of workers, 191–95;
    workers suppressed by
    Alemán, 191
Phillips, A. Z., 265
Pierson, Warren Lee, 334
Pincus, Goody, 32
Pineapple industry, 271–72;
    Veracruz project, 213–14, 242,
    271
PIPSA (Productores y
    Importadores de Papel S.A.),
    351, 354
Plan sexenio militar, 78
PNLM (Partido Nacional Liberal
    Mexicano), 225
PNR (Partido Nacional
    Revolucionario): Rubio and, 82
Polanco, José Vallejos, 186
Politics, 108–15, 150, 169, 299–300,
    361, 364; abuse of authority
    and, 259–63; in Acapulco, 274–
    76; Alemán and, 216–19, 257;
    business and, 207–12;
    Cárdenas and, 256–57; cinema
    and, 47–48; corruption and,
    253, 281–91; discrediting labor
    and, 276–80; effect on society,
    255; Gaxiola affair and, 124–
    31; governorship struggles,
    234; hidden deals, 266–68;
    inside information and, 270–
    73; kickbacks, 263–66; kinds
    of, 311–12; land conflicts and,
    8; Left wing, 109–10, 140–41,
    164, 177, 202–3, 226–30, 239,
    286, 330, 363, 365; looting and,

257–59; Maximino Avila Camacho and, 281–91; media and, 311–12, 350–52; payments for, 268–70; peasant conflicts with, 18; poverty and, 254; Right wing, 109, 141, 232–35, 363, 365; rule changing and, 280–81; social consequences of, 301–3; U.S. corruption and, 291–98; violence of, 151–54. *See also specific parties*
Polo, 106
Ponce, Manuel M., 57–58
Porfirian theory, 40–41, 44, 49, 60, 62
Porfiriato, 24, 65, 109, 111
Porter, Katherine Anne, 66
Portes Gil, Emilio, 81, 90, 141, 238, 257, 319–20; Article 123 and, 83; land reform and, 105; 1940 election and, 87–88; right wing and, 112–13
Portland Cement Company, 133
Posada, José Guadalupe, 40
Positivism, 38
Possi, Antonio, 225
Presente: inside information and, 273
PRI (Partido Revolucionario Institucional), 177, 226, 229–30, 261–62; Alemán Doctrine and, 223; anti-Communism and, 203; business and, 217; changes selection procedure, 206–7; clashes with FPPM, 242; falling standards of living and, 221; inside information and, 273; land reform and, 185, 186; Monterrey imposition and, 159; 1952 election and, 239; Tapachula election and, 233; television and, 215; troubles within, 237; women's vote and, 218
Price control, 209
Prieto, Carlos: MEXLIGHT and, 297
PRM (Partido Revolucionario Mexicano), 7, 79, 84; Avila Camacho and, 86, 89–91, 95; clashes with UCL, 153–54; COPARMEX and, 82–83;

corrupt elections and, 151; Gaxiola affair and, 126–27, 130; legitimacy questioned, 166; moderating of, 85; Monterrey imposition and, 159; 1940 election and, 87; 1952 election and, 239; political position of, 108, 110; right wing of, 112; Six Year Plan and, 80; violence and, 152, 155–58, 218–19; war shortages and, 131
Production, 24–28
Professionals, 32–33
Pro-México, 223
Propaganda, 15, 311–13; Allied Radio Network and, 337–39; by Britain, 314–27; Korean War and, 335–37; Office of Inter-American Affairs and, 333–35; by Soviets, 204; by U.S., 327–29; wartime advertising and, 329–33
Protectionism, 352–54
PSD (Partido Socialdemócrata), 110
Pulque, 15, 27

Quaker Oats Company, 190
Querétaro, 2
Quetzalcoatl Pyramid, 17
Quevedo Moreno, Rodrigo M., 87
¡Que Viva México! (film), 43–44
Quinn, Anthony, 49
Quintanilla, Luis: anti-Communism and, 200–202
Quiróz, Ignacio, 152–54, 158

Radio, 53–55, 352; allied network and, 337–39; Mexican, 324–25, 342–44. *See also* Media
Railroads, 10–11, 198
Raine, Phil, 335
Ramírez Rancaño, Mario, 103–4
Ramos, Samuel, 57
Rangel, Enrique, 190
Rangel Contla, José Calixto, 21
Rauschning, Herman, 320
Ray, Bill, 215, 343
Ray, Guy, 175, 287, 331–35, 346, 351; Allied Radio Network and, 337–38; León violence and, 157

Reader's Digest, 350
Reagan, Ronald, 210
Red Brigades, 18
Red Cross, 153–54
Redfield, Robert, 5
Reforma, 16, 18
Religion, 17–18. *See also*
    Anticlericalism; Catholicism
Rent control, 211–12
Republic Steel Company, 189
Reuters News Service, 322
Reveley, Paul J., 293, 294
Revueltas, José, 56
Revueltas, Silvestre, 58
Reyes, Alfonso, 37
Reyes, Bernardo, 82, 150
Rhuherry, F. B., 207
Rico, María Elena, 50
Rincón Gallardo, Carlos, 62–63
Río Escondido (film), 50
Ríos Chimal, Luis, 257–58
Rivas, Joaquín Méndez, 56
Rivera, Diego, 38–40, 66, 202;
    archaeology and, 41; invites
    Eisenstein, 44; Partido Popular
    and, 229
Rivero, Valentín, 82
Roads and highways, 10–12
Robertson, Sir Charles Grant, 321
Robertson, Thomas, 213
Rocha, Joel, 82, 343; opposes
    Cárdenas, 84
Rockefeller, Nelson, 32, 330; OIAA
    and, 333–35; Rivera and, 40
Rodeos, 61–62
Rodríguez, Abelardo, 90, 100, 141,
    170, 178, 235–38; anti-
    Communism and, 200; Gaxiola
    affair and, 124–30; 1940 elec-
    tion and, 88; right wing and,
    112; World War II and, 116
Rodríguez, Adolfo, 343
Rodríguez, Daniel, 284
Rodríguez, Herminio, 230
Rodríguez, José Martínez: anti-
    Communism and, 203
Rodríguez Lozano, Manuel, 38
Roja, Palomino, 276
Rojas, Juan José Rivera, 194
Romero, Emilio, 288
Romero, José Rubén, 56; attacks
    Cárdenas, 240

Ronfeldt, David, 266
Roosevelt, Eleanor, 335
Roosevelt, Franklin D., 101, 141;
    Avila Camacho's strategies
    and, 115
Rosoff, Samuel R., 166, 212
Ross, Arthur: MEXLIGHT and,
    297
Ross, Betty, 235
Ross, Charles G., 179
Ross, Sydney, 334
Royal, John, 337
Rubenstein, Anne, 58–59, 352
Rubin, Jeffrey, 256–57
Ruíz Cortines, Adolfo, 178, 213;
    background of, 241–42;
    corruption and, 279, 298–99;
    inside information and, 271;
    1952 election and, 237–44
Ruiz Galindo, Antonio, 26, 178–
    79, 208, 217, 275; Alemán's
    personal business and, 212;
    factory strike and, 92; inside
    information and, 273; petro-
    leum strike and, 191; political
    favors and, 132; tourist hotel
    of, 28, 132; trade practices and,
    133
Ruth, Babe, 176

Sabalo Transportation Company,
    295–96
Sada, Francisco, 82
Sada, Luis G., 82; opposes
    Cárdenas, 84
Sada, Roberto G., 82
Sáenz, Aarón, 37, 168; Alemán's
    personal business and, 212;
    corruption and, 267; inside
    information and, 273, 279;
    Monterrey Group and, 82–83;
    1940 election and, 88
Sáenz, José, 190
Sáenz, Josué, 3, 179, 190, 212
Sáenz, Moisés, 66
Sáenz Cournet, Aarón, 273
Sagaón, Carlos Romero, 196
Salas y López, Pablo, 82
Salesian Order, 225
Salinas, Gustavo, 292
Salvador, Jaime, 53
Samuelson, Paul, 221

San Angel, 29
Sánchez, Graciano: Avila Camacho candidacy and, 81
Sánchez, Jesús Salvador, 292–93
Sánchez Cano, Edmundo, 233, 234; corruption and, 258
Sánchez Pontón, Luis: labor disputes and, 107; removed by Avila Camacho, 95
Sánchez Taboada, Rodolfo, 261–62; Alemán Doctrine and, 223; land reform and, 185; women's vote and, 218
San Cristóbal, 7
Sandoval, Jorge Piño, 341
San Fernando de Asís, 17–18
San José de Gracia, 5
San Luis Potosí, 2
Santa (film), 43
Santos, Gonzalo N., 81
Saturday Evening Post, 141
Schuller, Friedrich, 85, 88, 116
Science, 31–35; agriculture and, 31; anthropology/archaeology, 41–42; health care and, 31, 32; professionals and, 32–33; reaction to atomic bomb, 33; underconsumption theory and, 33–34
Scott, H. L., 89
Sears, Roebuck Company, 27, 174, 208
Segura, Felipe Hernández, 154
Sensibar, Ezra: kickbacks and, 263–64
Serrano, Carlos I., 178, 212, 238, 260; corruption and, 259, 298–99; inside information and, 273; narcotics and, 216; prostitution and, 261
Sevilla, Ninón, 51
Sexuality, 14–15
Shaw, George P., 256
Sheffield, James R., 66
Silva Herzog, Jesús, 243, 244
Silverman, Joseph, 278
Simon, Andre, 131
Sinarquistas, 109, 232
Sinclair, Upton, 44
Sindicatos blancos, 103, 276–80
Sindicatos charros, 276–80
Siqueiros, David Alfaro, 38–39

SITMMSRM (Sindicato Industrial de Trabajadores Mineros, Metalúrgicos y Similares de la República Mexicana): declined membership of, 240; labor disputes and, 122; union fragmentation and, 195
Six Year Plan, 80, 219–20; Avila Camacho candidacy and, 81
Slutzker, Joseph, 278
SME (electrical workers): declined membership of, 240
Smith, Adam, 272
Smith, Ben, 65, 166, 212
SNTE (Sindicato Nacional de Trabajadores de la Educación), 37; Alemán Doctrine and, 223
Snyder, John W., 220, 296–97
Soccer, 64–65, 272–73
Social programs, 222–24
Sodi, Carlos Franco, 203, 288, 299
Solano, Noel Alrich, 346
Solís, Valencia, 336
Sonora dynasty, 254
Sorcini, Ricardo Hernández, 152
Sordo Noriega, Alonso, 214, 215, 263; media and, 343–44
Soustelle, Jacques, 315
The South American Handbook, 28
Souza, Mario: corruption and, 269; land reform and, 187; left wing and, 177
Sports, 60–65; *charreada*, 61–62; peasants and, 60. *See also by kind*
Spota, Luis, 57
Spratling, William, 66
Squire, J. D., 316
Stafford, Wander, 136
Stafford, Whitehead N., 136
STERM (Sindicato de Trabajadores Electricos de la República Mexicana), 97
Stewart, James B., 266
STFRM (Sindicato de Trabajadores Ferrocarrileros de la República Mexicana), 198; union fragmentation and, 195
STIC (Sindicato de Trabajadores de la Industria Cinematográfica), 47, 340–41

STPC (Sindicato de Trabajadores
de la Producción
Cinematográfica), 47, 340–42
STPRM (Sindicato de
Trabajadores Petroleros de la
República Mexicana): declined
membership of, 240; union
fragmentation and, 195
Street, Mary, 283
Street theater, 17
Suárez, Eduardo, 37, 190; Avila
Camacho and, 75; bankers'
convention and, 134; charges
against, 133–34; kickbacks
and, 264; MEXLIGHT and,
297; moderation of, 91–92
Suárez, Manuel, 274, 349;
Alemán's personal business
and, 212; corruption and, 263,
290; Gaxiola affair and, 124,
126; hotel project and, 214
Suárez, Mario, 102
Sullivan and Cromwell, 295–96
Supreme Court, 235, 364; autonomy of, 230–32; corruption
and, 299; land reform and, 103;
Monterrey imposition and,
158–59

Tabasco, 2; anticlericalism and, 18
Tacubaya, 29
Taft-Hartley law, 193
Tannenbaum, Frank, 66
Tapachula elections, 233
Tapado, 89, 279
Tapia, Sánchez, 87
Tárnava, Constantino de, 342
Taxes, 132–33, 210–11, 233, 234,
235, 242; tax concessions
(1947), 208
Taylor, Maxwell, 176
Tecate Brewery, 210; corruption
and, 268
Technocrats, 177–79
Teja Zabre, Alfonso, 331
Tejeda, Adalberto, 2; opposed by
Cárdenas, 89
Teléfonos de México, 214
Telegraph lines, 11
Telenovelas, 14; effects of, 366
Television, 27, 214–15, 344–46. *See
also* Media

Tello, Manuel, 179; anti-
Communism and, 202
Teotihuacán, 41
Tepache, 27
Tepoztlán, 5
Tepper, Harry, 278
Tequilíliztle: influence of, 17
Terrazas, Manuel: anti-
Communism and, 204
Terrorism, 261
Teyssier, Ezequiel, 198
Theater, 55
Thurston, Walter, 173, 260
Tiempo, 225, 350; Maximino Avila
Camacho and, 287
The Times (London), 316
Timón, 315, 319
Todo, 349
Tomich, Mrs. M. S., 26
Topete, Jesús: anti-Communism
and, 203
Torres, Blanca: corruption and,
255
Torres, José Martínez: corruption
and, 276
Torres, Miguel Contreras, 53
Torres Bodet, Jaime, 36, 56, 171,
176, 179
Toscano, Carmen, 26
Tourism, 28–31
Trade practices, 133
Traven, B., 56
"Treason of Tlaxcalantongo," 160
Trejo, Amado J., 124; Gaxiola
affair and, 129
Treviño, Jacinto, 273, 298
Trouyet, Carlos, 87, 270
Truman, Harry, 32; Alemán and,
175, 176, 236; anti-
Communism and, 200–205;
Messersmith corruption and,
297; Mexican loans and, 173;
O'Dwyer and, 274; Point Four
program and, 271; postage
stamps and, 253; visits Mexico,
175–76
Tula, 42
Tyne, L., 136

UCL (Unión Civica Leonesa):
clashes with PRM, 152–154;
León violence and, 155

Ugarte, José Gómez, 348
Ugarte, Salvador, 134
UGOCM (Unión General de Obreros y Campesinos de México), 230; declined membership of, 240; land reform and, 185, 186; petroleum strike and, 193; union fragmentation and, 195; violence and, 198–99
Ultimas Noticias, 323–24, 330
UNAM (Universidad Nacional Autónoma de México, or National University), 35, 140, 178, 204, 350; Alemán and, 160; student protest, 237
Underconsumption theory, 33–34
Unión de Camioneros, 164
Union of Workers of War Materials, 106–7
United States, 133, 159, 265, 362; Alemán and, 139, 171, 176–77; Allied Radio Network and, 337–39; anti-Communism and, 200–205; Army Air Corps scandal and, 291–93; Avila Camacho and, 80, 86, 102; Beteta and, 178; Britain and, 315–18; business and, 189–90, 206–7, 220; corruption and, 291–93; CROM and, 101; foreign debt and, 220–21; Hollywood and, 340–43; influence of, 35, 43, 53, 64–67, 367; Inter-Allied Propaganda Committee and, 315, 321–23, 326–31; labor conditions and, 123–24; land holdings and, 135–37; land reform and, 105; loans to Mexico, 173–74; Lombardo Toledano's allegations and, 157; Maximino Avila Camacho and, 284–85; Mexican media and, 327–29; Miller corruption and, 295–96; money diversion and, 265; National Labor Unity Pact and, 121; Navy scandal and, 293–95; newspapers and, 339; off-course missile and, 205; opposes Monterrey Group, 85–86; Partido Popular and, 228; petroleum strike and, 191–93;

political corruption and, 254; propaganda and, 329–33; protectionism and, 352–54; Rockefeller and, 333–35; Ruíz Cortines and, 242; Serrano's corruption and, 260; supplies corn, 141; Truman visits Mexico, 175–76; World War II and, 114, 130–31, 220
Uruchurtu, Ernesto P., 233, 239; corruption and, 299
U.S. Army Air Corps, 291–93
U.S. Department of Agriculture, 271
U.S. Department of the Treasury, 259–60, 272–73
U.S. Navy, 293–95

Valdez, Germán, 48–49
Valdez, José Ramón, 258
Valencia, Daniel V., 103
Valenzuela, Macías, 151, 152, 235
Vallarta, Manuel Sandoval, 33
Vámanos con Pancho Villa (film), 44
Vanguardia Nacionalista Mexicana, 109
Vasconcelos, Eduardo, 234
Vasconcelos, José, 124, 314–15
Vázquez, Gabino, 256
Vázquez, Manuel Ramírez, 161
Vejar Vásquez, Octavio, 95, 134; education and, 96
Velasco, Beatríz, 160–61
Velázquez, Fidel, 35, 47, 99, 227, 229, 236, 242–43, 340–41; corruption and, 277; encourages wartime cooperation, 122; Gaxiola affair and, 125; labor meeting and, 101; violence and, 198
Vélez, Jorge, 287, 288
Vélez, Othón, 338
Vera Estañol, Jorge, 133–34
Vidal, Manuel Gual, 178; Alemán's personal business and, 212; corruption and, 299
Viesca Palma, Jorge, 162, 168, 212; labor curbing and, 190–91
Villalobos, Antonio, 90
Villasana, Angel Raúl, 219
Villaseñor, Eduardo, 330; Article 27 and, 184; Avila Camacho

Villaseñor, Eduardo (*continued*)
cabinet and, 90; bankers'
convention and, 134; corruption and, 296, 297; shortages
from war and, 130
Villaseñor, Víctor Manuel, 126,
229, 236
Violence, 218–19, 362; electoral,
153–54; labor, 106–7, 109, 122–
23, 198, 230–32, 242; at Llera,
234; at Oaxaca, 233–34; at
Tapachula, 233
Virgin of Guadalupe, 18, 225
Volleyball, 61

Walker, Jimmy, 284
Wallace, Henry, 31, 284
War, Diplomacy, and Development
(Niblo), 33
Warman, Arturo, 94
Warren, Christopher, 316–17
Weed, Clyde E., 189
Weekly London Letter, 316
Welles, Orson, 49; encourages
wartime cooperation, 122
Wells, H. G., 325
Wenner-Gren, Axel Leonard, 140,
214, 265–66; Maximino Avila
Camacho and, 281–82, 284, 285
Westinghouse Company, 138, 189
Wilber, Vincent, 336
Wilkie, James, 2, 254
Wilson, Woodrow, 43
Winchell, Walter, 260

Wipple, G. C., 190
Wolfe, Bertram, 41
Womack, John, 40
Women: *el jaripeo* and, 61–62;
voting and, 217–19; work of,
14
World Bank, 174–75
World War II, 122, 141; advertising and, 329–33; banking and,
272; economy and, 3, 219–22;
industry and, 22–23; Mexico
joins U.S., 114–15, 291–93;
shortages from, 130–31;
wartime contracts, 265–66

Yáñez, Agustín, 56–57
Yglesias, Manuel Espinosa, 52
Yocupicio, Román, 78
Yucatán, 5
Yurén, Jesús, 103, 276, 277

Zacate, 13
Zamora, Juan, 277
Zapata, Emiliano, 18, 40
Zavala, Silvio, 37
Zendejas, Adelin, 218
Zengotita, Juan de, 221
Zertuche, Francisco, 343
Zevada, Ricardo J., 236
Zitácuaro, 232
Zogbaum, Heidi, 56
Zuazua, Fortunado, 84
Zubarán, Rafael, 124
Zuñiga, Francisco, 38

Latin American Silhouettes
Studies in History and Culture

*William H. Beezley and
Judith Ewell*
Editors

Volumes Published

Silvia Marina Arrom and Servando Ortoll, eds., *Riots in the Cities: Popular Politics and the Urban Poor in Latin America, 1765–1910* (1996). Cloth ISBN 0-8420-2580-4 Paper ISBN 0-8420-2581-2

Roderic Ai Camp, ed., *Polling for Democracy: Public Opinion and Political Liberalization in Mexico* (1996). ISBN 0-8420-2583-9

Brian Loveman and Thomas M. Davies, Jr., eds., *The Politics of Antipolitics: The Military in Latin America*, 3d ed., revised and updated (1996). Cloth ISBN 0-8420-2609-6 Paper ISBN 0-8420-2611-8

Joseph S. Tulchin, Andrés Serbín, and Rafael Hernández, eds., *Cuba and the Caribbean: Regional Issues and Trends in the Post-Cold War Era* (1997). ISBN 0-8420-2652-5

Thomas W. Walker, ed., *Nicaragua without Illusions: Regime Transition and Structural Adjustment in the 1990s* (1997). Cloth ISBN 0-8420-2578-2 Paper ISBN 0-8420-2579-0

Dianne Walta Hart, *Undocumented in L.A.: An Immigrant's Story* (1997). Cloth ISBN 0-8420-2648-7 Paper ISBN 0-8420-2649-5

Jaime E. Rodríguez O. and Kathryn Vincent, eds., *Myths, Misdeeds, and Misunderstandings: The Roots of Conflict in U.S.-Mexican Relations* (1997). ISBN 0-8420-2662-2

Jaime E. Rodríguez O. and Kathryn Vincent, eds., *Common Border, Uncommon Paths: Race, Culture, and National Identity in U.S.-Mexican Relations* (1997). ISBN 0-8420-2673-8

William H. Beezley and Judith Ewell, eds., *The Human Tradition in Modern Latin America* (1997). Cloth ISBN 0-8420-2612-6 Paper ISBN 0-8420-2613-4

Donald F. Stevens, ed., *Based on a True Story: Latin American History at the Movies* (1997). Cloth ISBN 0-8420-2582-0 Paper ISBN 0-8420-2781-5

Jaime E. Rodríguez O., ed., *The Origins of Mexican National Politics, 1808–1847* (1997). Paper ISBN 0-8420-2723-8

Che Guevara, *Guerrilla Warfare*, with revised and updated introduction and case studies by Brian Loveman and Thomas M. Davies, Jr., 3d ed. (1997). Cloth ISBN 0-8420-2677-0 Paper ISBN 0-8420-2678-9

Adrian A. Bantjes, *As If Jesus Walked on Earth: Cardenismo, Sonora, and the Mexican Revolution* (1998). ISBN 0-8420-2653-3

Henry A. Dietz and Gil Shidlo, eds., *Urban Elections in Democratic Latin America* (1998). Cloth ISBN 0-8420-2627-4 Paper ISBN 0-8420-2628-2

A. Kim Clark, *The Redemptive Work: Railway and Nation in Ecuador, 1895–1930* (1998). ISBN 0-8420-2674-6

Joseph S. Tulchin, ed., with Allison M. Garland, *Argentina: The Challenges of Modernization* (1998). ISBN 0-8420-2721-1

Louis A. Pérez, Jr., ed., *Impressions of Cuba in the Nineteenth Century: The Travel Diary of Joseph J. Dimock* (1998). Cloth ISBN 0-8420-2657-6 Paper ISBN 0-8420-2658-4

June E. Hahner, ed., *Women through Women's Eyes: Latin American Women in Nineteenth-Century Travel Accounts* (1998). Cloth ISBN 0-8420-2633-9 Paper ISBN 0-8420-2634-7

James P. Brennan, ed., *Peronism and Argentina* (1998). ISBN 0-8420-2706-8

John Mason Hart, ed., *Border Crossings: Mexican and Mexican-American Workers* (1998). Cloth ISBN 0-8420-2716-5 Paper ISBN 0-8420-2717-3

Brian Loveman, *For la Patria: Politics and the Armed Forces in Latin America* (1999). Cloth ISBN 0-8420-2772-6 Paper ISBN 0-8420-2773-4

Guy P. C. Thomson, with David G. LaFrance, *Patriotism, Politics, and Popular Liberalism in Nineteenth-Century Mexico: Juan Francisco Lucas and the Puebla Sierra* (1999). ISBN 0-8420-2683-5

Robert Woodmansee Herr, in collaboration with Richard Herr, *An American Family in the Mexican Revolution* (1999). ISBN 0-8420-2724-6

Juan Pedro Viqueira Albán, trans. Sonya Lipsett-Rivera and Sergio Rivera Ayala, *Propriety and Permissiveness in Bourbon Mexico* (1999). Cloth ISBN 0-8420-2466-2 Paper ISBN 0-8420-2467-0

Stephen R. Niblo, *Mexico in the 1940s: Modernity, Politics, and Corruption* (1999). ISBN 0-8420-2794-7

David E. Lorey, *The U.S.-Mexican Border in the Twentieth Century* (1999). Cloth ISBN 0-8420-2755-6 Paper ISBN 0-8420-2756-4

Joanne Hershfield and David R. Maciel, eds., *Mexico's Cinema: A Century of Films and Filmmakers* (2000). Cloth ISBN 0-8420-2681-9 Paper ISBN 0-8420-2682-7

Peter V. N. Henderson, *In the Absence of Don Porfirio: Francisco León de la Barra and the Mexican Revolution* (2000). ISBN 0-8420-2774-2

Mark T. Gilderhus, *The Second Century: U.S.-Latin American Relations since 1889* (2000). Cloth ISBN 0-8420-2413-1 Paper ISBN 0-8420-2414-X

Catherine Moses, *Real Life in Castro's Cuba* (2000). Cloth ISBN 0-8420-2836-6 Paper ISBN 0-8420-2837-4

K. Lynn Stoner, ed./comp., with Luis Hipólito Serrano Pérez, *Cuban and Cuban-American Women: An Annotated Bibliography* (2000). ISBN 0-8420-2643-6

Thomas D. Schoonover, *The French in Central America: Culture and Commerce, 1820–1930* (2000). ISBN 0-8420-2792-0

MEXICO in the 1940s

~~~

Attention to Mexico's history after 1940 stands in the shadow of the country's epic revolution of 1910–1923, and historians and scholars tend to bring their focus on the subject to a close with the end of the Lázaro Cárdenas presidency. *Mexico in the 1940s: Modernity, Politics, and Corruption* examines Mexican politics in the wake of Cardenismo and at the dawn of Miguel Alemán's presidency. Based upon a decade of intensive research, *Mexico in the 1940s* is the first broad and substantial study of the political life of the nation during this period, thus opening a new era to historical investigation.

Analytical yet lively, mixing political and cultural history, this volume captures the humor, passion, and significance of Mexico during the World War II and postwar years when Mexicans entered the era called "the miracle" because of the nation's economic growth and political stability. Stephen R. Niblo presents a mosaic of Mexico's national cultural life—its mass media, entertainers, and fads during what is described today as the golden age of movies, popular music, and radio. Niblo develops the case that the Mexico of today—politically and executively centralized, corrupt, and stressing business and industry while ignoring the needs of the majority of the population—has its roots in the fifteen years after 1940. Characters such as Manuel Avila Camacho and Miguel Alemán are sharply sketched, and the reader can see how their decisions and choices led the country to the crisis that Mexico has experienced in recent years.

Mexico in the 1940s offers a unique interpretation of the country's domestic politics during this period, including an explanation of how political leaders were able to reverse the course of the Mexican Revolution; an original interpretation of corruption in Mexican political life, a phenomenon that did not end in the 1940s; and an analysis of the relationship between the U.S. media interests, the Mexican state, and the Mexican media companies that still dominates mass communication today.